CHRISTIANITY, JUDAISM
AND
OTHER GRECO-ROMAN CULTS

PART ONE

STUDIES IN JUDAISM IN LATE ANTIQUITY

EDITED BY

JACOB NEUSNER

VOLUME TWELVE

CHRISTIANITY, JUDAISM
AND
OTHER GRECO-ROMAN CULTS

PART ONE

LEIDEN
E. J. BRILL
1975

CHRISTIANITY, JUDAISM AND OTHER GRECO-ROMAN CULTS

STUDIES FOR MORTON SMITH AT SIXTY

EDITED BY

JACOB NEUSNER
Professor of Religious Studies
Brown University

PART ONE

NEW TESTAMENT

LEIDEN
E. J. BRILL
1975

LIBRARY
McCORMICK THEOLOGICAL SEMINARY
1100 EAST 55th STREET
CHICAGO, ILLINOIS 60615

ISBN 90 04 04215 6
90 04 04216 4

Copyright 1975 by E. J. Brill, Leiden, Netherlands

All rights reserved. No part of this book may be reproduced or translated in any form, by print, photoprint, microfilm, microfiche or any other means without written permission from the publisher

PRINTED IN THE NETHERLANDS

TABLE OF CONTENTS

Foreword. IX

New Testament Introduction. A Critique of a Discipline . . . 1
   HELMUT KOESTER, Harvard University

Good News Is No News: Aretalogy and Gospel 21
   JONATHAN Z. SMITH, University of Chicago

A Fresh Approach to Q 39
   WILLIAM R. FARMER, Southern Methodist University

Blasphemy: St. Mark's Gospel as Damnation History 51
   T. A. BURKILL, University of Rhodesia

From Isaiah 61 to Luke 4 75
   JAMES A. SANDERS, Union Theological Seminary

Luke 12, 13-14, Tradition and Interpretation 107
   TJITZE BAARDA, Vrije Universiteit, Amsterdam

"Am I a Jew?"—Johannine Christianity and Judaism . . . 163
   WAYNE A. MEEKS, Yale University

The Kinship of John and Acts 187
   PIERSON PARKER, The General Theological Seminary

A Foreword to the Study of the Speeches in Acts 206
   MAX WILCOX, University College of North Wales, Bangor

L'hymne christologique de Col i, 15-20. Jugement critique sur
l'état des recherches 226
   PIERRE BENOIT, o.p., École biblique et archéologique française, Jérusalem

Paul and his Opponents: Trends in Research 264
   E. EARLE ELLIS, New Brunswick Theological Seminary

The Present State of Scholarship on Hebrews 299
   GEORGE WESLEY BUCHANAN, Wesley Theological Seminary, Washington

PART TWO

EARLY CHRISTIANITY

The Earliest Christian Communities as Sectarian Movement 1
    ROBIN SCROGGS, Chicago Theological Seminary
Power through Temple and Torah in Greco-Roman Palestine 24
    SHELDON R. ISENBERG University of Florida
Réflexions sur le Judéo-Christianisme 53
    MARCEL SIMON, Université de Strasbourg
Asia Minor and Early Christianity 77
    SHERMAN E. JOHNSON, Church Divinity School of the Pacific
Peter in Rome. A Review and Position 146
    D. W. O'CONNOR, St. Lawrence University
Une allusion de l'Asclepius au livre d'Hénoch 161
    MARC PHILONENKO, Université de Strasbourg
Christ in Verbal and Depicted Imagery: A Problem of Early Christian
Iconography 164
    S. G. F. BRANDON
Das Thema "Vertreibung aus dem Paradies" in der Katakombe der Via
Latina und sein jüdischer Hintergrund 173
    KURT and URSULA SCHUBERT, Universität Wien
Vox Populi Voluntas Dei and the Election of the Byzantine Emperor. . 181
    MILTON V. ANASTOS, University of California, Los Angeles
Hypatius of Ephesus on the Cult of Images 208
    STEPHEN GERO, Brown University
Contemporary Ecclesiastical Approaches to Biblical Interpretation:
Orthodoxy and Pseudorthodoxy 217
    ERNEST S. FRERICHS, Brown University

PART THREE

JUDAISM BEFORE 70

Joy and Love as Metaphorical Expressions of Willingness and Spontaneity in Cuneiform, Ancient Hebrew, and Related Literatures: Divine Investitures in the Midrash in the Light of Neo-Babylonian Royal
Grants 1
    YOCHANAN MUFFS, The Jewish Theological Seminary of America
On the Origins of the Aramaic Legal Formulary at Elephantine 37
    BARUCH A. LEVINE, New York University
Myth and Midrash: Genesis 9:20-29 55
    ALBERT I. BAUMGARTEN, McMaster University
The Jewish Historian Demetrios 72
    E. J. BICKERMAN, Columbia University
The Tales of the Tobiads 85
    JONATHAN A. GOLDSTEIN, University of Iowa
The *Acta pro Judaeis* in the *Antiquities* of Flavius Josephus: A Study
in Hellenistic and Modern Apologetic Historiography 124
    HORST R. MOEHRING, Brown University
The Archangel Sariel. A Targumic Parallel to the Dead Sea Scrolls . . 159
    GEZA VERMES, University of Oxford

TABLE OF CONTENTS VII

Qumran and Iran: The State of Studies 167
   RICHARD N. FRYE, Harvard University
The Multiform Jewish Heritage of Early Christianity 175
   ROBERT A. KRAFT, University of Pennsylvania
A Note on Purification and Proselyte Baptism 200
   R. J. ZWI WERBLOWSKY, Hebrew University Jerusalem
Sadducees *versus* Pharisees: The Tannaitic Sources. 206
   JACK LIGHTSTONE, Brown University
Masada: A Critique of Recent Scholarship 218
   LOUIS H. FELDMAN, Yeshiva University

PART FOUR

JUDAISM AFTER 70

Redactional Techniques in the Legal Traditions of Joshua ben Ḥana-
niah 1
   WILLIAM SCOTT GREEN, University of Rochester
The Artificial Dispute: Ishmael and ʿAqiva 18
   GARY G. PORTON, University of Illinois
Form-Criticism and Exegesis: The Case of Mishnah Ohalot 2:1 30
   JACOB NEUSNER, Brown University
Two Traditions of Samuel: Evaluating Alternative Versions 46
   BARUCH M. BOKSER, University of California, Berkeley
R. Abbahu of Caesarea 56
   LEE I. LEVINE, Hebrew University, Jerusalem
"Conjecture" and Interpolation in Translating Rabbinic Texts, Illu-
strated by a Chapter from Tanna debe Eliyyahu 77
   WILLIAM G. BRAUDE, Providence, Rhode Island

OTHER GRECO-ROMAN CULTS

Iconoclasm among the Zoroastrians 93
   MARY BOYCE, University of London
Quellenprobleme zum Ursprung und Alter der Mandäer 112
   KURT RUDOLPH, Karl-Marx-Universität, Leipzig
The Religion of Maximin Daia 143
   ROBERT M. GRANT, University of Chicago
Dositheus, Jesus, and a Moses Aretalogy 167
   STANLEY ISSER, State University of New York, Binghamton

BIBLIOGRAPHY

A Bibliography of the Writings of Morton Smith, to December 31, 1973. 191
   A. THOMAS KRAABEL, University of Minnesota

Index of Biblical and Talmudic References 201

General Index. 220

FOREWORD

Morton Smith was born on May 28, 1915, in Philadelphia, Pennsylvania. He prepared for university work at the Academy of the New Church in Bryn Athyn, Pennsylvania, then went to Harvard College, where he majored in English Literature and graduated A.B., *magna cum laude*, in 1936. After a year of travel, he returned to Harvard Divinity School and received the S.T.B., *cum laude*, in 1940, winning a Sheldon Fellowship for study in Jerusalem. He held the Sheldon Fellowship from 1940 to 1942, and was Thayer Fellow at the American School of Oriental Research, Jerusalem, in 1942-1943. In Jerusalem he enrolled as a research student in the Hebrew University, from 1940 to 1944, whence he received the Ph. D. in classical philology in 1948, for a thesis, written under the direction of Professor M. Schwabe, on *Tannaitic Parallels to the Gospels* (Hebrew: *Maqbilot ben haBesorot leSifrut HaTanna'im*). He had meanwhile returned to Harvard for postgraduate work under the direction of Professors A. D. Nock, Werner Jaeger, and, later, Robert Pfeiffer. This led in 1957 to a thesis on the history of Judaism in Palestine to the eve of the Maccabean revolt, published in 1971, after several revisions, under the title *Palestinian Parties and Politics that Shaped the Old Testament*. He began university teaching in 1950 and was Instructor in Biblical Literature at Brown University in 1950-1951 and Assistant Professor of Biblical Literature at Brown University from 1951 to 1955. He held the position of Visiting Professor of History of Religion at Drew University in 1956-1957. In 1957 he was appointed Assistant Professor of Ancient History at Columbia University. He was promoted to Associate Professor in 1960, and to Professor in 1962. He is now Professor of Ancient History at Columbia University. His studies since 1950 are indicated by the bibliography at the end of Volume IV. For some years past he has been collecting material for a history of magic in the Greco-Roman world.

He held a Fulbright Scholarship for post-doctoral research in Greece in 1951-1952, a Guggenheim Fellowship in 1955-1956, the Lectureship on the History of Religions of the American Council of Learned Societies in 1961-1962, a Fellowship of the American

Council of Learned Societies in 1963-1964, a Fellowship of the Bollingen Foundation in 1964, Membership in the School of Historical Studies of The Institute for Advanced Study in 1966-1967, and a Fellowship of the American Council of Learned Societies in 1966-1967. He was Visiting Professor of History of Religion at Wesleyan University in 1971, and in the same year gave the Max Richter Lectures at Brown University. He is a member of, among other learned societies, The American Academy of Arts and Sciences, American Historical Association, American Philological Association, American Schools of Oriental Research, American Society of Papyrologists, Archaeological Institute of America, Association Internationale de Papyrologues, Corpus Hellenisticum Novi Testamenti Colloquium, Israel Exploration Society, Phi Beta Kappa, Society of Biblical Literature, Studiorum Novi Testamenti Societas, and World Union of Jewish Studies.

The editor hopes that these papers, on themes of interest to Morton Smith, will contribute to the critical discussion of some problems of concern to him. Since Smith is one of the great scholarly masters of this generation, it is through scholarship, and not through encomia, that the editor and his colleagues choose to pay their tribute. The facts about the man, his writings, his critical judgment, intelligence, erudition and wit, his labor as selfless teacher and objective, profound critic speak for themselves and require no embellishment. We happily celebrate his reaching the age of sagacity: בן ששים לזקנה!

Each contributor took responsibility for proof-reading his contribution and for choices as to transliteration, abbreviations, and related matters. Mr. Arthur Woodman, Canaan, New Hampshire, prepared the indices.

Most of the cost of publishing these volumes has been provided by E. J. Brill. The subsidy added thereto, principally for setting type in foreign alphabets and other extraordinary costs, derives from several sources. Mr. Max Alperin, Providence, Rhode Island, and Mr. William Green, Manchester, New Hampshire, gave welcome and generous gifts. It is deeply heartening to the editor that, in these times of difficulty for universities and for scholarship, there still are individuals who wish to associate themselves with scholarly projects. The Jewish community of Rhode Island, through the Bureau of Jewish Education of the Jewish Federation of Rhode Island, made an important contribution. It is much appreciated that the townsfolk among whom the editor makes his life so indicate their concern and meaningful engagement in his work. The bulk of the subsidy derives from the editor's personal contributions to the Max Richter Foundation, of which he is president, from proceeds of lectures, book royalties, and other earnings. Accordingly, it is the editor's wife and children who ultimately have made the publication of these books possible, along with E. J. Brill. I hope that the quality of what follows will impress my teacher, Professor Morton Smith, and those scholars who care to read these volumes, as having been worth the immense efforts of all concerned.

J.N.

Brown University
Providence, Rhode Island
May 28, 1975

NEW TESTAMENT INTRODUCTION:
A CRITIQUE OF A DISCIPLINE

HELMUT KOESTER
Harvard University

I. *Some remarks about the history of the discipline*

The most striking feature of the discipline of "Introduction" is the unusually high degree of self-assured security and complacency which characterizes its presuppositions and its aims. If, for the moment, we allow as the starting-point of the discipline Richard Simon's *Histoire critique* (1689-93)[1] —there are reasons to dispute this (see below)—this peculiar feature appears already at this early stage. Simon begins a long series of scholarly Introductions written by generations of scholars who assume that their own possession of truth is perfect, even though the expression of this truth as it is preserved in the manuscripts of the New Testament is unfortunately not quite so perfect. Simon asserts that the truth which is the foundation of the established church, i.e. the Roman Catholic Church, is a sure and unchanging foundation of faith, whereas already the manuscript variants of the writings of the New Testament show, how uncertain and unreliable is a truth preserved in written books.

In the same way, the leading Biblical scholar of the period of rationalism, Johann Salomo Semler (1725-1791), had no desire to interfere with the truth of the divine word, when he subjected the writings of the Bible to critical questioning.[2] But he continued the process by which critical investigation on the one hand and edification on the other were separated from each other. Semler confronts the uncertainty of our own insights into the question of divine origin and inspiration of the Bible with the general and unchanging certainty and quality of the Christian religion and of

---

[1] Richard Simon, *Histoire critique du Nouveau Testament* (1689); idem, *Histoire critique des versions du Nouveau Testament* (1690); idem, *Histoire critique des principaux commentateurs du Nouveau Testament* (1693); cf. also Werner Georg Kümmel, *Das Neue Testament. Geschichte der Erforschung seiner Probleme* (1958), 41ff. (English translation 1972).

[2] Johann Salomo Semler, *Abhandlung von freier Untersuchung des Canon* (1772-76).

its true fundamental tenets. The parallelism of this enlightenment-position of Semler with Simon's Roman Catholic position is striking. It was on the basis of this position that the scholarly enterprise of the critical investigation of Biblical writings became possible; historical judgements as well as philological insights have been the result. But the price paid is exorbitant. Henceforth, critical theological scholarship was delighted to assert that the progress of cultural developments in general and of religious insights in particular was no longer subject to the knowledge and insight which resulted from a critical and historical investigation of the Biblical writings. Of course, the systematic theologian could continue to refer to the Biblical foundation of his theological enterprise; but he would go about this business without the benefit of the responsible scholarly methodology of critical Biblical scholarship. The Biblical scholars themselves had proclaimed that nothing they did would disturb the everlasting truths of Christian religion.

But in spite of such declarations of critical Biblical scholars that their work was not meant as a threat and was ultimately irrelevant, more conservative theologians supposed—not without reason—that this was not the case. A more conservative approach to the question of "Introduction" was willing to take up the challenge and worked to restore the historical authenticity of those Biblical writings which critical scholarship had dared to question. The culmination of these attempts is Theodore Zahn's (1838-1933) *Introduction* [3] which wants to demonstrate that all writings of the New Testament without exception were written by genuine Apostles. Zahn's work has never been surpassed in its erudition, shrewdness, sophistry, and hair-splitting argumentation, —and rarely has it been matched with respect to its assumption that all critical scholars are malicious.

It was Ferdinand Christian Baur who recognized that the real task was to reconstruct, on the basis of a critical evaluation of the sources, the primary issues of the historical process. It has become customary to castigate Baur for his adoption of the Hegelian schema (Thesis, Antithesis, Synthesis) into which he seems to have forced the historical developments of early Christianity. But, first, the basic historical issues had been identified by Baur in his *Die Christuspartei in der korinthischen Gemeinde* of 1831 one year

---

[3] *Einleitung in das Neue Testament*, vol. 1 and 2 (1897-99); English translation from the 3rd German edition 1909, revised 1917.

before the publication of Hegel's lectures on the philosophy of religion in 1832, and it was not until the publication of his *Die christliche Gnosis* in 1835 that Baur revealed any effects of his study of Hegel.[4] Second, Baur tried to demonstrate that Christianity's problem is a search for the criteria which lie embedded in the process of history itself, and that critical self-assertion of Christian beliefs within the developments of history is a task rather than a fixed inherited endowment of the theological endeavor. Third, Baur had no hesitation to include apocryphal and non-canonical material in his investigation; he was indeed a church-historian as much as a New Testament scholar. Fourth,—and this is of crucial importance—"Baur does not permit any other question than that which is historically intended. Apart from history, theology would belong nowhere."[5] Liebing concludes the article from which I just quoted with a paragraph in which he remarks: "What we have to learn from a new study of Baur is more than method. If it were only a question of method, we would have to say that he actually rendered the reception of the historical-critical method *more difficult*. Had theology learned from him earlier and better, then it would not have happened so easily that historical criticism was domesticated as a formal technique. It is understandable that theology was deeply shocked by Hegelianism; but innocence is no alternative to it."[6]

The tragedy of the subsequent development of the Tübingen School which derived from Baur's work and of scholarship thereafter is that the comprehensive task which Baur had formulated became divided into several separate enterprises which all rested on Baur's results rather than taking his methodological insights as a challenge. On the one hand, the discipline of New Testament Introduction proper, and with it a large segment of the historical-critical scholarship, slipped into a state of theological innocence—after a successful defense of the authenticity of the canonical writings against the radical and extreme positions which some students of Baur had taken. The serious historians of the Tübingen School were able to produce strictly historical descriptions of early Christianity in which each writing is explained on the basis of its

---

[4] Heinz Liebing, "Historical-Critical Theology," *Journal for Theology and the Church*, 3 (1967), 55-69.
[5] Liebing, *op. cit.*, 68.
[6] *op. cit.*, 69.

historical context. But non-canonical writings were becoming marginal again; the hypothesis of Baur about the basic antithesis of Jewish Christianity (the Jerusalem Apostles) and Gentile Christianity (Paul) had assumed the dimensions of an infallible dogma; and the historical questions had ceased to be critical theological questions. Most of the English and American scholarship up to the present time belongs in the same category, except that Anglo-Saxon scholars since Joseph Barber Lightfoot [7] have been less impressed by Baur's basic Jewish-Gentile Christian antithesis.

The more interesting developments of New Testament scholarship in our century seem to lie outside of the discipline of "Introduction." The older results of both liberal and conservative "Introductions" were repeated, supported by more detailed arguments and by an ever increasing amount of secondary literature. New discoveries tended to do no more than to amplify what is often still called the "background" of the New Testament. Adolf Jülicher's *Einleitung in das Neue Testament*, representing the liberal wing, had been published for the first time in 1894; almost 40 years later (1931) Erich Fascher published a new edition which made no substantial changes. Similarly, on the more conservative side, Paul Feine's *Einleitung in das Neue Testament* of 1913 appeared in a revised edition by Johannes Behm 1936 and was re-edited 1963 by Werner-Georg Kümmel (English translation 1966)—to be sure, enlarged to encyclopedic dimensions, but without a change in its basic orientation. Though this work, in its impressive erudition, easily surpasses most if not all other works in this discipline,[8] the limitation to the canonical writings of the New Testament seems more than surprising, and the refusal to engage in a thorough re-assessment of the presuppositions is somewhat disquieting. This is neither to deny that authors and editors of more recent Introductions have learned of more New Testament manuscripts, nor to say that they have not been aware of new methods such as form-criticism,

---

[7] Cf. especially his Commentary to *St. Paul's Epistle to the Galatians*, first published 1865.

[8] Cf. also such English language works as Morton Scott Enslin, *The Literature of the Christian Movement*, Christian Beginnings, Part III (1938); Ernest Findley Scott, *The Literature of the New Testament* (1932); A. H. McNeile, *An Introduction to the Study of the New Testament*, ed. by C.S.C. Williams (1953); Robert A. Spivey and D. Moody Smith, *Anatomy of the New Testament* (1969).—This is only a random selection, representing different types of New Testament Introductions.

history of tradition, and—more recently—redaction criticism. But scholars of the history-of-religions school had already demanded before the turn of the last century that the Apostolic Fathers and the New Testament Apocrypha be treated on the same level as, and together with, the canonical writings.[9] Yet the original title of the famous *Handbuch zum Neuen Testament* (ed. by Hans Lietzmann), "Handbook to the New Testament and its Apocrypha," never became a reality—even though commentaries to the Apostolic Fathers were eventually published. The reconstruction of the history of the origins of early Christian literature as a comprehensive task that must include all relevant writings of the period has not yet been realized in the discipline of New Testament Introduction. That this must also include an engagement of the theological perspectives, a critical discussion of the theological issues which determined the origin and tradition of such literature, is rarely recognized.

On the other hand, the theological orientation that appeared in a large segment of New Testament scholarship after the First World War has not been able to unite the theological concerns with the demands of historical reconstruction. Dialectical theology was a courageous answer to the experience of the First World War which had shaken the foundations of an optimistic cultural orientation of Christianity. It had become clear that history could no longer be seen as a long and continuous line of an evolution within which Christianity made its contribution by developing further and into more lofty clarity the great religious and social ideas embedded in its own primitive beginnings. On the contrary, since progressive "developments" themselves had proven to imply the possibility of eventual destruction—an insight which is very much with us today —one was tempted to turn to the great persons of history who had been able to stem the destructive tides of decline and fall again and again. One aspect of this trend was the renewal of Luther-studies by men such as Karl Holl. Consequently, the most significant accomplishments of this new theology with respect to the historical writings of the New Testament came to lie in the reconstruction of the thought-world of central figures, such as Jesus, John, and Paul, but often to the detriment of the reconstruction of the historical processes of which they were a part. The discipline

---

[9] The most prominent of these challenges was William Wrede's *Über Aufgabe und Methode der sogenannten Neutestamentlichen Theologie* (1897).

of New Testament Introduction was further distracted from its task that F. C. Baur had outlined, i.e. the theological assessment of the historical process. Instead, "Introduction" was abused to provide objective scholarly data about the reliability of source materials on which the presentations of the theology of such great personages could be based. Whatever was deemed as a "spurious" writing or tradition, fell by the wayside—what could a letter that was not actually written by Paul contribute to the reconstruction of the great Apostle's theology?

It is interesting to observe that still another significant development in Biblical scholarship, the history-of-religions approach, had no visible effect upon the discipline of New Testament Introduction, although it has played a significant role in the scholarly debate since the turn of this century. What one finds is at best a description of the "background" of the New Testament, divided into Jewish and Greek backgrounds. There are inherent tendencies in the history-of-religions approach which contributed to a certain disregard for questions of historical dating and distinctions in historical development. A convenient, albeit unjustified, consequence has been to describe these backgrounds as something strangely inflexible, that did not change its basic contours over the centuries. What really matters in this approach is an image of the basic and fundamental features of a particular religion. The religion of Judaism and of Hellenism thus is not seen as something that participates in the process of development and change which even the most conservative "Introduction" to the New Testament is willing to allow as a factor in the history which produced the early Christian literature. But even if such developmental features are recognized in Jewish and Greek religions of that period, they are rarely integrated into the picture of an ongoing process of history that produced the writings of early Christianity.

Thus, New Testament "Introduction," having preserved its purity and austerity as a discipline, among liberals and conservatives alike, in spite of its great erudition has never managed to become an enterprise which is central for the vital interests of religious, theological and historical understanding. At best, it has been useful as an ancillary discipline, helping to secure genuine source-materials for scholars who wanted to base their discussions on reliable information; or aiding theologians who wanted to affirm the authenticity of canonical writings on which they based their doctrines and dogmas.

II. *Theses for the reformation of this discipline as an "Introduction" to Early Christian history and literature*

1. New Testament Introduction as a theological discipline should not be afraid to disturb the complacent religious and cultural assumptions of the world in which Christians live and of its inherited prejudices. Only such an endeavor is worthy of the subject-matter of this discipline, i.e. of the treatment of early Christian writings, which themselves spearheaded a religious revolution in a time of cultural crisis and upheaval. It must also produce criteria for an evaluation of new cultural developments and their fascinating suggestion of a departure to new shores. If it fails to do so, it has failed to understand the cultural and religious conflicts which have produced the literature of early Christianity and it has misunderstood the purpose of the New Testament canon.[10]

2. It is wrong to fix the beginning of the history of this discipline in the enlightenment or pre-enlightenment period, even if we can re-assure ourselves that the methods of inquiry of that period have some resemblance with our own concept of what is "scientific" or "scholarly". Rather, the starting point of the history of the discipline must be seen in the earliest attempts to identify writings which could serve as critical canons in a situation of conflict, i.e. with Marcion and Irenaeus. The endeavors of these theologians were, by all means, "critical" and "historical" attempts. This is even more evident in the works of Origen and Eusebius who continued the critical and theological investigation into those source materials which were intended to determine the church's future. Their primary question was by no means: what was written by inspired Apostles and what is, therefore *historically* reliable? Rather they asked: which writings were used by the true believers from the beginning and have thus demonstrated their *theological* power as sources which sustained the life of the churches?

3. Therefore, the beginning of the discipline belongs in the period in which the New Testament canon was created. The canon was not invented in order to assure the undisputed possession of a

---

[10] Neither conservative nor liberal scholarship serves anyone today by emphasizing that the results of inquiry into questions of authorship and canonical status will not challenge the dogmatic assumptions of church, theology, and society. Scholarly disciplines which claim that the results of their research are ultimately irrelevant, demonstrate that they are neither faithful to their subject matter nor responsible to the culture which supports them.

body of writings apart from all conflicts. On the contrary, the canon was created as a critical weapon in a religious and cultural revolution. As such a weapon it wanted to assure historical continuity and it wanted to prevent departures into spurious cultural and religious objectives which were seen as alien to the origins of the Christian faith.[11]

4. The decision about canonicity cannot completely avoid uncertainty. It is probably wrong to assume that, because of some uncertainties about specific writings, the limits of the canon were not yet firmly drawn in the 3rd and 4th century. Almost all major New Testament writings were undisputed parts of the canon by the end of the 2nd century. Eusebius' Church History exemplifies the real reason for the uncertainties that still remained: The judgement depends upon one's own theological evaluation of the historical developments. Such evaluation requires an assessment of *all* writings from the early period of the church, canonical and apocryphal, and of the historical circumstances which lead to their production. There is also another element which invariably enters into the evaluation: the determination of theological content. The uncertainties which existed in the 2nd and 3rd century about the Revelation of John, e.g., are clearly uncertainties about its theological intentions rather than about its apostolic authorship.

5. Judgements about the exact time, place, and authorship of a particular writing are only preliminaries to the more important task, i.e. the reconstruction of history. To this task, all documents which are preserved must contribute equally, whether canonical or not. But this does not fully describe what is at stake. History is not reconstructed by accumulating objective statements about facts. Rather, this requires an assessment of theological purpose and of the intention of each and every document as part of an ongoing process. Ferdinand Christian Baur's *Tendenzkritik* is not so wrong after all. It is here, that theological questions can be formulated as historical questions. The historian who fails to do that does not only beg the vital theological concerns, he will also inevitably build up archives instead of history.

---

[11] It is to be noted that neither inspiration, nor apostolicity were recognized as criteria for canonization. Rather, the primary criterion was the usage of certain writings in the churches from the beginning, i.e. a criterion which emphasizes the integrity of historical purpose and the desire to make available for the future original insights which gave Christianity its initial distinctive features.

6. The questions with which Richard Simon and, in the subsequent century, the enlightenment initiated the formal discipline of "Introduction" were by no means unbiased and objective. They were typical and necessary questions of a conflict between Bible and religious tradition, or between Bible and the religious values of the enlightenment period. These questions can be dangerous, since they claim to be innocent and objective. If we adhere to them, they bind us unwittingly to the cultural problems of a period in history which is no longer ours (this includes the conservative approach to "Introduction"). They are even more dangerous because they suggest that religious options of our own time should not be made subject to the results of a critical inquiry into a historical authority, or that such critical inquiry should be limited to that portion of the historical authority which suits us well anyway; thus adherents of Luther's Reformation chose Paul, and liberals, pietists and revolutionaries chose Jesus as their authority—always claiming that there is objective support, based on scholarly investigation. But we have a right and a duty to expect that the texts will not only speak to us, advise us, but will also give their critical judgements about our thoughts. Otherwise history will remain mute and speechless and the historical inquiry an academic luxury.

7. A conflict of culture and religion is also documented in the sources with which we are dealing. What is required of us is the full investigation of *all* sources, Christian or pagan, orthodox or heretical, in their real historical perspective and constellation. History of religions is not a "background", but the movement of culture and religion, of which early Christianity was a part. If we can assess the direction of a Christian quest for meaning, we may be able to discern theological issues in their historical context. There is no doubt that this makes the scholarly task more difficult and more demanding. But it also makes it more worthwhile.

III. *Some perspectives and an example for a fresh approach*

Let me first list some of the established canons of the discipline of New Testament Introduction which must be abandoned:

(1) The restriction to the 27 canonical writings of the New Testament is no longer possible. In order to recognize and to appreciate the character and the peculiar message of these writings, they must be treated in the context of the early Christian literature as a whole.

(2) The treatment of writings in certain groups as suggested by traditional divisions of the canon, Gospels and Acts, Epistles, Revelation, is misleading. It can be justified only in the context of an inquiry that is devoted to the more limited study of genres and types of literature.

(3) The question of authenticity and authorship should be put into its proper perspective, i.e., it is a tool to determine with some certainty fixed points in relation to each other along the lines of continuing developments. But questions of authorship should never be construed in terms of value judgements such as "less genuine," "spurious," or "inauthentic."

(4) Another type of value judgements must be thrown out: we are too much accustomed to consider as secondary and late whatever is more "primitive" or more "miraculous", i.e., less agreeable to our enlightened tastes, and less likely in terms of modern natural sciences.

(5) The restriction of the consideration to literary critical questions (composition, sources, literary integrity) results in too narrow a perspective. If the interest is ultimately to determine the situation of particular writings in the life of the church, the methods of form criticism and tradition criticism become even more important.

The result will be different from the mere attempt to make only a few modifications in our traditional procedures. New approaches must be tried out. In the following I would like to suggest one possible procedure. I take my starting point from the observation that certain groupings of early Christian writings are suggested by their common use of the same "apostolic" authority, such as Paul, Peter, John and others. Such groups of writings also seem to point to similar geographical origins, and often they are directly dependent upon each other or they use the same kinds of traditional materials. From this perspective as my starting point I want to delineate a chapter of a New Testament Introduction that could be entitled: "The Pauline Literature".

The first step would be an assessment of all available materials. Under the name of Paul, or directly concerned with the work of this Apostle, the following writings have been preserved:

(1) More than a dozen letters,
(2) A book entitled the "Acts of Paul"
(3) The "Acts of the Apostles" by a certain Luke which, in its second part, is primarily dealing with Paul.

(4) An "Apocalypse of Paul", as well as writings like "Acts of Paul and Andrew", "Passion of Peter and Paul", which I will not consider here, since I do not want to complicate this trial run unnecessarily.

The first three, Letters, Acts of Paul, and Acts of the Apostles, seem to have a common geographical origin: they were apparently written in Asia Minor and Greece. For the letters this is shown by internal evidence (even though one or the other may have been written in Rome); for the Acts of Paul, this is evidenced by a reference which Tertullian makes to this book; with respect to the Acts of the Apostles, I am taking the common opinion of scholarship as my working hypothesis.

(1) The Letters: Of the Pauline letters a varying number occurs in the manuscripts of the New Testament. The oldest Papyrus containing the Pauline Epistles (P 46, Chester Beatty Papyrus) contains fragments of 10 letters: Rom, 1 and 2 Cor, Gal, Eph, Col (Phlm), Phil, I Thess, Hebr. There is no trace of 2 Thess and of the so-called Pastoral Epistles.[12] On the other hand, the old Latin manuscripts also include the Pastoral Epistles and a letter to the Laodiceans, i.e. a total of 15 Pauline letters.

The fact that the Greek manuscript tradition of the New Testament since the 4th century has adopted 14 Pauline letters, including the letter to the Hebrews but without the Laodicean letter, as part of the New Testament canon has resulted in the transmission of these 14 letters in hundreds of manuscripts from the 4th century onwards. Of these, the Epistle to the Hebrews does not even claim to be written by Paul; thus it can be left out of consideration here.

But there are several letters, in addition to the "non-canonical' letter to the Laodiceans, which have come down to us outside of the New Testament canon: an additional letter to the Corinthians (known as 3 Cor) included in the Acts of Paul and also transmitted independently in a Bodmer Papyrus; and a correspondence between Paul and the Roman Philosopher Seneca. Also these have to be considered as part of the Pauline letters from the ancient church.

(2) The Acts of Paul are first attested by Tertullian—an external attestation which is no worse than that for most of the canonical

---

[12] The actual order of the letters is Rom, Hebr, 1 and 2 Cor, Eph, Gal, Phil, Col, 1 Thess. It is uncertain whether also 2 Thess was included in this oldest collection. But there is no doubt that the Pastoral Epistles were not a part of it.

writings of the New Testament. The book never became part of the canon, and has, therefore, come to us in only very fragmentary form: a Greek Papyrus, written ca. 300 A.D. (Papyrus Hamburg), a coptic Papyrus from the 6th century (Papyrus Heidelberg); several Greek manuscripts as well as Latin, Syriac, Slavonic and Arabic translations of a portion of this work which is called "The Acts of Paul and Thecla"; Greek manuscripts and translations of the "Martyrdom of Paul". In addition, a large number of smaller fragments with parts of the text of this book exist. Obviously the book was well known and widely used among early Christians

(3) The Acts of the Apostles: the transmission of this book is very rich; however, it is preserved in two different versions, one represented by the Alexandrian texts of the New Testament, the other by the so-called "Western" Text. The latter is usually longer, and by some scholars it has been considered to be the original edition of the book by the author, though critical editions of the New Testament usually print the Alexandrian text.

With respect to the relationship of the various documents to each other the internal evidence is confusing. Some of the letters seem to be dependent upon others: Romans rehearses some of the themes contained in 1 Cor, Gal, and others; the Pastoral Epistles seem to depend upon a number of other Pauline letters; the letter to the Laodiceans looks like a compilation of quotes from other epistles; Ephesians and Colossians apparently discuss themes that the letters to the Romans, to the Corinthians and to the Philippians also raise.[13]

But the relationship among these letters is not something that can be considered without reference to the other "Pauline" writings. These also contain a number of rather interesting relationships. The Acts of Paul not only seems to use some of the Pauline letters, it also includes one of these letters, 3 Corinthians, as part of the narrative; furthermore, this book uses information about Paul's

---

[13] It can be further demonstrated that not all of these letters are direct copies of the autographs. Rather, a process of editing combined several older letters into new units. Rom 16 was originally sent to Ephesus as a letter of recommendation for the deacon Phoebe; Phil 3 must be a fragment of a letter later incorporated into the present Epistle to the Philippians; also Phil 4:10-20 was once an independent note of acknowledgement and thanks. What we now possess as the Second Epistle to the Corinthians is a composition of at least five different letters (see below). For relevant literature cf. Kümmel, *Introduction, passim*.

travel plans that was also available to the author of 2 Timothy. On the other hand, Luke's Acts of the Apostles seems to be completely oblivious of the fact that Paul wrote letters; the book never mentions any such letters. Whether "Luke" was Paul's travel companion, or whether he was some later author of the second generation of Christianity, this is strange indeed, because we have certain clues which indicate that collections of some of Paul's epistles were made very soon after his death.

One must further consider what normally is called the "external evidence" for the existence of any of these writings. The term is misleading, insofar as usage of any of these writings by some other author is not simply an "external" attestation to enable us to make conclusions about the time at which certain writings were already in existence; it also constitutes part of the living extension of Paul's activity, and witnesses to the continuing life of his work and to the various controversial issues which it had raised.

The first "external" evidence is found in the 1 Epistle of Clement which dates from the last decade of the 1st century and refers to Paul's epistles frequently. Even more abundant is the usage of such epistles in the letters of Ignatius of Antioch which were written about 110 A.D. Remarkably, both the 2nd Epistle to the Corinthians and the Pastoral Epistles are never referred to in either 1 Clement or in Ignatius. But that does not necessarily mean that these Pauline letters were not yet written at that time, nor can one conclude that all those Pauline epistles which are quoted here must therefore be genuine. The use of Paul's epistles in Ignatius demonstrates the lively continuation of the discussion of some of the central themes of Paul's theology, although the theme of "justification by faith" is completely missing (the term "righteousness" only appears once in Ignatius, namely in a gospel-quotation!). On the other hand, I Clement is primarily interested in Paul as a teacher of morality and proper conduct in the church. I Clement gives evidence for the knowledge of Pauline letters in Rome by the turn of the first century. But the apologist Justin Martyr half a century later never quotes anything from Paul, although he taught in Rome as did at the same time the shipowner Marcion from Sinope in Pontos, who edited the first canonical collection of Pauline Epistles, albeit without the Pastoral Epistles.

An introduction to these Pauline writings must discuss and analyze the historical developments and theological issues which have contributed to the various noteworthy phenomena which we have enumerated above. The necessary historical-theological quest also implies that one cannot—in the frequently observed fashion of New Testament "Introductions"—leave the decisive questions open and dangling: e.g. "this letter may or may not have been written by Paul, but we will proceed to harvest our theological fruits from the document anyway." One must insist that a writing and its content cannot be fully understood unless one is willing to assign— albeit hypothetically—a place to such a writing in the historical and theological developments of early Christianity.

A good starting point methodologically is the consideration of the form and function of a particular document or a group of writings. Several letters which have come to us under the name of Paul reveal that they are meant to be instruments of church organization.[14] They reflect directly the problems which must have arisen in the building up of only recently founded religious communities and they are either substitutes for personal visits or they are media which serve better than a personal visit and oral communication would at a particular political moment (e.g., in 2 Cor 10-13 Paul writes a letter, because a personal confrontation at that critical moment of the controversy could have had only negative consequences). We are well advised to assign such letters to Paul himself as long as we cannot detect any traces of imitation and pseudonymity in them (1 Thess, Gal, Phil, 1 Cor and the letters now compiled as 2 Cor belong in this category). Rom 16 and Phlm are additional examples of the use of the letter as political instrument. They are letters of recommendation for individuals which seek to influence the modes of mutual relationship in the church. It is noteworthy that the first of these pleads for the acceptance of a woman as an officer of the congregation, the second advises a master to welcome his runaway slave and to accept him as a Christian brother rather than a slave. Phlm 4:10-20 shows us a letter of acknowledgement and thanks for a gift which emphasizes at the same time the independence of the apostle. The interpretation of such letters must proceed together with the reconstruction of the history of the Pauline mission and of the controversies which arose in this process.

---

[14] For the insight into the use of the letter as a political instrument I am indebted to Dieter Georgi (lecture presented at Yale University, spring 1971).

Other documents have a distinctly different character. The Epistle to the Romans is a letter of introduction and an apologetic summary of Paul's theology. Such a summary of Paul's theology is also the letter to the Ephesians, although it lacks the element of the letter of recommendation which is so conspicuous in Romans. Both writings look back upon the other letters of Paul or upon their theological content as something that is already established. This is a perspective which they share with the use that Ignatius of Antioch makes of the Pauline epistles. Ignatius, however, shows yet another kind of dependence upon the Pauline letters: He uses the form of the Pauline letter as an instrument of church organization and of polemical controversy. But there is a conspicuous difference between Paul and Ignatius: Ignatius tries to influence already established Christian communities and attacks formulated heresies with respect to their false teachings, whereas Paul himself confronts critically theological problems which have arisen within the process of the establishment of new communities. That Ignatius is writing a letter of self-recommendation to the Romans shows that Paul's letter to the Romans has become a traditional norm. In Colossians and 2 Thessalonians we find that the genre of the Pauline letter has become an instrument of polemics against religious aberrations which threaten the integrity of the accepted Pauline teachings.

Of a different kind are those letters which turn the Pauline attempt to organize the life of his churches through written communication into the propagation of church orders. The tendency is clearly visible in the use that I Clement makes of the Pauline writings. It is well established in the Pastoral Epistles which are in fact church orders in the form of pseudepigraphical letters.[15] This indicates a development in which the form of the Pauline letters was used again, once it was established in those churches which emerged from the Pauline mission. However the purpose is quite different. The letter is still an instrument of church policy, but now it wants to communicate true doctrine and true order for the church. Also the letter to the Laodiceans and the 3rd letter to the Corinthians belong in this category.

There are a number of interesting parallels from the pagan

---

[15] Such letters to "individuals" as the Pastoral Epistles are, therefore to be distinguished sharply from the letter to Philemon or the correspondence between Paul and Seneca.

world.[16] Philosophical schools used the writing of fictitious letters under the name of a famous person as a literary frame for the promulgation of philosophical doctrine, inasmuch as also famous philosophers of that period had actually written letters to friends or to relatives (Cicero, Seneca) in order to propagate their philosophical views. This assumed life situation produced the "Correspondence between Paul and Seneca." A parallel for other Pauline letters are the letters of the Emperors through which they tried to instruct the officials in various provinces and cities with respect to specific important questions. The closest parallel to this is found in 1 Cor which gives instructions upon written request (cf. 1 Cor 7:1) and on the basis of other information (1 Cor 1:11). The Pastoral Epistles, on the other hand (Paul writing to Timothy and Titus instructions for the moral life and order of the church), are more closely related to the (usually pseudepigraphical) epistles of several philosophical traditions in which moral advice of a general nature is offered.

It is obvious that in several categories of "Pauline" letter production materials from the mission of Paul and from the letters he wrote have been used and re-used. Use of Pauline traditions also has been made by those writings which belong to an entirely different literary genre, i.e. the Acts of Luke and the Acts of Paul. However, the material that is used here is of a different character. It reflects patterns of early Christian mission in general and of mission in the Pauline churches in particular. Paul was remembered as a great and successful missionary, and that meant performance of miracles, documentation of the possession of divine spirit through powerful speeches in public and through deep scriptural exegesis. The literature which presents this image is almost entirely religious propaganda literature, and in this respect follows pagan examples of similar literary production (biographies, aretalogies, and romances), which are more typically "religious" than the genre of the letter which is either "political" or philosophical in character. The existence of such books as the Pauline Acts gives evidence for the continuation of a widespread early Christian pattern, i.e., the demonstration of the religious power of

---

[16] Cf. the recent publications in the SBL Dissertation Series 2, 4 and 5 (1972): John Lee White, *The Body of the Greek Letter*; Chan-Hie Kim, *The Familiar Letter of Recommendation*; John Lee White, *The Form and Structure of the Official Petition*.

the Gospel as a primary means of the further expansion of Christianity in the pagan world.

A second step in the elaboration of this approach would have to take into consideration two other elements, form-criticism, and the question of style and vocabulary.

Form-critical evaluation would have to show the particular status and development of traditional materials at the stage at which they were incorporated into the written documents in which they occur. Prayers and other liturgical materials, creeds and hymns as well as orally transmitted narratives (as miracle stories, novels, anecdotes) would have to be assessed with respect to their form and function in the life of the church. Fully developed credal formulations demonstrate that a writing belongs to a later generation of the church; those with still very primitive formulations of the creed are more likely of an earlier date. Novelistic development of miracle stories belongs to a comparatively late period, although some of the stories themselves could derive from very early stages of the tradition.

The investigation of vocabulary and style provides criteria for the relative dating of the various writings. The deutero-Pauline writings can be recognized insofar as they reveal a style of Pauline argumentation which has become stereotyped. Vocabulary is very sensitive with respect to certain fashions and also in view of an opponent's abuse. Once certain terms become key terms of the opponent's vocabulary, they only occur with certain qualifying attributes; e.g., the term gnosis/knowledge, frequently used by Paul, occurs in the Pastoral Epistles only once, and here with the modifier "falsely so-called" (1 Tim 6:20).

Also with respect to form and style the horizon must be expanded to include Jewish and pagan literature of that period. The Pastoral Epistles, to quote only one example, more than any other Pauline writing reflect linguistic elements very characteristic of the Greek which was typical of the literature of the 2nd century in general.

Only after the completion of such considerations and analyses will it be possible to reconstruct that section of early Christian history which has produced the literature of the Pauline Corpus at large. Historical and literary developments will have to be accounted for as well as the theological issues and controversies. The question of authorship in such a reconstruction will lose much of its mystique. Instead, the precise determination of the place both of the extant literature and of the development of traditions will have to be the main focus. To introduce the Pauline literature of early Christianity is a constructive task. Once the homework in the critical analysis of the sources is done, the "Introduction" will be able to present the topics of its subject matter in a way like the following:

(1) *The calling and the early mission of Paul* of which we can gain some fragmentary knowledge on the basis of his letters and of some older traditions in the Book of Acts. In this context belong typical features of the beliefs, the worship and the diversified religious convictions in the early Pauline churches, as they are visible in traditions which are quoted in Paul's letters.

(2) *The second period of Paul's ministry* which is directly related to the extant genuine letters. This will include a description of the effort of the organization of churches and the controversies with opposing interpretations of the Christian tradition; the role and function of the letters in their original form as part of these activities; and a theological evaluation of the work accomplished by Paul in this brief period, its problems and its ambiguous religious potential.

(3) *Early post-Pauline Christianity*: The development of tendencies which Paul had opposed; e.g. the use of the Pauline authority and of Pauline letters in the service of a gnosticizing Christianity and the renewal of the expectation of an impending parousia in the name of Paul. The letters to the Ephesians, Colossians, and 2nd Thessalonians seem to answer such problems, again under the authority of the great Apostle. At the same time, a tradition must have developed that transmitted stories of Paul as the great travelling miracle-worker in the interests of a continuing Christian propaganda.

(4) *First attempts to consolidate the Pauline tradition*: A first collection of the Pauline epistles was made that contained all letters which are now part of the New Testament canon except 2 Corinthians and the Pastoral Epistles. Ignatius of Antioch and Clement of Rome attest the wide circulation of this collection. The theological perspective which these letters present became influential also in the formation of the first written Gospel, Mark, which is distinctly Pauline in its sense of mystery and in its theology of the cross.

(5) The author of *Luke-Acts* is an important representative of the

next phase: against the paradoxical and enigmatic theology of the letters in which Paul appears as the representative of Christ's death in this world (Ignatius understood this just as well as Mark), Luke erects, on the basis of the tradition of Paul's miracle stories, a monument that pictures Paul as the successful missionary of the church who carries, guided by the spirit, the Gospel from Jerusalem to Rome; one may also note that Luke re-edits the Pauline Gospel of Mark in an analogous fashion. On the other hand, an unknown editor in Corinth seems to have composed several fragments of genuine Pauline writings into an impressive document which is known as the Second Epistle to the Corinthians; this collection reinforces, against Luke, the tradition that saw Paul as the messenger who represents in his life the secret and paradoxically human presence of the divine revelation rather than the public demonstration of impressive religious power.

(6) The line represented by Luke must have lived on strongly nevertheless; it makes its re-appearance in the *Acts of Paul* which does not use Luke's Acts, but depends upon a rich independent tradition. Here even the death of Paul became a demonstration of divine power (whereas Luke had not yet dared to conclude his work with an account of Paul's martyrdom). But although this work combined the miracle worker tradition with the image of the dying apostle, the existing corpus of Paul's letters itself still called for a solution, since by now it had become one of the most important books of the gnostic movement. The Acts of Paul had tried to solve this problem by inserting an anti-gnostic letter of Paul into the corpus (3 Corinthians). The attempt that was made in the invented correspondence between Paul and Seneca to present Paul as a philosopher was obviously no answer, though it shared the world-open attitude of the 2nd century apologists. Even less satisfactory must have been the letter to the Laodiceans, a patchwork of those quotations from Paul's epistles which were acceptable to the orthodox church.

(7) Two successful solutions emerged. They brought the epistles of Paul into a perspective in which they became documents which gave direction to the continuing life of religious communities, one by *Marcion*, the other by the author of the *Pastoral Epistles*. Marcion's revised edition, which tried to reconstruct the original form of these letters, makes Paul once again the apostle who proclaims a new message of salvation. In the Pastoral Epistles, on the other

hand, Paul is foremost a church-leader, teacher and organizer; some such traditions about his activities were apparently still available to the author, apart from the earlier letters. Within this horizon the transmitted collection of his epistles was allowed to survive in spite of inconsistencies and ambiguities in theological orientation within the collection itself.

It was this latter solution which the church later canonized. This was not done, because one believed in Paul as the great religious individual through which the Holy Spirit spoke with divine authority. Rather, this canonization came out of the confidence that the Holy Spirit is a gift that is given to the church, and that therefore usage by that church through the generations constituted enough grounds for accepting such writings as authority. The successors of those Christian communities in Asia Minor and Greece which Paul himself had founded and organized canonized this particular collection of Epistles together with the book of Acts, because these writings had proven to be forces which had sustained and nourished the life of these churches for several generations—and they promised to do so for many more generations to come.

GOOD NEWS IS NO NEWS: ARETALOGY AND GOSPEL

JONATHAN Z. SMITH
University of Chicago

> Crito: In what way shall we bury you?
> Socrates: In any way that you like, if you can catch me
> and I don't elude you.   (*Phaedo* 115C)

In recent years, sparked largely by the works of Morton Smith, Dieter Georgi, Hans Dieter Betz and Helmut Koester there has been a revival of interest in the question of the possible relationship between Greco-Roman aretalogies and Christian gospels. While others have made more extensive contributions to the implications of this relationship for the understanding of particular New Testament texts, Morton Smith, through his invaluable *Heroes and Gods* and his sophisticated and fulsome essay on the history of scholarship and the current state of the question, has provided the parameters for much of the current discussion.[1] However, I believe that further progress can be made only if we question two presuppositions that have shaped much of this research: that the aretalogy functions primarily as a model to be imitated and that the essential character of the aretalogy is that of a collection of miracle stories.[2]

I have taken my clue from a little noticed séance of the nineteenth century French magician, Eliphas Lévi. On July 24, 1854 as the culmination of a three week period of preparation, Lévi invoked the spirit of Apollonius of Tyana:

> The mirror which was behind the altar seemed to brighten in its depth, a wan form was outlined therein which increased and seemed to approach by degrees. Three times, and with closed eyes, I invoked Apollonius. When again I looked forth there was a man in front of me, wrapped from head to toe in a species of shroud, which seemed more grey than white. He was lean, melancholy and beardless, *and did not altogether correspond to my preconceived notion of Apollonius*

---

[1] M. Hadas and M. Smith, *Heroes and Gods: Spiritual Biographies in Antiquity* (London, 1965); M. Smith, "Prolegomena to a Discussion of Aretalogies, Divine Men, the Gospels and Jesus," *Journal of Biblical Literature*, XC (1971), 174-199.

[2] See, for example, D. L. Tiede, *The Charismatic Figure as Miracle Worker* (Missoula, 1972) who distinguishes between the aretalogy of the sage (model) and the aretalogy of the miracle worker (chapter 1, *passim*.).

... After the evocation I have described, *I re-read carefully* the Life of Apollonius ... and I remarked that towards the end of his life he was starved and tortured in prison. This circumstance, which perhaps remained in my memory without my being aware of it, may have determined the unattractive form of my vision.[3]

While there are many elements in the elaborate description of Lévi's ritual which are worthy of comment by an historian of religions, in the context of this article I would call attention only to the function of the *Vita Apollonii* in Lévi's account. The narrative of the Apollonius' life in the *Vita* inspired Lévi with the desire to 'meet' and gain wisdom from Apollonius. The ritual he employed was, he believed, a faithful repetition of one devised by Apollonius.[4] Yet Levi's 'experience' of Apollonius did not accord with his expectation. This drove Lévi to a reexamination of the *Vita* in the light of his experience and to a new understanding of his experience in the light of his reconsideration of the *Vita*.

I should like to suggest that this experience of discrepancy provides an important corrective to our usual understanding of aretalogies as models to be imitated by disciples. The devotee does not passively reenact or imitate. Rather he has an experience which *both validates and challenges* the model proposed by the "Life" and through a process of double-reflection, his understanding of both his experience and the "Life" requires reinterpretation. There is an interplay between text and experiential context and both are mutually challenged by this process. I would further argue that this sense of discrepancy, this interplay, is a major function of the aretalogy which is best expressed as the interplay between understanding and misunderstanding. In this paper, I shall explore this interplay in the *Vita Apollonii* by Philostratus and in the complex *Vita Pythagorae* tradition as represented by Iamblichus.

I

In his important study of the use of the terms "magician" and "sorcerer" in Western European literature, Robert-Léon

---

[3] E. Lévi, *Transcendental Magic*, A. E. Waite, transl. (London, n.d.), pp. 154-157 (emphasis, mine). Compare the use of this séance in W. Somerset Maugham's novel, *The Magician* (New York, 1909), pp. 81-86. E. M. Butler, *Ritual Magic* (Cambridge, 1949), pp. 283-293 is the only scholar I have seen who calls attention to the importance of Lévi's evocation.

[4] Lévi, esp. pp. 500f. Compare the recent occult interpretation of this document by J. van Rijckenborgh, *Het Nuctemeron van Apollonius van Tyana* (Haarlem, 1968).

Wagner noted the pains which his sources took to distinguish "les deux magiciens: le sincère et le roué."[5] This is, in fact, a far more significant and pervasive mode of division than the frequently employed functional typology which distinguishes a variety of forms of magic by the substance utilized or the action performed.[6]

There have been many suggestive theoretical contributions to the understanding and definition of magic.[7] One of the more important insights was suggested by the French Sociological School which argued that magic was not different in essence from religion, but rather different with respect to social position. In Durkheim's pithy formulation: *"There is no Church of magic ... A magician has a clientele and not a Church ... Religion, on the other hand, is inseparable from the idea of a Church."*[8] It is thus possible only to speak of the magician not of magic and to characterize his social and religious role as one of *mobility* (frequently expressed theologically by the charge that the magician is heterodox or politically by the charge that he is a foreigner or a subversive). The recent work of Peter Brown and Morton Smith has allowed us to describe this mobility with more precision.[9]

Both Smith and Brown have focussed attention on the one, universal characteristic of magic—it is illegal; within the Greco-Roman world it carried the penalty of death or deportation.[10] Smith concentrates on the implications of this for the magician and his

---

[5] R.-L. Wagner, *"Sorcier" et "Magicien": Contribution à l'histoire du vocabulaire de la magie* (Paris, 1939), esp. pp. 26-35.

[6] For a classic, and utterly unoriginal, example of this sort of functional typology, see Isidore of Seville, *Etymologies* VIII.9, *De Magis*.

[7] See the recent review article by M. and R. Wax, "The Notion of Magic," *Current Anthropology*, IV (1963), 495-518.

[8] E. Durkheim, *The Elementary Forms of the Religious Life* (London, 1954), p. 44 (original italics). Compare, M. Mauss, *A General Theory of Magic* (London, 1972), esp. p. 24 and H. Hubert's classic article, "Magia," in Ch. Daremberg and E. Saglio, *Dictionnaire des antiquités grecques et romaines* (Paris, 1873-1919), Vol. III:2 (1904), cols. 1494-1521, esp. 1494-1496.

[9] P. Brown, "Sorcery, Demons and the Rise of Christianity from Late Antiquity into the Middle Ages," in M. Douglas, ed., *Witchcraft: Confessions and Accusations* (London, 1970), pp. 17-45 (reprinted in P. Brown, *Religion and Society in the Age of St. Augustine* [New York, 1972], pp. 119-146); M. Smith, *Clement of Alexandria and a Secret Gospel of Mark* (Cambridge, Mass., 1973), esp. 220-237.

[10] See, in general, E. Massonneau, *Le crime de magie dans la droit romain* (Paris, 1933) and the Christian material collected by F. Martroye, "La répression de la magie et les cultes des gentils au IVe siècle," *Revue historique du droit français et étranger*, Sér. IV, IX (1930), 669-701.

disciples; Brown (influenced by contemporary anthropological theory) concentrates on the magician's accusers. Smith emphasizes that the terms magician, Θεῖος ἀνήρ and son of god all refer to "a single social type", that magician is the term applied to the figure by his "enemies", that "sceptical but reverent" admirers would use Θεῖος ἀνήρ and that his "believers" would call him son of god.[11] Brown emphasizes another distinction common in the literature, that between philosopher and magician,[12] and insists that these terms refer to a conflict for power. Both figures are competing for a 'place at the table' of "vested" Imperial-traditional power by claiming access to "inarticulate" non-traditional power, in particular the claim to possess an enlightened soul and powerful words. Thus the rhetor may bring a charge of magic against a religious adept or, himself, be charged with magic.[13]

These observations have a number of important implications for our understanding of the religious of late antiquity.[14] In this essay, I should like to focus only on their relevance to the way in which we read gospels and aretalogies. They suggest that for those figures for whom an ultimate religious claim is made (e.g. son of god), their biographies will serve as apologies against outsiders' charges that they were merely magicians and against their admirers' sincere misunderstanding that they were merely wonder-workers, divine men or philosophers. From Iamblichus' *De mysteriis Aegyptiorum* and Apuleius' *Apologia* to the Gospel of Mark (following T. J. Weeden and L. Keck),[15] the characteristic of every major religious biography (and associated autobiographical and dogmatic

---

[11] For a contemporary example, see Don Juan in C. Castenada, *The Teachings of Don Juan: A Yaqui Way of Knowledge* (Berkeley-Los Angeles, 1968) who is at pain to distinguish himself as a "man of knowledge" from the *brujo*. *Brujos* are shot according to Yaqui law (see R. L. Beals, *The Contemporary Culture of the Cáhita Indians* [Washington, 1945], p. 197).

[12] See the collection of terms in R. MacMullen, *Enemies of the Roman Order* (Cambridge, Mass., 1966), pp. 320f., n. 16.

[13] Examples in Brown, *loc. cit.* which may be multiplied, for example the rhetor Adrian οὕτω τι εὐδόκιμος, ὡς καὶ πολλοῖς γόης δόξαι in Philostratus, *Vita Sophisti* 590.

[14] I shall be developing some further implications in my article in the forthcoming *Festschrift* for N. A. Dahl edited by J. Jervell and W. Meeks.

[15] T. J. Weeden, "The Heresy that Necessitated Mark's Gospel," *Zeitschrift für die neutestamentliche Wissenschaft*, LIX (1968), 145-168; *Mark: Traditions in Conflict* (Philadelphia, 1971); L. Keck, "Mark 3.7-12 and Mark's Christology," *Journal for Biblical Literature*, LXXXIV (1965), 341-358.

materials) of the Greco-Roman period is this double defense against the charge of magic—against the calumny of outsiders and the sincere misunderstanding of admirers.

The solution of each group or individual so charged was the same, to insist on an inward meaning of the suspect activities. The allegedly magical action, properly understood, is a sign. There is both a transparent and a hidden meaning, a literal and an inward understanding required. At the surface level the biography appears to be an explicit story of a magician or a *Wundermensch*; at the depth level it is the enigmatic self-disclosure of a son of god.

The *double-entendre* character of the traditions extends from the most trivial detail to the most major incident. Every word, every gesture of the figure is pregnant with *possible* significance. The disciple, the reader, is obsessive and insane if he attempts to interpret every word and gesture as having a deeper meaning; he is a blind man and a fool if he fails to detect the deeper meaning.

This play between appearance and reality is not to be understood merely as an apologetic strategm to avoid unpleasant legal consequences. Code, the *double-entendre*, is the very essence of these figures. Whether revealed in a characteristic form of spells: "You are this, you are not this, you are that" "It is I, it is not I, it is so and so who says this" or in the equally characteristic use in the biographical tradition of riddle, aporia, joke and parable, these figures depend upon a multivalent expression which is interpreted by admirers and detractors as having univocal meaning and thus invites, again by admirers and detractors alike, misunderstanding. The function of the narrative is to play between various levels of understanding and misunderstanding, inviting the reader to assume that both he and the author truly do understand and then cutting the ground out from under this confidence. The figure for whom the designation son of god is claimed, characteristically plays with our seriousness and is most serious when he appears to be playing. This is a sign of his freedom and transcendence, the *sine qua non* of a religious figure of late antiquity worthy of belief.

This toying with the reader's confidence is especially prominent in traditions surrounding the chief disciples of the son of god. It raises for the reader the problem of the refraction of the figure through the reports of those who do not understand and those who misunderstand as in both the case of the Gospels and the aretalogies, it is these same not quite understanding disciples who are the major source of our knowledge of their master. For example, Philostratus' *Vita Apollonii* is alleged to be chiefly based on the "Memoirs" of Damis. The reader is presented with the claim (again as in the Gospels) of a retrospective understanding by the disciples which is relativised by their evident lack of understanding while their master was yet alive.[16] Philostratus introduces Damis with the revealing comment: "There was a man named Damis who was by no means stupid" (I.3)[17]; he was also, as the text repeatedly demonstrates, by no means wise! Damis lasts three hundred and twelve chapters of intimate acquaintance with Apollonius before he "first really" understood the true nature of Apollonius, that is, that it was divine and more than human" (VII.38)—or, Jesus' plaint to his disciples, "Do you still not understand" (Mt. 16.9 etc.).

Like Peter in Mark's Gospel (especially in the "Confession" of chapter 8) reversals with respect to the understanding and misunderstanding of the chief disciples are characteristic of the Greco-Roman *Vitae*. For example, in Philostratus I.18, Apollonius' disciples refuse to accompany him on his travels. He answers them:

> I have taken the gods into counsel and have told you of their decision; and I have made a trial of you to see if you are strong enough to undertake the same things as myself. Since you are so soft and effeminate, I wish you very good health so that you may go on with your philosophy; but I must depart whither wisdom and the gods lead me.

Three lines later he meets Damis who answers Apollonius immediately: "Let us depart, Apollonius, you following the gods and I [following] you." Damis thus appears to be the model of the true and understanding disciple in contradistinction to the previous group; but just as swiftly he reveals that he too does not truly understand. He offers to be of service to his master in that he

---

[16] Compare the attempts to understand (in a literal fashion) the characteristic riddle-speech of Apollonius in III.15 (cp. VI.11), IV.24 (cp. V.7) and IV.43 and the glosses by Damis and others in III.15, VI.32 etc. This material has been collected and discussed (without, I think, perceiving its central significance) by G. Petzke, *Die Traditionen über Apollonius von Tyana und das Neue Testament* (Leiden, 1970), pp. 111-116.

[17] I have cited Philostratus, *Vita Apollonii* according to the text in the Loeb edition by F. C. Conybeare (London, 1912) and have followed, with slight modifications, his translation. Attention should be called to the superb, lively translation by C. P. Jones in the Penguin Classics series (Harmondsworth, 1970) which is, unfortunately, abridged.

knows many of the languages of the peoples they will encounter on their journey. Apollonius replies: "I understand all languages, though I never learned a single one... I also understand all the secrets of human silence". Rather than comprehending, even now, Apollonius' rebuke, that the journey was not to be a tour and that Apollonius did not require the services of a guide, that the discussions they would have required no translation because human speech was inadequate for the matters to be discussed—Damis misunderstands Apollonius to be claiming *daimonic* status and "worshipped him".

Throughout the *Vita*, Damis functions like Peter in Mark's Gospel, the first and most cherished of the disciples who nevertheless consistently misunderstands. Like Peter, the last scene we have of Damis is a betrayal (VII.15)—and, like Peter, we have only the tradition that later reflection led to his final understanding.

What then is there to be understood about a figure such as Apollonius? It is here that the title of this essay's play on *euangelion* becomes *à propos*. The *Vita Apollonii* begins with a set of conflicting birth-stories, an aretalogical convention which apparently originated with Neanthes of Cyzicus (fl. 200 B.C.). After providing a series of portents, each of which testifies to Apollonius' divinity, but each of which reflects a different understanding of that divinity, Philostratus concludes: "The people of the country say that Apollonius was the son of this Zeus, but the sage called himself the son of Apollonius" (I.6). Regardless of the possible historical truth of the tradition that Apollonius' father bore the same name as his son, I find it impossible not to read a further meaning here. Apollonius is his own father, he is *sui generis*, he is himself, himself alone. All other definitions are inadequate.

From this introductory chapter where Apollonius is introduced as a new epiphany of Proteus ("the god of ever changing form, defying capture" I.4) to the last words of Apollonius, the Pythagorean, which relativise the central Pythagorean doctrine of the immortality of the soul (VIII.31), we are presented with a portrait of a powerful figure who muddles all models. The disciples (and his later readers) are incapable of being like him, even of truly understanding him, because he is fundamentally not like us. He is himself. He is an Other.

As is the case with John the Baptist or Jesus in the Gospels, there is a bewildering assortment of models projected upon Apollonius in Philostratus' account. But none of these is who he truly is. He is, as he constantly reiterates, Apollonius and it is up to disciple and reader to make what poor sense of that as they can. The disciple and the reader remain in the paradigmatic stance of the Babylonian satrap who asks Apollonius the question "From where have you come and who sent you?" (a question pregnant with possible meanings) and is toyed with for three times before the *egō eimi* pronouncement: "I am Apollonius of Tyana" (I.21).

Apollonius, as he functions in his *Vita*, remains opaque. He is a cipher. He has no teachings of his own. His philosophy, as represented by Philostratus, consists of neo-Pythagorean and Stoic commonplaces that may be found in any doxographical handbook. His own characteristic mode of speech appears to have been the riddle, the paradox or silence (see the programmatic statement in VI.11). Commanding enough to secure initial attention, he does not announce a new doctrine but rather seems to become invisible in any given situation. He is an αὐτοσχεδιαστής in the positive sense of the word (VII.30).

His opacity is equalled by his transparency. Neither providing a model nor a saving message, he does not overshadow a situation but rather dissolves from view. Every encounter is similar to that with the Emperor—he simply vanishes (VIII.15). He is able to step inside of every situation because he is, himself, outside of every situation. His biography as biography is not important. His message is given only in his free, playful and utterly transcendent intervention in specific situations which allowed for a moment the possibility of another point of view. The narrative of these situations could have been either immeasurably compressed or expanded, for each situation is essentially nonrepeatable. There can be no "Life" of Apollonius. He lives whenever and wherever a Lévi encounters him and can say "He did not altogether correspond to my preconceived notion" and reflect on this incongruity.

II

The traditions concerning Pythagoras are more complex, but the same general pattern may be discerned. Within the scope of this essay, I shall focus on the theme of understanding and misunderstanding within Iamblichus', *Vita Pythagorica*.[18]

---

[18] I have cited Iamblichus according to the text edited by L. Deubner, *De Vita Pythagorica liber* (Leipzig, 1937). Compare the rather free, English

The text begins with the declaration that "this book concerns the divine Pythagoras" (1, pg.5,2). A declaration that demonstrates that, as in the case of the superscription in Mark 1.1, the purpose of the work is not the gradual revelation of the divine nature of the protagonist—this is presumed from the beginning; but rather that its function is to play between a true and false understanding of this announcement on the part of *both* disciple and opponent.

The opening chapters, as in the *Vita Apollonii*, are given over to a set of conflicting birth stories.[19] Iamblichus presents a moralistic interpretation which stands, at times, in marked tension to the traditions he preserves. The progenitor of Pythagoras "it is said, was conceived by Zeus" which Iamblichus glosses "this was said either because of his virtues or his greatness of soul" (3, pg. 6, 5-7). It was "said" that Pythagoras was "conceived by Apollo" and it was because of this "nobility of birth" that a Samian poet refers to "Pythagoras whom Pythias bore to Apollo" (5, pg. 7, 5-8). He was educated in a way that made him "like a god". Although still young when his father died, he was reverenced by his elders because of his virtues—therefore "it was reasonable to call him the son of a god". His "divine nature" was exhibited in his virtues: his piety, his lack of anger and other violent emotions, his rational self-discipline. Hence it may be said that he lived at Samos as an ἀγαθὸς δαίμων (10, pg. 8, 20-30).

In offering these moralistic glosses on the traditions concerning Pythagoras as a son of god, Iamblichus is combatting what he considers to be the misunderstanding of Epimenedes, Eudoxus and Xenocrates that Apollo had sexual intercourse with Pythagoras' mother (7, pg. 7, 22-24). The text reveals considerable tension and is probably deliberately ambiguous (5, pg. 7, 9-23). The story is a version of the well-known literary motif and cultic fact of a childless couple visiting the oracle at Delphi and the subsequent birth of a *Wunderkind*.

---

translation by T. Taylor, *Iamblichus' Life of Pythagoras* (London, 1818). For the purposes of this paper, I have ignored a number of critical source problems in Iamblichus. Of special interest would be the vexed question of the degree to which Iamblichus is dependent upon an alleged biography of Pythagoras by Apollonius of Tyana!

[19] Note that Diogenes Laertius (VIII.1, 4) has organized his collection of traditions concerning Pythagoras' birth in a manner which more closely resembles that found in the *Vita Apollonii*—a set of conflicting birth-stories followed by an enigmatic self-testimony. I would take the intrusive material (VIII.2f.) to be the result of his editorial breaking of the form.

Mnesarchus went to Delphi, in Iamblichus' version, on a business trip accompanied by his wife who was not aware that she was pregnant. He asked the Pythia about the success of his commercial travels to Syria. He received the prophecy that his venture would be successful and the additional oracle that his wife was now pregnant and would bear a wonderful child of surpassing beauty and wisdom. When Mnesarchus reflected on the fact that the Pythia, without being asked, had volunteered the prediction that he would have a son possessing divine gifts, he named the child Pythagoras (i.e. "announced by the Pythia" ἀγορεύων τὸν Πύθιον)[20] and changed his wife's name from Parthenis (i.e. "virgin") to Pythais in honor of the oracle. Iamblichus hastened to add that one is not to think of physical intercourse.

Those whom he is combatting take the alternative understanding of the story. Pythagoras' mother was not pregnant at the time of the visit to Delphi. She became so as a result of the virgin having intercourse with Apollo (Παρθενίδι ... μιγῆναι τὸν Ἀπόλλωνα). For Iamblichus, such an understanding is crude superstition and is a misunderstanding of the true nature of Pythagoras' divinity. It is to be rejected as was the reverence paid by superstitious sailors with whom Pythagoras travelled who took him for a god, built an altar to him and offered sacrifices (15-17, pp. 11, 24-12, 26; compare Acts 14.11f.). It is to such a misunderstanding that Iamblichus juxtaposes a euhemeristic or moralistic interpretation. Pythagoras was called divine because of his virtues and conduct.

If Iamblichus is concerned to combat this outsider's misinterpretation, he is equally concerned with the misinterpretation of the insider, one who belongs to that outer circle of disciples whom he calls the *Akousmatikoi* and to whom he denies the title of "true Pythagorians".[21] Two themes predominate in their interpretation, both of which are strikingly parallel to elements in the lives of other sons of god such as Jesus and Apollonius: a variety of titles which are projected upon the figure in an attempt to 'locate'

---

[20] See the discussion in M. Delcourt, *L'oracle de Delphes* (Paris, 1955), pp. 235-239.

[21] Within the scope of this paper, it is not necessary to discuss the vexing question of the relationship between the *Akousmatikoi* and the *Mathēmatikoi*—on which, see W. Burkert, *Lore and Science in Ancient Pythagoreanism* (Cambridge, Mass., 1972), pp. 192-208. I have followed Iamblichus' polemical interpretation.

him and an interpretation of his divinity in terms of wonders and miracles.

The multiple titles play an analogous role to the multiple birth-stories. A chain of conflicting or competing testimony is capped by an enigmatic identification or self-testimony (compare John 1. 19-23).

> Some of them [the *Akousmatikoi*] spoke of him as the Pythian [Apollo], others as the Hyperborean Apollo, others as [Apollo] Paean. Still others thought him to be one of the *daimons* who inhabit the moon, others considered him to be one of the Olympian gods who sometimes appear to men in human form. (30, pg. 18, 12-17)

To such speculations, Iamblichus juxtaposes the insiders' interpretation—one of the traditions of the *Mathēmatikoi* or "true Pythagoreans" as preserved by Aristotle:

> Aristotle relates in his work on Pythagorean Philosophy that the following division was preserved by the Pythagoreans as one of their greatest secrets—that there are three kinds of rational, living creatures: gods, men and beings like Pythagoras (31, pg. 18, 12-16 = Aristotle, Fragment 192 [Rose]).[22]

Pythagoras, rightly understood, is *sui generis*, he is in a class by himself. It is a misunderstanding to classify Pythagoras either as a man (especially as a mere "magician") or as a god. Rather he is the mysterious 'included middle'. The history of the misunderstanding of Pythagoras could be written, in Iamblichus' view, from the same perspective as a history of Christian heresy, i.e., the emphasis on either the godhood or the manhood of the son of god and the failure to assert his paradoxical god-manhood.

There are those who exhibit one pole of this misunderstanding and relate Pythagoras to a variety of deities as an epiphany; there are those who focus too much upon the other pole and, conceiving of him as a man, narrative his miracles and thus run the risk of perceiving him as a magician and a fraud.[23]

The miracles of Pythagoras form a somewhat fixed catalogue which are capable of an independent, contextless circulation in

---

[22] Compare Iamblichus 144, pg. 80, 25f. "[they say that] man, bird and another third thing are bipeds—and the third thing is Pythagoras"; a play on the "man is a featherless biped" tradition.

[23] See Lucian, *Alexander* 4.

paradoxographical collections such as Apollonius, *Historia thaumasiai* 6 or Aelian, *Varia historia* II.26 and IV.17.[24] The most commonly recurring motifs are: (1) At the same hour Pythagoras was seen in two cities; (2) he had a golden thigh; (3) he told a Crotanite that in a previous existence he had been King Midas; (4) a white eagle permitted him to stroke it—in other versions, he converted a wild bear to vegetarianism or persuaded an ox to abstain from eating beans; (5) a river greeted him, "Hail, Pythagoras!"; (6) he predicted that a dead man would be found on a ship which was just then entering the harbor; (7) when asked for a sign, he predicted the appearance of a white bear before a messenger reached him bearing the news; (8) he bit a poisonous snake to death—in a more rationalistic version, he drove out a snake from a village. These stories are all presented without interpretation or explanation. They hint at the divine, the numinous, the ability to control the animal, the power of transcending space and time. But they do not define Pythagoras' divinity. "There is always something enigmatic about the meaning of these miracles ... explicitness is avoided".[25] They are hints; but they do not serve to prove or to demonstrate. Indeed, in a manner analogous to the ending of the Fourth Gospel (Jn. 20. 30f.), Iamblichus relatives their importance. They are outsiders' stories, they speak only περὶ τἀνδρός:

> Ten thousand other more divine and more wondrous things than these are related concerning the man by every source such as the prediction of earthquakes, the expelling of plagues and violent winds and the calming of rivers and seas so that his disciples may more easily pass over them. And similar wonders are narrated of others such as Empedocles, Epimenedes and Abaris... But these [that I have narrated] are sufficient as an indication of his piety (135, pp. 76, 19-77, 13).

and immediately Iamblichus turns to a 'higher' mode of discourse, characteristic of the *Mathēmatikoi*, which includes a complex discussion of the modes of reality in mythological and miraculous tales (138-140, pp. 78, 14-79, 12).

While the details of this discussion are not germane to this paper, two anecdotes, each of which Iamblichus narrates twice

---

[24] For an excellent discussion and rich bibliography, see Burkert, pp. 141-147. The collection apparently derives from Aristotle's lost work on the Pythagoreans.

[25] Burkert, p. 144.

during the course of this section on wonders, are revealing of the point of view of the "true" Pythagoreans towards signs and miracles.

> A shepherd feeding his flock near a tomb heard someone singing; but the Pythagorean to whom this was told was not at all incredulous, but asked what harmonic mode the song was in.

> Pythagoras, himself, was asked by a young man what was the significance of the fact that he had, while asleep, conversed with his dead father. Pythagoras said that "it signified nothing, for neither is anything signified by your talking to me". (Compare 139, pp. 17, 20-79, 3 and 148, pp. 83, 24-84, 7).

The miraculous is to be accepted as ordinary [26]; it has, in itself, no meaning unless it leads to insight or higher speculation. Each miracle is unimportant if interpreted univocally as a sign of divinity; its value come from the perception that it is a *double-entendre*.

The true understanding of Pythagoras is only hinted at by Iamblichus in a double-recension of the epiphany of Pythagoras. The first version (140-143) begins with one of the classic *akousmata*: "Who is Pythagoras? They say that he is the Hyperborean Apollo" (pg. 79, 13f.). In this version, which appears to be derived from Aristotle's rather credulous reporting of Pythagorean miracle-tales, "this is supposed to be proven" by two separate incidents: by Pythagoras accidentally showing his thigh while watching a dramatic performance and by his theft of the magic, gold arrow of Apollo from Abaris. The rest of the miracle-chain, discussed above, then follows. In this tradition, Pythagoras is the Hyperborean Apollo as demonstrated by his deeds.

Iamblichus' rejection of this understanding of Pythagoras depends upon his distinction between the *Akousmatikoi* and the *Mathēmatikoi* where the former are the outer circle of disciples, left with a set of enigmatic sayings (*akousmata*) and therefore lacking in true grounds for their beliefs.[27] It is from this outer circle that this misunderstanding derives. The nature of Pythagoras, for the *Mathēmatikoi*, cannot be disclosed or demonstrated from his miraculous deeds.

---

[26] Compare Aristotle, Fragment 193 [Rose], "The Pythagoreans marvelled at any city-dweller who said that he had never seen a *daimon*".

[27] Compare *Vita* 81-89 (pp. 46,22-52,19) with Iamblichus, *De communi mathematica scientia* 25 (N. Festa, editor [Leipzig, 1916], pp. 76,16-78,8), and see above, note 21.

The second recension (90-94) is attributed by scholars to Nichomachus, who was a critic of "mere" miracle-stories. It is representative of the interpretation of the *Mathēmatikoi*. Far more complex than the previous tradition, it joins in a free composition the episode of the golden thigh and the encounter with Abaris. Both the accidental nature of the disclosure in the theatre and the crude power-play of Pythagoras' theft are eliminated in favor of a dignified self-disclosure by Pythagoras. It is the transfiguration of Pythagoras before an equally divine witness who will not misunderstand. (It is thus parallel to the role of the heavenly witnesses at Jesus' transfiguration in contradistinction to the disciples who misunderstand).

The relationship between Pythagoras and Abaris in this version is one of immediacy. At first sight, Abaris immediately recognizes Pythagoras' true nature. Even though Abaris is not learned in the Greek philosophical tradition, Pythagoras sets aside his usual lengthy regimen and "immediately considered him capable" of learning his most esoteric doctrines. Abaris mastered them within the smallest possible space of time (pg. 53, 4-7).

To summarize the narrative: While travelling through Italy on his return to the North, Abaris, a priest of the Hyperborean Apollo, "immediately on seeing Pythagoras thought him like the god (εἰκάσας τῷ θεῷ) whose priest he was. And believing that Pythagoras was none other than the god himself, that no man was like him, but that he was truly Apollo (καὶ πιστεύσας μὴ ἄλλον εἶναι, μηδὲ ἄνθρωπον ὅμοιον ἐκείνῳ, ἀλλ' αὐτὸν ὄντως τὸν Ἀπόλλωνα)" Abarais gave him his golden arrow.[28] When Pythagoras received the miraculous arrow, he did not seem surprised nor did he inquire about it, but immediately, "as if he were the god himself (ὡς ἂν ὄντως ὁ θεὸς αὐτὸς ὤν)", he took Abaris aside and privately showed him his golden thigh as an indication that Abaris was not mistaken and that he had truly recognized him. Pythagoras declared that he had come on a mission of *therapeia* "and that it was for this reason that he had assumed human form (διὰ τοῦτο ἀνθρωπόμορφος) in order that men would not be disturbed by the strangeness of his transcendence (ἵνα μὴ ξενιζόμενοι πρὸς τὸ ὑπερέχον ταράσσωνται)". He then taught Abaris the esoteric, mathematical knowledge; but these things must remain secret (pp. 53, 10-54, 15).

---

[28] On the shamanistic elements in the Pythagoras-Abaris story, see M. Eliade, *Zalmoxis: The Vanishing God* (Chicago, 1972), pp. 21-75.

For mere mortals, a figure like Pythagoras must remain a cipher. They will be "disturbed by his strangeness" but they cannot overcome it. They will either be reduced to misunderstandings or dark riddles or complex and paradoxical theories such as that offered by Iamblichus:

> No one can doubt that the psyche of Pythagoras was sent from the kingdom of Apollo, though whether [he is related to the deity] as an attendant (συνοπαδόν) or through a more direct interpenetration (συντεταγμένην) we cannot know. (8, pp. 7, 29-8, 1)

The only possible means of obtaining true knowledge is through the principle of like knowing like. Thus Abaris and Pythagoras; or, in the Fourth Gospel, the Father and the Son. But even in these cases, what has been recorded by men is opaque and doubtless has been misunderstood.

What an Apollonius, a Pythagoras, a Jesus reveals in the narratives concerning them, is their own enigmatic nature, their *sui generis* character. What was said by one of these sons of god might have been said by the others: "You will seek me and you will not find me, where I am you cannot come" (Jn 7.34)—a saying which was misunderstood by opponent and disciple alike (compare Jn 7.35f. with 13.33).

III

As I have already noted, conclusions quite similar to these have already been reached with respect to the lives of Jesus.[29] Mark, it has been suggested, is concerned with combatting a θεῖος ἀνήρ christology which focussed on Jesus' miracles; the disciples are represented as misunderstanding Jesus as being merely a divine-man. The genre "gospel" is in the process of being redefined as a "reverse aretalogy".[30] I have tried to demonstrate that an analogous process is at work in Philostratus and Iamblichus. If we reserve

---

[29] See above, note 15. However there remains in the New Testament discussion some lingering notion that this is unique, i.e. that the theme of misunderstanding represents a Christian correction of a hellenistic mode of understanding Jesus. I would want to insist that the juxtaposition of the enigma of the son of god with misunderstandings is precisely characteristic of all hellenistic "gospels".

[30] I have taken this notion from an unpublished paper by Norman Peterson, Jr., "So-called Gnostic Type Gospels and the Question of the Genre 'Gospel'," manuscript page 66: "a gospel is a sub-type of Aretalogy, perhaps a polemical parody [of an aretalogy]."

the term "aretalogy" for those collections of model hagiographies and paradoxographies which are so widespread in the period of late antiquity, then I would want to reserve the term "gospel" for those works in which the adequacy of a magical or divine man interpretation of a son of god, in which the portrait of a life which can be imitated and the demonstration of divinity through miracles is relativized by the motif of misunderstanding and through the depiction of the protagonist as *sui generis*, as enigmatic and estranged. *A "gospel" is a narrative of a son of god who appears among men as a riddle inviting misunderstanding.* I would want to claim the title "gospel" for the *Vitae* attributed to Mark and John as well as for those by Philostratus and Iamblichus.

I would likewise relate my discussion of the content of the knowledge of the son of god transmitted by these "gospels" to the pioneering researches of Wayne Meeks on John. His description of the function of speech in the Fourth Gospel applies as well to the materials studied in this paper:

> The dialogue with Nicodemus and its postscript connected with John the Baptist constitute a virtual *parody* of a revelation discourse. What is 'revealed' is that Jesus is incomprehensible... The forms of speech which would ordinarily provide warrants for a particular body of information or instruction are here used in such a way that they serve solely to emphasize Jesus' strangeness. Yet it is not quite accurate to say with Bultmann that Jesus reveals only that he is the revealer. He reveals rather that he is the enigma ... [Only the initiate] can possibly understand its double entendre and abrupt transitions. For the outsider—even for the interested inquirer (like Nicodemus)—the dialogue is opaque.[31]

While the theme of hostility to the world and the dualism heaven/world is not as pronounced in the Greco-Roman *Vitae* as it is in the Christian, this description would hold as well for Apollonius and Pythagoras. In both the Greco-Roman and the Christian "gospels" we encounter an essentially contentless revelation, we encounter a figure who speaks and acts in a *sui generis* manner which breaks all previous cosmic and social structures. The Christian "gospels" appear to shrink from the full consequences of this enigmatic disclosure by introducing the category of the future when all will be clear and when the disciple and the son will be reunited. The

---

[31] W. Meeks, "The Man from Heaven in Johannine Sectarianism," *Journal of Biblical Literature*, XCI (1972), 44-72. I have taken the quotation from page 57.

Greco-Roman materials relativise the enigma by placing it within a context of public, philosophical rhetoric. But both require on the part of their readers a perception of discrepancy between their understanding and the protagonist's self understanding.

IV

I should like to conclude with one further set of reflections lest what I have written be misunderstood in a manner characteristic of New Testament theologians. I am not describing a shift from myth (i.e. "aretalogy") to *kerygma* or a process of existential demythologization. I would want to insist, as an historian of religions, that what I have attempted to describe is thoroughly consistent with a proper understanding of myth. I should like to affirm some 'hard-nosed' statements about myth—that it is a "category mistake" (Ryle) and that it is "that which gives worldly objectivity to that which is otherworldly" (Bultmann)—and reject some 'softer' statements such as those associated with the Frankfurt School which seek to maintain a distinction between the primal moment of myth as *Ergriffenheit* and a secondary application. I would propose that there is no such category as "pristine" myth but only application and that this application derives from the character of myth as a self-conscious category mistake. That is to say that the discrepancy of myth is not an error but the very source of its power.

My understanding of the nature of application has been much influenced by recent anthropological studies of divination. The diviner, by manipulating a limited number of objects and by rigorously interrogating his client in order to determine his "situation" arrives at a description of a possible world of meaning which confers significance on his client's question or distress. The diviner offers a plausibility structure, he suggests a possible "fit" between the structure he offers and the client's situation and both the diviner and his client delight in exploring the adequacy, the possibilities and implications of the diviner's proposal.[32]

Myth as narrative, I would suggest, is an analogue to the limited number of objects manipulated by the diviner. Myth as application represents the complex interaction between diviner, client and "situation". There is delight and there is play in both the 'fit' and

---

[32] For example, V. Turner, *Ndembu Divination: Its Symbolism and Techniques* (Manchester, 1961).

the incongruity of the 'fit', between an element in the myth and this or that segment of the world that one has encountered. Myth, properly understood, must take into account the complex processes of application and inapplicability, of congruity and incongruity. Myth shares with other genres such as the joke, the riddle and the "gospel" a perception of a possible relation between two different 'things' and it delights in the play in-between.

We have need of a rhetoric of incongruity which would explore the range from joke to paradox, from riddle-contest to myth and the modes of transcendence, freedom and play each employs. The "gospel" as I have described it stands in the closest relation to the joke which has been recently described by Mary Douglas as:

> A play upon form. It brings into relation disparate elements in such a way that one accepted pattern is challenged by the appearance of another which in some way was hidden in the first... The joke affords opportunity for realizing that an accepted pattern has no necessity. Its excitement lies in the suggestion that any particular ordering of experience may be arbitrary and subjective. It is frivolous in that it produces no real alternative, only an exhilarating sense of freedom from form in general.[33]

Given the religious situation which confronted the man of late antiquity, which described a world in which the archaic structures of order and destiny were discovered to be evil, confining and untrue, in which man strove to be free from being 'placed', such frivolity is, in fact, transcendence.[34]

---

[33] M. Douglas, "The Social Control of Cognition: Some Factors in Joke Perception," *Man*, n.s. III (1968), 365.

[34] See J. Z. Smith, "Birth Upside Down or Rightside Up?" *History of Religions*, IX (1970), 281-303; "The Wobbling Pivot," *Journal of Religion*, LII (1972), 134-149; "The Influence of Symbols upon Social Change: A Place on Which to Stand," in J. Shaughnessy, ed., *The Roots of Ritual* (Grand Rapids, 1973), pp. 121-143.

A FRESH APPROACH TO Q

WILLIAM R. FARMER

Southern Methodist University

The idea of 'Q' is currently exercising a significant influence on scholarship. That there was such an early collection of the sayings of Jesus, and that scholars have reliable access to this collection through the Gospels of Matthew and Luke is presupposed in most contemporary speculation about the Origins of Christianity, and in attempted reconstructions of early Christian history and theology. Ironically, never in the last half century has uncertainty concerning the content or even the existence of 'Q' been greater than it is at present.[1] This points to a serious difficulty amounting to a theoretical impasse for contemporary scholarship.

What follows is intended as a contribution toward the resolution of this impasse, and presupposes the viability of the Griesbach hypothesis. Few adherents of the two-document hypothesis are

---

[1] Richard A. Edwards in "An Approach to a Theology of Q", *Journal of Religion*, October 1971, pp. 247-269, represents the current tendency to build on 'Q'. He reviews earlier work in this tradition and cites the writing of Norman Perrin, M. Jack Suggs, James M. Robinson, William A. Beardslee, and Paul D. Meyer, among others. R. Schnackenburg in his review of D. Lührmann's *Die Redaction der Logienquelle*, Neukirchen, 1969, published in *Biblische Zeitschrift*, 1971, pp. 279-81, recognizes a new theological interest in 'Q' and surveys Roman Catholic work on the christology and theology of 'Q' recently completed and in progress. Support for the 'Q' hypothesis among scholars in recent years has come from E. L. Bradby, *Expository Times*, 1957, pp. 315-18; F. G. Downing, *New Testament Studies*, 1965, pp. 169-81; B. Martin, *Theology*, 1956, p. 1828. Critics dubious of 'Q' include A. W. Argyle, *Expository Times*, 1961, pp. 19-22; A. M. Farrer, *Studies in the Gospels*, ed. D. E. Nineham, Oxford, 1955, pp. 55-86; J. Jeremias, *New Testament Theology*, Part One, London, 1971, pp. 38f.; C. S. Petrie, *Novum Testamentum*, 1959, pp. 28-33; R. T. Simpson, *New Testament Studies*, 1966, pp. 273-84. In their "Once More-Statistics and Q," *Novum Testamentum*, 1968, pp. 95-147, Charles E. Carlston and Dennis Norlin are almost certainly correct in rejecting Jeremias' view that 'Q' material in Matthew and Luke can be explained by appeal simply to the hypothesis of their dependence on oral tradition. But their dependence on the work of A. M. Honoré for their confidence in the two-document hypothesis has been criticized by David Wenham whose analysis of the statistical work of Honoré raises serious questions about its reliability. See A. M. Honoré, "A Statistical Study of the Synoptic Problem," *Novum Testamentum*, 1968, pp. 95-147, and Wenham's analysis in "The Synoptic Problem Revisited," *Tyndal Bulletin*, Cambridge, 1973, pp. 13-17.

unaware of the serious difficulties that face the critic who attempts to explain all the synoptic data on that hypothesis, and a growing number of experts are becoming aware of the real advantages of the Griesbach hypothesis.[2] For this reason it may be a timely exercise for some critics (certainly including those who while continuing to adhere loosely to the two-document hypothesis are open minded on the question) to reflect on the problem of 'Q' from a fresh perspective. One way in which this can be done, and the way taken in this essay, is by attempting to explore the question: "How is material common to Matthew and Luke viewed on the Griesbach hypothesis?"[3]

On the Griesbach hypothesis the Gospel of Matthew was composed before Mark, Luke and John. In writing the first volume of his two-volume work, the author of Luke-Acts followed the general outline of Matthew but often substituted different tradition for that found in Matthew. Mark and John were written after Matthew and Luke, which accords with our earliest external evidence bearing on the question of the sequence in which the gospels were written, namely the testimony of Clement of Alexandria who reports that he "received it from the elders that the gospels with genealogies were written before those without genealogies."

The problem of understanding the relationship between Matthew and Luke is both constituted and complicated by the circumstance that, as Augustine noted, "no one of the evangelists did his work in ignorance of that of his predecessors." For those like Augustine, who believe that the Gospels were written in the traditional order Matthew, Mark, Luke, and John, the point at which to begin a study of their literary interdependence would be to consider the relationship between Matthew and Mark. On the Griesbach hypothesis, however, the point at which to begin is with the relationship between Matthew and Luke. There is some advantage, therefore, in concentrating attention upon the material common to Matthew and Luke. For on the Griesbach hypothesis, this material

---

[2] For the view that the Griesbach hypothesis has emerged as the chief rival of the two-document hypothesis, see Robert Morgenthaler, *Statistische Synopse*, Zurich, 1971, p. 27, *inter alia*, and "A Response to Robert Morgenthaler's Statistische Synopse," *Biblica*, Vol. 54, Fasc. 3, 1973, p. 420ff., by William R. Farmer.

[3] This essay was first prepared at the request of M. Jack Suggs, Chairman of the Gospel Seminar of the Society of Biblical Literature for the first meeting of the Task Group on the Sequence of the Gospels held in New York, 1970, and chaired by William Beardslee.

can be considered without reference to the complicated problem of what Mark and John may have done. However, before considering this material on the Griesbach hypothesis, we first need to consider how it has traditionally been treated on the two-document hypythesis.

On the two-document hypothesis, which presupposes that Matthew and Luke have independently copied Mark, the material common to Matthew and Luke is frequently divided into two categories: double tradition and triple tradition. On the Griesbach hypothesis, however, these categories are otiose. The double tradition is simply material taken by Luke from Matthew which Mark did not use. Whereas, the so-called triple tradition is material Luke took from Matthew which the author of Mark conflated into his gospel. In other words, on the Griesbach hypothesis, the "double" and "triple" tradition categories are artificial literary creations of the two-document proponents and have no meaning at all so long as one is restricting his attention to Matthew and Luke. For all those who conventionally think in "two-document" terms, it is important to grasp the point that on the Griesbach hypothesis the material common to Matthew and Luke is inclusive of what is regarded as the double *and* triple tradition on the two-document hypothesis. Once this point is firmly grasped, several matters which on the two-document view are perplexing, find a ready explanation.

For example, on the two-document hypothesis, it has often been noted that, although the double tradition has come to Matthew and Luke from some early written collection of the sayings of Jesus, this document seems also to have included material that would have been more appropriate in another gospel, e.g. John the Baptist tradition, temptation story, healing of the centurion's son, etc.

Speaking broadly, on the Griesbach hypothesis material common to Matthew and Luke includes whatever Luke took from Matthew, *plus* whatever Luke may have copied from other sources closely paralleling material copied by Matthew. Sometimes it appears that the author of Luke has conflated or combined texts he found in his special source material with the Matthean form of the same tradition. The Parable of the Talents may be a case in point (Lk. 19: 12-27//Mt. 25:14-30). In other cases, as for example with the Parable of the Great Feast (Lk. 14:16-24//Mt. 22:1-10) and the Parable of the Lost Sheep (Lk. 15:4-7//Mt. 18:12-14), the author of

Luke has simply chosen one form of the tradition to the exclusion of the other. That is, these parables in Luke have been taken from his special source material, and the form of the same parables in Matthew have exercised no visible influence upon the Lucan text. In all such cases where the author of Luke has had access to sayings of Jesus in his special source material which have parallels in Matthew, he was in a position to preserve these sayings in a form which plausibly could be closer to the original than the same sayings as found in Matthew.

As early as the first half of the 19th century it was noted that sometimes Luke and sometimes Matthew has a saying of Jesus that seems to be more original than the parallel form of the saying in the other Gospel. This led some of the 19th century advocates of the Griesbach hypothesis to postulate that behind Matthew and Luke was an extensive proto-gospel, known to both evangelists, and that sometimes one evangelist preserved the text of this proto-gospel more faithfully than did the other. Some advocates of the Griesbach hypothesis went so far as to hold that Matthew and Luke probably were entirely independent of one another, in which case all the material common to these two Gospels would have been derived from this imagined proto-gospel.

Our present two-document hypothesis developed out of this latter form of the proto-gospel hypothesis: namely Matthew and Luke have copied an extensive proto-gospel (much longer than Mark since it included such material as the sermon on the mount, etc.) *and* they were otherwise quite independent of one another. The essential new element which paved the way for the two-document hypothesis was the idea of an extensive collection of sayings copied by Matthew and Luke. This removed the necessity that the proto-gospel account for the great bulk of the sayings of Jesus common to Matthew and Luke, and paved the way for Holtzmann and his followers to think of the proto-gospel as an "Ur-Marcus." Sometimes the collection of sayings ('Q') was conceived as a second proto-gospel, i.e. a proto-Matthew, so that the two proto documents behind our canonical Gospels were Ur-Marcus and Ur-Mattaeus, as with Bernhard Weiss. As between Holtzmann and Bernhard Weiss, it was the former's views that prevailed in the form the two-document hypothesis had assumed by the time of Streeter; i.e. Matthew and Luke have independently copied Mark and 'Q'.

The never-ending problem of defining the content of 'Q', or

the problem of the overlap between Mark and 'Q', or the problem of whether 'Q' is a single written source or a plurality of written and/or oral sources, all these disappear on the Griesbach hypothesis, at least as that hypothesis can be understood and defended *today*. We must emphasize the word "today" because an important development in Gospel studies has taken place since the hey-day of this hypothesis in the 19th century. This development concerns Form Criticism.

Before the advent of Form Criticism there was a tendency to think in terms of dating all material in a document at the time of the composition of that document. Thus when it was discovered that what was believed to be the earliest Gospel (Matthew) was written after the eye witness period, a discovery effectively verified by 1832 in the work of Sieffert, the reliability of the Gospels as historical sources for a knowledge of Jesus was seriously challenged. The radical solution was to deny the possibility of reliable knowledge of Jesus, and out of this developed the Christ myth theory according to which Jesus never existed as an historical figure and the Christ of the Gospels was a social creation of a messianic community.

A reactionary solution to this development was to deny the validity of the historical-critical method and to retreat into Orthodoxy. However, most theologians chose what came to be called a mediating solution. They accepted a late date for Matthew and the other canonical Gospels but moved around these late Gospels in various ways to get to the earlier eye witness period. In moving around these late canonical Gospels, theologians still thought in terms of datable documents rather than in form-critical terms. The proto-gospel and sayings collection in which they believed were datable to the eye witness period by the external evidence of Papias. According to Schleiermacher to whom we are indebted for the origin of the Logia idea, when Papias referred to Mark it was not to our canonical Mark, obviously late, but to an Ur-Marcus. And when he referred to τὰ λόγια he referred to a collection of the sayings of Jesus made by the Apostle Matthew. By adhering to texts where two or three of the Synoptic Gospels agreed, scholars in the mediating school were confident that the texts of these "datable" (to the apostolic period) documents could be reconstructed in such a fashion as to constitute a reliable foundation for their theological systems.

The collapse of such 19th century liberal theologies is well known. Nineteenth century liberal theologies, however, did not die easily. They were replaced by dialectical theology only after considerable polemicizing during which the attempt to ground theology upon the historical Jesus was effectively discredited. This theological polemicizing has not only distorted our understanding of the importance of source criticism, it has also obscured the full importance of the discipline of form-criticism, which came to the fore at the very time when 19th century liberal theology was being discredited.

Only in recent times has it become clear that form-criticism can put the quest for the historical Jesus upon a secure basis. Form-criticism enables the critic to recognize that in a particular Gospel not all the material is to be dated at the time of that Gospel's composition. The Gospels preserve older traditions. Some of the sayings attributed to Jesus in the Gospels go back to Jesus himself. The task of delineating the origin and development of the Jesus tradition in the Gospels is not complete. But no one today who is engaged in this task labors under the assumption that he must discover some Gospel datable to the eye witness period—nor even some particular apostolic collection ('Q') of the sayings of Jesus. Form-criticism enables the critic to treat each literary unit separately, and frees the student to think in terms of a multiplicity of pre-gospel sources. Actually Herder in the 18th century, and later Schleiermacher in his classic work on Luke, anticipated this development. But not until Dibelius and Bultmann did this understanding of the development of the Gospel tradition begin to become normative among students of the Gospels.

All this has been said preliminary to our approaching the Gospels of Matthew and Luke on the Griesbach hypothesis. This historical note helps explain why today an adherent of the view that Luke copied Matthew, and that Mark worked with both Matthew and Luke, will generally work with the hypothesis somewhat differently than those 19th century scholars who held this same basic solution to the Synoptic Problem but oftimes combined it with the notion of a proto-gospel and its corollary, the independence of Matthew and Luke.

In any case, the 20th century adherent of the Griesbach hypothesis will not do as did F. C. Baur, and think of Matthew as a reliable recension of an earlier apostolic Gospel of the Hebrews.

Rather will he think of the author of Matthew composing his gospel out of a great variety of pre-existing materials including several important collections of logia material. As examples of such pre-existing collections we may consider those found in the following sections of Matthew: 5:1-7:29; 10:5-42; 13:3-50; 18:1-35; 23:1-39; 24:4-25:46. Some of these collections of sayings materials may have been known to the evangelist Matthew combined in one or more large composite sources from which he has made selections. However, it is equally likely that they all came to him first independently and probably from different communities. Or the evangelist may in some cases have combined even these sections of his gospel out of materials which came to him separately. Such questions must be decided upon the basis of redaction and tradition criticism. On the Griesbach hypothesis, there is no redactional evidence to suggest that the author of Matthew has composed any of the tradition in these collections. On the contrary they all seem to have been edited into his work largely unaltered from pre-existing texts written in Greek. These pre-existing Greek texts seem themselves to have been relatively late and represented the Jesus tradition at a rather advanced stage of its development (post-Pauline). Form-criticism, redaction, and tradition criticism, however, enable the student to work with these developed collections of the Jesus tradition and assist him in separating the earlier material from its later modifications.

To a considerable degree, on the Griesbach hypothesis, the study of Matthew can be carried forward with little regard to the Lucan text. However, this is certainly not the case in studying Luke. Here there must be frequent reference to the question of what the author of Luke may have done with the text of Matthew.

Luke's Treatment of Matthew on the Griesbach Hypothesis

The beginning of wisdom in dealing with the question of the relationship between Luke and Matthew on the Griesbach hypothesis is to recognize that in addition to having a copy of Matthew before him, the author of Luke also had access to other source material—not *another* "source"—be it noted, but a plurality of other written Greek texts. Much of Luke's special material has no parallel in Matthew. Some of it, however, as noted above, corresponds to the materials utilized by the author of Matthew, and in some cases this correspondence is so close as to suggest common written sources. In no case, however, are these latter indications of common written sources extensive enough to support the *conventional* 'Q' hypothesis. Most of what on the two-document hypothesis is called 'Q' material is best explained on the Griesbach hypothesis as material Luke copied from Matthew. This must not obscure the fact, however, that the Griesbach hypothesis affords support for the view that there were collections of the sayings of Jesus circulating in the churches at a very early date. For on the Griesbach hypothesis it is necessary to postulate such collections not only to explain a great part of the text of Matthew, but also to explain much of the text of Luke.[4]

---

[4] On the surface it may appear that to concede the necessity of positing the existence of collections of "sayings material" behind Matthew and Luke is to surrender the advantage of the economy of hypotheses. I do not accept this as a valid criticism of the Griesbach hypothesis. In chapter 6 of my book, *The Synoptic Problem*, I point out that while it is possible to multiply the number of hypotheses by imagining that the evangelists used hypothetical sources, and it might even be legitimate to do this, that procedurally one ought to try to explain the verbatim agreement between the synoptics without appealing to hypothetical sources. The reason for this procedure is not that the simplest explanation is necessarily the correct one, but it is wrong to multiply hypothetical possibilities unnecessarily. I do not say that it is wrong to hypothecate a hypothetical source if it is necessary. As indicated above, on the Griesbach hypothesis (and indeed on *all* historical-critical solutions of the Synoptic Problem), it is necessary to postulate collections of Jesus tradition. This is done because of the indications that the evangelists have copied such sources. This is clearly the case with Lucan parables. Many of these parables are not in Matthew. Where did the author of Luke get them? He must have gotten them from some source other than Matthew. So one is not in that case hypothecating source material unnecessarily. The evidence requires it. There is nothing wrong in hypothecating the existence of an otherwise unknown source or sources if there exists evidence that is best explained thereby. But for the sake of economy this is not to be done without good reason. This is not an infallible rule, but it is accepted procedure in literary criticism as well as in other disciplines, and one which commends itself by the results achieved when it is followed compared to those which are achieved when it is ignored. This relates to step one. In step three I take this matter up again. While it is possible to conceive of an infinite number of variations of the 18 basic relationships between these documents, by positing additional hypothetical documents, these 18 should be given first consideration. This does not mean that the investigator should assume that there were no additional hypothetical documents; on the contrary, he should be open to the possibility that such actually existed. There are instances in literary historical studies where circumstantial evidence requires the investigator to posit the existence of a document for which he has no direct evidence. But a critic should not posit the existence of hypothetical sources until he has made an attempt to solve the problem without appeal to such sources. In other words, on the Griesbach

If one makes a careful redactional and form-critical analysis of Luke on the view that its author had access to a copy of Matthew, it

hypothesis, in dealing with the parables in Luke, the proper procedure requires that one look at all parables in Luke that are parallel to Matthew, and consider the possibility that Luke has copied them from Matthew before concluding that they have not been copied from Matthew but in fact come from some source or sources quite independent of Matthew. One does not need to assume the existence of a source otherwise unknown until he has checked out the possibilities of accounting for these materials in terms of existing documents. In order to explain most of the vast amount of material common to Matthew and Luke on the Griesbach hypothesis one need not hypothecate an extensive collection of sayings copied by Matthew and Luke '(Q')', but it *is* necessary to hypothecate the existence of a large amount of parabolic material copied by Luke which material is quite independent of the source material copied by Matthew.

Only after the investigator has been unable to understand the relationship between Matthew, Mark and Luke without appealing to unknown sources, is he justified in hypothecating the existence of such unknown sources as may be required to explain phenomena which otherwise would be inexplicable. This is a very serious hang-up for those who hold to the Marcan hypothesis. They feel that this way of proceeding rules out in advance the two-document hypothesis. It does not, however, rule out in advance the Griesbach hypothesis. It simply says that before you consider the two-document hypothesis, if you are going to proceed in a sound way, consider explaining the phenomena without appealing to 'Q'. If you need 'Q', according to an arrangement where Matthew and Luke are dependent upon Mark, well, then see whether you can put Matthew first and Luke second and Mark third, or in some other arrangement and explain the phenomena, and if you find that as a matter of fact you can explain the phenomena in one or more of these ways, then there's no necessity for thinking that the true paradigm is provided by the one necessitating 'Q'. When I say explain all the phenomena, I mean all of the phenomena that is relevant to the synoptic problem and the synoptic problem classically is the problem of explaining the literary relationship between Matthew, Mark, and Luke.

There is in Chapter 17 of Luke some apocalyptical material that is parallel to apocalyptical material in Matthew 24 and it seems to me that the Lucan form of that material is more original than the form of the material in Matthew 24. Therefore, I cannot derive that apocalyptical material in Luke 17 from Matthew 24. At that point it is necessary for me to hypothecate, just as I do in the case of the special Lucan parabolic material, another source, an apocalyptical source, that Luke has copied. In my book I make the point that that source, copied by Luke on the one hand in Chapter 17, might have been copied by Matthew at an earlier period in Chapter 24. Professor Hare of Pittsburgh Theological Seminary has made the point that here I have a 'Q'. What I actually have is the acknowledgement of the possibility that in this one instance I may have a source common to Luke and to Matthew. That's not an impossibility. "But then why not broaden it," asks Professor Hare, "and use it to explain all the other agreements between Matthew and Luke." * I simply answer that I do not do that because

---
* "A Review of *The Synoptic Problem*," a transcription (mimeo) from tapes of a colloquy held at Pittsburgh Theological Seminary, April 3, 1967.

is not difficult to understand the problem of the relationship between these two Gospels. In general it may be said that the author of Luke is at no point required to behave in a manner unnatural to an author engaged in the production of a work like Luke-Acts. For example in working with Matthew, the author of Luke tends to move forward through this source. This is a natural literary practice for an author or editor to follow—especially when dealing with narrative material.

The fact that the author of Luke has utilized material in Matthew is obscured by the circumstance that he worked forward in Matthew not once, but repeatedly. A further obscuring factor is the circumstance that between chapters twelve and eighteen he abandons Matthean order rather completely and utilizes material from Matthew following the basic order of some other source or sources. In fact on the Griesbach hypothesis it becomes clear that essentially what the author of Luke did was to combine his sources, in general utilizing in a very free manner the basic outline of Matthew, except in that section of his gospel constituted by chapters 12-18. In so doing he freely alters Matthew's outline and frequently substitutes traditions from his other sources for corresponding material in Matthew, e.g. birth stories, genealogy, parables, gnomic material, stories, etc., and often compiles material from different sources according to an intelligible principle of association. In the successive

---

that is not the simplest way to explain the evidence. In most instances you can explain the text of Luke by simply recognizing that he has modified the text of Matthew. Now, if one can explain most of the text of Luke without hypothecating an extended 'Q' like source, with miracle stories, John the Baptist tradition, etc., in my view that is still a definite advantage of the Griesbach hypothesis over the Marcan hypothesis, where the whole of the agreement between Matthew and Luke not covered in Mark must be explained in terms of 'Q'. In other words, it is not simply a question, "How many hypothetical sources do you need?" but "How extensive is the dependence upon these hypothetical sources which is required in order to account for the evidence?" It would be possible to extend considerably the list of such passages in Luke and Matthew which call for a common source or sources, and one would still not be required to hypothecate anything like the 'Q' that has traditionally and conventionally been required by the two-document theory. If, however, one thinks of 'Q' not as a document written in Greek which, if it were available, would account for the verbatim agreement between Matthew and Luke where this agreement cannot be accounted for through the dependence of Matthew and Luke upon Mark, but rather thinks in terms of 'Q' as a loose term to refer generally to sayings materials commonly available to Matthew and Luke, the grounds for discussion are open on a new basis.

redactional movements of going back over and then moving forward through Matthew made while composing chapters 9-12, the author of Luke incorporates into his text material from his other sources while following the general sequence of this material in Matthew. For chapters 12-18, however, as has been pointed out, he appears to follow the order of another source or sources while continuing to compile material according to the same principle of association, thus further utilizing material remaining in his text of Matthew *but not at all in Matthean order*.

At 18:15 the author of Luke returns to Matthew and follows that narrative freely to the end of his Gospel. This is all perfectly in accord with intelligible literary practice. However, on the two-document hypothesis, where one attempts to view Lucan and Matthean order through dependence upon Mark, and treats their editiorial dependence on Mark separately from their dependence on 'Q', the whole procedure is obscured, and we consequently find the ironical and confusing situation where *differences* in the order between Matthew and Luke in so-called 'Q' material is appealed to as evidence that Luke did not know Matthew, thus lending credence to the existence of 'Q' (Streeter), while *similarity* in the order of 'Q' material is appealed to as evidence that Matthew and Luke did know 'Q' (Taylor), which again supports belief in the existence of 'Q'.[5] Such similarity as exists in order between Matthew and Luke is most naturally explained by direct dependence of Luke on Matthew, and such differences as exist seem to me to pose no serious problem for an author-editor responsible for a freely created work like Luke-Acts. In fact, the most unusual differences that do exist, when once properly understood in terms of Lucan dependence on Matthew, are actually supportive of the view that the author of Luke either had access to Matthew or to the text of a gospel very similar to the text of Matthew. The demonstration of this particular contention, however, requires a full exhibition of the redactional procedures of the author of Luke, and goes beyond the scope of this paper. This paper has been designed to

---

[5] B. H. Streeter, *The Four Gospels*, London, 1953, p. 183; Vincent Taylor, "The Order of Q," *Journal of Theological Studies*, 1969, pp. 1-23, and "The Original Order of Q," *New Testament Essays*, ed. A. J. B. Higgins, Manchester, 1959, pp. 246-69. Such partial, selective, and preferential treatment of the evidence by critics is clearly explained in Thomas Kuhn's discussion of the role of basic paradigms in scientific communities, in his book, *The Structure of Scientific Revolutions*, Chicago, 1962.

orient the reader (especially the reader who, while he is open to the Griesbach hypothesis, still tends to think in "two-document" terms), to the manner in which one approaches the general problem of explaining the material common to Matthew and Luke on the Griesbach hypothesis.

The import of this discussion for the resolution of the present impasse over 'Q' is that it opens up and initiates an exploration of a way in which theological and historical projects can continue to presuppose a considerable corpus of early Jesus *logia* tradition without necessitating any dependence on a dubious hypothetical document written in Greek, which, if we could find it, would help explain the differences between Matthew and Luke in passages common to those Gospels, but not paralleled in Mark. This description has for over one hundred years given scholars the technical meaning of 'Q'. In this sense 'Q' is not only problematic as most critics understand, but as this study has shown, it is unnecessary for the pursuit of responsible historical and theological study of early Christianity, providing one accepts the validity of form-criticism and/or the viability of the Griesbach hypothesis, or for that matter any solution of the synoptic problem which allows for and envisions the author of Luke having access to and making extensive use of the Gospel of Matthew.

BLASPHEMY:
ST. MARK'S GOSPEL AS DAMNATION HISTORY

T. A. BURKILL
University of Rhodesia

We take it that the Greek noun *blasphēmia* primarily denotes any defamatory pronouncement or any utterance meant to damage or denigrate the reputation of some individual or group;[1] and from this basic definition we may at once deduce that, although commonly ascribed to evil doers by biblical writers, *blasphēmia* is *per se* ethically neutral. The truth of such an inference finds inductive confirmation when attention is drawn to passages that expressly refer to divine maledictions, whence it follows that by scriptural standards to commit blasphemy is by no means necessarily unjust. For, besides blessing the good, God himself, the ultimate source of justice, also curses the wicked (cf. Gen. 1:28; 3:14). And in a broad sense cursing amounts to an intense form of blaspheming since it is directed not merely against the reputation of its object, be it an individual or a group, but against its very existence as a personal or societal entity. Moreover, *human* cursing may be either magical, relying simply on the supposed inherent dynamism of some verbal formula, or intercessory (imprecatory), relying on extrinsic supernatural power (divine or demonic) to effect the fulfilment of the wish behind the malediction concerned.[2] With

---

[1] While it is agreed that the *phēmia* in *blasphēmia* is cognate with *phēmē* ("speech"), the etymology of the *blas* is uncertain. One suggestion is that it derives from the same root as *blapsis* ("injury," "damage," "harm" or "harming"), but in this case would one not have expected the form *blapsiphēmia*? Several other proposals have been made, one of which, for example, points to a connection with *melas* ("black"); so J. B. Hofman, *Etymologisches Wörterbuch des Griechischen* (2nd imp., Munich, 1966), p. 36. Cf. E. Boisacq, *Dictionaire étymologique de la langue grecque* (3rd ed., Paris and Heidelberg, 1938), s.v.

[2] Strictly, for a monotheism such as eventually emerged in ancient Israel, *divine* cursing could hardly be imprecatory because there existed no higher power to which Yahweh might appeal: God speaks, and his word immediately comes to pass (Gen. 1:3). In this respect, Yahweh acts as a magician rather than as a person who comports himself prayerfully.—It goes without saying that the distinction between the magical and the intercessory applies to benedictions as well as to maledictions; cf. the paper by G. Vermes, "Hanina ben Dosa: A Controversial Galilean Saint from the First Century

regard to mockery, reviling or scoffing, it is normally a milder species of blasphemy than cursing, for its basic purpose is apparently to humiliate someone, to undermine his pretensions by holding him up to ridicule. It should also be borne in mind that derisive laughter may be avoked by blasphemous drama in which speech is subordinated to action—a point amply illustrated in such a scene as that offered in Mark 15:16-20.[3]

True, we must beware of applying our nicely contrived modern definitions too rigorously. Thus the distinction we have made between blaspheming and cursing is not to be construed as a hard-and-fast one, for in antiquity an individual's name was widely assumed to be somehow integral to his personal existence, not merely a convenient means of identification, performing much the same kind of function as a parcel's detachable label. Given such an assumption, to misuse a person's proper name or to damage his reputation could easily be understood as militating against his essential being.[4] Again, in pre-scientific cultures the limits

---

of the Christian Era" in *J.J.S.*, XXIII (1972), 28ff., where it is stated: "By contrast to the healing miracles in which Hanina asks God to intervene, here we encounter a quasi-command... This detail reveals the existence of a tradition depicting Hanina as God's agent, not merely as an intercessor" (p. 41). Cf. below, note 36.

[3] In general, see the articles "Blasphemy", "Blessings and Cursings", and "Curse" (by S. J. de Bries, W. J. Harrelson, and S. Gevirtz respectively) in *I.D.B.* I, 445, 446ff., 749f., and also our article "The Causes of Laughter" in *The Central African Journal of Medicine* (Salisbury, Rhodesia), XVII (1971), 113ff.—In his *J.B.L.* monograph *The Problem of 'Curse' in the Hebrew Bible* (Philadelphia, 1963; corrected reprint, 1968), H. C. Brichto makes a spirited attack on J. Hempel's thesis that magical factors are entailed in the ancient Israelite practices of blessing and cursing. Brichto contends that "the evidence for magical concepts underlying the biblical phenomena of curse (and of blessing) has been grossly overvalued" (p. 215); and he goes further a little later when he writes: "In the [Hebrew] Bible, good fortune and misfortune are traceable to God, and prayers of imprecations involving these are, even when not explicit in the text, addressed to the Deity" (p. 218). It seems to us, however, that if Hempel overstates his case, the same holds still more obviously of Brichto. In any event, magical motifs are certainly present in the New Testament, and so why should they be absent from the Old—a wide range of documents emanating from a varying culture that was no less syncretistic?

[4] For various pertinent examples of the substantial importance attributed to names or reputations, see Exod. 20:7 (Yahweh's name must not be misused), Ecclus. 39:9-11 (the righteous man wins immortality in the survival of a good name), Mark 1:24 (a demon would gain access to apotropaic power by announcing its knowledge of an exorcist's name), and Luke 1:57-66 (the miraculous naming of John the Baptist). Cf. the instructive paper by Isaac Rabinowitz, "'Word' and Literature in Ancient Israel" in *New Literary*

dividing the various orders of existence, such as the boundary between the organic and the inorganic or that between the human and the infra-human, were passed over with considerable ease. Much of primitive animism survived into New Testament times, and men could on occasion treat even material things as though they had psychological qualities analogous to their own. Thus, if a person may suffer acute disturbance through being possessed by an unclean spirit, so the water of the Sea of Galilee could be invaded by a storm demon; and if a person may suffer ruin through being blasphemed, so a fig tree could be cursed and thereby caused to wither and die.[5]

In the Markan passages where blasphemy or blaspheming is expressly referred to (2:7; 3:28-29; 7:22; 14:64; 15:29), the word (whether in a substantival or in a verbal form) is used in a bad sense. But this must not be taken to mean that, any more than in Old Testament usage, blasphemy, for St. Mark, is a monopoly of the wicked. Actually, the evangelist's thought on the matter is not without intricacy, and the relevant evidence calls for careful scrutiny. An attempt to meet such a demand is made in the following pages, where the problem is considered under five headings: 1. Unbelief and Blasphemy; 2. Reciprocity and Markan Inconsistency; 3. The Gospel as Damnation History; 4. Unbelief as Absolute and Relative; 5. The Degeneration of Relative Unbelief. The essay ends with a brief recapitulation of the main conclusions.

1. *Unbelief and Blasphemy*

In a noteworthy article [6] E. Grässer has argued that in Mark

---

History, IV (1972-73), 119ff.—Of course, when suggesting that the modern tendency is to regard a person's name as little more than a label, we do not overlook the fact that in contemporary Western society blasphemy, as in the form of persistent slander, can still bring about the downfall of its victim.

[5] See Mark 4:35-41; 11:12-14, 20-21, and cf. our *Mysterious Revelation* (Ithaca, New York, 1963), pp. 45-47, 54. In what follows this work is cited as *M.R.*—Admittedly, the empathy in which primitive animism is doubtless rooted continues to figure in modern scientific culture, not only among children, but also among mature people, as when the aesthetic attitude is adopted and a piece of sculptured stone, for instance, becomes (in the eyes of the observer) instinct with human emotion.

[6] "Jesus in Nazareth (Mark VI. 1-6a): Notes on the Redaction and Theology of St. Mark", *N.T.S.*, XVI (1969-70), 1ff., esp. 21. A German version of the article is presented in the *Z.N.T.W.* supplement (no. 40) *Jesus in Nazareth* by E. Grässer, A. Strobel, R. C. Tannehill, and W. Eltester (Berlin

6:6a the *apistia* ("unbelief", "lack of faith" or "distrustfulness"), a disposition to negate the authority of Jesus by drawing attention to his humble family connections, is to be understood as an indication that the Messiah's compatriots, like the high priest at 14:64, regards his presence among them as a *blasphēmia*, a heinous offence against God. Grässer here seems to bring out a significant facet of the evangelist's doctrinal stance. As we have previously suggested,[7] the story of Jesus' rejection in his *patris* (Mark 6:1-6a), which is immediately followed by an account of the mission of the twelve (6:6b-13, 30) may well be intended to anticipate the shape of things to come. In St. Mark's scheme of arrangement the story, coming as it does at the end of his reports concerning a more or less settled ministry in Galilee, is apparently meant as a representation on a small scale of the Christ's final rejection by his own nation, an act which resulted in the crucifixion and the subsequent world-wide mission of the apostolic church. So the evangelist probably takes the *eskandalizonto* in verse 3 (cf. 1 Cor. 1:23; Rom. 9:33) and the *apistia* in verse 6 (cf. Rom. 3:3; 11:20) to symbolise in advance the typical Jewish attitude to the apostolic doctrine of the crucified Messiah, in which case he again contravenes the strict requirements of his theory of the messianic secret.[8] Further tension is involved in verse 5, where the second clause conflicts with the first. Perhaps verse 5b was absent from the story as St. Mark received it, and we may confidently assume that it was introduced, not to illustrate the iupotence of Jesus in face of the disrespect of his compatriots, but to emphasise the baneful consequences of unbelief: those who fail to show the honour and reverence due to him thereby exclude themselves from the blessings that can come through *pistis* ("belief", "faith", "trustfulness"). Presumably the evangelist understood verse 5a in this way; hence he retained the phrase "he could not" (the blessings of faith cannot come through *apistia*) and interpolated verse 5b to make room for the fact that a minority of Jews did respond with *pistis* to the church's startling announcement of the resurrection of the crucified Christ.[9]

---

and New York, 1972), pp. 1ff.—It ought perhaps to be noted that in Mark 6:1 "native place" (*patris*), not "Nazareth", is the expression employed.

[7] See *M.R.*, pp. 137ff.

[8] For Markan inconsistency in general, see our *New Light on the Earliest Gospel* (Ithaca, N.Y., and London, 1972), pp. 1ff., 121ff. This work is hereinafter cited as *N.L.E.G.*

[9] He could also have had it in mind that the apostolic communities sprang from a societal nucleus that was entirely Jewish in its membership.

In all likelihood verse 6a ("And he marvelled because of their *apistia*") is also part of the Markan redaction, for in it there comes to characteristically paradoxical expression the evangelist's attitude in face of the relative failure of the gospel to win its way among the Jews. The element of paradox is clear: if a prophet is held in honour except in his *patris* and among his kinsfolk, why should the reaction of *hoi polloi* in verses 3f. occasion surprise?[10] St. Mark was evidently taken aback by the general Jewish refusal of what, as he felt, it was in their highest interest to accept, and he construed their negative response to be a sign of *apistia*, a hardened maliciousness that transformed good into evil.[11] *Apistia* induced human beings to disvalue distinctively Christian values, so that words of wisdom (*sophia*) and miraculous works of healing (*dunameis*) became a *skandalon* to them. Hence the Markan mode of depiction is here reminiscent of the Pauline declaration in 1 Cor. 1:23f. to the effect that the apostolic gospel is a *skandalon* to Jews and a *mōria* ("folly") to Gentiles, whereas the *klētoi* (those who accept God's salvific call) apprehend in the proclamation of the crucified Christ both divine power (*dunamis*) and divine wisdom (*sophia*).

Accordingly, the implication appears to be that, in St. Mark's view, any hostile expression of *apistia*—disbelief in Jesus as Messiah, the Son of God and the Son of Man—constitutes an instance of

---

[10] Similarly, if it is divinely decreed that the Son of Man must suffer at the hands of his fellow countrymen, why should the Jewish authorities be blamed for engineering the crucifixion? Cf. *N.L.E.G.*, pp. 3ff., 15ff., 100, 122ff., 228.

[11] Hence there is truth in the following statement made by T. W. Manson: "Blasphemy against the Holy Spirit is not merely a matter of bad language. It is far more deadly than that. It is the extremest form of opposition to God. He who blasphemes against the Holy Spirit has identified himself so completely with the kingdom of evil that for him evil is good, ugliness beauty, and falsehood truth; and so the workings of the Holy Spirit appear to him as madness." See *The Sayings of Jesus* (London, 1949), p. 110. Of course Manson is here referring specifically to Mark 3:28f., and he takes "the Son of Man" in the corresponding Q passage (Matt. 12:32/Luke 12:10) to denote any human individual. However, he disregards the primary exegetical question as to the precise significance of the saying within the editiorial framework of the Markan gospel; and, overlooking the awkwardness of the logion in its present context, he fails to differentiate biographical actuality from the data of tradition and redaction; cf. R. Scroggs, "The Exaltation of the Spirit by Some Early Christians", *J.B.L.*, LXXXIV (1965), 359ff., and M. E. Boring, "How May We Identify Oracles of Christian Prophets in the Synoptic Tradition? Mark 3:28-29 as a Test Case", *J.B.L.*, XCI (1972), 501ff. Boring concludes that the saying in question derives from the charismatic *milieu* of primitive ecclesial prophecy (p. 521).

blasphēmia. Such an exegesis finds confirmation in Mark 2:1-12, a pericope that entails an implicit contrast between *pistis* and *apistia*.[12] In verse 5 Jesus discerns the *pistis* of the paralytic and of those who transport him, and in verse 7 certain scribes who are in attendance adjudge that the healer blasphemes when he tells the patient that his sins are forgiven. Thus we have here a significant correspondence, not only to the reaction of the high priest at 14:64, but also to that of the majority of Jesus' compatriots in Mark 6:1-6a—and this despite the facts (a) that there is no express reference to blasphemy in the story of the rejection in the *patris*, and (b) that the word *apistia* occurs neither in the story of the healing of the paralytic nor in the report of the nocturnal trial.

2. *Reciprocity and Markan Inconsistency*

The foregoing considerations lead us to make the point that a certain reciprocity is involved in St. Mark's interpretation of the conflict between the opposing forces of good and evil. Those hostile to Jesus attribute to him the crime of blasphemy, and thereby they unwittingly lay themselves open to the self-same charge. And such a rendering of the matter, we submit, adumbrates an *odium theologicum* that had emerged in the evangelist's own ecclesial situation. The enemies of the apostolic gospel commit blasphemy in that they malign the name of God, confounding the workings of his beneficent Spirit with the workings of Beelzebul, the prince of the demons; they confound the good with the bad—and this, for St. Mark, is an unpardonable offence.[13] So we might be tempted to agree with F. W. Danker when he writes: "On the one hand, Jesus is declared

---

[12] We hold that in Mark 2:1-12 a straightforward account of a miraculous healing has been transformed into a controversy story. The change was effected by the interpolation of verses 5b-10, and perhaps this was mainly the work of a pre-Markan editor. If verse 9 is meant ironically, it could be an interpolation within an interpolation, inserted by the evangelist himself. See *M.R.*, pp. 126ff.

[13] Cf. above, note 11. In view of the parallelism between the two charges "He is beside himself" (3:21) and "He is possessed by Beelzebul" (3:22), the evangelist's note at 3:30 could refer to both accusations. The suggestion is that all who speak ill of Jesus are really blaspheming against the holy Spirit that inspires his words and deeds (3:29; cf. 1:10). Admittedly, in accordance with the evangelist's doctrine of the messianic secret, Jesus' opponents, like all outsiders, are divinely prevented from knowing the *mysterium* (4:11f.). But the people generally, besides being amazed at the Lord's words and deeds (1:22, 27), are favourably disposed towards him (12:12). Cf. below, Section 4, re absolute and relative *apistia*; also, *N.L.E.G.*, pp. 15ff., 173ff.

to be a lawless man, possessed by a demon. On the other hand, the human opposition making the judgment is itself the agent of demonic forces".[14]

However, Danker too easily assumes that the *apistia* which issues in blasphemy is, in the Markan view, always due to demonic influence. Demonism certainly plays an important part in our earliest gospel, but the prominence of this particular factor must not be allowed to blind us to the roles played by other categories of explanation in this general connection. As we have put it elsewhere, "there are various types of causal explanation in St. Mark's total philosophy, and he shows much facility for suddenly shifting his frame of reference from one type to another. Thus, with regard to the origination of evils of one sort or another, on a primary level of causation, they can be produced by human volition (as in 2:1ff.); on a secondary level, by demonic agency (as in 5:1ff.); and, on a tertiary level, by the ultimate predetermination of God (as in 8:31)".[15] Hence there is no warrant for jumping to the conclusion that the kind of *apistia* entailed in 2:7, 3:22, 6:3 and 14:64 is to be ascribed to the mode of secondary causation. In 2:1ff., for instance, the evangelist is obviously thinking of causation on the primary level. The suggestion is that the patient owes his malady to sins for which he is personally responsible: according to the diagnosis, the paralytic needs forgiveness, and as soon as this has been secured the cure is effected. And in verse 5 the *pistis* of the patient and his associates is esteemed as meritorious (for which the cure is a reward), and this has its counterpart in the implied *apistia* of the scribes, a condition that also seems to be assessed as a matter of personal responsibility: those who here accuse Jesus of blasphemy are blameworthy.[16]

---

[14] See "The Demonic Secret in Mark: A Reexamination of the Cry of Dereliction (15:34)", *Z.N.T.W.*, LXI (1970), 65.

[15] See *N.L.E.G.*, p. 177; cf. pp. 205ff.

[16] In this respect 2:1-12 stands in striking contrast to such passages as 1:23-28 and 4:10-12, where the general public's relative deficiency in spiritual insight is attributed to divine predetermination or causality on the tertiary level; cf. *M.R.*, pp. 62ff., 96ff.—Perhaps it should also be observed that St. Mark has no explicit idea of mechanical causality in the modern scientific sense, the three modes of causation he resorts to being all of a personal (volitional) character. For a philosophical proposal that seeks to combine the concepts of teleological and efficient (mechanical) causality with an axiology, see our work *God and Reality in Modern Thought* (Englewood Cliffs, N. J., 1963), pp. 83ff., 125ff.—A further point worthy of attention may be put thus: If, as R. Bultmann thinks (*Primitive Christianity in its Con-*

An exegesis on the same lines is required in the case of 14:55-65, the account of the Lord's nocturnal trial before the sanhedrin. Here the pressure exerted by St. Mark's religious conviction subjects his apologetic theory of the messianic secret to an irresistible strain, so that in 14:62 the *mysterium* of the prisoner's essential status is disclosed outside the circle of the initiated. While the evangelist believes that the passion was a provision of God's sovereign purpose (the tertiary level of causal explanation), he nonetheless desires to make it quite plain to his readers that the crucifixion was a crime for which the Jewish (in contradistinction to the Roman) authorities were *de facto* responsible (the primary level of causal explanation). The effective operation of such a motive makes for a tension that occasions acute inconsistency in St. Mark's treatment of his materials. Thus, insofar as he is concerned to stress Jewish culpability, he tends to contravene the strict requirements of his secrecy doctrine by allowing what he conceives to be the true character of Jesus to come to open manifestation. It is doubtless in this way that we should understand the synthetic declaration at 14:62 ("I am; and you shall see the Son of Man sitting at the right hand of Power and coming with the clouds of heaven"), a confession made in response to the high priest's direct enquiry, "Are you the Messiah, the Son of the Blessed?"[17] The Jewish leaders who oppose the prisoner are in an inexcusable position since what they do is done not in the absence of revelation but in the face of a clear opportunity to recognise what he truly is or that for which he truly stands. They are guilty not merely because they let the opportunity pass them by, but because they confuse truth with falsity; and, allying themselves with the latter, the high priest and his colleagues stand under the

---

temporary Setting [New York, 1965], p. 70), Pharisaic (and Talmudic) Judaism is to be censured for construing faith in terms of merit, the same kind of judgement must in a considerable measure be passed on the author of our earliest gospel.

[17] Cf. *N.L.E.G.*, pp. 12, 67, 93, 126, 134, 138f., 260f. It is unlikely that in fact the high priest would have seriously put the question of 14:61b; for, as the tenant of Israel's supreme politico-religious office, he would regard himself as the Messiah, that is, as God's anointed heir of David's kingly rule.—For the general thesis that the Markan account of the nocturnal trial is a dramatised theological construction introduced by the evangelist into the traditional record of the passion, see *M.R.*, pp. 242f., 259, 280ff., and *N.L.E.G.*, pp. 104, 229, 249.

prospective judgement of the Son of Man. The judges who condemn are destined to be condemned.[18]

Thus the idea of an eschatological double reversal is involved here as it is elsewhere, providing indeed one of the organising principles of the evangelist's total literary production. The first shall be last, and the last first (10:31). If the faithful must receive adequate compensation for their voluntary privations (10:28-31), those who prefer worldly gain to persistent compliance with the moral implications of the *mysterium* must suffer perdition on that account (8:36), for whoever is ashamed of Jesus and his words amid prevailing sin and faithlessness, the Son of Man shall be ashamed of him when the Kingdom of God comes with power (8:38—9:1). But the sanhedrinists who convict the prisoner in 14:55-65, while responsible for their action (a product of hostile *apistia*), cannot presently feel shame in doing what they do since their complete failure to recognise the now revealed secret of the Lord's person must debar them from any consciousness of humiliation in their forthright repudiation of his claims.[19] So, as the evangelist understands the matter, the court's decision to condemn Jesus to death on a charge of blasphemy is itself an instance of shamelessly wilful *blasphēmia*; and this in turn means that, no less than the demons,[20] the Jewish authorities are doomed to destruction.

---

[18] Hence, for the evangelist, the fate of all the sanhedrinists is analogous to that of the demons. However, whereas the latter, being supernatural, are well aware that their doom is imminent (1:24), the former are only incensed at the christological confession of 14:62 and unanimously agree to return a verdict of blasphemy, a capital offence (14:63f.). In his exasperation the high priest may tear his robes, but his is not the desperate agitation of the silenced demon in 1:23ff.—a creature that immediately knows the *mysterium* without any confession on Jesus' part. Such knowledge could scarcely spring from *pistis* as St. Mark understands it, for demonic behaviour in his presentation is always nefarious, while *pistis* issues in action that conforms with the will of God (cf. 3:35). *Prima facie*, therefore, it seems improbable that the evangelist would have endorsed the statement in Jas. 2:19, "Even the demons have faith (*pisteuousin*) and shudder". Presumably, he would have opted for *oidasin* ("know" or "cognise") rather than *pisteuousin* (see 1:24). On the other hand, Mark 3:35 implies much the same as Jas. 2:20 — *pistis* without righteous action is devoid of salvific value. Cf. *M.R.*, p. 78, n. 17.

[19] Perhaps they will be moved to experience a sense of shame at the last judgement, but then it will be too late for repentance! Cf. below, notes 28 and 48.

[20] We adjudge the second clause of the demon's apotropaic address in Mark 1:24 to be not a question but a categorical statement ("You have come to destroy us"); see *M.R.*, pp. 63, 72ff., and cf. below, note 44.

Such a hermeneutic seems to find corroboration in St. Mark's redactional intercalation of the story of the so-called cleansing of the temple between the earlier and later parts of the account of the cursing of the fig tree (11:12-25): Israel stands under the Messiah's censure, a protestation that brings about not only Jesus' arrest and eventual execution but also the disintegration of the Jewish nation as an organised community with divinely and imperially endowed privileges. In other words, the crucifixion of the Christ entails the ruin of Israel as the elect people, and, from another point of view, the ruin of Israel entails the Messiah's infamous death.[21] Moreover, in view of the implied correspondence between the ill-fated fig tree and the Jewish authorities, we may assert that, according to the evangelist's way of thinking, Jesus actually does commit blasphemy, though not in the sense supposed by the presiding judge at the nocturnal trial (14:64). It is not the name of God that the Messiah brings into discredit, but rather the name of his prestigious opponents; and, indeed, so potent are his words that the very life of their time-honoured theocratic leadership must wither and die.[22]

3. *The Gospel as Damnation History*

Because of the mutual blaspheming involved in the operative *odium theologicum*, a viable exegesis can scarcely construe St. Mark's assessment of the cosmic process exclusively in terms of so-called *Heilsgeschichte* ("salvation history"). In that assessment the future of the Jewish authorities is evidently no brighter than that of Judas Iscariot (14:21); in their case, as in that of the hosts of Beelzebul, the apostolic gospel is really bad news and the career of Jesus itself fundamentally amounts to a *Verdammungsgeschichte* ("damnation history"). Thus despite his eschatological hope, the

---

[21] For this reciprocity, cf. *M.R.*, pp. 120ff. A consideration of Mark 14:1f. in the light of 11:18, 27f. and 12:12 suggests that the evangelist regards Jesus' violent action in the temple as the immediate occasion of his arrest in a place that was named Gethsemane (14:32ff.).

[22] The parable of Mark 12:1ff. exemplifies a strikingly analogous motif: the wicked husbandmen fail to deliver the fruit required of them and even go so far as to slay their landlord's beloved or only son, the consequence being that they are destroyed and the vineyard is entrusted to the care of others. In this instance, however, the destruction is effected *via* the direct intervention of the landlord (12:9), not *via* any malediction on the part of his son; cf. the relative taciturnity of Jesus in the Markan trial narratives (14:55ff., 15:1ff.).

evangelist is by no means an unqualified optimist,[23] those assigned to the category of the lost being far more numerous than scholars usually acknowledge. As in Palestine so elsewhere, *hoi megaloi* ("the great ones") are commonly motivated by unworthy ambitions, forcing their way to governmental power out of an inordinate lust for personal aggrandisement (10:42f.). St. Mark's sympathies are primarily on the side of the masses as distinct from those of high estate,[24] and yet it remains that *in toto* his contemporaries constitute an adulterous and sinful generation (8:38), ordinary folk being only too easily misled by the nefarious machinations of their political leaders (10:42; 15:10f.). As for the chosen race, its doom is sealed; the cursed fig tree inevitably perishes (11:21), or, as the point is otherwise made, the care of the Lord's vineyard is confided to others (12:9). But what of these others? Although now the divinely appointed elect of a new dispensation (13:20), they are nonetheless still liable to be led astray (13:5, 22), and collectively they make up but a persecuted and scattered minority (13:9, 27) whose existence can be maintained only at the cost of self-denial and persistent vigilance (10:21; 13:33). Thus even the Messiah's true kinsfolk, the multiracial heirs of erstwhile Israelite privilege (3:35), do not escape the weakness of the flesh (14:38), their capacity for holding out under stress being severely limited (14:37). And, since salvation is the reward for endurance to the end (13:13), we can safely infer that for the most part the prospective coming of the Son of Man will bring shame rather than joy (cf. 8:38).

Accordingly, the term *euaggelion* ("good news") belongs to the tendentious vocabulary of the early church; and *mutatis mutandis* much the same holds of the German expression *Heilsgeschichte*, which has come to be so widely used among biblical theologians during recent decades. As Morton Smith acutely observes,[25] in each instance the word "expresses the viewpoint of the elect. But the elect were a minority (Lk. 13.23f. and par.; Acts 4.12; II Thess. 1.8; etc.). From the viewpoint of most of the expected participants, as expressed by Celsus, the predicted events seemed rather a *Verdammungsgeschichte* (Adv. Cels. 3.16; 4.23, 73; 5.14; 7.9; 8.48).

---

[23] Cf. *N.L.E.G.*, pp. 129f.
[24] See *N.L.E.G.*, pp. 173ff.
[25] See "Pauline Problems apropos of J. Munck, 'Paulus und die Heilsgeschichte'" *H.T.R.*, L (1957), 109, n. 6.

G. Wetter, Der Sohn Gottes, Göttingen, 1916, 123, has conjectured that it was the doctrine of the coming judgment which brought upon the early Christians the charge of being enemies of mankind. (Consequently, John's insistence that Jesus is not to be the judge of the world, may be apologetic, ib.120-4)." This passage, we submit, brings out a significant aspect of primitive Christian thought that has been unduly neglected, and, unless our evaluation of the relevant data is seriously at fault, the earliest canonical gospel provides ample additional evidence for the validity of Morton Smith's general contention.[26]

Looking more closely at the Markan treatment of conspicuously hostile forces, we recall that it is largely governed by a *lex talionis* such as is nicely formulated by the Apostle Paul when he writes, "God certainly deems it just to repay with affliction those who afflict you" (2 Thess. 1:6). There has to be a final settling of accounts. Regarding St. Mark's depiction of the demonic agents of Satan, he makes it obvious that, while knowing the *mysterium*, they have no saving *pistis*.[27] They immediately apprehend that the coming of Jesus heralds their imminent destruction, and their encounter with the terrible truth sends them into wild extravagances of convulsive agitation (Mark 1:26; 5:13; 9:20, 26). They are dismayed, but being inherently evil they cannot bring themselves to repentance, a radical change of mind that would effect a localised suspension of the normal operations of nemesis, the divinely constituted law of retribution.[28] Moreover, the evangelist apparently takes it for granted that the words as well as the deeds of the unclean spirits bear witness not only to their special faculties of

---

[26] Re the continuing neglect in question, see, for example, M. R. Playoust's article "Oscar Cullmann and Salvation History" in *The Heythrop Journal*, XII (1971), 29-43; in it such of Cullmann's works as *Christ and Time* (3rd ed., London, 1962) and *Salvation in History* (London, 1967) are carefully dealt with, but no reference whatsoever is made to the datum that for most people the apostolic gospel signified their damnation.

[27] See above, note 18.

[28] Probably St. Mark never considered the question whether the demons are by nature incapable of feeling shame, an emotional reaction which seems to be partly conditioned by an awareness of some standard of decency or loyalty. But it might be noticed that in 3:22-30 the implied notion of "no honour among thieves" (v. 22b) is dismissed as inapplicable to Beelzebul and his demonic subordinates; these latter stand solidly behind their satanic leader (vv. 25f.), and such loyal commitment may at least allow room for the possibility of demonic shame. Cf. *M.R.*, p. 136, n. 42; also, above, note 19, and below, note 48.

cognition but also to their utter depravity, a corruption which indeed mars their ethical vision. Although they have supernatural powers of locomotion and can see the *mysterium* and its damnatory implications, they fail to understand the inner workings of the Kingdom of God. Thus in 5:7b the demons that dement a hapless Gerasene, speaking collectively as a single individual, address Jesus blasphemously in the following terms: "I adjure *(horkizō)* you by God, torment me not".[29] This injunction, imperiously made under the threat of a divine curse should it be disobeyed, presupposes that the Most High could repudiate his own Son, the Beloved with whom he is well pleased (1:11; 5:7a). So God's name is here taken in vain, the demons failing to grasp that, if their own satanic forces are not divided against themselves (3:23ff.), neither are those of the Most High; and the calamitous outcome of their blasphemous adjuration is that they are promptly despatched to the depths of the sea.[30]

The Jewish leaders are also conspicuously hostile to the truth, and their fate is no better than that of the hosts of Beelzebul; but whereas the latter know what lies in store for them, the former unwittingly contrive their own liquidation. For, as indicated earlier, in attributing to Jesus the crime of *blasphēmia* (14:63f.), they themselves blindly commit the very offence of which they speak. Their unanimous verdict, like the concerted adjuration of 5:7b, presupposes that God's Kingdom is divided against itself, and so it amounts to the unpardonable offence of blasphemy against the holy Spirit (3:29), the Spirit that descended upon Jesus at the commencement of his earthly ministry (1:10). However humble his family connections, a person so inspired could never blaspheme against the heavenly source of his manifest wisdom and power; and to be scandalised at such an individual is itself a most odious *skandalon*, an astonishing response that inevitably brings the privations of *apistia* ("unbelief") in its train (6:1ff.). Hence St. Mark's interpretation in this context adumbrates the same concept of a retributive reciprocity as that discernible in his treatment of the demons. The crucial decision to damn Jesus for blasphemy must react violently upon those who make it, the result being that all the chief priests and the elders and the scribes (14:53b) expose

---

[29] The N.E.B. translation, "In God's name do not torment me", is too mild a rendering of the Greek.
[30] Mark 5:13. In general, cf. *M.R.*, pp. 86ff.

themselves to a divine curse, a condemnation apparently to be ultimately ratified at the great assize held in prospect at 14:62. And if at this juncture something of the resplendent glory of the *parousia* is allowed to pierce the gloom of the Lord's humiliation,[31] from another point of view the coming of the eschatological Son of Man casts ominous shadows before it. In other words, those who blaspheme are necessarily blasphemed, and therefore the evangelist already at 11:14 can depict Jesus as prefiguring the final verdict of the victorious Son of Man by permitting him to curse the fig tree because of its unfruitfulness.[32]

4. *Unbelief as Absolute and as Relative.*

In a certain sense St. Mark puts the sanhedrenists in much the same position as that in which he places the disciples after his report of Peter's confession (8:29). While the fact of Jesus' Christhood is deliberately concealed from the public by the injunctions to silence and by parabolic cryptology (3:11f; 4:11f.), it is discovered at Caesarea Philippi, whereupon its implications are expounded to the twelve, and in the transfiguration scene something of its inherent splendour is made manifest to the especially privileged three (9:2ff.). The veil of the flesh is temporarily withdrawn in the presence of the chosen few, but persistent *apistia* and resultant fear (4:40f.; 9:6; cf.16:8) impair their intelligence and must continue to do so until the Son of Man is raised from the dead (9:9), a happening which, in the evangelist's philosophy of history, inaugurates the period of enlightened *pistis*, wherein, pending the final diviue intervention, the saving and damning truth of the gospel is confidently proclaimed on a world-wide scale.[33]

The high priest and his colleagues also conduct themselves as they do, not in the absence of revelation, but in face of a clear opportunity to grasp the *mysterium* of the Lord's real status (14:62ff.). However, whereas they respond with a malicious *apistia* that mistakes good for evil and issues in blasphemy against the

---

[31] See *M.R.*, pp. 242f., 322f. In this perspective St. Mark is seen as again breaking the barriers set by his doctrine of the messianic secret, freely giving direct expression to his confidence in the transcendent dignity of the crucified Christ of the apostolic gospel.

[32] Of course Israel—here symbolised by the fig tree—responds to this imprecation by consigning Jesus to the curse of crucifixion (cf. Deut. 21:23; Gal. 3:13). But the latter will have the last word at the *parousia* (Mark 8:38).

[33] Cf. *N.L.E.G.*, pp. 108, 144ff.

holy Spirit, the disciples (Judas apart) react with an *apistia* that issues in fear and bewilderment, and they take flight on the occasion of Jesus' arrest (14:50). For the time being their *apistia* prevents them from comprehending the meaning of their master's private instruction concerning the ordained necessity of the passion (8:31ff; 9:30ff; 10:32ff.). Nonetheless, it is mild enough to permit them to retain the content of such instruction as authentic tradition and thereby to prepare themselves for their post-resurrection role as doughty missionaries of the church's decisive message (13:9ff.; 16:7). So H. Riesenfeld rightly insists that the fear ascribed to the disciples (4:40; 6:50; 9:6, 32; 10:32; cf. 16:8) is a dogmatico-theological rather than a psychological phenomenon. To use his own words: "Leur crainte est rapportée dans l'intention de faire ressortir un manque de foi [*apistia*], l'incapacité de comprendre la portée messianique des paroles et des actes de Jésus".[34] Riesenfeld further suggests that the disciples' *apistia* in the Gethsemane scene is indicated by sleep (not fear) because in this episode a fearful anguish characterises the Christ himself.[35]

It appears, therefore, that the evangelist distinguishes between the deep-seated *apistia* of the Jewish leadership, a stubborn malevolence that issues in culpable blasphemy, and the less radical and less reprehensible *apistia* of the disciples, an incredulity that usually comes to expression in perplexity and fear. Jesus' followers may run away from the scene of the arrest (14:50), but with the exception of Judas (14:21) they commit no unforgivable sin, as it seems. Thus, so far as the betrayer and the sanhedrinists are concerned, St. Mark places particular emphasis upon their blameworthiness, tending to think basically on what we have termed the primary level of causality, an inclination doubtless bound up with his evident desire to shift responsibility for the crucifixion

---

[34] See his *Jésus transfiguré* (Copenhagen, 1947), p. 285. In Mark 5:36 the advice given to the ruler of the synagogue ("Fear not, only believe") implies that *pistis* expels *phobos*. On the other hand, in 1 John 4:18 it is *teleia agapē* ("perfect love") that banishes fear.

[35] *Ibid.*, p. 286, n. 27. Another possibility is that St. Mark introduces the sleep motif into his Gethsemane story with 13:36 in mind. Also, it should be noted that neither *phobos* nor any of its cognates occurs in 14:33. But one may reasonably infer that the Lord's distress involves *phobos*, a dread induced by a sense of impending catastrophe. Hence the evangelist does on occasion understand *phobos* in an ordinary psychological sense, and probably, as in the case of sleep, he here connects it with the weakness of man's carnal nature (14:37f.). Cf. *N.L.E.G.*, pp. 68, 258f.

from the Roman prefect to the Jewish authorities and their treacherous accomplice, Judas Iscariot. On the other hand, regarding the disciples generally, the evangelist is predominantly thinking on the tertiary level of causation, interpreting events in terms of the predeterminism of God's overruling programme for the current order of creaturely existence.

But the distinction between the two kinds of *apistia* is not consistently maintained, and this incoherence arises from St. Mark's habit of making sudden transitions from one frame of causal reference to another. A remarkable example of this is provided in 14:21, where a solemn affirmation of the effectiveness of God's predeterminism ("For the Son of Man goes in the way prescribed for him in the scriptures") is immediately followed by a blasphemous utterance which damns a person for playing the part assigned to him in the divinely devised programme ("But woe to that man by whom the Son of Man is betrayed"). Two opposing stances are here combined in a single sentence, an explanation on the tertiary level of causation abruptly giving place to a malediction that presupposes an understanding of Iscariot's treachery on the primary level.[36] In allying himself with the hierarchs (14:10f.), Judas comes to exemplify the same kind of *apistia* as they—the *apistia* that has damnation for its sequel.

With an eye on their post-resurrection role in the formation of the apostolic church, St. Mark evaluates the milder *apistia* of the eleven largely in terms of the tertiary type of causation. During the Messiah's earthly career they have to grope their way since they are not yet meant to grasp the *mysterium* that is being entrusted to them. Their divinely appointed lot is such that, only after their master's resurrection, can they clearly apprehend and openly proclaim the fateful truth now being privately received with an *apistia* manifested in fearfulness and bewilderment. Hence their unbelief, in contradistinction to that of the hierarchs and their

[36] As in the case of 5:7b (see above, note 29), the N.E.B. translation of 14:21b ("but alas for that man by whom the Son of Man is betrayed") is much too tame. The pronouncement is analogous to the damning of the fig tree in 11:14 (cf. 11:21), although this, unlike 14:21b, is blasphemy in the form of an imprecatory, not a magical, curse. In 11:14 Jesus comports himself prayerfully as a religious being, whereas in 14:21b he speaks as the ultimate disposer of the historical course of events. Cf. above, note 2, and *M.R.*, pp. 232ff.—It is of interest to recall that St. Mark, unlike the third and fourth evangelists (see Luke 22:3; John 13:2), nowhere resorts to the secondary type of causation in his treatment of the betrayal.

accomplice, is temporary and not finally inexcusable. However, in this regard as in others, the evangelist sometimes switches from the tertiary to the primary level of causal explanation, so that the disciples are occasionally reproached for the obtuseness engendered by an *apistia* to which they are predestined. In 8:14-21, for example, Jesus, as if in a state of exasperation, rebukes his followers somewhat disdainfully by subjecting them to a searching interrogation. In all, nine questions are addressed to them, the last one being, "Do you not yet understand?"[37] Although there is one loaf with them in the boat (v. 14), the disciples, apparently prompted by the twofold mention of leaven in the warning against the Pharisees and Herod, engage in a paradoxical conversation about the fact that they have no bread (vv. 15f.). Then comes the interrogation (vv. 17-21), and, as we have argued in greater detail elsewhere,[38] the content and form of the nine questions are such as to suggest that the disciples are already expected to comprehend the secret import of the miracles of the loaves. That is to say, they ought to understand what the evangelist means his readers to understand, namely, that Jesus is none other than the Christ in his capacity as Risen Lord of the church's eucharistic cultus, the One who imparts spiritual food for the nourishment of those who possess *pistis*. Thus we are confronted with what seems to be an anticipation of the Johannine notion of the bread of life (John 6:35), Jesus himself being the one true loaf that is with the disciples in the ship. So at this juncture St. Mark, momentarily setting aside his concept of God's governing programme for the world, expresses himself directly in terms of the apostolic faith and holds the disciples responsible for an *apistia* which, from the standpoint of the tertiary level of causality, cannot be superseded by *pistis* until the Son of Man is raised from the dead.

5. *The Degeneration of Relative Unbelief*

If Judas Iscariot loses himself in an unpardonable *apistia* through joining forces with the Jewish leadership, how exactly, in the light of St. Mark's total redactional performance, is Simon Peter's

---

[37] The first two clauses of verse 18 properly constitute two questions, not one—and so the series of nine enquiries illustrates the evangelist's liking for triads; cf. *M.R.*, pp. 123 n.16, 203, 205 n.36, 232 n.24, 236, 243ff., and *N.L.E.G.*, pp. 256 ff.

[38] *N.L.E.G.*, pp. 84ff., 147.

threefold disavowal (14:54, 66-72) to be assessed? *Prima facie* the degeneration of the latter's relative *apistia* may seem to be no less grave than that of Iscariot, for in 14:71 we read: "And he began to curse (*anathematizein*) and to declare under oath (*omnunai*), 'I am not acquainted with this man of whom you speak.' " If the treachery of Judas amounts to blasphemy against the holy Spirit, does not the same equivalence apply in this instance? The answer is negative; for unlike his erstwhile colleague (14:21f.), so far from being definitively damned, Peter is the only disciple to be mentioned by name in the angelic promise of a rendezvous with the risen Jesus in Galilee (16:7). One might seek to account for this rather striking discrepancy by referring to competing external pressures: on the one hand, the evangelist was influenced, indirectly if not directly, by Pauline hostility towards those apostles who made much of the privilege of having associated with Jesus prior to the crucifixion;[39] and, on the other hand, he could scarcely neglect the widely established tradition that Peter was historically the first representative of the church's post-resurrection faith.[40] However, while such a hypothesis may offer a partial explanation of the discrepancy in question, any attempt at an adequate explanation primarily requires a consideration of possible determinants that are more or less clearly native to St. Mark's way of thinking and method of redaction. It is to a consideration of this kind that we now address ourselves.

Approaching the problem from the standpoint of style, we note that, despite the roughness of his Greek, the evangelist is something of a literary artist with a keen sense for the dramatic and with a liking for vivid contrasts.[41] At the beginning of his passion narrative, for example, the luminous story of a woman's anointing Jesus' head with costly perfume is set on a dark background of malicious scheming and treachery (14:1-11). Also, the account of Peter's threefold denial (14:54, 66-72) is itself made to constitute a framework for the report of the nocturnal trial (14:55-65), doubtless a literary device to emphasise the contrast between Jesus' sustained

---

[39] Cf. A. Loisy, *The Birth of the Christian Religion* (London, 1948), pp. 99ff.
[40] The Markan gospel shows no trace of the claim, which may have been made by one party in the primitive church, that James, the Lord's brother, was the first person to whom a post-resurrection christophany was vouchsafed; for the possible existence of such a party, see P. Winter's article on 1 Cor. 15:3b-7 in *Nov.T.*, II (1957), 142ff.
[41] See *M.R.*, pp. 121, 228ff.

composure and his disciple's moral disintegration.[42] And the lower the latter sinks, the greater becomes the contrast—and coincidentally the more impressive becomes Peter's postresurrection reinstatement heralded in the angelic promise of 16:7.

Of course one might seek to save Markan consistency by so interpreting 14:71 as to mitigate the gravity of the offence it indicates. One possibility would be to argue that the *anathematizein* is to be construed merely in a psychological sense: Peter suddenly bursts out into profane language simply to relieve his pent-up feelings of vexation; he is annoyed with the bystanders for teasing him, not with his master now being tried on a capital charge.[43] But do not the words that immediately follow the *anathematizein* militate against such an exegesis? Peter goes on to disclaim all knowledge of the man to whom the bystanders refer, and this he does under oath (*omnunai*). How can a swearing of this kind be less reprehensible than the demonic adjuration *(horkizō)* of 15:7? Another possibility would be to take the *anathematizein* reflexively, as in the R.S.V. rendering. Even so, in invoking a curse upon himself Peter must invoke it upon his former self as allied with the Christ who presently suffers disgrace before the supreme court of the nation, and this must mean that Jesus falls within the scope of the malediction. Ashamed of his relevant past, the disciple who here curses that past is seeking to neutralise its continuing baneful effect in the present, and one would therefore expect that he is due to be reciprocated by becoming an object of shame at the last judgement (8:38).

Perhaps, therefore, at 14:71 Peter's relative *apistia* becomes absolute, in which case it could be inferred that the evangelist, defying the requirements of logical coherence, gives way to his liking for the extravagances of dramatic contrast. A similar inference might be made apropos of 8:33, where the same disciple is actually rebuked as an agent of Satan because of his inability to grasp the mysterious meaning of the secret messianic fact which he has just discovered (8:29). Here indeed we have a juxtaposition of extremes, and if *in loco* Peter has identified himself with the

---

[42] A similar effect can be produced in the cinema by the technique of the divided screen; see P. Winter, *On the Trial of Jesus* (Berlin, ²1974), p. 32.

[43] A psychologising hermeneutic seems to underlie the N.E.B. translation of *ērxato anathematizein*, "he broke out into curses".

forces of Beelzebul, his perdition is inevitable.[44] Again, in 14:27f. the solemn prediction of the eleven's forthcoming disorderly retreat (14:50) is immediately followed by the assurance of a post-resurrection reunion with Jesus in Galilee. This contrast is made all the more remarkable when two points are borne in mind. Firstly, in 14:27 the verb *skandalizein* is used in a passive form as it is in the report of the rejection in the *patris* at 6:3c; and if in this latter instance the verb signifies a reaction that bespeaks an absolute *apistia* (6:6a), ought not the same apply to the disciples' hasty withdrawal from the scene of the arrest? [45] Secondly, in 8:35 and 38 we learn that whoever would save his life (at the expense of the gospel) will lose it and that whoever is presently ashamed of Jesus will become an object of shame at the last judgement. By these criteria, should not the eleven be finally condemned? For at 14:50 they forsake their master and flee for their lives, and at 14:71 Peter is ashamed of his past association with the Messiah. Should not such conduct be tantamount to what the evangelist understands by blasphemy against the holy Spirit? [46]

---

[44] In his article, "Prolegomena to a Discussion of Aretalogies, Divine Men, the Gospels and Jesus", *J.B.L.*, XC (1971), 197, Morton Smith makes the interesting suggestion that the second clause of 1:24 ("You have come to destroy us") is redactional; coming as it does at the head of St. Mark's first exorcism story and being unparalleled in the subsequent stories, the statement was added in the interest of the evangelist's eschatological view that the miracles of Jesus were signs of the approach of the Kingdom of God. But can we be sure that such a view did not antedate St. Mark? Cf. Matt. 12:28/Luke 11:20 (Q); also, above, note 20.

[45] The N.E.B. translation of 14:27a ("You will all fall from your faith") is quite misleading, for, according to St. Mark, the typical attitude of the disciples generally is that of relative *apistia*; genuine faith (*pistis*) comes only after the Son of Man is raised from the dead (9:9).— Incidentally, it might be noted that the N.E.B. should be used with extreme caution. Apart from the few examples we have already cited, a glaring instance of N.E.B. unreliability is the rendering "but we proclaim Christ—yes, Christ nailed to the cross" (1 Cor. 1:23); for, despite the LXX translation of Psalm 22:17 (English versions, 22:16), the fourth evangelist is the first (and only) New Testament writer definitely to imply that Jesus was *nailed* to the cross; the likelihood is that he was roped thereto; cf. M. Dibelius, *From Tradition to Gospel* (London, 1934), pp. 184f., 188f., and P. Winter, *op. cit.*, pp. 95f.

[46] In his contribution, "Peter's Curse", to the C. F. D. Moule Festschrift, *The Trial of Jesus* (ed. E. Bammel; London, 1970), pp. 66ff., H. Merkel argues that in the last resort the anathematisation of Mark 14:71 must be directed against Jesus, and this hermeneutic seems sound enough specifically respecting the significance of the passage within the cadre of the redaction. But Merkel's concluding inference is hardly warranted; he writes: ".... it is quite unthinkable that the community should have invented a story about

Accordingly, it seems that our tentative proposal is not without secure foundation: in his treatment of the disciples' shortcomings St. Mark does allow his lively interest in the presentation of dramatic contrasts to violate the rigorous demands of logical coherence. And this ought to occasion no surprise, since in numerous other regards he contravenes the requirements of rational consistency.[47] Nonetheless, if justice is to be done to the evangelist's mode of thought in this connection, it must be recognised that, not minimising the moral depths to which the eleven are allowed to sink, their characteristic *apistia*, even in its most degenerate condition, never quite matches that of Judas Iscariot when he betrays his master and allies himself with the national leadership.

Thus, although at 8:33 Peter is severely rebuked and addressed as if he were an embodiment of Satan, he continues to stay at his master's side until the arrest has taken place—and this despite his bewilderment and unreliable behaviour (9:5f.; 14:37). Again, while the verb *skandalizein* is used in the prediction of 14:27 (as it is at 6:3c), in the report of its fulfilment (14:50) the eleven simply take flight. Offended they may be, but not to the extent that they participate in the chorus of the multitude that calls for the Messiah's crucifixion (18:13f.). Their *apistia* is still an *apistia* of fear and uncertainty. Moreover, the disavowal at 14:71 takes on a slightly less sinister aspect when carefully considered in the light of its total context. It is from afar off that Peter follows Jesus into the high priest's courtyard (14:54), the suggestion being that he is at once fascinated and repelled by the turn of events. In the evangelist's dramatic portrayal, that is to say, natural fear (like sleep, a weakness of the flesh—14:38) combines with the divinely predetermined fear of relative *apistia*. Subjected to a searching cross-examination Peter becomes increasingly agitated, envisaging the terrible possibility of his having to suffer a humiliation similar to that which has already overtaken the Messiah. His natural fear intensifies, and release from the emotional tension is eventually

---

her recognised leader which humbled him so deeply, unless something of the sort had actually taken place". In making this deduction, besides neglecting the primary exegetical question of St. Mark's theologico-literary aims, Merkel disregards the evidence for the existence of rival factions in the ambit of primitive Christianity. Cf. above, notes 39 and 40; also, M. Goguel, *H.T.R.*, XXV (1932), 1ff., where it is hypothecated that the story of Peter's denial was fabricated out of an unfulfilled prediction made by Jesus.

[47] See above, note 8.

sought in the blasphemy of a curse that would nullify the continuing effect of a past that has now become for him an object of shame (14:71). However, the Markan motif of a predestined relative *apistia* at once reasserts itself. Prompted by the second cock-crow, Peter recalls Jesus' solemn prediction, and he breaks down and weeps (14:30, 72). This tearful denoument signifies that he is finally ashamed of his having been ashamed of an erstwhile allegiance to the prisoner now being charged with the very crime he himself has just committed.[48] Hence, by so quickly forestalling what is to be the normal response of the exalted Son of Man in such cases (8:38), Peter is enabled personally to rescind his momentary lapse into a form of blasphemy that is commonly unpardonable (3:29). In other words, the evangelist's general notion of the disciples' relative *apistia* regains its usual prominence; and Peter is sufficiently equipped for the post-resurrection reunion in Galilee (14:28; 16:7), a triumphant experience that will transform his

[48] See 14:63f.—Re the sense of shame (cf. above, notes 19 and 28), it can be occasioned either directly or indirectly. Directly evoked shame presupposes a humiliating realisation of one's having contravened some standard of morality, decency, propriety or modesty, and such is the kind of shame evinced in the regretful tears at 14:72c (cf. the firm promise made in 14:31). Indirectly evoked shame presupposes a feeling of superiority (differently expressed in sarcasm and snobbishness), and it entails a disdain of one's inferior connections; this is the kind of shame that presumably lies behind the blasphemy in 14:71.—Of course it is indirect shame that is referred to (twice) in the ominous saying of 8:38 ("For whoever is ashamed of me and of my words..., of him will the Son of Man be ashamed..."). This pronouncement probably has a forensic connection in the protasis as well as in the apodosis, and it could be a post-ressurection construction designed to warn members of a persecuted church against apostatising when facing accusations in courts of law; see P. Vielhauer, *Aufsätze zum Neuen Testament* (Munich, 1965), pp. 76ff., 101ff., and E. Haenchen's article on the composition of Mark 8:27—9:1, *Nov.T.*, VI (1963), 81ff. That St. Mark was well aware of the perils to which representatives of the apostolic gospel were exposed, is vividly shown in 13:9-13.—As for 14:71, H. Merkel, *op. cit.*, pp. 69f., (see above, note 46) aptly points out that judicial authorities, both Jewish and Roman, came to regard the cursing of Jesus as a proof of innocence when a person was indicted for the crime of professing Christianity .The *birkath haminim*, introduced into the liturgy of the synagogue perhaps c. 90 A.D., is also of interest in this regard; see *N.L.E.G.*, p. 228, n. 66.—Also regarding Mark 14:71, Merkel writes: "The Gospel of the Nazarenes uses, in place of *anathematizein*, the verb *katarāsthai*. This verb, too, always has a transitive meaning. Therefore it was not understood in the sense of self-cursing". But may it not be that the Peter of Mark 14:71, dissociating the present from the past, regards his relevant former self as an object? It should also be noted that *katarāsthai* (which means much the same as *anathematizein*) is the verb used at Mark 11:21 (re the fig tree).

relative unbelief into the genuine *pistis* of the apostolic church.[49]

So we come to the end of our examination of the passages relating to St. Mark's notion of blasphemy in its bearing upon his attitude

[49] Hence T. J. Weeden grossly exaggerates when he writes that (in St. Mark's gospel) the disciples *en bloc* "finally reject Jesus as completely as the Jewish hierarchy;" see his *Mark—Traditions in Conflict* (Philadelphia, 1971), p. 163; cf. pp. 38ff. Actually, there are other respects in which Weeden shows himself to be an unreliable guide, as, for example, when he lists R. H. Lightfoot among the defenders of the *parousia* interpretation of Mark 14:28 and 16:7 (p. 111, n. 13), but fails to note that Lightfoot came to repudiate this view; see *M.R.*, p. 256, n. 7. We offer a few further illustrations of our point: (a) Weeden upholds that the *parousia* exegesis of Mark 14:28 and 16:7 (pp. 110, 114)—and yet he also maintains that, for St. Mark, the second advent is not a localised but a ubiquitous phenomenon, heralded by the collapse of the entire cosmos (pp. 97, 167). (b) Weeden contends that, in view of the women's silence (Mark 16:8c), the disciples, in the evangelist's interpretation, "never received the angel's message, and thus [*sic*] never met the resurrected Lord, and consequently [*sic*] never were commissioned with apostolic rank after their apostasy" (p. 50; cf. pp. 117, 164).—as if the prediction of Mark 14:28 did not have the same import as the promise made in Mark 16:7 (see *M.R.*, pp. 245ff., 252ff.), and as if the disciples had not already been apostolically commissioned by Jesus in Mark 3:13ff. (cf. 6:7, 30). (c) Weeden posits that the notions of Jesus as thaumaturge and as suffering servant are diametrically opposed to each other (pp. 165f.)—but could it not be that the two ideas were deliberately combined by the evangelist in an effort to bring out the greatness of Jesus' self-humiliation, the crucifixion being evaluated as a supreme act of divine condescension? (see *M.R.*, pp. 41f.). (d) Weeden deems that the Markan concept of a divine man who exercises miraculous power is Hellenistic, opposing it to the church's primitive Palestinian tradition (pp. 55, 165)—as though, after centuries of exposure to it the Jewish inhabitants of Palestine had assimilated next to nothing of Hellenistic syncretism, with its thaumaturgic implications (see *N.L.E.G.*, pp. 199ff.). (e) Weeden lays it down that the representation of Jesus as a thaumaturge is "reduced to a low key" in the second half of St. Mark's gospel (p. 164, n. 5)—as if the predetermining of destiny and the occasioning of darkness at noon (during the paschal season) were less miraculous than, say, the curing of diseases (see *M.R.*, pp. 232ff., 245). (f) Weeden asserts that in Mark 15:39 the centurion is prompted to make his confession "solely [*sic*] on the basis of Jesus' suffering and death", believing "Jesus to be the Son of God because he died as a suffering servant" (p. 167) —but if such were the evangelist's view, would the confession be immediately preceded by a report of the rending of the temple curtain? (see *M.R.*, pp. 246ff.). (g) Weeden regards the cry of Mark 15:34 as voicing unqualified despair (p. 167, n. 8)—whereas in all likelihood St. Mark took it to denote that to the very last moment of his earthly career the Christ comported himself in accordance with God's sovereign purpose (see *M.R.*, pp. 239ff.). (h) Weeden claims that, in the evangelist's estimation, during the period following the crucifixion the Christ is never present among "the company of believers until the kingdom of God has come, an event still awaited at the time of Mark" (p. 114)—and yet he does recognise that, according to Mark 13:11, "the spirit that animated Jesus" will come to the assistance of

to forces hostile to the church's mission. Our various investigations go to show that, while blasphemy as such is ethically neutral, the evangelist primarily associates it with unbelief; that his treatment of the matter reflects the reciprocity entailed in an *odium theologicum* of his own ecclesial situation; that he uses conflicting frames of reference in his causal explanations of evil; and that he implies a distinction between absolute and relative unbelief, the latter being a volatile condition subject either to complete degeneration or to radical transformation into salvific faith. But perhaps most noteworthy for present-day biblical scholarship, with its recent stress on so-called *Heilsgeschichte*, is the further conclusion that St. Mark provides ample evidence favouring Morton Smith's thesis regarding the severely limited number of the elect: for the majority of mankind, as for the totality of the hosts of Beelzebul, the apostolic gospel means damnation.

---

persecuted exponents of the apostolic gospel (p. 168); apparently Weeden here unduly assumes that the evangelist was more of a theological systematician than, say, the Apostle Paul, a writer who did not differentiate the Spirit of God or the holy Spirit from the living Christ when referring to the divine inspiration of believers (see 1 Cor. 12:3; Gal. 2:20; and re the unsystematic character of St. Mark's thinking, see *N.L.E.G.*, pp. 121ff.). (i) Weeden holds that the disciples in Mark 2:18-20, figuratively appearing as guests at a wedding reception, represent "the Christian community" (p. 114)—but, if, as Weeden thinks, the Markan disciples *in toto* are no better than the Jewish leadership (p. 163) and stand for "a theological cancer that must be destroyed" (p. 164), must it not follow that, according to St. Mark, "the Christian community" is destined for damnation? (j) The evangelist is far from being a systematic philosopher who carefully defines his main ideas and brings them together in a coherent whole— but this affords no excuse for a confused exegesis such as Weeden presents: thus, while he supports the *parousia* interpretation of Mark 16:7b (pp. 110, 114), he can still on occasion argue as if it refers to one or more appearances of the risen Jesus in the Galilean region (pp. 50, 164); and Weeden's contention that, had they repented of their apostasy, Peter and his colleagues "could have joined... in the reunion of Jesus with his elect at the parousia" (p. 117) is quite untenable, since, for St. Mark, the coming of the Son of Man with great power and glory is willy-nilly a divinely appointed object of expectation, not a possible object of retrospection (see *N.L.E.G.*, pp. 127ff.).

FROM ISAIAH 61 TO LUKE 4

JAMES A. SANDERS
Union Theological Seminary

The present study will attempt to sketch a history of function of Isaiah 61:1-3 from its appearance in the Tanak to its role in the Lukan account of Jesus' appearance and sermon in the Nazareth synagogue.* The method employed in the study is that of Comparative Midrash. Comparative Midrash differs from the method which has been called "history of interpretation" in two particulars. Whereas the latter emphasizes how an OT passage was interpreted in its several uses in post-biblical literature, Comparative Midrash emphasizes the role an ancient authoritative tradition, whether or not actually quoted or cited as scripture, played in the life and history of Judaism and Christianity. What function did a particular tradition have in the life of the community where and when it was called upon by that community? What need of theirs was it called on to meet? Secondly, close attention is paid in Comparative Midrash to the manner in which the tradition is contemporized by the community to meet that need: this aspect of the work involves hermeneutics in *sensu lato*, i.e., the manner in which the

---

* The present paper, in an early form, was presented at Yale Divinity School as one of the Shaffer Lectures of April 1972. I wish to thank Dean Colin Williams and colleagues and friends at Yale whose reactions and criticisms have been very instructive; I wish also to thank Prof Moshe Greenberg of the Hebrew University for the opportunity to read it there in March 1973. But my greatest thanks go to Prof Morton Smith, whom we honor in this volume, who has graciously read other papers in the making and is the most thorough and helpful such critic I know. Because he could not read this one for me—what is a Festschrift?—not only he must suffer this time, but others as well.

The transliterations in this article do not follow any system of which I am aware, but are, I think, both simple and clear. For those who need guidance the chart inside the front cover of each issue of *CBQ* may be consulted save for the following deviations from it: *v* stands for *vav* (or *waw*), *z* for *tsade*, *sh* for *shin*, and *ks* for *ksi*; all vocal *shevas* are noted by the short-vowel sign (e.g., *ĕ*), but *iota* subscript is not in any way indicated. *Dagesh forte* is indicated by doubling the letter except in the case of gutturals and *shin*; in the latter cases a hyphen is inserted between the article and the first root letter. Such citations, as are given in transliteration, are not intended as substitutes for text-editions but serve only to specify what words and phrases of the ancient texts are being treated.

tradition is woven by the exegete with other materials at his disposal to draw benefit from the citation, reference or allusion.

All translations, and not only the targumim, are more or less relevant to the community for which the translation is effected. Early manuscripts of biblical books, such as those from Qumran, exhibit variantiae which cannot be overlooked in such a study. The most fruitful field for study is the so-called sectarian literature, whether this be Qumranian, Christian, proto-rabbinic or that of some other Jewish denomination from which we may have inherited literature without knowing more about them (such as certain apocrypha). By comparing the available instances of contemporization of authoritative traditions in the Second Temple Period, and by considering them one in the light of the other, considerable light may be shone on the whole and on particular instances that may otherwise be unavailable.

Comparative Midrash properly begins by a recognition of the peculiar role of scripture in the life and history of Judaism. While much benefit derives from comparison with rhetorical-critical work on non-Jewish literature in the eastern Mediterranean area of the same time period, the peculiar role of Torah in the life of Judaism must be recognized before valid work can begin. Experts in the field of Greek and hellenistic studies recognise that a considerable difference exists between the role or function of a Torah tradition in Judaism and the role of classical mythology in the hellenistic world.[1]

In both cultures traditions are called on for the authority they may offer to the writer who cites them. And many of the rhetorical or midrashic methods of the two worlds are similar. This is so much the case that it is quite proper to speak of the eastern Mediterranean area in this regard. As Morton Smith has recently shown, "hellenization" meant not only Greek influence in the Semitic world of the time but also Semitic influence in the Greek and hellenistic worlds of the time.[2] Nonetheless, for all the work being done in the area of the broader sense of Comparative Midrash,[3]

---

[1] See the study by Henry A. Fischel in the *Semicentennial Volume of the Middle West Branch of the American Oriental Society* (1969) 59-88; also Fischel's article on "Rabbinical Knowledge of Greek and Latin Languages" in the *Encyclopaedia Judaica*, 16 volumes (1972), ad loc., under "Greek", and now see his *Rabbinic Literature and Greco-Roman Philosophy* (1973).

[2] Smith, the chapter on "Hellenization" in his *Palestinian Parties and Politics that Shaped the Old Testament* (1971) 57-81.

[3] See the seminal article on "Midrash" by Renée Bloch in Supplement V

there is no phenomenon outside Judaism quite comparable to Torah. Integral to the very essence and character of Judaism is the historic memory of the role the Torah traditions played in her death and resurrection experience of the sixth and fifth centuries B.C.E.[4] In crucial ways, that experience of the death of old Israel and the resurrection/birth of Judaism helped to shape the old pre-exilic traditions into the Torah and Prophets and Psalms, as we know them, or, at least, into the shape they now have (though much was added in and after the exile without altering the basic shape). Jews, wherever they have been, have somehow always known this about their Torah: it has Life-giving power. It and it alone, it was thought, provided the survival power through the Babylonian exile, and then through Persian dispersion and hellenistic temptations: it told them who they were in the face of despair and of the temptation to assimilate. And Torah, in the mind of the Jew who knew who he was, was not just the Pentateuch, but also the Prophets and the Psalms and eventually the Writings, and beyond that the oral "Torah" as well as the written, the Talmud as well as the the Bible. Torah in this sense came to mean Judaism itself. To understand Judaism, indeed, to understand midrash, one must begin with this wellspring of life, Torah.

I

Study of the function of a biblical tradition begins properly with the Bible itself. Biblical scholarship has over the past two centuries developed a number of tools whereby to understand a biblical passage in its biblical setting. Literary criticism helps to locate the source of the material under study and to determine if it is a unity or if composed by some later editor from more than one source.

(1957) col. 1263-81 of *Dictionnaire de la Bible*. Cf. also Roger Le Déaut, "Apropos a Definition of Midrash," *Interpretation* 25 (1971) 259-82 (with introduction by the present writer); the pertinent bibliography by my former student, Merrill P. Miller in *Journal for the Study of Judaism* 2 (1971), esp. pp. 36-78; and the essays by R. Bavier and J. Townsend in Jacob Neusner, ed., *The Study of Judaism* (1972) 7-80.

[4] Sanders, *Torah and Canon* (1972) and "Adaptable for Life: The Nature and Function of Canon" forthcoming in the G. Ernest Wright Festschrift. The metaphors of re-birth and death/resurrection were used by Jeremiah and Ezekiel. The process of the selection of material and shaping of canon must be traced primarily in the experiences of the believing communities and *not* in councils and lists. The latter derived whatever authority they had from accurate reflection and expression of the former.

Formcriticism, a branch of literary criticism, attempts to define the basic literary units under consideration, both the smaller component units a biblical author may have used and the larger units he himself may have penned or uttered. Formcriticism is often used to probe back of a principal biblical author to the way in which material he has quoted or adapted was understood before he himself made use of it. Historical criticism has both a large meaning and a more refined one: it may mean the whole enterprise of biblical scholarship in the sense of the quest for the meaning of the Bible in its own historical settings; or it may mean, as over against enthusiastic Formcriticism, the need to reconstruct as nearly as possible the historical settings in which the biblical literary units under study scored their basic, primary points.

Traditioncriticism studies a basic tradition, which can be located in more than one biblical passage, by carefully noting through synoptic study of the several loci where it appears, the different ways that tradition was used and the different functions it had and roles it played in the hands of the different biblical authors who used it (Jahwist, redactor, prophet, psalmist, or whoever). Traditioncriticism is, in a manner of speaking, the intra-biblical counterpart of Comparative Midrash, which simply carried on the same kind of study into the later period. Finally there is Redactioncriticism, a tool of study whereby one attributes to the last editors of the larger literary units of the Bible their own basic intelligence and motives. Redactioncriticism, as over against the assumptions of old literary criticism, which thought of them as faithful collectors, grants to these later contributors to the Bible their own theological and political ideas which can be found in the way they arranged and edited the smaller literary units which they received and collected.

Canonical Criticism, the latest and most engaging of the sub-disciplines of biblical study, carries on beyond Redactioncriticism, beyond the conscious efforts of actual individuals (or discrete schools), to those all-crucial moments in the canonical process after the largest literary units have been molded by geniuses to the filtering process of the faithful who, to put it bluntly, either continued to read what the geniuses handed on or, finding them irrelevant to their needs, left them lie in *genizot* or, less dramatically, simply in drawers throughout the eastern Mediterranean basin to discolor and decay from disuse. Here was where distinctions were made as to what was Torah and what was Prophets, here was where the real criteria for canonization lay—in a massive but intensive historical process where neither benevolence nor malice aforethought of any genius or any council played a hand, but where the real test of canonization lay. Does it give life to the people where they are? Later councils could but ratify such a plebiscite, nor could they foist onto the people what the people in their collective innocence, wisdom and honesty had simply set aside. Canonical Criticism studies such times and moments in the history of the biblical process to try to understand what needs were being met by the stuff we call canonical. Judaism was principally a diaspora people in these times, the largest communities living in Babylonia and Egypt until well into the Middle Ages.[5] Either an old tradition met the people out there where they were, at some point or other, earlier or later, or we have it not.

Midrash Criticism then picks up with that observation and, using all the available instances of the use of such a tradition, attempts to understand the various ways in which a given passage or tradition met the people where they were, precisely the ways in which it was adaptable. If a tradition was canonical in any sense, it was adaptable: that is its nature; hence no biblical passage has only that meaning which modern biblical scholarship assigns to it.[6] To recover the original meaning of a biblical passage is extremely important, but it is only the beginning of a serious study of that passage. The reason it is in the Bible may well be due to a meaning derived from the passage by a later generation in the canonical process beyond the last editors! Comparative Midrash raises the legitimate question as to what is meant by the expression "original meaning". Do philologists not tend to assign meanings to words which antedate the period of the original biblical author, thus by-passing the "original meaning" in the opposite direction?[7]

Nonetheless, a valid history of Isa 61:1-3 begins, properly, with the meaning the biblical author intended.

---

[5] See the comprehensive work of the editor of the present volume: Neusner, *A History of the Jews in Babylonia*, four vols (1966-69).

[6] Note the different "original meanings" assigned to crucial biblical passages within the short history of modern biblical scholarship. Even the "original meaning" varies with the Zeitgeist of our own times.

[7] This is evident in the work of Mitchell Dahood: see especially his *Psalms*, 3 volumes, in the Anchor Bible (1966-70).

II

The efforts of modern biblical scholarship have not rendered clear judgments about the meaning of Isa 61:1-3 at the first stages of its formation and history. There seem to be three major positions on the literary nature, or form, of the pericope. But whether or not it should be seen as the opening strophe of the fuller poem, 61:1-11, the first three verses are commonly seen as the basic small unit.[8]

Some scholars view it as an Ebed Yahweh poem.[9] D. Michel and others view it as influenced by the Ebed poems, an early poetic midrash on the Ebed idea.[10] A third opinion is that, formcritically, it presents the call of a prophet, perhaps the Third Isaiah.[11] Part of the reason for such diversity of opinion about the passage is that of the difficulty in determining the nature of Isa 56 to 66; much of what one thinks of our passage depends on a prior judgment about the larger body of material in which it is imbedded.

But equally important in contributing to the uncertainty is content analysis of phrases in the text. As Bernhard Duhm pointed out, the author has mixed the figures of herald of good news and prophet.[12] Whether or not it is a confusion depends considerably on one's understanding of either Gestalt. Another reason is that, as Westermann remarks, this is surely the last time that a prophet so freely and surely expressed the certainty that God had sent him with a message to his people. Such a view depends, of course, on the date one assigns to the basic unit. Another reason for scholarly uncertainty is that the author clearly draws on earlier material, especially Isa 42:3 and 7. And D. Michel has seen this better than most. In Isa 61 we have a good example of what Renée Bloch called biblical midrash in the Bible itself. Zimmerli, who

---

[8] James Muilenberg sees the basic poem as including 61:1-11 and having five strophes, of which vv. 1-3 form the first, *Interpreter's Bible* 5, 708-16.

[9] W. W. Cannon, *ZAW* 60 (1929) 284-88; O. Procksch, *Theologie des AT* (1950) 290; others have had similar but modified views, such as von Hoonacker and J. Morgenstern: cf. Robert Koch, *Biblica* 27 (1946) 396-401, and Morgenstern, *HUCA* 40-41 (1969-70) 109-21.

[10] D. Michel, *ThViat* 10 (1966) 213-30; and see also Walther Zimmerli in *Archäologie und AT* (Galling Festschrift 1970) 321-32.

[11] K. Elliger, *ZATW* 49 (1931) 112-41; cf. Westermann, *Das Buch Jesaia, Kapitel 40-66*, *ATD* 19 (1966) 290-92; and see also the study of Zimmerli, cited above, whose position is rather complex but would not rule out the formcritical category of a call of a prophetic figure; cf. B. Duhm, *Das Buch Jesaia* (1892) 425-26.

[12] *Ibid.*, Cf. Westermann, *op. cit.*, 290.

disagrees with Michel in part, concludes with a view very similar when he suggests the passage is the essence of an exilic sermon based on both Lev. 25:10 and Deutero-Isaianic traditions![13]

From philology there are two suggestions about the one difficult reading in MT, though these are rather mutually exclusive. The one bids us turn to Egyptian documents and the other to Babylonian. The problem the text presents is that the verb *pqḥ*, in 61:1, is elsewhere in the Bible used only of the opening of eyes or ears. [14] In 1947 the Egyptologist A. S. Yahuda cited the portion after the *maqeph* in the Isa text, *qôaḥ*, as a loan word which in New Egyptian means, according to Yahuda, "a wooden collar, especially used to be fastened tightly around the neck of the prisoners (*Aeg. Wb.* V 66)". He takes the whole phrase to mean "to open the collars of the prisoners", and excuses the use of *pqḥ* instead of *ptḥ* as a purposive literary device of the author.[15] And we must admit that this is a very attractive explanation: biblical authors did precisely that sort of thing to score points in their brilliant rhetoric.

But did they go that far out of their way to accomodate an Egyptian word which we cannot be at all sure the first hearers or readers would have known? The answer to that question depends on a number of factors. In the meantime another very attractive explanation has been advanced by the renowned Assyriologist, Shalom Paul.[16] Pointing out that Isa 42:7 has already equated opening the eyes with liberation from prison, Paul suggests the prophet made *pqḥ-qḥ* parallel to *dĕrôr* and thus used it also to mean freedom. Paul cites a cuneiform inscription in which Sargon declares that in liberating Dur-Yakin he destroyed the prisons in it and "let the prisoners see the light". Such a phrase Paul states was the equivalent of "I set them free". Paul translates Isa 61:1f.,

---

[13] Cf. Zimmerli, *op. cit.*, 330-32. This, I think, is right; see below.

[14] In Isa 42:20 it is used for opening ears. Note the very same problem with respect to the Greek verb, *dianoigō*, which though elsewhere is used only for the opening of eyes, or of the heavens (some sort of vision), in Luke 24:32 is used, after its normal use in 24:31, to mean opening a scroll! This was clearly an effective rhetorical device used by Luke to stress that one can "see" (open the eyes) in the present only after one "sees" (opens) the scriptures. This point is more certain than the so-called proleptic eucharist celebrated in Emmaus: the breaking of bread as study of Torah is very ancient.

[15] A. S. Yahuda, *JBL* 66 (1947) 86-87.

[16] S. Paul, in W. W. Hallo, ed., *Essays in Memory of E. A. Speiser* (1968) 180-86, esp. 182

then, "to proclaim liberty to captives and to prisoners freedom". This explanation has the advantages of recognizing the import of Isa 42:7 for our passage and of suggesting a Mesopotamian idiom as an extra-biblical parallel: it fits a broad view of the exilic or post-exilic Mesopotamian provenance of the passage.

III

Early witnesses to the text betray patterns familiar in text criticism. They all exhibit keen interest in the *pqḥ-qḥ* reading, clearly indicating to the trained observer that they were all struggling with the text (whether one word or two) represented by MT, and not with a genuine variant. IQIs a and b leave no space for a *maqeph*, suggesting perhaps a duplicated form of the last letters of the root, or perhaps indicating, with the MT tradition, an early confusion both about the form and the meaning. Classical and traditional grammarians have most often taken it to be a hapax noun form based on *pqḥ* with an intensive sense of eyeopening.[17]

Apparently the LXX took it in this way in translating it by the noun *anablepsis* and in translating the previous word by *tuphloîs*, rendering the phrase *kai tuphlois anablepsin* continuing the predicate construction after the verb *kēruksai-liqrō'*, which is precisely the text of Luke 4:18. Modern scholarship has suggested that LXX, and hence Luke, read *vĕlassanverîm* instead of *vĕla'ăsûrîm*.[18] I think such a reading highly unlikely as Vorlage for the LXX. On the contrary, because of similar expressions in Hebrew Isa 42:7, 18, 22 and 43:8, the Greek translator had no difficulty whatever in understanding and conveying the metaphor of blindness for prisoners.[19] The burden of proof rests on those who would defend a

---

[17] Most modern scholars have also taken it as a noun, as already suggested by the ancient translators except the Targum: see BDB *ad loc*. P. Volz in *Jesaia II* (1932) 254 thought, on the basis of 10 medieval MSS, that *qḥ* alone stood in an early text and was corrected above the line by the addition *pqwḥ*, the two of which then flowed together. Zimmerli, *op. cit.*, goes in the opposite direction and sees *pqhqwḥ* as a dittography of *pqwḥ*. Ibn Ezra, in contrast to both, had defended MT grammatically by citing other verbs where the last two root letters are doubled, the so-called *peʿalʿel* form. Qimḥi and Mezudat Zion allow of the possibility of a noun while Targum Jonathan, Ibn Ezra and Rashi are very clear about its being a verb in form, if not in function.

[18] Cf. first apparatus of BH³ (> BHS).

[19] Isa 29:18 and 35:5 refer apparently to actual healing (cf. Matt 8:1-9:34; Matt 15:31; Luke 7:22, etc.) and not, as in the Deut-Isa passages, to prison blindness.

variant Vorlage behind the LXX reading. If I read Seeligman correctly, this phrase in 61:1f is hardly surprising as a translational effort of what was understood by the LXX as a metaphor in the Hebrew text before him.[20] Luke, as already noted, followed the LXX at this point, which is hardly suprising from what is known of OT quotations in Luke-Acts elsewhere. The Lukan citation reflects the LXX verbatim save for two variations: Luke omits the fourth of the six colons of 61:1 and reads *kēruksai* instead of *kalesai* as the first word of 61:2. But we shall return to these and other observations about the Lukan citation.

Where the LXX translator met a genuine difficulty in his Vorlage he resolved it by tanslating the phrase (*vĕla'ăssûrîm pĕqaḥqôaḥ*) metaphorically, precisely because he thought the original author had intended it that way; and I think he would have based his defense on the same metaphors already cited in Isa. 42-43. These chapters represent different authors in antiquity, the so-called Second and Third Isaiahs. But as Zimmerli has suggested, the later author may well have been developing an idea of the earlier author. I would even suggest that in 61:1 an Isaianic disciple was engaging in a very early midrashic reflection on the Deut-Isa materials cited, and that the later LXX translator of Isa 61 understood quite well what he was doing.[21]

Other points of interest arise when one compares LXX with Vulgata, for almost invariably the latter follows the MT tradition where it differs from LXX. The Vulgate follows the MT verbatim in the difficult opening phrases of v. 3, as over against a translational attempt in some MSS of the LXX to facilitate the transfer into the receptor Greek: the inclusion of *Dominus* in v. 1b where LXX lacks *kurios* for MT tetragrammaton; and the inclusion of *Deo nostro* in v. 2b, after *diem ultionis*, where LXX lacks *tō theō'ēmōn* (most MSS) for MT *lē'lōhēnû*. One such point, however, is intriguing, and belongs, I am convinced, to the study precisely of history of midrash rather than to that of textual criticism. And this again,

---

[20] I. L. Seeligmann, *The Septuagint Version of Isaiah: A Discussion of its Problems* (1948) 95-121. Seeligmann does not deal with Isa 61:1-3 directly.

[21] It should be remembered that a translator has the advantage of a vertical reading of a biblical book, and the LXX translator of the later chapters of Isaiah was in all likelihood the same as for Deut-Isa, at least; cf. Seeligmann, *op. cit.* He would have translated chapter 61, therefore, only a comparatively short time after chs. 42 and 43. (The Syriac in this whole section seems to be a faithful daughter of LXX.)

is in v. 1f, the *pqaḥ-qôaḥ* difficulty. Here the Vulgate reads *clausis apertionem*,[22] which is just as interpretative in its own way as LXX *tuphlois anablepsin*, but in a different tradition, namely, that represented later on by Rashi and Qimhi: the opening of prisons instead of, with LXX, the opening of eyes of the blind in prison. Of course, the Rabbis often go on to interpret the prison as *galut*, which one cannot attribute to Jerome. I do not think that Jerome had a variant Vorlage before him: he simply wanted to make sense in Latin of a Hebrew cryptic expression, and in doing so he showed himself a good student of the Bethlehem rabbinate.

Also interesting is where the Latin appears to go along with the LXX vs. MT. There seem to be two such cases: *indulgentia* in v. 1e seems to stress a certain connotation of the LXX *'aphesis* rather than the plain meaning of MT *děrôr*;[23] and *fortes iustitiae* in v. 3e is certainly closer to LXX *geneai dikaiosunēs* than to MT *êlê hazzedeq*. However, it is very interesting to note that in this too, Jerome seems to anticipate rabbinic interpretations recorded in *Mezudat Zion* and *Mezudat David* where "oaks of righteousness" are viewed as *gědōlîm běma'ăsēh ẓedeq*—precisely *fortes iustitiae*.[24]

Some MSS and editor of MT read *ēlê*, in Isa 61:3e, gods, without the first *yod*. 1QIs[a] has the *yod* while 1QIs[b] has a lacuna and is therefore indeterminate. Milik, in 11Q Melch 14 (see below), reads *ēlê* [haẓẓedeq] as a citation of our passage. 11QMelch, however, cannot be taken as textual witness since it is clearly a midrash and, according to the midrashic rules of the period, was perfectly free to read *ēlê* for *êlê*. In point of fact, no ancient witness is in this case determinate for what either the translator or the midrashist had as Vorlage; for all the witnesses available, including the targum (see below), could have as well read the one or the other to derive

---

[22] Vetus Latina apparently had it *vinctis apertionem* (understand *carceris*). Jerome in his commentary remarks that the sense of the Hebrew could be either that "the blind might see" (*caecis ut videant*) or that "prisons be opened" (*clausis apertionem*). Note that Aquila chose *diablepsin* (seeing clearly), Sym. *apolusin* and *dianoiksin*. All ancient traditions, except the Targum, understood *pěqaḥ-qôaḥ* as a noun form.

[23] *Aphesis* is, of course, absolutely correct for Heb *děrôr* since the LXX here but follows the practice of the LXX in Lev 25 and elsewhere (cf. Jer 34:8); but in those passages the Latin usually has *libertas* and not *indulgentia*: cf. Suzanne Daniel, *Recherches sur le vocabulaire du culte dans la Septante* (1966).

[24] Aquila, Sym. and Theod. read *'ischuroi tou dikaiou*, with variant *tou laou* (sic), which seems to be a mid-term understanding between LXX *geneai* and Lat. *fortes*.

the sense they convey. On the other hand one must leave open the possibility that *ēlê* was a very early, genuine variant, even, possibly, that MT *êlê* is a hidden tiqqun for *ēlê*. The greater likelihood, nonetheless, is that the author fully intended "oaks of righteousness" as parallel to "a planting of Yahweh" but stylistically allowed for the possible poetic ambiguity: see *êlê hā-'āreẓ* in Ezek 17:13 and II K 24:15, where the meaning clearly is "powerful men".

It is difficult to date the Targum Jonathan to Isa 61, but it is interesting to compare the effort there with those of Qumran and the LXX to understand *pĕqaḥ-qôaḥ*.[25] The Targum reads precisely *vĕlid'ăsîrîn* for *vĕla'ăsûrîm* of MT but for *pĕqaḥ-qôaḥ* we are offered in direct discourse the very words the herald is to proclaim to the prisoners: *'itgĕlû lĕnêhôr*, "Come forth to the light". It would appear that the Targumist reflects the tradition of the *maqeph*, which is not surprising, and that he took *pĕqaḥ* to be a collective imperative, strengthened perhaps by the *qôaḥ* enclitic, on which he simply threw in the towel. If one reads *pĕqaḥ* as a verb, "Open the eyes", it may, in the context of prisoners, say to them what the Targum says, "Come out into the light".

But, in contrast to LXX, there are other points of interest in the Targum for our study. The Targumist makes clear at the beginning of 61:1 that this passage was spoken by the prophet Isaiah, *'ămar nĕbîyā'*. He understood this passage as indeed rabbinic Judaism after him has understood it (see below), as a reflection by the prophet on his vocation and hence on his source of authority. Scholarly discussions about the Ebed Yahweh, or about the office of *mĕbassēr*, or about Trito-Isaiah, would have been strange to the Targumist. For him Isaiah was here saying something about his own vocation. That's the peshat; and there's an end of it.

For the Targumist *rûaḥ 'ădōnāy 'ĕlōhîm 'ālāy* becomes *rûaḥ nĕbû'āh min qădām 'ădōnay 'ĕlōhîm 'ălay*, which specifies the sense of the passage rather narrowly. A spirit of prophecy would have gone forth from the presence of God to settle like a mantle on the prophet. In later rabbinic literature, this passage is cited to stress the peculiar authority of Isaiah as distinct from all other prophets. Though they do not, like the Targum, introduce the idea of a spirit of prophecy, the midrashim and the commentators

---

[25] Editions used were the *Miqra'ot Gedolot* of Vilna 1892 and A. Sperber, *The Bible in Aramaic*, Cf. J. F. Stenning, *The Targum of Isaiah* (1949) 202-05.

do not depart far from this basic interpretation by the Targum. The elimination of the word *māshaḥ* and the substitution of *dĕrabbê yātî ʾădōnay*, "The Lord has appointed me," and, then reading it with the following, *Lĕbassārāʾ ʿinvĕtānayyāʾ*, effectively eliminated the whole notion of anointing: "The Lord has appointed me to bear good news to the afflicted." Rashi, and Mezudat Zion say that it does not mean anointing but being made important or great.[26] Ibn Ezra and Qimhi cite Ps 105:15 (I Chron 16:22; cf. II Sam 1:14-16) to insist that the passage refers to the prophet himself and none other.[27] Three times the Targum uses the expression *qădām ʾădōnay* in interesting ways. The first we have seen is in speaking of the spirit of prophecy *min qădām ʾădōnay*. The second instance is in the first colon of v. 2 where the text says *liqrōʾ shĕnat rāzôn laʾ-dōnāy*. The Targum translates the *lamed* by *qădām*, so that the sense of the colon becomes, "To proclaim the year of acceptance before the Lord and the Day of Puranut before our God". Here we have a consistent picture of a *mĕbassēr*, a herald-prophet, who goes forth from the presence of God to proclaim exactly what God wishes him to proclaim. All messianic overtones are eliminated making the Targum possibly an indirect witness to earlier messianic interpretations. Whereas the LXX and Qumran indicate some interest in the *lameds* in v. 2, [28] the Targum shuts out all options with its *qădām ʾădōnay*.

Finally in v. 3 the Targum, in translating the phrase *êlê hazzedeq*, understands *rabrĕbê qushtāʾ*, "princes of righteousness" instead of "oaks of righteousness".[29] This is, as noted above, interesting in the light of the possibility that 11QMelch 14 read the phrase "Gods of Righteousness", or of Justice.[30]

---

[26] Muzudat Zion, like Rashi, uses the expression *ʿinyan gĕdûlāh*, but then cites Isa 45 and Cyrus to explicate. All this would appear to argue for an anti-Christian Tendenz as one tradition of Jewish interpretation. The Christian use of Isa 61 was the foil for this tradition.

[27] "Do not touch my annointed ones; do my prophets no harm."

[28] Cf. the Göttingen LXX Isaiah, ed. by J. Ziegler (1939) where *ʾeniauton kuriou dekton* has the variant *eniauton tō kuriō dekton*. At Qumran the reading becomes *shĕnat hā-rāzôn lĕmalkî ẓedeq* in 11QMelch 9: see the discussion below.

[29] Targum reads *vĕyiqrôn* for MT *vĕqōrāʾ* where 1QIs[a] has *vĕqārĕʾû* or perhaps *yiqrĕʾû*.

[30] According to J. T. Milik, *JJS* 23 (1972) 98 and 106. And I agree; see the Theodor Gaster Festschrift. The original editors had read *êlê mĕrômîm*; see below.

IV

Before turning to Qumran (where interest in Isa 61:1-3 was as great as in the NT), we might for a moment look to the various rabbinic sources though the interest there was clearly not as great as among the sectarians. According to Heimann, Isa 61:1 is cited nine times down through Ibn Bakudah, which he includes in his index, and Isa 61:3 five times.[31] In about half of these instances there is a mere passing reference to the Isa material in which it is clear that there is no real interest at all in Isa 61 except perhaps in asmakhta to something else quite different. These I omit from consideration. Very like these is one I shall mention nonetheless. In the Zohar (II 136b) the Sabbath is presented as the reflexion of the *'ôlām habbā'*; on the Sabbath the souls of the just enter Paradise on high and at a given moment, after a Sabbath promenade in Paradise, recite either Isa 61:1 or Ezek 1:21. Both passages have to do with the activity of the spirit. The Ezek passage, which is so closely associated with the Merkabah traditions, needs no explanation in the Zohar at this point.[32] What is interesting is that our passage in Isa should be viewed in the same category. The Zohar is not an eschatalogical text but a mystical one; it nonetheless deemed it wise to martial Isa 61 to support its speculations.

The Mekilta to Ex 20:21 [33] claims that the text there which speaks of Moses entering the *araphel* or deep darkness, really concerns Moses' humility. In doing so Isa 61:1 is cited alongside Num 12:3, Isa 66:2 and Ps 51:14 to establish Moses' great humility.

In this same line is a passage in Abodah Zarah 20b, duly recorded as well in Yalqut Shim'oni and Yalqut Mechiri,[34] which, after providing in the name of Pinhas ben Ya'ir a sort of scale of cause and effect in ascending ranks of piety and reward, states, in the name of Joshua ben Levi, that humility is the greatest of all of these and cites as *dictum probantium* our passage, noting that the text does not say *lĕbassēr ḥasîdîm* but *lĕbassēr 'ănāvîm*. They are the *'ănāvîm* who will receive the good news; hence humility,

---

[31] Aaron Mordechai Heimann, *Sefer Torah ha-ketubah veha-mesorah 'al torah nebi'im vĕketubim*, ad loc.

[32] J. Neusner, "The Development of the *Merkavah* Tradition," *JSJ* 2 (1971) 149-60.

[33] Par. Jethro 9. This same midrash is recorded also in Yalqut Shimoni II, remez 302, remez 485, and remez 954.

[34] The Yalqut Sh. and Mechiri references are *ad loc.*, Isa 61:1.

88 JAMES A. SANDERS

ʿănāvāh, is *gĕdôlāh mikkulām*. The assumption is that *ʿănāvāh* earns the reward entailed in the message of the herald.

In Lev Rabbah 10:2, [35] there is recorded the familiar tradition, with slight variants in each, that in contrast to all other prophets, Isaiah alone received the spirit of God himself, or as Pesiqta has it, "out of the mouth of God" (cf I K22: 20-23). While these do not stress, as does the Targum, a spirit of prophecy from before God, they do not contradict the Targumic tradition.

Isa 61:1 is at least twice cited along with Isa 32:14 and Isa 60:22 as one of the three passages where we find the holy spirit spoken of in relation to the redemption of the End Time. The one is Midr ʾEkah to 3:50 (73a). In Yalqut Mechiri *ad loc.*, Lam 3:49 appears in the place of Isa 60:22.

Finally, Isa 61:1 is linked in Targum Ps-Jonathan to Num 25:12 with Mal 3:1 in a view of the mission of Elijah when he comes to announce the End Time and the coming of Messiah.[36]

In three of the six basic rabbinic traditions in which Isa 61:1-3 figures, with any import at all, it is seen in relation the eschaton: the mission of Elijah, final redemption by the *rûaḥ haqqōdesh*, and the exalted place of humility in receiving the good news of the final herald. Note that in none of these is the passage itself interpreted messianically in the strict sense of the term; but the evidence is very clear that it was not unimportant in rabbinic traditions in discussions of the End Time.

What originally was an exilic text referring to an historical situation, in which, in all probability an Isaianic disciple refers to himself as having the authority of the spirit of God to announce a Jubilee release from the oppressive aspects of diaspora, became in some rabbinic traditions an eschatological reference.

This is, of course, especially the case at Qumran and in the NT, to which we now turn.[37]

---

[35] Also in Pesiqta 125 b; Yalqut Mechiri *ad loc.*; Yalqut Shimoni II, remez 443; Pesiqta de Rab Kahana 125b-126a.

[36] The phrase *pĕʾēr taḥat ʾēpher* in 61:3 is cited numerous times in the literature as proof-text for where the ashes of mourning for the temple should be put, i.e., on the same place on the forehead as the tefillin (Midr. Tehillin 137.6; Taanit 16a, and Yalqut Shimoni II, remez 404 and 685). For those interested in literary style, and for those interested in later hermeneutics, there is a rare observation about rhetorical devices in Deut-Isa: cf. Pesiqta de Rab Kahana 126a. Also there is quite a literature from the middle ages emanating from the *ʾăvēlê ẓîon*, who took their name from Isa 61:3.

[37] The only passage I have so far been able to locate in (what used to be

V

Until 15 years ago the importance of Isa 61:1-3 at Qumran was largely unrecognised. What use the Essenes made of these verses had gone virtually unnoticed except by David Flusser in an article entitled "Blessed are the poor in Spirit...."[38] In his article Flusser signaled allusions to Isa 61:1-2 in Matt 5:3-5; but he also pointed out an "enriching" juxtaposition of Isa 61:1 and Ps 37:11 in 1QH xviii 14-15 and in 4QpPs37. Flusser's translation of the former emphasizes his point:

> To (have appointed) me in Thy truth
>   a messenger (of the peace) of Thy goodness,
> To proclaim to the meek the multitude of Thine mercies
>   to let them that are of contrite spirit
>   he(ar salvation) from (everlasting) source
>   and to them that mourn everlasting joy. (1QH xviii 14-15)

Flusser's work on 4QpPs37, however, can be complemented considerably since the work of Stegemann on the pesher in 1963 and 1967, the full publication of the pesher in *DJD* V in 1968, and John Strugnell's review of the latter in 1970.[39] But Flusser's essential observation is still valid: the pesher on Ps 37:11 clearly reflects Isa 61:1-2 by the midrashic technique of "enrichment' common in all Judaism of the period.[40] A fresh translation of the pesher, in the light of the work of Stegemann and Strugnell would read as follows:

---

called) the Apocrypha and Pseudepigrapha is Sirach 48:10-11 where it is said in the Greek that Elijah was filled with his spirit (certain MSS and Syr-Hex have 'holy spirit') and in the Syriac that Elijah received a double portion of prophecy. Unfortunately the Cairo MSS are mutilated or non-existant at this point of ch. 48 and the Masada fragments simply do not extend this far. My own judgement would be that Ben Sira is not thinking either of Isa 61 or of the eschaton in this famous passage. H. L. Strach, *Die Sprüche Jesus: des Sohnes Sirachs* (1903); R. Smend, *Die Weisheit des Jesus Sirach*: text (1906) 55-56 cf. Vol. I (1906) 461-63; M. Z. Segal, *Sefer Hakmat ben Sira ha-shalem* (1953) 80.

[38] *IEJ* 10 (1960) 1-13. Cf. Keck *ZNTW* 56 (1965) 108-29 and 57 (1966) 54-78 who criticizes Flusser. Keck's argument is unconvincing at this point.

[39] H. Stegemann, *RQ* No. 14 (1963) 235-70 and No. 22 (1967) 193-210; *DJD* 5 (1968) Pls. 14-17; J. Strugnell, *RQ* No. 26 (1970) 211-18. Cf. J. Fitzmyer, *CBQ* 21 (1969) 65-67.

[40] Gertner, *BSOAS* (1962) 1-27 and *JSS* 7 (1962) 267-92. Cf. E. Ellis, in *Neotestamentica et Semitica* (1969) 61-69.

> But the *ʿănāwîm* shall inherit the earth and delight in abundant peace. Its pesher concerns the congregation of the *ʾebyōnîm* who accept the season of affliction but will be saved from the snares of Belial and thereafter all who inherit the earth will delight and luxuriate in all the delights of the flesh. (4Qp Ps 37, II 9-10)

But the redemptive aspect of the *shĕnat rāzôn la ʾdōnai* is not the only facet of this passage reflected in Qumran thought. The *yôm nāqām* of Isa 61:2 is stressed in 1QS ix 21-23 where the *maskîl*, or instructor at Qumran, is described as a man zealous for the *ḥôq*, law, and its time of fulfillment which is paraphrased as the *yôm nāqām* when he will do nothing but *rāzôn* in that day.[41] This *rāzôn*, of course, means doing the pleasure of God, or doing what is *dektos* to God, at the End Time. This passage alone makes clear the dual aspect of the *shĕnat rāzôn la'dōnai* of Isa 61:2 as understood at Qumran—bliss for the true Israel but utter damnation for Qumran's enemies.[42] The *yôm nāqām* of Isa 61:2 also appears in 1QM vii 4-5; there the men of Qumran who are to fight with the holy angels in the great final battles are described as "volunteers, pure of spirit and flesh, and eager for the *yôm nāqām*".[43] This line in 1QM follows immediately on the passage which lists those who are forbidden to come near the battle field on that day, the halt, blind, lame and those of impure or injured body.[44]

These indications of the use of Isa 61:1-2 at Qumran were dramatically supplemented in 1965 in the publication of 11QMelch by Adam S. van der Woude.[45] A former student of mine, Merrill Miller, shows in an article published in 1969 that Isa 61:1-2 "stands behind the unfolding pesher material" of 11QMelch.[46] It is not just a part of the enriching biblical material but "is woven into the fabric of the commentary material and is in fact its formative element".[47]

Miller in his paper, which had been a seminar presentation at Union Seminary the year before, convincingly demonstrates that the citations in 11QMelch from Lev 25:13, Dt 15:2, Isa 52:7 and

---

[41] Cf. 1QH x 19.

[42] Mezudat David interprets the phrase *shĕnat rāzôn leyisrāʾēl*.

[43] Yigael Yadin, *The Scroll of the War of the Sons of Light Against the Sons of Darkness* (1962) 291.

[44] See my study, in *Essays in Old Testament Ethics* (J. Philip Hyatt, *in Memoriam*), ed. by J. Crenshaw and J. Willis (1974) 245-71. "The Ethic of Election in Luke's Great Banquet Parable."

[45] A. van der Woude, *OS* 14 (1965) 354-73; M. de Jonge and A. van der Woude, *NTS* 12 (1966) 301-26; J. Fitzmyer, *JBL* 86 (1967) 25-41.

[46] M. Miller, *JBL* (1969) 467-69.

[47] Ibid., 469, n. 13.

Ps 82:1-2 and 7:8-9 [48] are all related to phrases from Isa 61:1-3 which in effect links the citations in such a way as to demonstrate the unity of the scriptures. Words and phrases from Isa 61:1-3 appear in lines 4, 6, 9, 13, 14 and 18-20 at points quite crucial to the fabric of the whole piece.[49] The words from Isa 61 which appear there are as follows:

Line 4 *ha-shĕbûyîm* (*lishbûyim*)
      6 *wĕqārā' lāhem dĕrôr* (*liqrō' lishbûyim dĕrôr*)
      9 *shĕnat ha-rāzôn lĕmalkê zedeq* (*shĕnat rāzôn la'dōnay*)
     13 *noqmat mishpĕtê 'ēl* (*yôm nāqām lē'lōhênû*)
     14 *'ēlê [hazzedeq]* (*êlê hazzedeq*)
     18 *hamĕbassēr* (*lĕbassēr*)
     18 *mĕshîah ha-rû[ah]* (*māshah YHWH 'ōtî*)
     19 *[lĕnahēm kol 'ăbēlîm lasûm la'ăbēlê zîōn]*
     20 *lĕnah[em] ha'[ăbēlîm]* (as above)

It is Isa 61:1-3 which in 11QMelch eschatalogizes the Jubilee Year proclamation of Lev 25 and Dt 15 and which shows the unity of scripture, according to Miller.[50]

In 11QMelch it is Melchizedeq, a heavenly judgment and redemption figure, perhaps the chief figure in the Qumran view of the heavenly council whom Milik now calls "une hypostase de Dieu" (as over against Melkiresha', his evil antagonist), who proclaims *shĕmittāh* (l. 3) and *dĕrôr* (l. 6) for the captive, that is for the Essenes, but proclaims the *yôm nāqām* for the forces of Belial.[51] It is Melchizedeq who proclaims or announces the End Time (i.e. *melkî-zedeq* is the subject of the verb *qārā'* of Isa 61:1 and 2), and it is also Melchizedeq who executes the judgment of God of the Eschaton. Melchizedeq is also identified as the evangelist, or *mĕbassēr* (lines 16 and 18) who is anointed by the spirit (l. 18). What he proclaims, in effect, is the "acceptable year of Melchizedeq (l.9);[52] four times is Melchizedeq called the *'ĕlōhîm* (ll. 10, 16,

---

[48] Isa 8:11 in line 25 of 11QMelch should be added to the list.

[49] See my study, "The Old Testament in 11QMelchizedek," in the Theodor Gaster Festschrift, *The Journal of the Ancient Near Eastern Society of Columbia University* 5 (1973) 373-82.

[50] Miller saw allusions to Isa 61:1-3, only in 11QMelch lines 4, 6, 9, 13, and the first noted above in line 18. For the others here listed see my study already cited in the Gaster volume. One of the remarkable aspects of Zimmerli's study, cited above, is that he has seen Isa 61:1-3 as a a reflection on Lev 25:10 and Isa 42:7 by the tradition-critical method without reference to Qumran or the rabbis. This suggests how complementary the two methods are if handled properly.

[51] I agree with Milik against Carmignac in *RQ* No. 27 (1970) 343-78.

[52] Recall that Rashi and Ibn Ezra interpreted 61:2a as *gĕ'ûlāh*, as over

24 & 25), or heavenly being [53] who on that day will reign and execute judgments against the forces of Belial but redemption for the "captives" (*shěbûyîm*), or Essenes.[54] "Captives" in 11QMelch becomes an epithet for the convenanters like "poor" or "pure' or "good" in other Qumran texts.[55]

VI

The quotation of Isa 61:1-2a is peculiar to Luke; it is lacking in the Mark 6 and Matt 13 parallels.[56] Luke has made of the Rejection pericope a very important statement about what in Jesus' teachings offended his contemporaries. In Mark and Matthew, both of which explicitly state that the folk at Nazareth *'eskandalizonto 'en 'autō*, the offense is that of a prophet not being honored in his own country nor by his own kin: his general wisdom and his works appear pretentious for a hometown *tektōn* (carpenter). But in Luke, by contrast, we attend a synagogue service, see Jesus given an *'alîyāh* to the *bîmāh*, hear him read a Haftarah portion from Isaiah, and hear him do biblical midrash on it based on Elijah and Elisha.[57] Luke makes it very clear, *pace* Jeremias,[58] that the offense taken by the faithful of Nazareth was at Jesus' midrash on the Isaiah passage. What in Mark and Matthew is a rejection by Jesus of the people's *'apistia*, in Luke is a rejection of Jesus by the people be-

---

against Qimhi and Mezudat David who interpreted it to mean *shěnat haggālût* and *shěnat rāzôn leyisrā'ēl*. Rashi and Ibn Ezra could be messianic whereas the others appear quite political.

[53] In 11QMelch he is the *'ělōhîm* of Ps. 82:1 and the *'ělōhayik* of Isa 52:7.

[54] The key word for the Essenes in 11QMelch is the *shěbûyim* of Isa 61:1.

[55] See 11Q Ps 154 for a significant clustering of such appellatives for the sect: Sanders, *DJD* 4 (1965) 68-69 and *The Dead Sea Psalms Scroll* (1967) 108-09.

[56] Isa 61:1-2 in Luke has been treated by Larrimore Clyde Crockett in a 1966 dissertation at Brown University. This very fine work came to my attention only after the first draft of this study was completed, and is still available only through University Microfilms. See also Crockett, *JBL* 88 (1969) 177-83. An important study which Crockett overlooks in this article is that of A. Strobel, *TLZ* 92 (1967) 251-54 on the relation of Isa 61:1-2 and Lev 25:10 in Luke 4:16-30. However, neither Strobel nor Crockett saw the importance of Isa 61 (not to mention Lev. 25:10) in 11QMelch, and 11QMelch for Luke 4.

[57] The critique, of Aileen Guilding's theory (*The Fourth Gospel and Jewish Worship* 1960) about a triennial lectionary cycle in the first century, by R. Brown, *CBQ* 22 (1960) 259-61 and others, should shift attention to the work of P. Billerbeck, *ZNTW* 55 (1964) 143-61 which I have not seen mentioned by anyone dealing with this problem.

[58] J. Jeremias, *Jesus' Promise to the Nations* (1958) 44-45, following Bruno Violet, *ZNW* 37 (1938) 251-71.

cause of his sermon. The ambiguous reaction of the people after Jesus reads the passage from Isa 61, plus 58:6, is shown in their single question (contrast parallels) "Is not this Joseph's son?" The people were both pleased and puzzled by Jesus' acclamation that this very familiar and key passage of scripture was being fulfilled on that very day. To say that that particular passage was being fulfilled was to proclaim the acceptable year of the Lord. The people would have been exceedingly pleased to hear that the great day had arrived, but they would have been puzzled that Jesus, a familiar local personage, would have arrogated to himself the role of *mĕbassēr*, herald of the Great Day, a role which at Qumran was, as we have seen, reserved for Melchizedeq, the chief *'ĕlôhîm* of the heavenly council. But that which in v. 22 is pleased puzzlement, in v. 29, seven verses later, becomes threatening anger. Jesus' cousins and familiar friends turn from a puzzled but receptive audience into a lynching party. Luke forces us to ask what it was that happened within verses 23 to 27 that would cause a receptive congregation to turn into an angry mob. It is the same kind of question forced upon us by Baruch when Jeremiah's cousins and familiar friends at Anathoth turned against him, stoned him, chased him out of town and threatened to lynch him (Jer 11, etc.) What had the man said that made them so mad?

In Luke it is not Jesus' general wisdom nor even his works which offend the people, as is apparently the case in Mark and Matthew: in Luke it is the specific application Jesus makes of the Isaiah passage. There are many problems, as everyone knows; but the force of them focuses our attention on the question of the hermeneutics involved in this sermon at Nazareth as reported by Luke; indeed, the discovery of the importance of Isa 61:1-3 in 11QMelch fairly rivets our attention on the hermeneutical question.

However, the hermeneutic techniques which Luke used are not as significant as the hermeneutic axioms which underlie those techniques.[59] Before one can attribute true value to the herme-

---

[59] M. Gertner lists six midôt employed by NT writers (*'al tiqrey, tartey mashma', enriching, muqdam me'uḥar*, syntactical inversions and *midrash shēmōt*) in *JSS* 7 (1962) 270, and the larger rubrics of midrash (*gezerah shavah, peshat [dianoigon], midrash haggadah*, etc.) in *BSOAS* (1962) 1-27. William Brownlee listed 13 "presuppositions", or what we should now call hermeneutic techniques, evident in 1QpHab, in *BA* 14 (1951). A recent look at midrashic technique at Qumran is by E. Slomovic, *RQ* No. 25 (1969) 3-15 (*gezerah shavah, zēker ledāver* and *asmakhta*). (See Gertner's excellent

neutic techniques which an ancient midrashist used, he must first try to recover what the hermeneutic axioms were on which the hermeneutic techniques were based. My recent work on midrash at Qumran, as well as that of some of my students, suggests that there were two hermeneutic axioms operative at Qumran.

The first axiom was the principle which has been recognized by nearly all scholars who have worked on the Qumran pesharim but which was well expressed by Karl Elliger in *Studien zum Habakkuk-Kommentar vom Toten Meer* in 1953: "Der Ausleger hat ein ganz bestimmtes hermeneutisches Prinzip als Richtschnur. Und dieses lässt sich in zwei Sätzen zusammenfassen: 1. Prophetische Verkündigung hat zum Inhalt das Ende, und 2. die Gegenwart ist die Endzeit." [60] In other words, at Qumran prophecy had as its content the End Time, and the present is the End Time. B. J. Roberts has recently extended this basic observation to show how the Qumran sectarians believed that the Bible generally, and not just prophecy, had as its object the End Time and how the convenanters believed that they were to fulfill the role of the central *personae dramatis* of the End Time. "The Bible was their concern and constituted their whole being ... What we have here (in the scrolls) is the literature, the actual self-expression, of a people who regarded themselves and everything surrounding them, as the embodiment of the fulfillable word of God." [61] They believed themselves the true Israel of the End Time.

However, these are but different ways of expressing the first hermeneutic axiom at Qumran. The second hermeneutic axiom at Qumran has not been as clearly recognised by scholarship but is in my opinion just as important as the first. It was expressed by one of my students in a seminar paper in the following manner: "All words of woe, curse, judgment, disapproval, etc., are to be directed against those outside the community, especially those in Jerusalem; but all words of blessing, praise, salvation, confort, etc., are to be directed towards those inside the community".[62] Put

---

caveat in the *BSOAS* [1962] 20-21, following Torczyner in Ben-Yehudah's Thesaurus, that the meaning of *peshat* is not "literal" but "contextual" or "wide-spread-meaning.")

[60] Elliger, *Studien* (1953) 275-87, a remarkable early statement of Qumran ideology.

[61] B. J. Roberts in *Words and Meanings* ed. by P. Ackroyd and B. Lindars (1968) 195 and 199.

[62] James Bresnahan, an STM candidate at Colgate Rochester Divinity School.

more simply, the second hermeneutic axiom at Qumran required that scripture be so interpreted as to show that in the Eschaton God's wrath would be directed against an out-group while his mercy would be directed toward the in-group. This does not mean that the covenanters viewed themselves as sinless or exempt from God's temporal judgments. The Qumran doctrines of man and sin were very high indeed, and the sect daily confessed their woeful sins and executed their ablutions. But it was in part because they viewed themselves as having a proper orthodox doctrine of sin, and also viewed themselves as judged betimes, that they had faith that when the great day came they would be the objects of the blessings the Bible would allow. Put another way, the Essenes never in their commentaries interpreted scripture as judgmental of themselves in terms of their basic claims. That is, there was no prophetic realism or prophetic critique at Qumran. No scripture is ever interpreted as a judgment or challenge to their own theology or ideology, or to their confidence in their blissful destiny in the End Time. By prophetic realism I mean a challenge from within the group's own self-understanding. They apparently had no Jeremiah who so interpreted the tradition, as Jeremiah interpreted the Exodus covenant traditions, so as to force his own people to face the essential and existential question of whether they really were the true Israel they claimed to be. Prophetic realism is that dimension within a community which challenges its identity, and challenges it on the base and authority of the very tradition on which that identity is based. There was clearly no prophetic hermeneutic at Qumran. They apparently followed the hermeneutic tradition of what John Bright calls the "official theology" as well preached by the ancient court prophets and so-called false prophets, who represented the normal, reasonable theology of their time. Prophetic critique does not challenge simply the ethics of a community but challenges the very *ethos*, or interpretation of the *muthos* of the community—its self-understanding, without, however, rejecting the community.

The first hermeneutic axiom at Qumran was eschatological. The second was constitutive; that is, it marshalled scriptural authority in service of Qumran ideology. It is only after the importance of these two hermeneutic axioms is perceived that the various hermeneutic techniques at Qumran, have any significance.

VII

When Jesus says, in Luke 4:21, "Today this scripture is fulfilled in your ears", he was saying what the good folk at Nazareth so much wanted to hear. He was observing, according to their "ears", the first hermeneutic axiom. But, in doing so he went beyond anything we have in the scrolls. There is no similar phrase in Qumran literature. Near the end of 1QM occurs the famous prayer to be recited at the end of the seventh great battle against the forces of Belial when the final victory shall be won. But even there where *hayyôm* in the sense of "today" does occur the context is still a prayer, *hayyôm hôphiaʿ lānû*, "Today, appear Thou to us". Like the Essenes the early Christians were convinced that the pertinence of scripture was to the End Time of their day the *ʿēt haqqēz*; i.e., the Law and the Prophets and Psalms were subjected to the first hermeneutic axiom of Christian midrash which was the same as at Qumran. And the early church also employed constitutive hermeneutics in order to demonstrate that Christ was the true Israel and, in Him, the Church the New Israel of God.[63] In their belief, the truth of the OT was revealed only when contemporized to their day through the Christ figure as initial fulfillment of all that was there. To rephrase B. J. Roberts: what we have here (in the NT) is the literature, the actual self-expression of a people who regarded Christ and everything surrounding him as the embodiment of the fulfillable Word of God.

So, the first hermeneutic axiom in the NT is the same as that at Qumran, i.e., eschatological, but intensified and heightened. The actual fulfillment had begun, they believed, and nowhere in the NT is this more sharply put than in this hapax in Luke 4:21, *sēmeron peplērōtai ʿē graphē ʿautē*. Following this, Luke omits the Markan report that the congregation were scandalised, but suggests that they were amazed, as we have seen. Jeremias, following Violet, interprets this puzzlement or wonderment, by retroversion to Aramaic, as anger at Jesus for omitting the phrase "and day of vengeance for our God".[64]

Jeremias' basic point that Luke omits the phrase *kai ʿēmeran*

---

[63] J. Sanders, *JR* (1959) 232-44; and "The Dead Sea Scrolls — A Quarter Century of Study," *The Biblical Archaeologist* 36 (1973) 110-48, esp. 144-48.

[64] See above n. 58.

'antapodoseōs in Jesus' citation of Isa 61:2 is of great significance as we shall see in a moment, but not for the reasons that Jeremias cites! And this brings us to review the second axiom in Essene hermeneutics. That the End Time meant blessings for the Essenes but only woe for their enemies is clear in all Qumran literature; and it is especially clear in 11QMelch where Melchizedeq on that great and final day is to wreck divine vengeance upon Belial and all other enemies.

If Jesus omitted this all-important phrase, in his recitation of Isaiah, it is considerably more significant than his omitting the earlier phrase in v. 1, "to bind up the broken-hearted" which has its synonymous parallels in the phrases preceding and following. The addition of the phrase, *'apostelle tethrausmenous 'en 'aphesei*, from Isa 58:6, necessitated the elision of one such colon for the dual purpose of establishing a kind of parallelism between the occurences in Greek of *'aphesin* in 61:1 and *'aphesei* in 58:6, and of emphasizing the idea precisely of release, as indeed 11QMelch also does. The whole of the first half of 11QMelch is a midrash on the idea of release in the Jubilee texts of Lev 25, Deut 15 and Isa 61. Here. 11QMelch and Luke 4 are in striking harmony and seem both quite faithful to the ancient fabric of Isa 61:1-3 itself.[65]

Where they differ radically is in Jesus' midrash on *who* the poor, the captives and the blind would be. Whereas 11QMelch, by citing Lev 25:10 and Isa 52:7, clearly is based on the second Essene axiom that the captives to be released are the in-group, or Essenes, Jesus' citation of the gracious acts of Elijah and Elisha toward the Sidonian widow and the Syrian leper shows that he does not subscribe to the Essene second axiom. Far from it, by this enriching juxtaposition of the acts of Elijah and Elisha and Isa 61, Jesus clearly shows that the words meaning poor, captive, blind and oppressed do not apply exclusively to any in-group but, on the contrary, apply to those to whom God wishes them to apply. God sent (*ēlias 'epemphthē*) Elijah and Elisha to outsiders, the Sidonian Widow and the Syrian Leper.

Jesus' second axiom, if we read Luke correctly, is the contradiction of the Essene second axiom. It is precisely the dimension of prophetic critique in the NT which we have seen is so significantly lacking in the Qumran literature but is an integral part of Luke's gospel, or, perhaps, his Jesus sources. If the second axiom in the

---

[65] See above nn. 10 and 50.

early church was largely the same as that at Qumran, as it surely was, then all the church needed do in its polemic with Judaism, about which of them was the true Israel, was to transmit Jesus' prophetic challenges to his fellow Jews fairly intact but read them as rejection of Jews and acceptance of Gentiles: thus the *ipsissima vox Jesu*, read by a diametrically opposed hermeneutic axiom (the constitutive rather than prophetic), would say something like the opposite of what Jesus had intended. A simplified view of the operation of these two axioms would be as follows:

	Qumran	*Jesus and* NT (?)	*Early Church and* NT (?)
First axiom:	Eschatalogical	Eschatalogical	Eschatalogical
Second axiom:	Constitutive	Prophetic	Constitutive

It would seem to me that the long-standing debate over the place and significance of the proverb in Luke 4:24 and parallels, that a prophet is either '*atimos* or not *dektos* in his own *patris* should now be reviewed in the light of the recognition of the prophetic dimension of the hermeneutic second axiom underlying much of the scripture by Jesus in Luke.[66]

There are two salient observations necessary about the Lukan form of the proverb. First, only Luke, like Papyrus Oxyrhynchus I 6, has the adjective *dektos*; Mark and Matt have '*atimos*, and John in 4:44 has the noun *timê*. Second, Luke's citation of Isa 61:2 ends on the climactic '*eniauton kuriou dekton—shĕnat rāzōn la'-dōnai*—which, *pace* Jeremias, is the proper explanation for the omission of the following phrase, about God's day of vengeance, in Isa 61:2. Luke thus anticipated, by citation of the Wisdom tradition about the non-acceptance of prophets, the exegesis which, through recalling the acts of grace of Elijah and Elisha, he was going to give to the Isa 61 lection: the year of the End Time is determined by God alone. *Dektos* normally is used to express God's pleasure; only in this proverb apparently is it used to speak of man's acceptance of another man. Just as '*eudokia* in the *bat-qōl* in the Bethlehem theophany in Luke 2:14 expressed God's *rāzôn*, so also the *dektos* of Isa 61:2 refers to the *rāzôn* of God alone. By the midrashic technique of gezerah shavah, the Lukan Jesus not only emphasizes the climactic position he had given to the concept

---

[66] See the review of the problem in a different light by Hugh Anderson, *Interpretation* 18 (1964) 259-75, esp. 263ff.

of *dektos/rāẓôn* in the Isaiah reading, but he also emphasizes that it is not what man has pleasure in, or accepts, but what is acceptable to God that matters in the Eschaton. The proverb in Luke, "No prophet is *dektos* in his own *patris*" is not only much more likely the original, as the Oxyrhynchus citation would indicate, it is a far stronger and more offensive statement (if from Jesus) than the flaccid form of the proverb in Mark and Matthew.

But the proverb in Luke has a far greater function than to emphasize God's will in the Eschaton as over against man's will. The proverb signals which hermeneutic second axiom Jesus intended to subscribe to in his exposition of Isa 61 (and not only here, as I shall show in another study on Luke 9-18, but in his whole ministry, which Luke claims began with this midrash on Isa 61). No prophet, that is, no true prophet of the Elijah, Amos, Isaiah, Jeremiah type is *dektos* by his own countrymen precisely because his message always must bear in it a divine challenge to Israel's covenantal self-understanding in any generation. In other words, a true prophet of the prophet-martyr tradition *cannot* be *dektos* at home precisely because of his hermeneutics. Just as the so-called true prophets of old cited the ancient Mosaic and Davidic Torah traditions of Israel's origins not only as the very authority of Israel's existence, but as a judgment upon and a challenge to the official ideology of their day; so the Lukan account of the Rejection pericope shows Jesus in that same prophetic tradition vis-à vis *his* contemporaries: by the prophetic-hermeneutic second axiom Jesus turned the very popular Isa 61 passage into a judgment and a challenge to the definitions of Israel of his day. The reason, the whole passage makes clear, that the proverb is true is not only that a hometown figure is over-familiar and lacks the authority that a measure of strangeness might bring, but it is true principally because of how a true prophet, in a certain Elijah-type biblical tradition, must cast a light of scrutiny upon his own people from the very source of authority on which they rely for their identity, existence and self-understanding. It is in this sense of the word "prophet" that I understand Otto Michel's dictum, recently cited by Asher Finkel: "Jesu Messianität ist prophetisch. Sie erhebt sich auf prophetischer Gundlage, sie lebt von prophetischen Gesetzen... Es liegt eine innere Notwendigkeit in Jesu Gang zum Kreuz: Der Prophet ist Märtyrer."[67]

---

[67] See Asher Finkel in *Abraham Unser Vater*, ed. by Otto Betz, *et al.* (1963) 115.

Larrimore Clyde Crocket, in a 1966 doctoral dissertation done at Brown University on the Gospel of Luke, asks whether the controversy between Jesus and John the Baptist, as reported in Luke 7:22-23, might not have been because Jesus interpreted the crucial words, "poor" "captive" "blind" and "oppressed" to mean those whom the Essenes viewed as impure of spirit and flesh.[68] John, who would have gotten much of his own eschatological orientation at Qumran in his youthful years spent there, apparently disagreed with Jesus on this vital point. Jesus' question *ti 'exēlthate 'idein* in Luke 7:24-25 is perhaps the vital one. It is indeed a question of what one looks for that is axiomatic in how one reads a situation. The Jesus in Luke's sources apparently meant that if the word poor means poor, and the Eschaton really means good news for them, whether they are in the in-group or not, then living in the desert in sack cloth and ashes, fasting, or, living in the desert a spartan existence embracing poverty while rejecting the blemished victims of poverty, is somehow missing the point. It would appear as though John had his doubts as to whether Jesus was indeed *'o 'erchomenos, hā-bā'*, and I suspect that his doubts arose precisely because John basically agreed with the Essene second axiom. If one expected the *měbassēr* to come like Melchizedeq, in a blaze of glory with heavenly armies, then Jesus' saying that Elijah when he comes will act like Elijah when he was here—bless outsiders—would have been offensive indeed.[69] "Blessed is he who takes no offense at me" (7:23) would mean that one's second axiom could not have been exclusivist, and *ptochoi/'anāwîm* could not be *in-group appellatives*. If this construction of the encounter or controversy between Jesus and John is sound, then we may have pierced back to a pre-resurrection tradition.

VIII

In the face of the kind of comparisons available in the midrashic history of Isa 61 in the Second Temple Period, especially between Luke 4 and 11QMelch, can we any longer have confidence in a purely Redaktionsgeschichtlich approach to the source of the midrash

---

[68] See above n. 56.

[69] Offensive to Jews, spoken to them by a fellow Jew who was an eschatological prophet, but encouraging, of course, to early Christians when later read by constitutive hermeneutics to mean Judaism was rejected and the young church (mostly made up of Gentiles) was elect.

on Isa 61 reported in Luke 4? Who provided this prophetic dimension resident in the Nazareth sermon? Whose gift to the NT is *its* prophetic, second axiom? Luke's? Or the man Luke reports as having offended his compatriots to such an extent that they tried to lynch him? I confess to an innate reverse skepticism. I grant that. But why should I attribute this prophetic dimension to Luke? Is it not possible that Jesus might have used the *Essene second axiom as a foil* against which he gave his prophetic understanding of the judgements and grace of God in the End Time—and thereby so deeply offended some of his compatriots (was not *dektos* in his own *patris*).[70] If we then can recover the foil over against which a NT concept comes to full vitality, have we not satisfied one of the most rigorous criteria by which historical reconstruction of the thrust of Jesus' didache, his prophetic critique, is made possible? Whether we agree with Jeremias, or not, that the parables were directed by Jesus at his critics, we must concede that Jesus' prophetic critique of the common inversion of the Deuteronomic ethic of election was correctly understood by his critics and provoked reactions from them.[71]

This sketch of the history of the function of Isa 61:1-3 in the Second Temple Period provides a context for understanding its function in Luke 4. It provides, I think, a breakthrough for understanding what in Luke 4 are otherwise inconsistencies in the text as emphasized by Source Criticism.[72]

It is the position of this paper that none of these so-called inconsistencies actually exist in the text of Luke if approached using the method of Comparative Midrash as a supplement to other methods.

Whether Luke correctly understood Jesus' own second (prophetic) axiom or himself shared the early churches' second (constitutive) axiom, he clearly intended to stress the disproportionality of the earlier and later reactions of the congregation. He clearly wanted

---

[70] Recent studies by J. A. Fitzmyer, CBQ 32 (1970) 501-31 and J. A. Emerton, *JTS* 24 (1973) 1-23 clearly leave open the possibility that Jesus himself may even have been responsible for the word plays on '*aphesis* and *dektos* in Greek; but what is important is not the origin of the hermeneutic technique but the source of the second, prophetic, axiom. My thesis is quite congruous with that of W. D. Davies in *The Setting of the Sermon on the Mount* (1964) 252-6.

[71] See above n. 44.

[72] See my effort with respect to the *Ursprung* of the *Carmen Christi* of Phil 2, in *JBL* 88 (1969) 279-90.

to say that it was Jesus' exegesis of Isa 61 by means of the material from Kings on Elijah and Elisha which disturbed his family and friends at Nazareth. At the point just after Jesus' reading from Isa 61 the people would have interpreted the passage favorably to their own position; but when Jesus then used the hermeneutic of prophetic critique the people were deeply offended.[73]

One could hardly blame the congregation at Nazareth for expecting Jesus to interpret the *logoi tēs charitos* or *divrê ḥesed*, which he had read from Isa 61, as favorable to themselves, particularly when he had stressed *'aphesis-děrôr* by the interpolation of Isa 58:6 (which also ends in *'aphesis-ḥophshîm*) and insisted immediately upon sitting down, that they should be understood in the eschatological or, at least, penultimate situation they, like the faithful at Qumran, believed themselves to live in.

Already the LXX indicates, as Seeligmann points out in discussing similar passages in Isa 9, 11 and Deut-Isa, that the *děrôr* of which the prophet spoke in ch 61 pertained to the Galut which would walk from the darkness of dispersion to the light of life in Eretz Israel. Later the rabbinic traditions pick up the same interpretation and expand it even to the point of interpreting the *shěnat rāzôn la'dōnai* as *shěnat rāzôn lěIsrāēl*. While it is difficult to date the origins of the midrashic and talmudic passages in which Isa 61 figures with the same interpretation, Jerome's translation indicates they date at least from the 4th century C.E., and the LXX and Targum indicate they date from much earlier times indeed. The uniqueness of Isa 61 for reference of prophetic authority directly from God, rather than from prophetic predecessors, is also part of this tradition. The eschatological re-interpretation is indicated by the passages in Midrash Ekah and the Palestinian Targum (Ps-Jon) to Numbers.

The material from Qumran, which provides ample evidence that all these interpretations were current in Jesus' day in Palestine and fully held by the covenanters there, however, offers the necessary foil for understanding how Jesus' exegesis of Isa 61 would have shocked the people at Nazareth and angered them— and justifiably so. At Qumran the *měbassēr* was interpreted as the

---

[73] It is not necessary to belabor the point clarified by C. F. Evans in *Studies in the Gospels*, ed. by D. E. Nineham (1955) 37-53, that Luke viewed Jesus, on a primary level, as "the prophet like Moses" (Deut. 18:15 reflected in Luke 9:51-53; 10:1; 11:27-28; 12:47-48 *et passim*, and Acts 3:22).

Melchizedeq of Ps 110:4, a heavenly judging and redeeming figure who would come at the head of the angelic armies to redeem the true Israel, i.e., Qumran, and wreak vengeance and retribution on all her enemies, human and cosmic.

Jesus, by contrast, arrogates this passage of unique prophetic authority (which Qumran had already apotheosized to a heavenly figure, Melchizedeq) to himself and apparently insists that the *'aphesis* of which it speaks will pertain in the End Time to those outside Israel, and insists that what is *dektos, 'eudokia* or *rāzôn*, is totally God's free choice alone. It must be emphasized that in the highly charged eschatalogical atmosphere of Qumran and the NT, this would not have been divine largesse to outsiders on the way to final truth, it would be, as so often elsewhere in Luke, the final demonstration of the meaning of election.

In Luke's effort to expand the petty opposition between Capernahum and Nazareth (which one gets more miracles?) to the tension between three early understandings of the mission of Jesus—that to Israel alone, that to the Gentiles—and the prophetic tension which arises out of that, far from there being an inconsistency in the pericope (between vv. 24 & 25-27) about who rejects whom, Luke's point is that the Nazareth congregation rejected Jesus precisely because he preached Isa 61 in the way he did—by applying the hermeneutic axiom of prophetic critique even to the End Time. Little wonder that the faithful at Nazareth rejected not only fhis interpretation but the preacher-interpreter as well. The offense was intolerable. It went against all they believed in.

The method of Comparative Midrash supplements other methods to render clarity, perhaps for the first time, in the study of this Lukan pericope. From the perspective afforded by this method of study, there are no such inconsistencies in the pericope, but rather a text of introduction to Jesus' prophetic ministry in an eschatological age, which proleptically rehearses the end of that ministry at its beginning.

Often scientific exegesis is largely a search for the ancient question to which the text before us provided answers; for it is the finding of the question or concern addressed which unlocks the full significance of a text and the "quest for the question" can be aided by a) sketching a midrashic history of the passages of scripture cited in that text so as b) to recover the foil against which the midrash in the text comes alive.

Specifically, Luke's Nazareth pericope is the foundation stone of his gospel, which he wrote in large measure to answer the embarrassing question of why Jesus was crucified: Jesus was the eschatalogical prophet, anointed by the spirit (Luke 3:21-22 where Ps 2:7 is interpreted in a midrashic complex with Isa 42:1 and 61:1) who so challenged his compatriots' assumptions about divine election that he met the prophet-martyr's end. His message as *měbassēr* was both a prophetic challenge to such assumptions *and* the announcement of the End Time, not just one or the other alone. The combination was strange indeed. The angry reception his message received in Nazareth anticipated, according to Luke, the reception it would finally receive at its end.

This method of Comparative Midrash by which one seeks the foil to which a prophetic critique is directed can be an aid, it seems to me, in piercing back of Luke to Jesus himself. What may appear anti-Jewish or anti-Semitic in Luke, in Jesus himself would have been simply a challenge leveled at the theological ideology or political theology of one's own countrymen or *patris*. Hence, our final suggestion is that the gospels, and especially Luke, I think, like the books of the prophets of old, if read out of context, appear anti-Jewish.[74] But read in full original context they are together part of the glory of a common past.[75]

---

[74] See Nils Dahl, "The Story of Abraham in Luke-Acts," in *Studies in Luke-Acts*, ed. by L. E. Keck and J. L. Martyn (1966) 139-58 and more recently J. Jervell *Luke and the People of God* (1972), as well as the dissertation by Crockett cited above.

[75] After completion of the above, five publications came to my attention which merit comment.

H. Schurmann, "Zur Traditionsgeschichte der Nazareth Perikope Lk 4, 16-30," *Mélanges Béda Rigaux*, ed. by A. Descamps and A. de Halleux (1970) 187-205. This is a study done in the classical source-critical mode and results in the conclusion that Luke 4:17-21 (23a) and 25-27 come from Mark, and 4:16, 22, 23b, 24 and 28ff., from the *Redequelle*: hence, one must not attribute to Luke everything not in Mark, nor should one build up a Redaktionsgeschichtlich theology therefrom. The advice is cautionary and therefore to some extent valuable, but the method precisely exposes the need for a history of midrash approach.

J. Bajard, "La Structure de la péricope de Nazareth en Lc iv, 16-30," *Ephemerides Theologicae Lovanienses* 45 (1969) 165-71. This is a very valuable study which coincides with my own at two essential points. After analyzing the so-called incoherencies in the Lukan material Bajard concluded (and this is his thesis) that Luke so transformed the structure of the account, as it appears in Mark, that the so-called incoherencies appear only if one studies Luke taking Mark as his point of departure. If one takes Luke on his own ground, one sees that he has precisely ordered his material so as to demonstrate that Jesus was rejected at Nazareth (contrast Mark and Matthew) at the beginning of his ministry for the same reason that he was put to death at its end—his refusal to limit salvation to his own fatherland. Bajard correctly sees that the rupture between Jesus and his compatriots takes place in Luke only at v. 27 after the sermon, and not at all at vv. 22-23. The bulk of Bajard's article is a study of three key words in Luke's account, *marturein*, *thaumazein* and *dektos*. These lead him to a view of vv. 22-23 which coincides with the one presented here, as well as to a view of the importance of *dektos* in vv. 19 and 24, which is very encouraging indeed. Bajard apparently knows nothing about midrashic techniques but by the word-study method sees the immense importance of the key word *dektos*.

David Hill, "The Rejection of Jesus at Nazareth," *Novum Testamentum* 13 (1971) 161-80. After reviewing the various problems presented by the Lukan account and the inadequacies of earlier studies, Hill correctly sees that *dektos* plays a crucial role in the pericope. Hill then suggests that Luke is here presenting a programmatic prologue to Jesus' ministry and thereby makes two important points: a) Jesus' gospel of "release" will achieve success outside the confines of Judaism; and b) rejection by the Jews and acceptance by the Gentiles is not wholly a matter of free choice but are principally phases in the overall purposes of God and essential stages in the Lukan Heilsgeschichte. After a review of the first-century synagogue lectionary problem (in which he cites L. C. Crockett's *JJS* 17 article but not his dissertation—alas, no one seems to know of it) Hill draws six conclusions: a) Jesus stresses, through Luke, that the prophetic ministry that will win acceptance (with God, of course) has to transcend the limits of one's own land and people; b) this is Luke's, similar to Paul's, Heilsgeschichte which attempts to account for the failure of the gospel among Jews but its success among Gentiles; c) one cannot pierce back to Jesus by means of observations about lectionary cycles; d) nonetheless, it is fair to suggest that Jesus preached and taught in Nazareth and received less than enthusiastic reception (the rest is Luke's); e) Jesus probably applied Isa 61:1 to himself at sometime as seen by 11QMelch 18 (sic); f) the Beatitudes in Matt 5 and the Nazareth pericope in Luke 4 indicate that both the First and the Third Evangelists put peshers on Isa 61 at the start of Jesus' ministry (Hill fails to cite Flusser).

The works of Bajard and Hill are both very encouraging indeed. They both have seen the importance of *dektos* without specifically using the method of Comparative Midrash, which means that each fails to press through to see its full importance (though Hill rightly sees the Lukan stress on divine will) in terms of Jesus' role in Luke as eschatological prophet. Each wants to offer some suggestion about the contribution of Jesus to the Lukan account (and Hill rightly denies that either linguistic criteria or studies in the calendar will avail), but neither has put the crucial question of whether the point being scored in the episode better fits, or has a foil, in Jesus' time or in Luke's time.

This all-crucial question cannot be put without engaging in Comparative Midrash. And if one does attempt to trace a history of the function of Isa 61:1-3 he must, of necessity, find himself emphasizing its importance at Qumran, for locating its significance in the Lukan story. Hill alone refers to 11QMelch in work to date on Luke 4, but, even so, quite misses its significance altogether: he cites only line 18 and comments only that it is the only instance at Qumran of a single prophet being designated "anointed". Hill fails to see the very basic position Isa 61 occupies in 11QMelch and further fails to understand the basic similarity-yet-contrast to its function there and in Luke 4. He also fails to see how the heavenly Melchizedeq as *mĕbassēr* is a foil par excellence to the role of *mĕbassēr* played by Jesus in Luke.

Appearing far too late to take into consideration, even in this postscriptum, is the symposium volume of four essays entitled *Jesus in Nazareth* (1972), which I have just seen (at a moment of editorial grace well beyond the deadline the present article should have been submitted). Erich Grässer writes on "Jesus in Nazareth (Mc 6:1-6a)," August Strobel on "Die Ausrufung des Jobeljahres in der Nazareth-predigt Jesu; zur apokalyptischen Tradition Lc 4:16-30," Robert C. Tannehill on "The Mission of Jesus according to Luke iv 16-30," and Walther Eltester on "Israel im lukanischen Werk und die Nazareth-perikope." Prof Tannehill made some very helpful comments on the occasion of the first exposure of my work in this regard at an annual Society of Biblical Literature meeting in New York in 1970, and I am very pleased to see his own work now available. A glance at the four studies indicates great promise. Strobel deals at some length with 11QMelch and Tannehill with the Isaiah quotation, though none of the articles can be said to engage in Comparative Midrash.

Finally, I am very pleased to take note of the triple-issue of *Revue des Sciences Religieuses* 47 (1973) 157-419, entitled "Exégèse biblique et judaïsme". Though I cannot, before mailing off these pages, study each of the eleven articles with care enough to make a general comment, I see enough even now to be greatly encouraged that recently developing methods of study of the New Testament are moving apace. Of special interest in the volume is a study by Charles Perrot entitled "Luc 4:16-30 et la lecture biblique de l'ancienne Synagogue". He carefully and judiciously makes his way through the maze of arguments and suggestions (including Billerbeck's mentioned above) but then advances the bold hypothesis, on the basis of the triennial cycle and Mann's data, that the service in which Jesus read and preached may well have been Yom Kippur in Tishri. The great value, in my mind, of Perrot's remarks is in his taking the Jubilee Year theme as key.

LUKE 12, 13-14
TEXT AND TRANSMISSION
from Marcion to Augustine

TJITZE BAARDA
Vrije Universiteit Amsterdam

Εἶπεν δέ τις ἐκ τοῦ ὄχλου αὐτῷ·
Διδάσκαλε, εἰπὲ τῷ ἀδελφῷ μου
μερίσασθαι μετ'ἐμοῦ τὴν κληρονομίαν.
Ὁ δὲ εἶπεν αὐτῷ·
Ἄνθρωπε, τίς με κατέστησεν
κριτὴν ἢ μεριστὴν ἐφ' ὑμᾶς;

And someone out of the multitude said to him: 'Teacher, tell my brother to divide with me the inheritance'. And He said to him: 'Man, who appointed me a judge or a divider over you?'.[1] The anecdote of the dissatisfied heir and of Jesus' rejection of his request is one of the well-known short stories in Lucan tradition. History of exegesis tells us that ever since this apophthegma found a place in the Gospel of Luke the readers were puzzled by two questions: First: why did Jesus not wish to enter into the merits of the case? Why did he so brusquely reject the appeal? And what did he mean to say by his decision not to interfere? *Second*: what made people remember such an episode afterwards? What caused them to hand the story down to a later generation? Or, in other words, what was for them the authoritative meaning of Jesus' reaction to this request? One may say that even the answers to the first question are generally focused on the problem of whether there was a general law which might fully explain the attitude of Jesus and which also could then be applied to every new situation. The need of such general principle comes to light, if some exegete deals with the story as if it were a mere incident in the life of Jesus and does not define some basic truth; in that case later commentators feel that this exegesis is somehow deficient and try to rectify this lack. I came across an example of this procedure in Syriac literature. Īshōʻdād of Merw, in his commentary on Luke, presents us with a characteristic specimen of Antiochian exegesis

---

[1] For the text, cf. K. Aland, M. Black, B. M. Metzger, A. Wikgren, *The Greek New Testament*, Stuttgart 1966, 264.

(which might possibly go back to the interpretation of Theodore of Mopsuestia) [2]:

Said to Him one out of the multitude: 'Tell my brother to divide with me the inheritance'.—Now it is likely that this man's brother was one of those who followed our Lord. And because our Lord always commanded those who obeyed Him to despise the visible things, he thought (and) supposed for that reason that he would find an opportunity to deal falsely with his brother, as if He would immediately say to him: 'If you have chosen to be my disciple, give all that you have to your brother'. But our Lord knew that the time for this had not yet come, and also that if He would rightly command that the affairs should be arranged, that man would cherish an irreverent idea and say to our Lord, as his brother in Egypt (said) to Moses: 'Man, who has appointed you a judge and divider over us?'. Now this is exactly the reason why our Lord also gave precisely the answer which (that man) would have given to Him, if He would rightly have commanded that the inheritance should be divided'.

Three centuries later, Dionysios bar Ṣalībī, offers the same exegesis,[3] but he concludes his observations with the fundamental principle that our Lord 'did not come to divide *earthly* inheritances, but to separate and divide the believers from the unbelievers'.[4] On this construction, Jesus' answer to the dissatisfied heir that he was not a judge or divider has actually been detached from its original setting and has now become a general rule: Jesus has nothing to do with such *earthly* affairs as inheritances. This procedure, however, is not restricted to the 'exegetes', since those who in one way or another transmitted the text of this Lucan passage sometimes betray the same eagerness to hear in Jesus' answer a general principle which is in accordance with their own conviction.

In Search of the Original Text

2.1. κριτὴν ἢ μεριστήν.

Our translation of the Lucan episode was based upon the text which modern editors have adopted as the probably original text.

---

[2] M. D. Gibson, *The Commentaries of Ishoʿdad of Merv*, Horae Synopticae VII, vol. III, Cambridge 1911, 43:20-44:12.

[3] A. Vaschalde, *Dionysii Bar Salibi Commentarii in Evangelia* II, 1, C.S.C.O 95 (= Syr. 47), Louvain 1953 (= 1931), 340:13-26.

[4] A. Vaschalde, *o.c.*, 340:26-28.

This form of the text contained the reading κριτὴν ἢ μεριστήν, which was introduced for the first time by C. Lachmann,[5] apparently on the basis of Ms. B alone. He was followed by editors such as C. Tischendorf,[6] S. P. Tregelles[7] and B. F. Westcott & F. J. A. Hort,[8] whose preference for this reading resulted mainly from their new understanding of the history of the text, which meant the overthrow of the *Textus Receptus*.[9] Their chief witnesses were Ms. B and Ms. ℵ, which were held to be relatively or even almost free from textual corruption. Later discoveries presented us with another important witness, namely P75, a manuscript of a very early date which seems to a large extent to have escaped corruption.[10] If we follow the classical division of textual witnesses we find support for the reading in question in the following recensions:[11]

1. *The Alexandrian Text*: P75 ℵ B L 0191 [12] *33 892 1241*; this form of text still extant in the tenth century was known in Egypt as early as the beginning of the third century. The fact that it is also found in Sahidic manuscripts (ⲛ̄ⲕⲣⲓⲧⲏⲥ ⲁⲩⲱ ⲛ̄ⲣⲉϥⲡⲱⲣϫ) provides additional proof of its early presence in Egypt.

2. *The Caesarean Text*: the Lake-family, viz. *1-118-131-209* (if we may believe H. von Soden [13] also their relatives *1192 1210 1582 2193*), the Ferrar-family, viz. *13-69-346* (not *124*),[14] supported

---

[5] C. Lachmann(-Ph. Buttmann), *Novum Testamentum Graece et Latine*, t. I, Berlin 1842, 433 (... κριτην B D, δικαστην A Q ς ... η μεριστην A B Q ς).

[6] C. Tischendorf, *Novum Testamentum Graece*, I, Leipzig ⁸1872, 581.

[7] S. P. Tregelles, *Greek New Testament*, II, London 1861, 299; idem, *An Account of the Printed Text of the Greek New Testament*, London 1854, Collation, 29.

[8] B. F. Westcott, F. J. A. Hort, *The New Testament in the original Greek* I, London 1898, *Text*, 153.

[9] Cf. e.g. Von Soden (1913), Vogels (1920), Souter (rev. ed. 1947), Merk (¹1951), Bover (³1953), Nestle-Aland (²⁵1963), *The Greek New Testament* (1966).

[10] Cf. A. F. J. Klijn, *A Survey of the Researches into the Western Text of the Gospels and Acts*, Leiden 1969, 49.69f.

[11] The survey of manuscripts is mainly based upon the Apparatus of the *Greek New Testament*, 264; the versions are checked in the respective editions (cf. *ibid.*, xlix-lv).

[12] MS 0191 was part of a larger 6th century manuscript which can partly be restored with the uncial fragments 070 0110 0124 0178 0179 0180 0190 0191 and 0202, cf. K. Aland, *Kurzgefasste Liste der griechischen Handschriften des Neuen Testaments* I, Berlin 1963, 13. 43³. 53¹. Its character is certainly Alexandrian.

[13] H. von Soden, *Die Schriften des Neuen Testaments in ihrer ältesten erreichbaren Textgestalt*, Berlin 1913 (*Der Text*), 313 mentions fam. I^η without an exception.

[14] H. von Soden, *o.c.*, 313: I^ι exc b 1211.

by their adherents *230 543 788 826 983 1689*. If the origin of the Armenian (հատուոր կամ բաժանարար) and Georgian (მსჯულსა ან გამყოფელსა) texts is not in the Syriac Vulgate, it is highly probable that the so-called Caesarean recension was their ultimate source. If this is true, there would be sufficient reason to suppose that the presence of the Caesarean reading, which is found only in late cursives (most of them dating from the 11th-15th centuries; the relatively independent Caesarean text of minuscle *700* [15] dates from the 11th century) could be established for the fifth century. The origin of the Caesarean text—or rather of the proto-Caesarean text—seems to lie in the Egyptian text of the third century,[16] so that this type of text may be nothing else than another witness to the so-called Alexandrian text. Therefore, it would be of great importance if we could find another, unambiguously independent text which could present us with the certainty that the Alexandrian text is more than a local recension. It seems to me that we might find such evidence in the early Latin tradition.

3. *The Old Latin Text*: the Old Latin manuscripts *aur e f l q*—the same is true for the Latin Vulgate—have the reading *iudicem aut divisorem*, while another manuscript—*b*—offers the synonymous reading *iudicem aut dispensatorem*. As a matter of fact, it is not absolutely certain that *iudicem* renders the word κριτήν; however, if my solution of the origin of the variant δικαστήν is valid,[17] it is very probable that it is not this word, but the word κριτήν which occasioned the rendering *iudicem*. In that case the second century Old Latin version (or versions) would produce at least some evidence that the spread of the reading κριτὴν ἢ μεριστήν was wider than in Egypt only.

2.2. δικαστὴν ἢ μεριστήν.

It is true that in itself the Old Latin rendering like ours could serve as a translation of another textual reading: δικαστὴν ἢ μεριστήν. This is the form transmitted by the *Textus Receptus*,[18] which was

---

[15] For this codex, cf. B. H. Streeter, *The Four Gospels*, London ⁸1953, 32, 81 n. 2 and passim.

[16] Cf. A. F. J. Klijn, *A Survey*, 34; B. M. Metzger, *The Text of the New Testament*, Oxford 1964, 215.

[17] See below, par. 3:5.3.

[18] Cf. F. H. A. Scrivener, *Novum Testamentum Graece*, Textus Stephanici A.D. 1550, Cambridge-London 1891, 176f.

an exponent of the wide-spread Antiochian or Byzantine recension. Among the witnesses to this text we find several uncials— A K Q R W X Γ Δ Θ Λ Π Ψ—and a multitude of cursives [19] and lectionaries. The close relationship between the Antiochian recension and the Syriac Vulgate may be an indication that the text of the latter (ܪܝܫܐ ܕܡܦܠܓܢܐ) has been dictated by the former's δικαστὴν ἢ μεριστήν; if so, the readings of the Arabic Diatessaron and some Arabic versions (حاكماً وقاسماً) and also that of the Persian version (داوری کن یا بخشاینده) may have their ultimate source in the Byzantine text. The influence of that recension is even traceable in northern Egypt, for the Bohairic version (ⲛ̄ⲣⲉϥϯϩⲁⲡ ⲓⲉ ⲛ̄ⲣⲉϥⲫⲱϣ) seems to be an adequate rendering of δικαστὴν ἢ μεριστήν.[20]

It is evident from an examination of the external testimony for the reading of the Byzantine text that the manuscript witnesses are on the whole of more recent date than those which contain the rival reading κριτὴν ἢ μεριστήν,[21] although the problem of the versions ought not to be skirted. The translators of these versions were often confronted with the same difficulty we have, namely how to find a way to express the "difference" between the words κριτής and δικαστής. Originally, there was a clear difference between them, for in classical Greek ὁ κριτής was the arbiter,[22] ὁ δικαστής the criminal judge.[23] This distinction, however, gradually

---

[19] The *Greek New Testament, loc. cit.*, lists 565 1009 1010 1071 1079 1195 1216 1230 1242 1253 1344 1365 1546 1646 2148 2174.

[20] The word ⲡⲉϥϯϩⲁⲡ may render δικαστής as can be deduced from one Sahidic manuscript with the reading ⲛ̄ⲕ[ⲣⲓⲧⲏⲥ ⲁⲩⲱ ⲛ̄ⲣⲉϥ]ϯϩⲁⲡ; it seems unlikely that the second word renders κριτής. The reading κριτὴν ἢ δικαστήν is actually found in one cursive, viz. 69 (see below). We may also refer to the reading in Exod 2, 14: ⲛⲓⲙ ⲡⲉ ⲛ̄ⲧⲁϥⲕⲁⲑⲓⲥⲧⲁ ⲙ̄ⲙⲟⲕ ⲛ̄ⲁⲣⲭⲱⲛ ⲁⲩⲱ ⲛ̄ⲣⲉϥϯϩⲁⲡ ⲉϩⲣⲁⲓ ⲉϫⲱⲛ (R. Kasser, *Papyrus Bodmer XVI*, Genève 1961, 34); the word ⲡⲉϥϯϩⲁⲡ occurs also in Acts 7, 27.35 (cf. M. Wilmet, *Concordance du Nouveau Testament sahidique*, C.S.C.O. 185, Subs. 15, vol. II.3, Louvain 1959, 1462). Absolute certainty cannot be achieved, however, for in the New Testament κριτής is transliterated as ⲕⲣⲓⲧⲏⲥ eleven times, but it has been rendered as ⲡⲉϥϯϩⲁⲡ no less than seven times.

[21] The oldest manuscripts with the Byzantine reading are A, Q and W. all of them dated in the fifth century.

[22] Cf. F. Büchsel, Κριτής κτλ., *T.W.N.T.*, III (1938), 949, n. 1.

[23] *Ibid.*

vanished so that in Hellenistic times any difference of meaning seems to have been lost.[24]

2.3. Κριτής *and* Δικαστής *in biblical Greek*.

The question may arise whether it was justifiable, on merely statistical or chronological grounds, to abandon the reading of the *Received Text* in favour of the text now generally accepted. One might, for example, object to this abandonment by arguing that the less frequent occurrence of the word δικαστής in the O.T. Greek (if compared with κριτής)[25] speaks in favour of the originality of δικαστής. In the New Testament, δικαστής occurs only twice, both times in a Lucan text—Acts 7,27.35.[26] Would it not have been possible for an early scribe to replace the rare, Lucan word δικαστήν by the more common word κριτήν? It should be borne in mind, however, that the word δικαστής as found in Acts 7 occurs both times in a quotation from Exod. 2,14. Therefore, the word is not really characteristic for Luke. At best, one can say that the quotation from Exodus which happens to contain the word δικαστής was important for Luke in composing Stephen's 'midrashic' apology. It seems to me more likely that the word δικαστής rather than being ascribed to Luke should be attributed to a scribe who—probably under the influence of an exegetical tradition[27]—wished to make the text which he was copying conform more closely to the text of Exod 2,14:[28] τίς σε κατέστησεν ἄρχοντα καὶ δικαστὴν ἐφ' ἡμῶν.[29] Moreover, the substitution of δικαστής for κριτής could

---

[24] Cf. W. Bauer, *Griechisch-Deutsches Wörterbuch zu den Schriften des Neuen Testaments*, Berlin ⁵1963, 393.896, who even reports the occurrence of δικαστής as 'Schiedsrichter' and of κριτής as 'Richter' (Diodorus Siculus).

[25] Cf. E. Hatch, H. A. Redpath, *A Concordance to the Septuagint*, Graz 1954 (= Oxford 1897), vol. I, 335b: Δικαστής (= שֹׁפֵט) 8x; II, 791a-b: Κριτής (= שֹׁפֵט or דִּין) over a column.

[26] W. F. Moulton, A. S. Geden, *A Concordance to the Greek Testament*, Edinburgh (repr.) ⁴1967, 562: Κριτής 19x: 4x Acts, 5x Luke (2x *Sondergut*, 18, 2.6; 3x Q: 11, 29/Mt 12, 37; 12, 58 bis//Mt 5, 25); 219: Δικαστής twice.

[27] See below, par. 3:5.3.

[28] Cf. C. Tischendorf, *o.c.*, I, 581: 'non incredibile est hanc lectionem ex Act. 7, 27.35 (Exod 2, 14) . . . fluxisse'; H. Alford, *The Greek New Testament*, I, Cambridge 1898, 563 app.: 'The element of confusion has been . . . Acts 7, 27.35: hence the variations'.

[29] A. E. Brook, N. McLean, *The Old Testament in Greek*, I, 2, Cambridge 1907, 159 (some 15 cursives have ἡμᾶς; the addition of εἰς ἄνδρα (= לְאִישׁ) before ἄρχοντα is found in *one* cursive, in the Armenian text and in the Syro-Hexaplaric version under ※).

help us avoid the difficult problem thrown up by the rhetorical question in the answer of Jesus, the problem whether or not Jesus had denied being a κριτής.[30]

2.4. Other harmonistic readings.

If it is true that the reading δικαστήν was introduced by an early scribe who wished to harmonize Lk 12,14 with Exod 2,14, it is only reasonable to assume that other variations that contain also the word δικαστήν originate in the same eagerness for harmonization. We may list the following readings:

(3)   δικαστήν *28*
(4) μεριστὴν ἢ δικαστήν *472* Lect *1642*,
            cf. Eth ኀፋለ መኰንኖ፨ (?).[31]
(5) κριτὴν ἢ δικαστήν *69*,
            cf. SahMs ⲛ̄ⲕ[ⲣⲓⲧⲏⲥ ⲁⲩⲱ ⲛ̄ⲣⲉϥ]ϯϩⲁⲡ.[32]
(6) ἄρχοντα καὶ δικαστήν *157*, cf. *Liber Graduum* II : 2 ܪܝܫܐ ܘܕܝܢܐ.[33]

The last reading contains not only the word δικαστήν, but also the other word in the Exodus text: ἄρχοντα. This very word occurs also in two other readings, namely

---

[30] Cf. below, par. 3 : 3.3 a.o.

[31] According to B. Walton's Polyglot edition; it is not impossible that 'arbitrum et iudicem' in Rufin's translation of the Pseudo-Clementine *Recognitiones* (ed. E. G. Gersdorf, in *P.G.* I (1857), 1443), Lib. X : xlviii, may be a rendering of μεριστὴν καὶ δικαστήν (καὶ l. ἢ also in Eth).

[32] As for cursive 69, cf. W. H. Ferrar, T. K. Abbott, *A Collation of Four important Manuscripts of the Gospels*, Dublin 1877, 243 app. The Sahidic text is mentioned in G. Horner, *The Coptic Version of the New Testament in the Southern Dialect*, vol. II, Oxford 1911, 242 App.—The same reading is found in Ms. A of the text of 1 Clem IV, 10 (O. de Gebhardt, A. Harnack, *Clementis Romani ad Corinthios quæ dicuntur Epistulae*, Patrum Apostolicorum Opera I, 1, Leipzig ²1876, 10) as the text of Exod 2, 14 (the text of the edition agrees with LXX). The *Epistula Clementis* 5, 3 (B. Rehm, *Die Pseudoklementinen* I, *Homiliae*, Berlin 1969, 9 : 8) has also κριτὴν καὶ δικαστήν (the Latin translation of Rufin: *iudicem aut cognitorem*), when the author applies Lk 12, 14 to the office of a bishop: Christ does not want to appoint you a κριτής and a δικαστής in matters of money etc. As to the conjunction καί (instead of ἢ), it is found in 157, Syᵖ, *Liber Graduum*, in Tᴬ, Arab, Eth (cf. n. 27).

[33] Cf. M. Kmosko, *Liber Graduum*, Patrologia Syriaca III, Paris 1926, 29 : 7-8. Von Soden, *o.c.*, 313 app. mentions also Old Latin l; H. J. Vogels, *Codex Rhedigeranus*, Collectanea Biblica Latina II, Roma 1913, 209, however, does not give support for that reading, for his text reads thus: *quis me/constituit iudi/cem aut diviso/rem super vos*.

(7) ἄρχοντα ἢ μεριστήν Cyril of Alexandria,[34] Eusebius of Emesa.[35]
(8) ἄρχοντα ἢ κριτὴν ἢ μεριστήν *1012*

It is quite obvious that all these harmonistic readings can easily be consigned to the *apparatus criticus* as secondary or tertiary readings which have been substituted for or rather have corrupted the original text.

2.5. *The residue*

The *first* reading, κριτὴν ἢ μεριστήν, seems to stand a good chance of keeping the place assigned to it by modern editors. There remain, however, two other readings, which cannot be dismissed as obviously harmonistic readings or evidently scribal errors, namely

(9) κριτήν *and* (10) μεριστήν

It is true that they do not have the cloud of witnesses to which the *first* and *second* readings could lay claim. But quantity cannot always be the determining factor in solving questions of originality. These two readings present us with the two components of the first reading; one might possibly ask thus, whether this first reading could have been a mere conflation of two early, competing readings. This possibility makes it necessary for us to deal with each of these two readings in the following investigation of both the Syro-Latin text and the text of the Gospel of Thomas.

The Syro-Latin Text

3.1. *Manuscripts and Versions*

The choice between the *first* and *ninth* reading seems to me the most difficult one. The latter reading is found in the bilingual *Codex Bezae* both on the Greek page—D: κριτήν—and on the Latin side—*d: iudicem*. It seems quite natural to connect D-*d* with *c*, Codex Colbertinus, which also omits *aut divisorem*. These 'Western' witnesses do not stand alone, for the same reading may be supposed to be behind the wording of the Old Syriac witnesses Sy^s and Sy^c, ܕܝܢܐ 'judge'.[36] It is obvious that we have here an example of the

---

[34] Cf. the fragments of the commentary on Luke in J. A. Cramer, *Catenae Graecorum Patrum in Novum Testamentum* II, Oxford 1844, 100; (J. P. Migne), *Sancti Cyrilli Explanatio in Lucae Evangelium*, P. G. LXXII, Paris 1859, 475-950, 732 (the *lemma* has T.R., the text itself the remarkable variant reading).

[35] According to the files in Beuron, which refer to Eus-E 15, 1: *Quis me constituit super vos principem et divisorem* (E. M. Buytaert, *Spicilegium Sacrum Lovaniense* 26 (1953), 344:14).

[36] A. Resch, *Aussercanonische Paralleltexte zu den Evangelien* III (Lucas), T.U. X: 3, Leipzig 1895, 316 retranslated the Syriac word of Sy^c (under the

so-called *Syro-Latin* text of the Gospels. While the roots of this text seem to lie in the obscure textual history of the second century, it has sometimes been asserted that they reach even deeper than this stage of textual tradition, perhaps even into the original text of the Gospels.[37]

3.2. *Tatian*

(1) Among the suggested sources of the Syro-Latin text the Diatessaron of Tatian occupies a special place; and, indeed, there is reason to consider it as a possible source of the passage in question. In his Commentary on the Diatessaron, Mar Ephraem refers to the text of Luke 12,14 when discussing the episode in which John the Baptist denied that he was Elijah or the Messiah.[38] Ephraem observes, however, that Jesus himself called John Elijah. John's express denial does not imply that he was not a prophet, Elijah or an Anointed One, but that he was unwilling to be anyone of these for his questioners—for them he was only the Voice. In this connection, Ephraem refers to two similar denials of Jesus; Jesus said: 'I am not a judge', although He was a judge, and: 'I am not good', although He certainly was good.[39] The latter is apparently a paraphrase of Mk 10,18//Lk 18,19, τί με λέγεις ἀγαθόν; Consequently, it is not necessary to look for the pronouncement 'I am not a judge' in Gospel or Apocryphal traditions,[40] for that statement is likewise a paraphrase of what Jesus said according to Lk 12,14. Ephraem reformulated the rhetorical questions of Jesus (which expect negative answers) into negative pronouncements.

---

influence of Crowfoot?) into δικαστήν, just as J. Mill, *Novum Testamentum Graecum* (ed. L. Kustereus), Rotterdam 1710, Prolegomena, par. 33, p. 292, did in the case of the Latin text of *Codex Bezae* and of Tertullian: δικαστήν ἐφ' ὑμᾶς; Both scholars mention, however, the reading κριτήν as reading of resp. Sy^c (Resch in his comments) and 'Cant. Barb. I, Colb 8' (Mill, *o.c.*, 162). This ambiguity illustrates the difficulty of retranslating Syriac or Latin into Greek. As a matter of fact, the introduction of the reading δικαστήν must have been rather late: the terminus ante quem is the fifth century (cf. A.W.Q.), the terminus post quem about the time that the Marcionite antithesis became influential in orthodox exegesis, I would guess ca. the middle of the third century, cf. below 3:5.3.

[37] J. Wettstein, *Novum Testamentum Graecum*, Amsterdam, 735 observes that J. Mill, *o.c.*, 292, 423 (W. refers to the second edition of Leipzig) had already interpreted the word μεριστήν as a 'graft' from vs. 13.

[38] L. Leloir, *Saint Éphrem, Commentaire de l'Évangile concordant*, C.S.C.O. 137 (Arm 1), Version arménienne, Louvain 1953, 42:8ff. (= III:10), cf. *idem.*, C.S.C.O. 145 (Arm 2), Traduction, Louvain 1954, 31:16ff.

[39] L. Leloir, *o.c.*, 43:9-24 (= III:12); trad., 32:8-21.

[40] Cf. The Gospel according to Thomas, logion 72 (below 4.1 a.o.).

(2) As a matter of fact, Mar Ephraem mentions only the word ֿզատաւոր = ܕܝܢܐ 'judge'; he did not reproduce the word 'divider' (բաժանարար). It is true that an *argumentum e silentio* cannot be construed as sufficient evidence for the thesis that the Diatessaron text lacked the word 'divider'; Ephraem could have omitted it because it was not relevant for his discussion in the commentary. On the otherhand, however, if the word stood in the text of the Harmony he was using, would he not have mentioned it in his commentary in the interest of drawing a full, triple parallel between the negations of Jesus and those of John the Baptist?

(3) It seems to me that the Persian Harmony, in spite of its late and mixed character, may have preserved the reading of the Syriac Diatessaron, since it offers a text in which the 'divider' has been omitted: [41]

ای مرد مرا بر شما بقاضیتی که نشاند

'O man, who posed me over you in the office of Qādī?' which presupposes a Syriac original ܐܢܫ ܐܩܝܡܢܝ ܥܠܝܟܘܢ ܕܝܢܐ. I am inclined to believe that the agreement between Mar Ephraem's paraphrase (only ֿզատաւոր 'judge') and the Persian Harmony (only قاضیتی 'office of Qādī, judgeship') makes it highly probable that the same Syriac text was found in the original Syriac Diatessaron.[42] If this is true, the two Old Syriac recensions, Sy^c and Sy^s, which have the very same text, may have been influenced by the early Syriac Harmony.

(4) The question with which we are now confronted is whether we ought indeed to seek the origin of the Syro-Latin text in the Diatessaron. We know there is reason to suppose not only that the Harmony of Tatian influenced the early Syriac textual traditions but also that it affected the Latin Gospel tradition and possibly even Codex Bezae.[43] Therefore, we must bear in mind that the Dia-

---

[41] G. Messina, *Diatessaron Persiano*, Roma 1951, 72:5-6.

[42] Previous reconstructions of the Diatessaron completely neglect the Ephraemic text (Th. Zahn, *Tatians Diatessaron*, Erlangen 1881, L. Leloir, *Le Témoignage d'Éphrem sur le Diatessaron*, C.S.C.O. 227, Louvain 1962, have no reconstruction at all; I. Ortiz de Urbina, *Vetus Evangelium Syrorum, Diatessaron Tatiani*, Madrid 1967, 230 reproduced the text of *Liber Graduum* as Tatian's text).—The Western witnesses to the Diatessaron attest the reading *iudicem aut divisorem* (so *Codex Fuldensis*, cf. T^V: zudese o partidore, T^T: giudice o dividatore, T^Ahd: duomen odo teilari) or *iudicem et divisorem* (cf. Pepysian Harmony: juge and partener, T^N(L): richtre ende deilre, T^N(H): richter ende enen deylre, T^N(S): rechtre ende deilre).

[43] This is the opinion of such scholars as H. J. Vogels, D. Plooij, A. Baumstark, C. Peters (cf. C. Peters, *Das Diatessaron Tatians*, Roma 1939, ch. XI and XVII).

tessaron *could* have been the root of the Syro-Latin reading which we found in D-*d*-*c*-*Sy*c-*Sy*s. Does this imply that Tatian was responsible for the *ninth* variant? Was he the one who abbreviated the longer text κριτὴν ἢ μεριστήν, or was he himself dependent on a copy of Luke which contained already the short form κριτήν? Tatian was not always the great textual corruptor he is often taken to be. In many cases he has simply transmitted the text which he found in his copy. In the case of the locus presently under consideration there is reason to assume that the text he was using contained κριτήν alone.

3.3. *Marcion*

(1) A second possible source of the Syro-Latin text is the Gospel of Marcion, whose influence is traceable both in Western and Eastern texts of the Gospels.[44] Moreover, there is a good deal of agreement between Marcion's revision of Luke and Tatian's Harmony of the Gospels, which may be explained by the fact that Tatian probably borrowed several peculiarities from the Gospel of Marcion.[45] This latter Gospel was a dogmatical recension of the Gospel according to Luke, a revision attuned to a dualistic Paulinism in which the other sounds of early Christianity were drowned.

(2) One of the sources for the reconstruction of the text of Marcion's Gospel is Tertullian's polemical work, *Adversus Marcionem*. In dealing with the twelfth chapter of Marcion's Luke, Tertullian refers to a strong antithesis between Moses and Jesus:[46]

---

[44] Cf. E. Blackmann, *Marcion and his Influence*, London 1948, Appendix 7 (esp. 158f.), Appendix 8 (esp. 169f.); but see also *o.c.*, 58ff.

[45] E. Blackmann, *o.c.*, 170f. (in Appendix 8).

[46] Cf. E. Evans, Tertullian, *Adversus Marcionem*, vol. II, Oxford 1972, 422:19-30, 424:1ff. (= Adv. Marc. IV:28, 9-10): 'Ecce plane diversum exemplum Moysi et Christi: *Moyses rixantibus fratribus ultro intercedit et iniuriosum increpat: quid proximum tuum percutis? Et reicitur ab illo: quis te constituit magistrum aut iudicem super nos? Christus vero postulatus a quodam, ut inter illum et fratrem ipsius < de > dividenda* (so ed. Aem. Kroymann; Evans: dividunda) *hereditate componeret, operam suam, et quidem tam probae causae, denegavit.* Iam ergo melior Moyses meus Christo tuo, fratrum paci studens, iniuriae occurrens. (10) *Sed enim optimi et non iudicis dei Christus: quis me, inquit, iudicem constituit super vos?* Aliam vocem excusationis invenire non potuit, ne ea uteretur, qua improbus vir et impius frater adsertorem probitatis atque pietatis excusserat? Denique probavit malam vocem, utendo ea, et malum factum, pacis inter fratres componendae declinatione ... etc.'. (Cf. A. Harnack, *Marcion*, Leipzig ²1924, 280*).—It is clear that Tertullian converted Marcion's antithesis so as to demonstrate how silly Marcion was in contrasting Moses with Jesus.

'Moses intervened between quarreling brothers long ago, and he cried to the unjust one: Why do you beat your neighbour? And that man returned: *Who has appointed you a master or a judge over us?* Christ, however, when someone asked him to arrange the affairs with regard to the dividing of the inheritance between him and his brother, refused to give his assistance even in such a just case ... The Christ of the good God—who is not a judge—said: *Who has appointed me a judge over you?*'.

On the basis of this antithesis between Exod 2,14 and Luke 12,14 the text of Marcion may be reconstructed as follows: [47]

... τίς με κατέστησεν κριτὴν ἐφ' ὑμᾶς;

It seems certain, therefore, that the Syro-Latin reading was not created by Tatian; it appears to have been present in textual history some forty years earlier in Marcion's revision of Luke.

(3) The personal cachet of Marcion's Gospel becomes visible in this recension text of Luke 12,14. The omission of ἢ μεριστήν places all the emphasis on the word κριτήν. The implication of Jesus' question: 'Who has appointed me a judge over you?' is that he absolutely denied being *a judge*. Such a denial fits in well with Marcion's conviction that judgment as such was a characteristic feature of the righteous god of the law.[48] Jesus, however, is not a judge. The omission of 'divider' may be less harmles an alteration than it seems at first sight. It is not an omission of a rare and superfluous word,[49] but rather a doctrinal and deliberate correction of the original text. Moreover, for Marcion the knife cut both ways: Jesus denied with great emphasis that he was *a judge*[50]— he did not, however, deny that he was a *divider*. The words in Luke 12,51.53 [51] in which Jesus acknowledged that he came to bring *division* were certainly of great importance for a leader of a separatist movement.

---

[47] Th. Zahn, Marcions Neues Testament, in *Geschichte des neutestamentlichen Kanons* II.2, Erlangen-Leipzig 1892, 475; A. Harnack, *o.c.*, 213*.

[48] For Marcion's distinction of the good and the righteous god, cf. E. C. Blackman, *o.c.*, 66f.; Th. Zahn, *Geschichte des neutestamentlichen Kanons*, I.2, Erlangen-Leipzig 1889, 588, 692; A. Harnack, *o.c.*, 139 (cf. the expositions on Marcion's text of Lk 12, 58; 11, 42; Rom 11, 33).

[49] Th. Zahn, *Das Evangelium des Lukas*, Leipzig-Erlangen 1920, 496, n. 15.

[50] The same thing is implied in the text of the *Liber Graduum*, where the following references are quoted one after another: Lk 7, 37; 12, 14; Jn 8, 16; 19, 39.

[51] Cf. A. Harnack, *o.c.*, 216* (cf. also Th. Zahn, *o.c.*, I.2, 604).

3.4. Luke?

(1) My interpretation of the short text—κριτήν—is that it is the product of dogmatical revision. There are scholars, however, who hold the view that Marcion was not responsible for this alteration; in their view, Marcion was dependent on a text of Luke 12,14 with κριτήν only, a text which was already circulating in his day. They hold the view that the early Western texts D-*d-c* and the early Eastern texts Sy^s-Sy^c were independent witnesses—alongside Marcion and Tatian [52]—to an archaic text which existed already before Marcion, for example in Rome.[53] In this conception, therefore, Marcion is not the inventor of the *lectio brevior*, but simply one witness, besides others, to this short text κριτήν. Some of these scholars would even plead in favour of the thesis that this reading could have been Luke's own wording.[54]

(2) A. Merx, who defended the opinion that the Old Syriac text (as represented by Sy^s) was a faithful witness to a very early, if not to the original text of the Gospels, argued that Sy^s had also preserved the original reading of the passage in question. He emphasized the fact that the word μεριστής was a *hapax legomenon*,[55] and in addition he pointed to the fact that Jewish Law did not know the figure of special "executor" of the division of inheritances, but only that of the 'judge' (דַּיָּן) who could function as a qualified administrator of such affairs.[56] If Merx is justified in his conclusions, the Syro-Latin text did not only preserve the original reading of Luke at this point, but also continued the (Semitic) tradition behind Luke's wording: דַּיָּן or דַּיָּנָא.

(3) I do agree with Merx that the *judge* was the only person who might be considered as an authority in these matters. As far as I can see, the appellative חוֹלֵק or מְחוֹלֵק does not occur as the designation of a special officer in charge of the division of inheritances.

---

[52] A. Merx, *Die vier kanonischen Evangelien nach ihrem ältesten bekannten Text*, II, 2 Markus und Lukas, Berlin 1905, 302 does not even mention Marcion or Tatian.

[53] Cf. E. Nestle, E. von Dobschütz, *Einführung in die Textkritik des Neuen Testaments*, Göttingen 1923, 11; A. Resch, *o.c.*, 316 ('in der ältesten Redaction des Evangeliencanons').

[54] Cf. A. Merx, *loc. cit.*; F. Blass, *Evangelium secundum Lucam*, Leipzig 1897, 58, cf. also lxx.

[55] A. Merx, *loc. cit.*: 'Das Hapax legomenon μεριστής wird auch von Syrcrt verworfen wie von D 28 33 c . . .'.

[56] *Ibid.*: 'Das jüdische Recht kennt keinen besonderen Erbteiler, es war höchstens Aufgabe eines דַּיָּן = 'Richters'.

It is the father who *apportions* (מְחַלֵּק) his property;[57] the heirs *take their share* (חוֹלְקִין) according to the rules of the Law in the Thorah and the Mishnah, they take their *portions* (חֲלָקִים) of the *inheritance* (נַחֲלָה), which they *inherit* (מוֹרִישִׁין נוֹחֲלִין).[58] The persons who could act in *cases of property* (דִּינֵי מָמוֹנוֹת) were the *judges* (הַדַּיָּנִין).[59]

(4) Though in itself correct, the observation of Merx cannot solve the textual puzzle represented by Luke 12,14. For he merely tells us what the situation was in Jewish Law, and consequently what *could* have been the wording of Jesus or at least that of the Palestinian tradition of what Jesus said. The line between Jewish Law (and what Jesus said) *and* the reading of the Syro-Latin text does not necessarily run via the original text of Luke. It seems to me quite possible that Jesus (according to the tradition known to Luke) mentioned only the word 'judge' (דַּיָּנָא //κριτήν) in his answer to the complaining heir, whereas it was Luke who could not resist adding the explanatory words 'or divider' (ἢ μεριστήν).[60] The fact that the word μεριστής is a *hapax legomenon* cannot in any way be brought forward against the originality of the addition.[61]

3.5. Conclusions

If my observations are justified, we may conclude the following:

(1) the Syro-Latin text originated in the Marcionite revision of the Gospel according to Luke. The influence of Marcion is palpable

---

[57] Cf. *Baba Bathra* VIII.5a; IX.7, W. Windfuhr, *Baba Bathra*, in: *Die Mischna*, IV:3, Giessen 1925, 72.84.

[58] Cf. *Baba Bathra*, passim (e.g. I:5.6; VIII:1.3; IX:1.8.9).

[59] Cf. *Sanhedrin* III.1 (S. Krauss, *Sanhedrin-Makkoth*, in *Die Mischna* IV:4-5, Giessen 1933, 114f).

[60] The conjunction ἤ can be used in such a way that one might replace it by καί, e.g. Mt 5, 17.18.36. It implies that the two connected words are chosen as examples of a larger group. In Mt 10, 11, πόλιν ἢ κώμην means 'any place, smaller or larger, in which you come...'; 17, 25 τέλη ἢ κῆνσον 'any kind of tax which the sovereigns are to impose...'. The same use is found in Luke, cf. 13, 15; 14, 12; 16, 7. It seems to be Lucan idiom, however, to use the conjunction as an introduction of an explanation, e.g. Acts 4, 7 c(f. H. Conzelmann, *Die Apostelgeschichte*, Tübingen 1963, 37); 10, 28; 11, 8 (κοινὸν ἢ ἀκάθαρτον, cf. 10, 14 (καί), cf. also Mk 7, 2: τοῦτ' ἔστιν—F. Hauck, *T.W.N.T.* III, 791:31f.; M. Smith, *Tannaitic Parallels to the Gospels*, Philadelphia, Penns. 1951, 31ff.); Lk 9, 25 (... ἢ ζημιωθείς), 10, 42 (... ἢ ἑνός), cf. 12, 47.

[61] A. Plummer, *A critical and exegetical Commentary on the Gospel according to Saint Luke*, Edinburgh ⁵1922, liii lists μεριστής among ca. 200 hapax legomena.

in both Western and Eastern textual traditions, not impossibly via the Diatessaron of Tatian.

(2) The wording in Marcion's text was an abbreviation of the longer reading κριτὴν ἢ μεριστήν. In other words: Marcion, Diatessaron and the Syro-Latin text as a whole are an indirect testimony for the originality of the reading that has been preserved in the (proto-)Caesarean and (proto-)Alexandrian manuscripts.

Perhaps we may also recommend a third conclusion:

(3) Marcion, who introduced the reading κριτήν into the history of the text, was also responsible for the appearance of the other reading, δικαστήν. The antithesis between Moses and Jesus, that is, between Exod 2,14 and Luke 12,14, has influenced the subsequent history of exegesis, and so it became the ultimate source for the harmonization of the Lucan text with its counterpart in Exodus (ἄρχοντα καὶ δικαστήν) in the textual readings 2-3-4-5-6 (δικαστήν) and 6-7-8 (ἄρχοντα).

The original reading of Luke 12,14 is κριτὴν ἢ μεριστήν. The last two words seem to have been Luke's own explanatory addition to the word which has been transmitted to him by tradition.

The Gospel of Thomas

4.1. *Saying 72*: ⲣⲉϥⲡⲱϣⲉ = Μεριστήν.

The tenth reading—μεριστήν—is not found in any Greek manuscript; it would, thus, likely be difficult to find a scholar who would wish to defend the thesis that Luke wrote only this word in his text. The main support for this reading is found in Coptic texts. Surprisingly, G. Horner,[62] neglecting the manuscripts with the Alexandrian textual form ⲛ̄ⲕⲣⲓⲧⲏⲥ ⲁⲩⲱ ⲛ̄ⲣⲉϥⲡⲱⲣϫ, based the text of his edition exclusively on the *one* MS of the Sahidic version of Luke's Gospel which offers the reading ⲛ̄ⲣⲉϥⲡⲱⲣϫ, 'divider'; it seems to me that he made the wrong choice in this case. Nevertheless, the reading 'divider' commanded new interest in more recent times through its occurrence— ⲛ̄ⲣⲉϥⲡⲱϣⲉ —in another Coptic text, namely in Saying 72 of the Gospel of Thomas:[63]

[*A man said*] *to Him*: '*Speak to my brothers, that they divide my father's possessions with me*'. *He said to him*: '*O man, who made me a divider?*'. *He turned to his disciples and said to them*: '*I am not a divider, am I?*'.

---

[62] G. Horner, *The Coptic Version*, 242.
[63] Cf. B. M. Metzger's translation in K. Aland, *Synopsis Quattuor Evangeliorum*, Stuttgart, 1964, 526.

The discovery of the Gospel of Thomas among the many writings of the Nag Hammādi find is undoubtedly one of the most exciting events that happened within the area of Gospel research of the last three decennia. This apocryphal collection of some 114 sayings of Jesus comprised no less than fifty logia closely related to materials in the Synoptic Gospels. Inevitably, the question arose whether or not these fifty sayings were dependent on these Gospels. If they were not, they could possibly throw light upon the origin and growth of the earliest traditions of the Gospel kerygma. The problem of relationship between the apocryphal document and the canonical writings has not yet been solved, but is still a matter of intensive discussion. This paper will not suggest an answer to that general question, since our observations, and consequently our conclusions, are limited to logion 72. This restriction is necessary to avoid premature generalizations.[64] Our sole task here is to analyze the interrelationship of Luke 12, 13-14 and logion 72, and to search for an explanation of the remarkable reading 'divider' in the text of Thomas. This analysis will have to reckon with four different approaches to the problem of relationship.

4.2. Source Criticism

(1) One of the ways of investigating the problem of relationship between Thomas and Luke takes its departure from the analysis of *sources*. A large part of the Synoptic materials in the Gospel of Thomas is in agreement with Luke, especially the non-Marcan traditions thereof.[65] If one takes the line that Thomas is *not* dependent on Luke, one is obliged to assume a common source for them. The usual approach to Luke's sources distinguishes (apart from Mark or some proto-Mark) between traditions in common with Matthew—Q—*and* materials peculiar to Luke—L—.[66] Starting from this rather schematic classification, one might be tempted to

---

[64] Cf. O. Cullmann, Das Thomasevangelium und die Frage nach dem Alter der in ihm enthaltenen Tradition, *Theologische Literaturzeitung* 85 (1960), 331-334, 333, who warned against 'vorzeitige Verallgemeinerungen im negativen oder positiven Sinne'.

[65] H. Schürmann, Das Thomasevangelium und das lukanische Sondergut, *Biblische Zeitschrift* 7 (1963), 236-260, reproduced in his *Traditionsgeschichtliche Untersuchungen zu den synoptischen Evangelien*, Düsseldorf 1968, 228-247, 228; cf. also O. Cullmann, *a.c.*, 333. Recently: B. Dehandschutter, L'Évangile selon Thomas: témoin d'une tradition prélucanienne?, in: *L'Évangile de Luc*, Mémorial Lucien Cerfaux, Gembloux 1973, 287-297.

[66] Cf. e.g. E. E. Ellis, *The Gospel of Luke*, London 1966, 25ff.

suggest either Q or L, or both, as possible common sources of Luke and Thomas, the more so because in each of these sources the 'sayings'-tradition, which is so characteristic for Thomas, is clearly discernible.[67] Remarkably enough, those scholars who hold the opinion that Thomas is *not* dependent on Luke sometimes deny that Thomas could have used such sources as Q or L. They rather voice the opinion that the apocryphal Gospel is based upon a distinct 'Jewish-Christian' source, viz. some Aramaic Gospel,[68] or to put it more vaguely, pre-Q, Pre-L or pre-Gospel collections of ΛΟΓΟΙ-traditions.[69]

(2) Luke 12, 13-14 is an example of Lucan 'Sondergut' whose origin is difficult, if not impossible to trace. If the episode were Luke's own invention in order to provide the narrative of the rich fool with an occasion,[70] the dependence of Thomas on Luke need not be proved; but there is not the slightest bit of evidence to indicate that this 'occasion' is a mere redactional fabrication of the Evangelist. H. Schürmann, who made a thorough investigation of the relationship between Thomas and Lucan 'Sondergut',[71] was convinced that Luke 12, 13-14 originated in Q.[72] Since his argument is not closely-reasoned in my view, I prefer to identify the episode merely as special Lucan material without attempting to give a sharper definition.[73] Moreover, even if the origin of this material was Q, we are still left with its Lucan form (*without* a

---

[67] Cf. e.g. T. Schramm, *Der Markus-Stoff bei Lukas*, Cambridge 1971, 14f.

[68] Cf. e.g. G. Quispel, Some Remarks on the Gospel of Thomas, *New Testament Studies* 5 (1958/9), 276-290, 278.281.290; L'Évangile selon Thomas et le Diatessaron, *Vigiliae Christianae* 13 (1959), 87-117, 116f.; *Makarius, das Thomasevangelium und das Lied von der Perle*, Leiden 1967, 79ff., 81; *Het Evangelie van Thomas en de Nederlanden*, Amsterdam/Brussel 1971, 70.

[69] Cf. esp. H. Köster, ΓΝΩΜΑΙ ΔΙΑΦΟΡΟΙ, *Harvard Theological Review* 58 (1965), 279-318, 298ff. (298: Thomas does not continue Q, but represents the Eastern branch of the Gattung "Logoi", the Western branch being represented by the Synoptic Logoi of Q).

[70] Cf. A. Loisy, *L'Évangile selon Luc*, 1924, 345.

[71] H. Schürmann, *o.c.*, wished to answer the question 'Ist hinter Thom. und speziell dem Luk. S(ondergut) eine gemeinsame Quelle anzunehmen, oder ist Thom. hier direkt oder indirekt vom Lukasevangelium abhängig?' (229).—His conclusion is that only the latter alternative is possible, cf. 246 (under 2). I cannot understand why G. Quispel, *Makarius*, 80 writes 'Nun hat aber H. Schürmann gezeigt, dass "Thomas" das Lukasevangelium gar nicht gekannt hat'.

[72] H. Schürmann, *o.c.*, 232f.

[73] Cf. E. E. Ellis, *o.c.*, 25f. (The Sources of Luke) attributes 12, 13-34 partly to Q, partly to L.

Matthaean counterpart) *and* its parallel in Thomas. Are we able to deduce anything from the deviations (omissions, additions or alterations) between Thomas and Luke with regard to their relationship? Was there a common source behind them? And did Thomas eventually preserve the wording of that source in a more correct form than did Luke? Or is the text of Thomas nothing other than a retouching or development of Luke's redaction? Before we are able to answer these questions in our comparison of the two Gospels [74] we must give our attention to the other approaches to the problem.

4.3. *Search for Aramaisms*

(1) A *second* approach, which is closely connected with the former, is that which tries to ascertain the presence or absence of a Semitic colouring of parallel texts in Thomas and Luke. Such a search for identifiable Semitisms, or rather: Aramaisms, in the two existing recensions of the episode of the dissatisfied heir may certainly be of some importance. Aramaic was admittedly the language of Jesus and of the earliest stage of tradition of his sayings. Therefore, the discovery of Aramaisms or at least of some Semitic colouring that may shine through the Greek or Coptic wording may be helpful in reconstructing the pre-Synoptic and pre-Greek tradition.[75] Several scholars have claimed to have discovered hard-core Aramaisms in other logia of Thomas which would carry us back to these early stages of oral or written Aramaic tradition.[76] In some cases the measure of Semitic flavour seemed to be even greater than in the Synoptic parallels.[77] The conclusion is then obvious: if this state of affairs can be established, we are 'on safer ground' [78] in establishing the independence of the Gospel of Thomas.

(2) It may be useful to demonstrate the need for caution in any attempt to trace Aramaisms in the Coptic Thomas. An example

---

[74] Cf. below, *Collation* 6:2.2; 2.3; 2.7; 2.8; 4.1; 4.3; 4.4 and the discussion thereof.

[75] Cf. J. Jeremias, *Neutestamentliche Theologie* I, Gütersloh 1971, 13ff.

[76] E.g. G. Quispel, Some Remarks, 282 (and passim); L'Évangile selon Thomas, 87ff.; W. H. C. Frend, The Gospel of Thomas: is Rehabilitation possible?, *Journal of Theological Studies* 18 (1967), 13-26, 15.

[77] Cf. e.g. C.-H. Hunzinger, Unbekannte Gleichnisse Jesu aus dem Thomas-Evangelium, in *Judentum, Urchristentum, Kirche,* Festschrift für J. Jeremias, Berlin 1960, 209-220, 220 (n. 48); J. Jeremias, *Unbekannte Jesusworte,* Gütersloh ³1963, 19.

[78] Cf. O. Cullmann, *a.c.,* 333.

of carelessness is found in the treatment of logion 113, which has a close parallel in Luke 17, 20f.[79] The difficult Lucan expression μετὰ παρατηρήσεως 'with/by observation' has a parallel in the wording ϩⲛ ⲟⲩ ϭⲱϣⲧ ⲉⲃⲟⲗ, 'in an expectation', of Thomas. It has been asserted that the two different expressions can be explained as translation variants of the underlying Semitic root חור,[80] which might be interpreted—according to this view—both as 'observe' and as 'expect'. This explanation simply begs for some criticism. First of all, one should keep in mind that the Coptic verb ϭⲱϣⲧ does not lack the connotation of 'observing'; its actual meaning is 'to see, to look', and with ⲉⲃⲟⲗ it means 'to look for, to expect'.[81] On the other hand, the Greek παρατηρεῖν does not wholly exclude the idea of 'expecting'; it means 'to watch closely, to observe', sometimes even 'to lie in wait for, beobachtend abwarten'.[82] Therefore, one cannot exclude the possibility that the Coptic expression is nothing more than a tentative rendering of the Lucan text. But let us assume that Thomas and Luke are two different traditions at the root of which an Aramaic wording might be conjectured, could this be the suggested verb חור? The problem is that the verb

[79] G. Quispel, Some Remarks, 288; L'Évangile selon Thomas, 115; H.-W. Bartsch, Das Thomasevangelium und die synoptischen Evangelien, *New Testament Studies* 6 (1960), 249-261, 257; see also H. Schürmann, Das Thomasevangelium, 238 n. 61 (hesitating).

[80] G. Quispel, *loc. cit.*; no effort has been made to conjecture some noun corresponding to the Greek or Coptic forms.

[81] Cf. W. E. Crum, *A Coptic Dictionary*, Oxford 1939, 837f.: ϭⲱϣⲧ, βλεπεῖν, ὁρᾶν, θεωρεῖν, σκοπεῖν, etc.; ϭⲱϣⲧ ⲉⲃⲟⲗ, ὁρᾶν, προσδέχεσθαι, ἐπιδεῖν, ἐλπίζειν etc.

[82] For the first meaning ('observe'), cf. H. G. Liddell, R. Scott, *A Greek-English Lexicon*, Oxford ⁹(repr.) 1953, 1327; for the second meaning, cf. *ibid.* (Aristoph., Rh. 1384ᵇ 7); H. Riesenfeld, παρατήρεω, *T.W.N.T.* VIII (1969), 147:13f. (Test. Sal. 6.4 94*30)).

[83] G. Dalman, *Aramäisches-neuhebräisches Handwörterbuch zum Targum, Talmud und Midrasch*, Frankfurt a.M., ²1922, 140 does not differentiate between the two branches of the language (חור a. sehen); C. Brockelmann, *Lexicon Syriacum*, Halle ²1928, 426, designates it as AR, i.e. as occurring both in East and West Aramaic. As a matter of fact, it occurs as Pe'al form in the Targum on Proverbs 23, 33 (conj.), 4, 25 (?) and 17, 24; it is clear, however, that these occurrences are from Eastern Aramaic origin (imperfect with *nun*-prefix). As to the occurrences of חור Pi'el 'to make clear, to make evident' in Talmud Yerushalmi (cf. J. Levi, *Chaldäisches Wörterbuch über die Targumim*, Leipzig 1881, 244) it must be observed that these occurrences are partly problematic and that their origin is perhaps from a different root (cf. M. Yastrow, *Dictionary of Talmud Babli, Yerushalmi, Midrashic Literature and Targumim*, New York (repr.) 1950, vol. I, 438f.). I did not find occurrences of the verb in other languages of Palestina or Syria.

חור is, as far as I can tell, not present in *Western* Aramaic dialects.[83] As a matter of fact, it is found in *Eastern* Aramaic, especially in Syriac.[84] If the solution proposed by G. Quispel were correct, it would be necessary to seek in the direction of *Syriac* as the origin of the ambiguity which caused the two renderings in Luke and Thomas. But this is apparently not Quispel's intention.[85] Although I am inclined to defend the Syriac background of the Coptic Gospel of Thomas, I would not care to defend the position that finds the solution in an original ܚܘܪ. As a matter of fact, the origin of the Lucan μετὰ παρατηρήσεως is most probably the expression בִּנְטִיר,[86] but I would not suggest that the Gospel of Thomas is dependent on that wording. The Syriac versions of Luke present us with the rendering ܒܢܛܘܪܬܐ 'with observation' (Sy[s.c] *sing.*, Sy[p] *plur.*). The Aramaic root *n ṭ r* has a variety of meanings: 1. *to observe*, 2. *to watch*, 3. *to wait*, and—at least in Syriac—4. *to expect*.[87] Still, in some Arabic dialects of Syria, the verb نظ *'to watch, to guard'* also has the meaning of *'to expect'*.[88] So, in my view, one cannot rule out the possibility that the Coptic expression ϩⲛ ⲟⲩ ϭⲱϣⲧ' ⲉⲃⲟⲗ is a specific, possibly even dogmatical [89] interpretation based on the very Syriac wording which we found in the Syriac versions: ܒܢܛܘܪܬܐ. G. Quispel's expectation of finding support for his thesis (חור !) in the Arabic Diatessaron remains unfulfilled. He refers to the wording 'par l'attente' of that harmony,[90] but here he is deceived by Marmardji's (in itself correct) translation, since the Arabic wording بالانتظار is nothing more than an interpretative transliteration [91] of the original Diatessaron wording ܒܢܛܘܪܬܐ (=Sy[s.c.p]) 'with

---

[84] Cf. R. Payne Smith, *Thesaurus Syriacus*, vol. I, Oxford 1879, 1226f.: 'inspexit, contemplavit..., expectavit...'.

[85] A Syriac substrate of the tradition in Thomas has been suggested by A. Guillaumont, Sémitismes dans les logia de Jésus, rétrouvés à Nag Hammadi, *Journal Asiatique* 246 (1958), 113-123.

[86] Cf. J. Levy, *Chaldäisches Wörterbuch* II, 107 (ref. to Job 4, 12); for the conjecture, cf. A. Meyer, *Jesu Muttersprache*, Freiburg-Leipzig 1896, 87. I agree with Meyer's solution 'heimlich', 'in secrecy'.

[87] R. Payne Smith, *o.c.*, vol. II, Oxford 1901, 2353; C. Brockelmann, *o.c.*, 426 ('observavit, custodivit, ... expectavit, animadvertit').

[88] *Al-Faraid*, Beyrouth [17]1955, ٨٢٧ (cf. نظ 'observe' and 'expect', *o.c.* ٨٣٦), Cl. Denizeau, *Dictionnaire du parlers arabes de Syrie, Liban et Palestine*, Paris 1960, 521.

[89] Cf. H. Schürmann, *o.c.*, 238 n. 61.

[90] G. Quispel, L'Évangile selon Thomas, 95.115.

[91] Interestingly enough, A.-S. Marmardji, *Diatessaron de Tatien*, Beyrouth 1935, 380, follows his puristic inclinations here also and proposes to

observation'[92] which accurately renders the Greek μετὰ παρατηρήσεως.

(3) There is no reason, however, to abandon this approach as such. We ought to continue examining the respective texts of Luke and Thomas for eventual Semitisms and form a conclusion only after an evaluation of their respective relationship to (either Western or Eastern) Aramaic traditions.[93]

4.4. Thomas and Jewish-Christian Documents

(1) The *third* angle from which scholars have approached the question of dependence or independence is that of those early writings which are supposedly containing Jewish-Christian traditions.[94] First of all, proposals have been made as to a possible rapport between Thomas and the remains of the well-known Judaeo-Christian Gospels such as the Gospel according to the Hebrews, the Gospel according to the Ebionites and the Gospel of the Nazarenes.[95] Due to the fragmentary character of these remains it is almost impossible to reach definite conclusions with respect to their interrelationship on the one hand and to their respective relations to the canonical Gospels on the other hand. Their harmonistic character, especially in the case of the Ebionite Gospel, sometimes gives the impression that they were written not without knowledge of some of the canonical Gospels.[96] However, the specific Lucan material is scanty in them.[97] Therefore, it is not strange that these texts produced neither the text of Luke 12, 13f. nor a parallel to it.[98]

---

read the more 'adequate' بمراقبة 'by observation'; this conjecture, however, wholly neglects the peculiar nature of the Arabic harmony which should not be judged by classic rules.

[92] A paper on Luke 17, 20f. in the Diatessaron by the present author is in preparation.

[93] See below, esp. *Collation* 6:1.7; (4.4); 2.2; 2.6; 4.1; 5.1.

[94] G. Quispel, *Makarius*, 79ff.; idem, The Discussion of Judaic Christianity, *Vigiliae Christianae* 22 (1968), 81-93, 85.

[95] G. Quispel, *Makarius*, 19; W. H. C. Frend, The Gospel of Thomas, 15. 21ff.

[96] H. Schürmann, *o.c.*, 244.

[97] H. Schürmann, *o.c.*, 245.

[98] G. Quispel, *Makarius*, 79 finds a stilistic parallel to the addition of Thomas in the Gospel according to the Hebrews (fragm. 11): 'et conversus dixit Simoni . . .' (E. Klostermann, *Apocrypha* II, Berlin 1929, 9). There is a Lucan parallel in 10, 23 (cf. esp. H. Schürmann, *o.c.*, 233, n. 30). Quispel denies any influence of Luke on Thomas here, although he himself acknowledges the secondary character of the addition of Thomas (see below par. 6, n. 10).

(2) The next document that was qualified to give support to the view that Thomas was independent of the canonical Gospels and was based upon a Jewish-Christian Gospel were the so-called Pseudo-Clementine writings, since there seemed to be a large measure of agreement between this literature and the logia of Thomas.[99] It has been suggested that this agreement can only be explained by the assumption of a common Aramaic source which originated in a Jewish-Christian milieu.[100] The identification of that common-source document is not so easy; it is not very probable that it was the Gospel according to the Ebionites,[101] but it might have been an apocryphal Aramaic source underlying both Thomas and the Ebionite Gospel, which source has influenced the Gospel materials in Justin, Clement of Alexandria, II Clement and the Codex Bezae.[102]

(3) Unfortunately, none of these documents have a parallel to logion 72. This absence seems to be completely compensated for by the presence of a parallel in a recently discovered Muslim writing. According to some scholars this writing contains a long passage of markedly Jewish-Christian origin. The document in question is a large apologetic and polemical work of ʿAbd al-Gabbar to which we shall give attention in a separate paragraph of this paper.[103]

4.5. *Thomas and the Western Text*

(1) The studies of G. Quispel have underlined the importance of the Western Text for the study of Thomas. His investigation of the Pseudo-Clementine literature forced him to pursue his inquiry in the direction of the Western Text and the Diatessaron traditions. He was convinced that along these lines one might trace a homogeneous non-canonical tradition of the sayings of Jesus, which then also comes to light in the Gospel of Thomas.[104] There is, in

---

[99] Cf. G. Quispel, L'Évangile selon Thomas, 181ff.; *Makarius*, 19.
[100] G. Quispel, L'Évangile selon Thomas, 192.
[101] *Ibid.*, 194.
[102] *Ibid.*, 195.
[103] Cf. par. 5 and par. 6 (passim), esp. *Collation* 6:4.—The reading κριτὴν καὶ δικαστήν in the Pseudo-Clementine 'Epistula Clementis' 5, 3, cf. above par. 2, n. 28, is not of any help here.—The function of 'Clement' is not that of a judge, but rather of one who separates (χωρίζειν) with the word of Truth the better people from the worser. Is that the reason why the author could not use the reading μεριστής?
[104] G. Quispel, L'Évangile selon Thomas, 196; cf. *Het Evangelie van Thomas*, 70ff.; *Makarius*, 19f.

fact, a large measure of agreement between Thomas and the Western Text.[105] The cause of that agreement, however, has not always been explained in the same way. One might, for example, interpret this phenomenon in such a way that Thomas is another snapshot of the vivid and uncontrolled development of the Gospel text during the second century, a stage of textual history of which also Marcion and Tatian seem to be representatives.[106] Others have conjectured that Marcion and even Tatian could have influenced the textual shape of the logia of the Coptic Thomas.[107] But those who champion the independence of Thomas and its traditions argue, as we have seen, that the link between Thomas and the Western Text is fundamental: Western traditions are largely affected by Jewish-Christian pre- or non-canonical materials of the synoptic type. The agreement between Thomas and the Western Text leads us back into a stage of tradition which lies behind or beside that of the Synoptic Gospels. And so, the Western Text becomes one of the channels through which the archaic Jewish-Christian traditions flowed into the bed of later church literature.[108]

(2) The limitation of our investigation to logion 72 precludes further discussion of this charming hypothesis. This paper has a closely defined purpose, namely, the examination of the relation between logion 72 and Luke 12, 13-14, and in the course of that examination due attention will be given to the occidental tradition of the Lucan text.[109] The situation is rather complex here, however, since Thomas (= μεριστήν) and the Western (or Syro-Latin) text (= κριτήν)[110] are antipodal in their most important variation. The question before us now is whether the Syro-Latin ring (Marcion-Tatian-Vetus Syra-Vetus Latina-Codex Bezae) presents us with the *only* 'Western' reading. Our observations with respect to the reading *iudicem aut divisorem* suggest that there was also an early occurrence of the *original* text of Luke 12, 14 in the Old Latin Gospel tradition. And again, is it possible that a *third* reading

---

[105] Cf. T. Baarda, Thomas en Tatianus, ch. 6 in R. Schippers, *Het Evangelie van Thomas*, Kampen 1960, 135-155; G. Quispel, L'Évangile selon Thomas et le Diatessaron, *Vigiliae Christianae* 13 (1959), 87-117, 89-95.

[106] Cf. e.g. E. Haenchen, *Die Botschaft des Thomasevangeliums*, Berlin 1961.

[107] Cf. my Thomas and Tatianus, 155.

[108] G. Quispel, *Makarius*, 20; Tatianus Latinus, *Nederlands Theologisch Tijdschrift* 21 (1967), 409-19, 416f.

[109] Cf. Collation 6:2, 6; 3.4; 4.1; 4.3.

[110] Cf. par. 3.

(only: *divisorem*) existed in early Latin manuscripts? St. Augustine's wording 'Quis me constituit divisorem haereditatis inter vos?'[111] has been adduced as a testimony for such a text—an *African* 'Western' text—which, just as the Coptic text, had preserved the very Jewish-Christian tradition that had been the source of the Gospel of Thomas.[112] In a separate section we shall investigate the real contribution of St. Augustine's text to the textual problem of Luke 12, 14.[113]

'Abd al-Ğabbār

5.1. *An important discovery*

Several years ago there was a press report on an important discovery which would throw new light on the troubled history of the Jewish-Christians in the early ages of Christianity.[114] A manuscript was found in Istanbul which contained the text of an unknown work of the Muʿtazilite author ʿAbd al-Ğabbār, the chief Qadī of Rayy; the work is entitled *Tathbīt Dalāʾil Nubuwwat Sayyīdina Muḥammad*.[115] It was written in 385 a.H. (995 A.D.) with the avowed object of defending the prophethood of Muhammad against every sort of criticism of those who had not welcomed the Muslim faith. The first part of this writing contains a long passage devoted to Christianity in order to demonstrate how justified Muhammad was in what he had said about Jesus and the Christians.[116] The sensational thing of the discovery was exactly this section on Christian faith and history. The first scholar to publish a study on the passage, Shlomo Pines of the Hebrew University of Jerusalem, expressed the opinion that a great deal of this material was not Islamic in origin, but rather represented the contents of a

---

[111] G. Quispel, *Het Evangelie van Thomas*, 93 (ref. to *Sermo* 359.3).

[112] G. Quispel, *o.c.*, 93.

[113] See below, par. 7.

[114] The first announcement which I found was in the *Jerusalem Post* of 22-6-1966: '10th Century text sheds new light on early Christians'; G. Quispel gave an interesting report on this 'Belangrijke Ontdekking over de Oorsprong van het Christendom' in *Elsevier* 19-11-1966 (p. 45), 26-11-1966 (p. 53).

[115] Edited by ʿAbd al-Karim ʿUthman, Beirouth 1966.—A description of the work is found in S. Pines, *The Jewish Christians of the early Centuries of Christianity according to a new Source*, Jerusalem 1966, 1ff.; S. M. Stern, Quotations from apocryphal Gospels in ʿAbd al-Jabbār, *Journal of Theological Studies* 18 (1967), 34-57, 34ff.; idem, New Light on Judaeo-Christianity?, *Encounter* May 1967, 53-57.

[116] Folia 42-105 (cf. resumé in S. M. Stern, Quotations, 34-39).

Syriac treatise of the fifth or sixth century written by Jewish Christians as an apology against the Orthodox, Jacobite and Nestorian parties in the church.[117] The original document had been accommodated to the purposes of the Muslim author in a few passages, but these emendations and interpolations were certainly not of such a nature or extent that they cut off access to the original Syriac writing. The importance of Pines' thesis becomes even more evident when it is realized that this Arabic document presents us with an interpretative description of the history of Christianity from its beginnings up to the fourth century. Could it be possible to read in an Arabic writing of the tenth century an independent piece of historiography which confronts us with the Jewish-Christian understanding of the early ages of Christianity? If so,[118] these Jewish-Christians had "a bitter and disenchanted view" of that history in which "the early Christian missionary work in Antioch and the activity of Paul and after him of Constantine and of his successors" were mere factors of the corruption and Romanization of an originally pure Christianity.[119] In spite of their somehow prejudiced evaluation of history, their apology may preserve a good many reliable traditions. Certain parts of the text may transmit traditions that go back to a very early period of the Jewish Christian sect, a period when it still had memories of the Jerusalem community and its flight from Jerusalem to Mesopotamia.[120]

5.2. *Luke 12, 13-14?*

(1) The second chapter of 'Abd al-Ǧabbār's large book [121] deals with the argument that Muhammad was wholly justified in saying that the Christian religion was not in accordance with the teaching of Jesus. For Christians honoured Jesus as a divine being, although Jesus himself never claimed divinity or divine authority; on the contrary, by his own words he made sufficiently clear that he was inferior to Allah.[122] This statement is proved by several quotations

---

[117] S. Pines, *o.c.*, 8, 11f., 21, and passim.

[118] The positive answer of S. Pines is also found in his paper "Israel, my Firstborn" and the Sonship of Jesus, a theme of Moslem anti-Christian Polemics, in *Studies in Mysticism and Religion* (Festschrift for G. G. Scholem), Jerusalem 1967, 177ff.

[119] S. Pines, *The Jewish Christians*, 64f. (and passim).

[120] S. Pines, *o.c.*, 32 (cf. 21ff.).

[121] Folia 50b-56b (S. M. Stern, Quotations, 35).

[122] Cf. S. M. Stern, a.c., 36.

from the four Gospels;[123] one of these proof texts reads as follows:[124]

And said to Him a man: 'Master, let my brothers share (divide) with me the inheritance of my father'. And He said: '(And) who appointed me over you a divider?'.

This text was dealt with in Pines' book, but it was identified by G. Quispel,[125] who in collaboration with D. J. Hoens, gave a more correct translation of the Arabic text. The translation given above is based upon the edition of ʿAbd al-Ǧabbār's book by ʿAbd al-Karīm ʿUthman.[126]

(2) ʿAbd al-Ǧabbār's contribution was warmly welcomed by Quispel, who had no doubts that the new source, in spite of some legendary accretions, contained many valuable memories and traditions from the past of the suggested Jewish-Christian sect.[127] The parallels with the Old Syriac text, the Gospel of Peter and the Pseudo-Clementine writings seem to warrant the claim that the document underlying the Arabic text had been written in Syria at a much earlier time. In the view of Quispel, there may be a good deal of reliable tradition in the document; it may even contain very archaic elements. This is especially true for the sayings of Jesus that are transmitted by ʿAbd al-Ǧabbār, for they often differ from the wording of the canonical Gospels. The recension

---

[123] Stern mentions Mk 10, 45 parr.; 10, 17f. parr.; 13, 32; Lk 11, 41f.; 12, 13f.; 18, 18f.; 22, 42ff.; Jn 5, 30; 7, 38; 8, 40; 11, 41f.; 12, 24; 14, 24; 17, 3.6.8.—It is not improbable that the author was dependent on such works as ʿAli b. Rabban al-Ṭabari's 'Refutation of the Christians' (the author was a Christian physician who became a convert to Islam), cf. S. M. Stern, *a.c.*, 36; idem, ʿAbd al-Jabbār's Account of how Christ's Religion was falsified by the Adoption of Roman Customs *Journal of Theological Studies* 19 (1968), 128-185, 129.

[124] In the edition of ʿUthman, 113 (fol. 53a)—for the Arabic text cf. below, the *Synopsis*, col. 3.—The transcription of S. Pines, *o.c.*, 13, n. 35, was incorrect (S. Pines, "Israel, my Firstborn", 177 n. 2; and again in a letter of October 1973); cf. S. M. Stern, ʿAbd al-Jabbār's Account, 129. According to Pines (*loc. cit.*) the numbering of the folia in ʿUthman's edition must be wrong; he locates the text on fol. 52b.

[125] G. Quispel, Belangrijke Ontdekking II, 53.

[126] The edition reads *tarka* or *tarika*, litt. that which is left, viz. the inheritance. S. Pines, "Israel, my Firstborn", 178 n. 3, acknowledges that reading ('in all probability') against his own guess, *The Jewish Christians*, 13 n. 35, *barakāt*, which occasioned such translations as 'wealth' or 'rijkdommen' (G. Quispel).

[127] For the following, cf. G. Quispel, Belangrijke ontdekking II, 53; The Discussion of Judaic Christianity, 85f.; *Het Evangelie van Thomas*, 90-94; Tatianus Latinus, 416f.

of the dissatisfied heir and the answer of Jesus, for example, is greatly different from the Lucan wording; it was apparently the version of the story that circulated among the descendants of the early community of Jerusalem, the Jewish Christians who had moved from Palestine to Mesopotamia.

(3) Now, this recension, Quispel argues, is almost completely identical with logion 72 of Thomas. This proves that Thomas must have used a Jewish-Christian source. The proof is decisive, he continues, for this new source makes it once for all clear that the Gospel of Thomas contains sayings of Jesus [128] which are independent from the canonical Gospels and which were preserved by Jewish-Christians who brought their own traditions from Jerusalem to Edessa. The final conclusion is: 'the game is up'; [129] those who hold another view with respect to the origin of the traditions in Thomas will have to reconsider. Even though he became slightly more careful upon becoming aware of the severe criticism evoked by Pines' thesis,[130] he continues to maintain his position: 'Although further publications must be awaited, we must agree with Pines that this wording ultimately goes back to a Jewish Christian source. But then we must conclude that the Gospel of Thomas too derived this Saying and others from a Jewish Gospel tradition'.[131] The thesis is abundantly clear: the variations of the Arabic version of the story are not to be registered in the Apparatus of a New Testament edition as variant readings of Luke 12, 13-14; in fact, they are indications of an independent, pre- or non-canonical tradition. And so ʿAbd al-Ǧabbār's text becomes the *keystone* of Quispel's approach to the Gospel of Thomas.

5.3. *Questions*

(1) I do not think that it would be fair to try to destroy this

---

[128] G. Quispel, Tatianus Latinus, 416 (cf. *idem*, The Latin Tatian or the Gospel of Thomas in Limburg, Journal of Biblical Literature 88 (1969), 321-330, 327) is not justified in saying that the document contains 'words of Jesus, which are practically in agreement with logia in Thomas'. As far as I can see, only logion 72 has a parallel in ʿAbd al-Ǧabbār.

[129] G. Quispel, Belangrijke Ontdekking II, 53: 'Deze strijd is nu beslist' cf. I, 45 where he writes that his own views did not please everyone, so that books were written against his view of 'independence'. But now, with Pines' booklet in hand, it is possible to discover who was on the right track, he says.

[130] G. Quispel, The Discussion of Judaic Christianity, 85; *Het Evangelie van Thomas*, 91 ('Deze hypothetische ... bron is niet geheel waardeloos' betrays his apparent hesitation).

[131] G. Quispel, The Discussion of Judaic Christianity, 86.

keystone merely by having recourse to the evaluation of Pines' ingenious theory by S. M. Stern.[132] The latter acknowledged the charming enthusiasm behind that theory, but at the same time qualified the results of Pines' investigations as mere 'fantasies' arising from 'a regrettable act of folly by a distinguished scholar', which cannot hold against 'sound judgement' (although 'there will always be people ready to believe the craziest theory'): nothing is left to us but to abandon 'the chimaerical Judaeo-Christians' of Pines. Quispel's keystone deserves a better hammer and chisel than such general and unnecessary pronouncements as these.

(2) Nevertheless, it is obvious that Quispel's treatment of the 'new source' is too rash. He did not take into account the context in which the Arabic version of the story occurs, namely, a florilegium of Gospel quotations whose purpose was to demonstrate that Jesus did not wish to be honoured as God.[133] These quotations are taken from at least three canonical Gospels, one of them being unmistakably the Gospel of Luke.[134] Why should an exception be made in the case of the story of the man who wished to have a share in the inheritance? One cannot base himself here on the fact that the narrative in the Arabic text differs from the Greek text of Luke, for deviations from the canonical wording are usual in ʿAbd al-Ǧabbār, even where the influence of apocryphal traditions is impossible. One has only to look at the wording of Luke I, 1-4 ('I know your desire for good, for knowledge and instruction, so I have composed this Gospel according to what I knew. For I was close to those who have served the Word and have seen it')[135] to know how easily quotations could be transformed by ʿAbd al-Ǧabbār or by his spokesman.

(3) Even if it were true that a Jewish-Christian tract of the fifth or sixth century was the ultimate source, it would hardly be reasonable for an author of that time to have based his argument against the Christians on other Gospels than those which were in

---

[132] S. M. Stern, ʿAbd al-Jabbār's Account, 129f.—Stern did not recognize the influence of Syriac sources on ʿAbd al-Ǧabbār; they may explain some details in the Arabic text, for example when it speaks of eighty Gospels from which the four have been selected. This is not a 'whim' of the author (so Stern, 184) but a well-known Syriac tradition, cf. my Het ontstaan van de vier Evangelien volgens ʿAbd al-Djabbār, *Nederlands Theologisch Tijdschrift* (1974) 215-238.

[133] Cf. S. M. Stern, Quotations, 36; S. Pines, *The Jewish Christians*, 6, 60f.

[134] Four quotations are from Luke.

[135] Het Ontstaan van de vier Evangelien volgens ʿAbd al-Djabbār,

LUKE 12, 13-14

use among them. If, however, the florilegium was a Muslim product, composed either by ʿAbd al-Ǧabbār himself or by a predecessor with the help of some Syriac (Nestorian?) source of christological proof texts, the inaccuracies and deviations from the canonical texts could easily be explained.

For example, the rendering of John 5, 36b: [136]

الاعمال التي أعملهن من الشاهدات لى
بان الله أرسلنى الى هذا العالم.

('the deeds that I will do, *they* are witnessing of me/ that *God* has sent me *into this world*') could be explained as follows: the substitution of 'Father' by 'God' may be attributed to the Islamic author; the place of αὐτά(هن) before μαρτυρεῖ [137] is found in a Syriac text, viz. in Mar Ephraem's commentary on the Diatessaron (XIII:11): [138]

ܚܒܪ̈ܐ ܕܥܒܕ ܐܢܐ ܗܢܘܢ ܣܗܕܝܢ ܥܠܝ.

which is in complete agreement with the first line of the Arabic text; and the addition 'into this world' may have been someone's paraphrase under the influence of similar phrases in 3,17; 10,37 and 17,18.[139]

It is also true that not all of the quotations can be explained in this easy way. For example, another text reads thus: [140]

وقال انى انا لست أدين العباد
ولا احاسبهم باعمالهم
لكن الذى أرسلنى هو االذى يلى (؟) ذلك منهم

i.e., 'And He said: "I shall not judge men/nor shall I call them to account for their deeds,/but He who sent me He is the one who shall settle that with them". Pines made this a proof text for his verdict that ʿAbd al-Ǧabbār's quotations are *as a rule* taken from non-canonical Gospels. This thesis seems to be founded partly on

---

[136] Ed. ʿUthmān, 113 (fol. 53a; Pines: 52b), 1-2.
[137] One Greek text, 047, has this reading.
[138] L. Leloir, *Saint Éphrem, Commentaire de l'Évangile concordant, Texte syriaque*, Dublin 1963, 110:16.
[139] The addition of 'this' before 'world' (which is Johannine, cf. 9, 39; a.o.) is not infrequently found in Syriac texts, cf. 12, 47 (TE-arm XVIII: 11), 15, 19 (Sy^pal, cf. Dial. of Adamantius). How easily such an addition as 'into this world' could creep into a text after the verb 'to send' is evident from 17, 3 where D alone reads εἰς τοῦτον τὸν κόσμον.
[140] Ed. ʿUthmān, 112:10f. Cf. S. Pines, *The Jewish Christians*, 6.60.

faulty identifications,[141] partly on faulty considerations. Pines found a clear contrast here between the Arabic saying and the word of Jesus in John 5,22, and concluded that the former originated in an apocryphal tradition. Apparently he did not take account of the slight tension in the various pronouncements concerning judgment in the fourth Gospel. The first line of the Arabic text might be a rendering of John 8,15 ἐγὼ κρίνω οὐδένα (cf. 3,17; 12,47) and the third line might preserve a reminiscence of John 8,16 ἀλλ' ... ὁ πέμψας με (without ὁ πατήρ, cf. ℵ* D Sy$^{s.c}$). The text does remain rather obscure, of course; still there is no reason to make the conjecture of an apocryphal origin. In any case, the author himself (or his source) is not aware of such an apocryphal source, for he attributes the text to the fourth Gospel (هذا فى انجيل يوحنا), i.e., 'this is in the Gospel of John').[142] Pines' thesis requires a more thorough inquiry than we are able to make here. Here again, we must limit ourselves to the text of Luke 12, 13-14 and its parallel in ʿAbd al-Ǧabbār. The next question is whether it is necessary to view Quispel's conclusions as correct. An answer to this question requires an investigation of the various texts and their respective relationships.

Luke, Thomas and ʿAbd al-Ǧabbār, a Comparison

6.1. The Divider

(1) Quispel's contention that the texts of ʿAbd al-Ǧabbār is almost completely identical with the version of Thomas [143] cannot be sustained. It is true that they share the remarkable reading 'divider' (cf. our *Collation* 6:1.7; 4.4), but our *Synopsis* and *Collation* reveal that there are also some important differences between them. First of all, we should observe that there is a good deal of agreement between Luke, Thomas and ʿAbd al-Ǧabbār, for their common material, i.e.

> ... said to Him: ... (my brother/s) divide with me ...
> ... He said ...: Who ... me a divider ... ?

contains the rudiments of a dialogue. As for the remainder, one cannot say that the Coptic and Arabic completely agree with each

---

[141] This is true for his connecting of the parallel to Lk 12, 13f. with the Zebedee question of Mk 10, 35ff. parr.

[142] Ed. ʿUthmān, 112:10.

[143] G. Quispel, *Belangrijke Ontdekking*, 53 ('vrijwel letterlijk'); *Het Evangelie van Thomas*, 91 ('... woordelijk').

other against Luke. It is true that in addition to the reading 'divider' they have some other important elements in common (sc. 6:4.1; 4.3) which differ from the Lucan text, but, on the other hand, there is a large measure of agreement between Luke and 'Abd al-Ǧabbār against Thomas (four major items, 6:2.2(?); 2.3; 2.7; 2.8) and between Luke and Thomas against 'Abd al-Ǧabbār (cf. esp. 6:3.2; 3.4). Even apart from that, the differences between Thomas and 'Abd al-Ǧabbār—about 14 out of 25 elements to be compared—are so numerous that it hardly seems probable that they represent *one* particular tradition. A closer investigation, however, will be necessary for a final judgement.

(2) The agreement between the three texts in 6:1.7 is only apparent, for it is exactly in this common reading that the texts differ (cf. 6:4.4). It may be useful to deal with both the agreement and the difference in this first stage of our comparison.

(3) According to Quispel [144] the word 'divider' is the word originally present in the tradition before Luke and even in the original saying of Jesus himself. It was the translation of the Hebrew word חוֹלֵק or of the Aramaic expression בַּעַל פְּלֻגְתָּא, he says. Initially, Quispel traced this remarkable word, μεριστής, back to a Semitic background in collaboration with D. Gershenson.[145] They were convinced that Jesus deliberately used either חולק or בעל פלוותא, since there was an ambiguity in these words. The verbs חלק or פלג could denote the division of inheritances, but they could also have the connotation of 'teaching controversial or schismatic ideas',[146] and this was exactly the point of Jesus' word. As a matter of fact, Jesus did not mean to indicate that he was not willing to act as a divider of an inheritance, but rather that he did not want to introduce dissenting opinions or to found a new school.[147] He was punning. Later on, Quispel explained the

---

[144] G. Quispel, *o.c.*, 92f.

[145] D. Gershenson-G. Quispel, Meristae, *Vigiliae Christianae* 12 (1958), 19-26.

[146] D. Gershenson-G. Quispel, *a.c.* 24f.; G. Quispel, *o.c.*, 92.

[147] D. Gershenson-G. Quispel, *loc. cit.*; I have my doubts with regard to the partic. *Qal* (חוֹלֵק) which means 'dividing' in the sense of 'taking a share' or (with עַל) 'differing from (someone's opinion)'. Does it also mean 'schismatic'? It seems to me that partic. pass. חָלוּק or partic. act. *Paʿel* מְחַלֵּק could mean 'asserting a different opinion'; as to פלג, partic. *Hifʿil* מַפְלִיג 'differing' or partic. *Peʿal* פָּלִיג (with עַל) may mean 'differing in opinion (from) . . .' and can be used for school differences, but the *Paʿel* is used in the sense of 'to divert the mind of people' (= 'schismatic').

	Synopsis	
Thomas log. 72	Luke 12, 13-15[a]	ʿAbd al-Ǧabbār fol. 53[a]

	Thomas log. 72	Luke 12, 13-15[a]	ʿAbd al-Ǧabbār
1	[ⲡⲉϫ]ⲉ ⲟ[ⲩⲣⲱⲙⲉ]	εἶπεν δέ τις	وقال له رجلٌ
2		ἐκ τοῦ ὄχλου	
3	ⲛⲁϥ ϫⲉ	αὐτῷ·	
4		διδάσκαλε,	مُرْ
5	ϫⲟⲟⲥ	εἰπὲ	
6	ⲙ̄ⲡⲁⲥⲛⲏⲩ	τῷ ἀδελφῷ μου	أخي
7	ϣⲓⲛⲁ ⲉϥⲛ[ⲁ]ⲡⲱϣⲉ	μερίσασθαι ⎫	يُقاسِمَني
8		μετ' ἐμοῦ ⎭	
9	ⲛ̄ⲛⲉϩⲛⲁⲁⲩ ⲙ̄ⲡⲁⲉⲓⲱⲧ	τὴν κληρονομίαν	تَرِكة أبي
10	ⲛ̄ⲙ̄ⲙⲁⲉⲓ		
11	ⲡⲉϫⲁϥ ⲛⲁϥ ϫⲉ	ὁ δὲ εἶπεν αὐτῷ·	فقال
12	ⲱ ⲡⲣⲱⲙⲉ	ἄνθρωπε,	
13	ⲛⲓⲙ ⲡⲉ	τίς	ومن
14	ⲛ̄ⲧⲁϩⲁⲁⲧ'	με κατέστησεν	جعلني
15			عليكم
16		κριτὴν ἢ	
17	ⲛ̄ⲣⲉϥⲡⲱϣⲉ	μεριστὴν	قاسماً
18		ἐφ' ὑμᾶς;	
19	ⲁϥⲕⲟⲧϥ ⲁ'		
20	ⲛⲉϥⲙⲁⲑⲏⲧⲏⲥ		
21	ⲡⲉϫⲁϥ ⲛⲁⲩ ϫⲉ	εἶπεν δὲ πρὸς αὐτούς·	
22	ⲙⲏ ⲉⲓⲉϣⲟⲟⲡ'		
23	ⲛ̄ⲣⲉϥⲡⲱϣⲉ		
24		ὁρᾶτε καὶ φυλάσσεσθε	
25		ἀπὸ πάσης πλεονεξίας	

meaning of Jesus' pronouncement as follows: the regulations of the Law were given in Deut. 21,15ff; Jesus refuses to entertain the actual query of the dissatisfied heir, because such matters were already settled by the Law.¹⁴⁸ The Semitic wording behind the Greek μεριστής, either חולק or בעל פלגותא must have been transmitted by the Gospel according to the Hebrews ¹⁴⁹ or by the Jewish-Christian tradition as preserved among the Syrian descendants of the early Palestinian community of Christians.¹⁵⁰ According to this view, Luke found only μεριστής or its Semitic equivalent in his source and added the word κριτής, which makes the whole thing less understandable: the word 'judge' is beside the point, since this was certainly not a case of lawsuit.¹⁵¹

(4) We are confronted with the strange situation that a champion of the Western text, i.c. A. Merx, defends an original reading κριτήν, arguing that this word accurately renders דִּין (דִּינָא) and that *this* word was the only proper one for the situation described in the anecdote, whereas a defender of the independence of Thomas, i.c. G. Quispel, objects to the idea that Jesus could have used that term, and maintains that it was introduced by a mistake on Luke's part. I cannot function as a judge in this case, since I have already shown my preference for the opinion that דינא was present in the Aramaic tradition (cf. 3:4.3-4): Luke found דינא or κριτήν and he added ἢ μεριστήν to explain to his readers that the Jewish *judge* could function as an executor.

(5) The Gospel of Thomas does not merely attest the reading 'divider', but it lays all emphasis on that word, and consequently on the fact that Jesus clearly denied that he was a *divider*. Moreover, this emphasis is augmented by the addition (6:2.8) in which Jesus asks his disciples whether or not He is (or shall be) a divider. This addition is admittedly a secondary development ¹⁵² by which the author of the apocryphon wished to underline the point of the narrative. Gershenson and Quispel believed that the addition presents us with the pun: Jesus' answer to the dissatisfied heir ('I cannot take a hand in the division of property') has been brought to another level through this addition ('because He is not one ...

---

¹⁴⁸ G. Quispel, *o.c.*, 93; cf. also D. Gershenson-G. Quispel, *a.c.*, 24: 'Jesus' strict adherence to the Law'.

¹⁴⁹ D. Gershenson-G. Quispel, *a.c.*, 25.

¹⁵⁰ G. Quispel, Belangrijke Ontdekking, 53f.

¹⁵¹ G. Quispel, *Het Evangelie van Thomas*, 93.

¹⁵² W. Schrage, *Das Verhältnis des Thomasevangeliums zur synoptischen Tradition und zu den koptischen Übersetzungen*, Berlin 1964, 151; even G. Quispel, *o.c.*, acknowledges that it is not authentic (under influence of the short text in ʿAbd al-Ǧabbār?).

who introduces dissenting opinions').[153] Quispel does not seem to have maintained that interpretation in his later studies, where he finds the pun in Jesus' answer to the heir too, and not only in his rhetorical question to the disciples.[154] It seems to me that the addition has no other aim than to reinforce the meaning of Jesus' answer to the heir.[155]

(6) We should take note of the fact that the omission of κριτήν ἤ is not the only variation. Thomas also has no equivalent to ἐφ' ὑμᾶς// عليكم (6:2.7). The omission of ⲉϫⲱⲧⲛ 'over you' is not without significance, for its absence gives to the answer of Jesus a more general and universal meaning. His denial is not only true in this particular case between this man and his brothers (cf.6:2.3), but it is in a general sense a characteristic of the Christ in whom the author of Thomas believes.[156]

(7) Jesus' unwillingness to be a divider is in harmony with the general idea that *division* was the essence and product of the powers of darkness. In logion 61b the author has Jesus say:[157]

> Therefore I say:
> If he is (of?) the same (ⲉϥ-ϣⲏϣ(?)),
> he will be filled with light;
> but if he is divided (ⲉϥ-ⲡⲏϣ)
> he will be filled with darkness.

Division is, according to the Gnostic idea, a characteristic feature of the realm of darkness, that is, of ignorance.[158] Unity means salvation.[159] Jesus is the Unifier (ἑνωθῆναι θέλω καὶ ἑνῶσαι θέλω),[160]

---

[153] D. Gershenson-G. Quispel, *a.c.*, 24f.
[154] G. Quispel, *o.c.*, 92f.
[155] B. Gärtner, *The Theology of the Gospel of Thomas*, London 1961, 174f.
[156] W. Schrage, *o.c.*, 152 ('grundsätzliche Bedeutung').
[157] Cf. A. Guillaumont, H.-Ch. Puech, G. Quispel, W. Till, Y. ʿAbd al-Masīḥ, *L'Évangile selon Thomas*, Leiden 1959, 34 (Pl. 91:31-34). Ms.: ⲉϥϣⲏϥ, cj. ⲉϥϣⲏϣ, apparently on the basis of the foregoing lines (28f.): ⲁⲛⲟⲕ ⲡⲉ ⲡⲉⲧϣⲟⲟⲡ ⲉⲃⲟⲗ ϩⲙ ⲡⲉⲧϣⲏϣ 'I am he who is of (from?) the Same' in which the identity of the earthly and heavenly Son of Man has been expressed.
[158] Cf. M. Malinine, H. Ch. Puech, G. Quispel, *Evangelium Veritatis*, Zürich 1956, 29:1-5 (ⲡⲱϣⲉ); cf. B. Gärtner, *o.c.*, 135, 221.
[159] Cf. Logia 22, 106; B. Gärtner, *o.c.*, 223.
[160] Cf. M. Bonnet, *Acta Apostolorum Apocrypha* II:1, Leipzig 1898, 198, where these words from the Acta Johannis 95 (the hymn of Christ) are found.

who wants man to become *One*.[161] The real Gnostic, therefore, is undivided, the non-Gnostic is divided and rent.[162] Jesus removes the separation and gives Life in unity.[163] The seed of the Logos is unifying power.[164]

(8) Such ideas may have been present in the mind of the author of Thomas when he abbreviated the Lucan phrase. So we have the reverse here of the situation that we found with Marcion. Marcion wished to deny that Jesus was or would be a *judge*; therefore, he left out ἢ μεριστήν. Thomas, on the other hand, wished to make explicit that Jesus had nothing to do with *division*, so he deliberately omitted the words κριτὴν ἢ.

(9) Something ought to be said at this point about the striking parallel to Thomas in ʿAbd al-Ǧabbār's text. We have mentioned the fact that the Gospel quotations in this author's chapter on Christianity are of a free and loose nature. The author (or his predecessor?) has cited his source texts 'in his own way'.[165] Abbreviation is one of the characteristics, cf. *Collation* 6:3.1; 3.3; 3.5). It may have been the cause of *this* omission as well: Jesus' answer is sufficient if it speaks only of 'divider', for it was division that the man was asking for.

The episode figures in a series of proof texts, however, which are meant to demonstrate that Jesus is not the divine being which the Christians claim He is. The question now arises whether *al-qāsim* is a name or title of Allah. In Islam, Allah is the Allotter of Fate, *al-Mānī*, who distributes succes and failure, sweet and bitter, riches and poverty to mankind.[166] This allotment of fate, usually designated as *manīyah*, could also be expressed by derivatives of the root *qsm* (esp. II: qassama), which emphasizes the idea of distribution in the apportioning of fate.[167] Two phrases used by

---

[161] E. Haenchen, *o.c.*, 53f.; B. Gärtner, *o.c.*, 174f.

[162] W. Schrage, *o.c.*, 153.

[163] Cf. W. Till, *Das Evangelium nach Philippos*, Berlin 1967, 118:12ff. (= Ev. Phil. 78).

[164] *Excerpta ex Theodoto* 2, 2, O. Stählin, *Clemens Alexandrinus* III, Leipzig 1909, 116:3.

[165] This is the expression which ʿAbd al-Ǧabbār uses, when he writes: 'None of these Gospels is a commentary upon another Gospel—as someone who writes afterwards comments on a book of someone who wrote before him and quotes the words of the latter *in his own way* (على وجهه) and then gives his comment ...'.

[166] Cf. H. Ringgren, *Studies in Arabian Fatalism*, Uppsala-Wiesbaden 1955, 14.46f. (ref. to Wellhausen).

[167] Cf. H. Ringgren, *o.c.*, 151, 156, 162.

Collation

(6.1) *Luke = Thomas = ʿAbd al-Ǧabbār*

1	(1/3)	εἶπεν ... αὐτῷ	ⲡⲉϫⲉ ... ⲛⲁϥ	قال له
2	(7)	μερίσασθαι	(verbum) ⲡⲱϣⲉ	(verbum) قاسم
3	(8/10)	μετ'ἐμοῦ	ⲛⲙⲙⲁⲉⲓ	– ني
4	(11)	ὁ ... εἶπεν	ⲡⲉϫⲁϥ	قال
5	(13)	τίς	ⲛⲓⲙ (ⲡⲉ ⲛⲧⲁ=)	من
6	(14)	με	-ⲧ-	ني –
7	(17)	μεριστήν	ⲛⲣⲉϥⲡⲱϣⲉ	قاسما

(6.2) *Luke = ʿAbd al-Ǧabbār contra Thomas*

1	(1)	δέ	omitt.	و
2	(4)	διδάσκαλε	omitt.	مر
3	(6)	τῷ ἀδελφῷ μου [sing.]	ⲛⲛⲁⲥⲛⲏⲩ [plur.]	[sing.] احى
4	(8/10)	μετ'ἐμοῦ post verbum	ⲛⲙⲙⲁⲉⲓ post obiectum	ني post verbum –
5	(11)	δέ	omitt.	ف
6	(14)	κατέστησεν	-ⲁⲁ-	جعل
7	(15/18)	ἐφ' ὑμᾶς	omitt.	عليكم
8	(19-23)	omitt.	Addition of a second question	omitt.

(6.3) *Luke = Thomas contra ʿAbd al-Ǧabbār*

1	(5)	εἶπε	ϫⲟⲟⲥ	omitt.
2	(6)	τῷ ἀδελφῷ μου	ⲛⲛⲁⲥⲛⲏⲩ	[nominat.?] احى
3	(11)	αὐτῷ	ⲛⲁϥ	omitt.
4	(12)	ἄνθρωπε	ⲱ ⲡⲣⲱⲙⲉ	omitt.
5	(13)	omitt.	omitt.	و

(6.4) *Luke contra Thomas = ʿAbd la-Ǧabbār*

1	(1-2)	τις ἐκ τοῦ ὄχλου	ⲟ[ⲩⲣⲱⲙⲉ]	وجل
2	(7)	μερίσασθαι (inf.)	ϣⲓⲛⲁ ⲉϥⲛ[ⲁ]ⲡⲱϣⲉ	يقاسم –
3	(9)	omitt.	ⲙⲡⲁⲉⲓⲱⲧ	ابى
4	(16)	κριτὴν ἤ ...	omitt.	omitt.

(6.5) *Luke contra Thomas contra ʿAbd al-Ǧabbār*

1	(9)	τὴν κληρονομίαν	ⲛ̄-ⲡⲣⲁⲛⲁⲁⲩ	تركة

'Abu'l 'Atāhiyah (in the early period of the Abasside era) may serve to illustrate this: 'The shares of the *manāyā* are *distributed* share by share' and 'The *manaya* have been distributed among men'.[168] The *qismah* becomes the share or portion which Allah attributes to a man or the act of apportioning fate on the part of Allah.[169] It seems to me that 'Abd al-Ǧabbār may have interpreted the answer of Jesus to have meant that Jesus was disclaiming the divine right of apportioning fate to men, because this belongs to the sovereign will of Allah alone.

(10) There is no need, therefore, to adduce 'Abd al-Ǧabbār as a chief witness for a particular Jewish-Christian tradition of the story of the dissatisfied heir. The agreement between Thomas and 'Abd al-Ǧabbār in this regard may be nothing else than an odd coincidence, just as the agreement between Thomas and the one Sahidic manuscript (resp. ⲡⲉϥⲡⲱϣⲉ and ⲡⲉϥⲡⲱⲣϫ) may be a casual one.[170] The fact that someone could find a text with 'Judge or divider' and still copy only the word 'divider' is not strange. The quotations of St. Augustine, to which we shall turn our attention in a separate paragraph, tend to substantiate this.[171]

6.2. *Luke and 'Abd al-Ǧabbār against Thomas*

(1) Besides two or three less important variations between Luke// 'Abd al-Ǧabbār *and* Thomas (*Collation* 6: 2.1; 2.4; 2.5).[172] there are several elements which seem quite important. Two of them have been discussed in our observations on the pivot word 'divider', namely, the omission of ἐφ' ὑμᾶς (2.7) and the addition of Jesus' word to the disciples (2:8); both of these variations tend to stress the essence of the saying in Thomas.[173] It is possible that a third variation (2.3) points in the same direction: here we have to do

---

[168] *o.c.*, 162 (ref. to 249, 1 and 34, 5).

[169] *o.c.*, 151.156.

[170] W. Schrage, *Das Verhältnis*, 152; Schrage takes for granted that Horner's text (cf. par. 4, n. 1) contains the original Sahidic reading (cf. 152, n. 2: 'Allerdings ist ein Teil von *Sa* nachträglich ausgefüllt worden'); moreover, he does not sufficiently deal with the various differences between *Sah* and *Thomas* (including the difference -ⲡⲱⲣϫ and -ⲡⲱϣⲉ).

[171] Cf. par. 7.

[172] The omission of δέ is found both in vs. 13 (Sah[129] Geo Old Latin *f*) and vs. 14 (Old Latin *a*).

[173] The introduction of this addition partly agrees with Lk 12, 15 (εἶπεν δὲ πρὸς αὐτούς) especially in the version of Sy^pT^A (= vs. 22): 'Said . . . to his disciples' (contra Sy^s.c (— vs. 14): 'Said . . . to the crowds'); for the agreement with H. E. fragm. 11, cf. par. 4, n. 37.

not with a case between a man and his brother but rather between someone and his *brothers*; the brothers are probably the members of the religious brotherhood to which the author belongs.[174] The quarrel has to do not with an earthly affair between two men but with a religious question of a more general importance.

'*Master . . .*'

(2) The omission of διδάσκαλε in Thomas may be quite interesting. There is a difficulty in the interpretation of 'Abd al-Ǧabbār's text. Pines' first reading of the manuscript resulted in the transcription *murā*, which he interpreted as a rendering of Aramaic *mārā* ('master', 'sir') as it was pronounced—*mōrō*—in one branch of the Syriac language.[175] The usual Arabic transcription of the word, however, is مار (= ܡܪܐ) or ماری (= ܡܪܝ), although the reading مُرّ is also possible.[176] 'Uthman's edition actually offered the reading مر to which Pines has given his approval, although he insists upon his own vocalization مُرْ (*mur*).[177] The translation of the Arabic word is usually 'Master' (so Pines and Quispel), but it should be kept in mind that ܡܪܝ is κύριε, not διδάσκαλε.[178] Of course, one may say that مر is nothing more than a free rendering of the underlying Syriac word (ܡܠܦܢܐ ?), but one cannot be certain.[179]

(3) If the omission of the word διδάσκαλε represents a preservation of the original, *pre-Lucan* tradition here, one might conclude that the addition of the address in Luke was merely a *Lucan* redaction. If this were true, the addition of an address in 'Abd al-Ǧabbār might have been inspired by the *canonical* text of Luke. But it is doubtful that the omission of Thomas originated in the Aramaic, pre-synoptic stage of tradition.

(4) Διδάσκαλε is not a favourite Lucan term. If he did in fact

---

[174] W. Schrage, *Das Verhältnis*, 152.
[175] S. Pines, *The Jewish Christians*, 13, n. 35.
[176] Cf. G. Graf, *Verzeichniss Arabischer kirchlicher Termini*, Louvain 1952, 103.
[177] S. Pines, "Israel, my Firstborn", 177, n. 3 (= 178).
[178] A substitution of διδάσκαλε by κύριε is already found in Mt 8, 25 (//Mk 4, 28).
[179] My first impression was, on the basis of the reading مرا, that the author (or his spokesman) was acquainted with Hebrew מוֹרֶה and transliterated it in Arabic *mura*.

use it, he merely adopted the wording of his sources, Q: 6,40, or G (=Mk or proto-Mk): 8,49; 9,38; 10,25; 18,18; 20,21; 20,28; 22,11. It occurs in his *special* matter five times, namely 7,40; 11,45; 19,39; 20,39 and 21,7; in two of these instances it was Luke's editorial hand which added the term to his source text. The *first* occurrence is Lk 20,39, where Luke concluded the dispute concerning the resurrection (=G) with a touch of his own, viz. 'and some of the scribes answered and said: *Teacher*, you have spoken well'. It is clear that he merely repeats the address which in his source was already present at the beginning of the episode (Lk 20, 28// Mk 12,19//Mt 22,24). The *second* instance is found in Lk 21,7, a phrase not present in Matthew or Mark; but here again he was led by his source, cf. Mk 13,1. This dependence on his sources, even where he added a touch of his own, makes it reasonable to assume that he was also guided by his sources in the three other places, 7,40; 11,45; 19,39.

Luke omitted the word διδάσκαλε in one Q-passage, namely, 9,57//Mt 8,19; and he replaced the word διδάσκαλε of his source (cf. Mk 4,38; 9,38) by the term ἐπιστάτα (8,24; 9,49), which is a favourite word of his.[180] He used the latter term also as a substitution for ῥαββί (9,33//Mk 9,5) and once (in 8,45) he added it where his source (cf. Mk 5,31) did not have an equivalent. Moreover, the word ἐπιστάτα is found twice in Luke's *Sondergut*, 5,5 and 7,13. On the basis of this it is reasonable to make the conjecture that the address διδάσκαλε in Lk 12,13 was not Luke's own invention; it probably stood in the tradition passed unto him.

(5) On the other hand, there may be an explanation of why Thomas omitted the word in the address. In logion 13, which closely ressembles the episode of Mt 16,13ff.,[181] we are told how Jesus asked his disciples to say what He was like. An angel, says Peter; a philosopher, is the predicate given by Matthew. But Thomas answers: '*Master*, my mouth is totally incapable of saying what You are like'. Jesus replies: 'I am not your *Master* (ⲁⲛⲟⲕ ⲡⲉⲕⲥⲁϩ ⲁⲛ), because you drank and became drunk from the bubbling spring which I have measured out'. Thomas is to be congrat-

---

[180] Cf. A. Oepke, ἐπιστάτης, *T.W.N.T.* II (1935), 619f.; O. Glombitza, Die Titel διδάσκαλος und ἐπιστάτης für Jesus bei Lukas, *Zeitschrift für die Neutestamentliche Wissenschaft*, 49 (1958), 275-278; T. Schramm, *Der Markusstoff bei Lukas*, Cambridge 1971, 58f.
[181] A. Guillaumont a.o., *L'Évangile selon Thomas*, Pl. 82:30-34, 83:1-14.

ulated, for he gave the right answer. Jesus is beyond comparison and words. He who knows this truth is no longer a disciple. For him the necessity of saying 'Master' [182] no longer exists. Jesus' reply does not mean to indicate that he refuses to accept the title 'Master', but only that there is a time when one is a disciple (so Peter and Matthew, who remain disciples) and a time when one is beyond discipleship (so Thomas). The man who asks Jesus to intervene against his brothers, however, is apparently not or not yet a disciple, and thus neither is Jesus his Master.[183]

'appointed'

(6) G. Quispel, in tracing Jewish-Christian traditions in the Gospel of Thomas, was very interested in two variant readings which Thomas shared with the Pepysian Gospel harmony: first, the addition 'of my father' (*Collation* 6:4.3), secondly, the reading 'made' instead of 'appointed' (6:2.6).[184] With regard to the latter it may be said that the medieval English harmony text ('Who makeþ me judge and partener over ȝou')[185] seems to be a good representative of the Western Diatessaron, for the same reading is found in other witnesses:

Diatessaron Venetum (c. 98)[186]   *chi m' ha fatto zudese . . .*
Diatessaron Leodiense (c. 144)[187] *wie heft mi ghemakt richtre . . .*
Diatessaron Theodiscum   *wer hat mich gemachet richtere . . .*
(c. 134)[188]
Diatessaron Haarense (c. 134)[189] *wie heef mi ghemaect rechter . . .*
Diatessaron Stuttgartensis   *wie heift mi gemaect rechtre . . .*
(c. 134)[190]

I agree with Quispel that there must have been an (original?) Latin harmony having the text 'quis me *fecit* iudicem . . .', instead of

---

[182] W. Schrage's reference (*Das Verhältnis*, 152, n. 4) seems to imply this.
[183] Papyrus Egerton II ro (A. de Santos Otero, *Los Evangelios Apocrifos*, Madrid 1956, 105) has Jesus say τί με καλεῖτε τῷ στόματι διδάσκαλον.
[184] G. Quispel, *Het Evangelie van Thomas*, 93f.
[185] M. Goates, *The Pepysian Gospel Harmony*, London 1922, 40:27f.
[186] V. Todesco, *Il Diatessaron Veneto* (Studi e Testi 81, part I), Città del Vaticano 1938, 91:24.
[187] C. C. de Bruin, *Het Luikse Diatessaron*, Leiden 1970, 144:27f.
[188] Chr. Gerhard, *Das Leben Jhesu*, Leiden 1970, 88:5.
[189] C. C. de Bruin, *Het Haarense Diatessaron*, Leiden 1970, 61:36.
[190] J. Bergsma, *De Levens van Jezus in het Middelnederlandsch*, Leiden 1898, 144 (the Hague MS.: 'wie heift mi gemaect enen richter . . .').

'quis me *constituit* iudicem ...' (Codex Fuldensis).[191] The question is, however, whether this reading—even if it were the reading of the *original* Latin Diatessaron—was also the reading of the *Syriac* Diatessaron.

(7) Unfortunately, the text of the Syriac Diatessaron has not been preserved. The proposal of I. Ortiz de Urbina,[192] namely, that the *Liber Graduum* presents us with the text of the harmony, seems hardly acceptable since its text, ܡܢܘ ܐܩܝܡܟ ܥܠܝܢ ܪܝܫܐ ܘܕܝܢܐ 'Who has appointed me over you a head and a judge',[193] is apparently a paraphrase of the parallel in Exod 2,14. As we have seen, it is more probable that in his copy of the Diatessaron Mar Ephraem found the same text as that presently contained in Sy[s] and Sy[c].[194]

(8) Interestingly enough, the Syriac Pentateuch in Lee's recension offers a text of Exod 2,14 which contains the reading 'made':[195]

ܡܢܘ ܥܒܕܟ ܠܓܒܪܐ ܪܝܫܐ ܘܕܝܢܐ ܥܠܝܢ
'Who has *made* you a chief man and a judge over us?'

It is sometimes suggested that the redactor of the Diatessaron usually borrowed his Old Testament quotations or references from the Syriac Bible, or at least that he was influenced by its diction. According to this argument, thus, the original Diatessaron could have contained the verb 'made' influenced by Exod 2,14 Peš. Apart from the fact that there is no specific indication that the Diatessaron text differed from that of Sy[s] and Sy[c], however, there is the difficulty that we do not know which Old Testament text the author of the harmony had at his disposal. In my opinion it is possible to postulate three different fourth century versions of Exod. 2,14:

1. (Lee/Barnes) ܡܢܘ ܥܒܕܟ ܠܓܒܪܐ ܪܝܫܐ ܘܕܝܢܐ ܥܠܝܢ
2. (*Liber Graduum*)[196] ܡܢܘ ܐܩܝܡܟ ܥܠܝܢ ܪܝܫܐ ܘܕܝܢܐ
3. (Aphrahat)[197] ܡܢܘ ܐܩܝܡܟ ܥܠܝܢ ܫܠܝܛܐ ܘܕܝܢܐ

---

[191] G. Quispel, *o.c.*, 94. He wrongly reconstructs the Latin text with 'aut' (= Cod. Fuld.); it should be 'et' (cf. par. 3, n. 7).

[192] I. Ortiz de Urbina, *Vetus Evangelium Syrorum*, 230; cf. par. 2, n. 29, par. 3, n. 7.

[193] M. Kmosko, *Liber Graduum*, 29:7-8.

[194] Cf. par. 3:2-3.

[195] W. E. Barnes, *Pentateuchus Syriace*, London 1914, 101.

[196] We may reconstruct this form of text if we consider the N.T. quotation as a paraphrasis of the O.T. text.

[197] *Demonstratio* II: 8, ed. J. Parisot, *Patrologia Syriaca* I, 1894 Paris, 64:25f.

Lee's text agrees with Targumic tradition in having the rendering ܓܒܪ ܪܒ (= גבר רב) [198] for the Hebrew אִישׁ שַׂר, but Aphrahat's text contains a reading which has its parallel in Codex Neofyti I.[199] One might say that the place of the term ܥܠ within the quotations of Aphrahat and *Liber Graduum* (as opposed to the place in Lee's text = M.T. & Targums) was influenced by the place of the reading ܥܠܝܟ in Sy[s.c.p], but since Sy[s.c.p] differ from the Greek text of Luke in this regard, one could as easily maintain that these versions have been influenced by a biblical text of type 2 or 3. As for the verb, the Hebrew wording מִי שָׂמְךָ allows various renderings, such as מִן שׂבאתך (Sam. Pent.), מִן שׁוִיך (Onk.), מן שוי יתך (Neof. I), מאן הוא דמני יתך (Ps.-Jon.) and the Syriac renderings found in 1 and 2-3. It is not impossible that ܥܒܕ was found in manuscripts of the second century. It cannot be concluded with any certainty, however, that Tatian knew this word and used it for his harmony. Likewise, the fact that the Western Diatessaron witnesses presuppose the reading 'fecit' does not necessarily imply that it was the verb ܥܒܕ that was used by Tatian for his Diatessaron.

(9) But let us assume that the verb ܥܒܕ was in his Diatessaron text. Does that mean that there was a Jewish-Christian tradition which contained the verb עבד? Was it *this* verb that gave rise to two different translations, namely ἐποίησεν/'made' (Thomas and Diatessaron) *and* κατέστησεν (Luke). I doubt it—not so much because the Hebrew verb עבד *never* became καθίσταναι in the LXX,[200] but even more because I think we are not entitled to make such sharp distinctions. In a Sahidic text of Acts 7,27.35 [201] we find respectively ⲡⲉⲛⲧⲁϥⲕⲁⲑⲓⲥⲧⲁ and ⲡⲉⲛⲧⲁϥⲣⲣⲟ as renderings of κατέστησεν. There is not a single reason to suggest that the Greek copy used by the Coptic translator contained both κατέστησεν and ἐποίησεν. Therefore, the possibility ought not to be excluded that

---

[198] Cf. A. Brüll, *Das Samaritanische Targum zum Pentateuch*, Hildesheim-New York (repr.) 1971, 64; A. Sperber, *The Pentateuch according to Targum Onkelos*, Leiden 1959, 91; M. Ginzburger, *Pseudo-Jonathan*, Berlin 1903, 100; A. Díez Macho, *Neophyti I: II. Éxodo*, Madrid 1970, 9.

[199] ܥܠܝܟ, cf. שליט in Targum Neophyti I.

[200] In Deut 16, 18, the LXX renders שֹׁפְטִים ... תִּתֶּן־לְךָ with κριτάς ... καταστήσεις σεαυτῷ, but Ms.B reads ποιήσεις. This may be an example of how easily καθίσταναι 'to appoint', could be converted into ποιεῖν.

[201] E. A. Wallis Budge, *Coptic Biblical Texts in the Dialects of Upper Egypt*, London 1912, 156f.

the Greek text underlying the wording of Thomas, ⲛⲓⲙ ⲡⲉⲛⲧⲁϩⲁⲁⲧ, could have been τίς με κατέστησεν.[202]

6.3. *Luke and Thomas against ʿAbd al-Ǧabbār*

(1) The agreements between Luke and Thomas against ʿAbd al-Ǧabbār are not very impressive. The Arabic text reveals a tendency toward abbreviation (6:3.1; 3.3; 3.4).[203] Omissions of words such as αὐτῷ (cf. cursive *1241*) and ἄνθρωπε (cf. cursive *69*) easily occur in transmissions of a text. The alteration of 'say to my brother' to 'let my brother' is not based upon a non-synoptic or pre-Lucan tradition, but is merely a paraphrase of the text found in Luke and Thomas. The only addition (6:3.5)—of 'and' before 'who'—is idiomatic.[204]

'*Man, . . .*'

(2) The agreement between Thomas and Luke in 6:3.4 may be significant. One should not stress the small incongruity between (ⲱ ⲡⲣⲱⲙⲉ) and Luke (ἄνθρωπε alone). In keeping with Koine usage, the use of the vocative particle ὤ is not frequent in the New Testament (cf. Rm 2, 1.3; 9,20; James 2,20).[205] In textual tradition, however, the bare vocative invites the addition of an interjection.[206] This is especially true for the versions. In our passage we read 'O homo' in Old Latin *b r¹ δ gat* Augustine (once), Missale Mozarabicum (PL 85,257), Diatessaron Venetum; 'la man' in the West-Saxon Gospels, and يااانسان in the Arabic version of Walton's Polyglot (V,325).

(3) The agreement is especially important because there is reason to assume that the vocative ἄνθρωπε is a 'favourite' word of Luke.[207] Here it is found in his 'Sondergut', but elsewhere a comparison is possible: in 5,20, where the parallels (Mt 9,2/Mk 2,5)

---

[202] R. Kasser, *L'Évangile selon Thomas*, Neuchâtel 1961, 95, reconstructs the Greek text thus: τίς με ἐποίησεν μεριστήν;, but he admits in a note: καθέστησεν pas impossible.

[203] Cf. vs. 13: omitt. αὐτῷ 1241 *b ff² i 1*.

[204] Preceeding 'and' is frequent in Arabic; it occurs also in Hebrew and Aramaic, *and* in Greek too, cf. W. Bauer, *Wörterbuch*, s.v. καί (I.2.h), 712.

[205] F. Blass, A. Debrunner, *Grammatik des neutestamentlichen Griechisch*, Göttingen ⁹1954, par. 146.

[206] In Augustine's quotations, the introductory word *dic(, homo, quis . . .)* deliberately contrasts Jesus' saying with the request of the man *dic(fratri meo . . .)*, see par. 7:2.

[207] Cf. J. C. Hawkins, *Horae Synopticae*, Oxford 1899, 14.29.

have Jesus saying τέκνον [208] to the paralytic man, and in 22,58.60, where the parallels (Mt 26,72.74; Mk 14,71; Jn 18,25) have no equivalent, the vocative ἄνθρωπε is used. I am not qualified to judge whether the use of this form of address is 'un-Jewish',[209] but that it is accepted Greek usage may be concluded from its frequent use in such Diatribe texts as the 'Discourses' of Epictetus.[210]

(4) It is true that ἄνθρωπε occurs in some apocryphal traditions, namely: in the famous addition of *Codex Bezae* to Luke 6,4, which in its present form is a Marcionite version of an (Palestinian?) agraphon;[211] *and* in the story of the rich youth as found in the Gospel according to the Hebrews, fragment 11.[212] Was it present in the original texts of these traditions? In the latter passage, we must reckon with the possibility that the word slipped into the text when it was translated from Aramaic into Greek or from Greek into Latin.

(5) It can be argued that here and elsewhere in Luke ἄνθρωπε comes from the hand of the author and not from his sources. This would make it highly probable that Thomas is dependent on Luke at this point.

6.4. *Thomas and ʿAbd al-Ǧabbār against Luke*

(1) This fourth series of comparisons shows some very interesting variations, which are important because they could potentially reveal the particular Jewish-Christian tradition that some scholars

---

[208] The address Τέκνον to someone who has no intimate relationship with the speaker (such as son, slave or pupil) occurs only here in the N.T.; it is found in Greek texts (cf. W. Bauer, *o.c.* s.v. τέκνον 2a, 1469) and in Semitic texts (cf. Sifra 26, 9, M. Smith, *Tannaitic Parallels*, 170 (n. 40), cf. also G. Dalman, *Jesus-Jeschua*, Leipzig 1922, 182f).

[209] Cf. G. Dalman, *loc. cit.*; *Worte Jesu I*, Leipzig ²1930, 32 ('Graecismus'), 370; J. Jeremias, *Unbekannte Jesusworte*, Gütersloh ³1973, 61 (and n. 48).

[210] Cf. Epictetus, *The Discourses* (ed. W. Oldfather, *Epictetus II*, London-Cambridge (Mass.) 1966, III, 14.2-5; 15, 9; 19, 5; 20, 16 and passim.

[211] Marcion and Codex Bezae agree with respect to the post-position of vs. 5 (after vs. 10); for the Palestinian origin, cf. J. Jeremias, *o.c.*, 61f.

[212] K. Aland, *Synopsis quattuor Evangeliorum*, Stuttgart 1964, 340 (64-71), G. Quispel, *Makarius*, 79f.; J. Jeremias, *o.c.*, 47ff.—Quispel makes it one of the stylistic arguments for the theory of Thomas' dependence on a Jewish-Christian source: Thomas 72: ... O man, ... He turned to his disciples ... ; H.E. fr. 11: ... homo ... et conversus dixit Simoni discipulo suo ... It is clear, that this similarity cannot support that theory. Quispel, on the other hand, refuses to accept a dependence of Thomas on Luke 10, 23 στραφείς πρὸς τοὺς μαθητάς (he may be right in this) on account of the fact that Thomas did not know Luke (*quod erat demonstrandum*, T.B.), cf. par. 4, notes 10 and 37.

contend as a source for Thomas. The main locus in terms of which that contention is argued—*Collation* 6:4.4—has already been dealt with in par.6:1, and our investigation there did not lessen our hesitations with respect to this construction of matters. Another interesting agreement between the Coptic text and the Arabic document is the addition: 'of my father' (6:4.3), which we shall discuss later. The deviation registered under 6:4.2 is only a seeming one: the infinitive μερίσασθαι, which after the verb εἰπέ has the same intrinsic value as constructions with ὅπως or ἵνα, could easily be rendered with ϣⲓⲛⲁ ⲉϥⲛⲁⲡⲱϣⲉ (ἵνα + fut. III) or with يقاسم (subj./imperf.).

'A man out of the multitude'

(2) The first variation (6:4.1) requires some preliminary remarks. The Coptic words are found in the topline of fol. 94, or rather, they are largely missing there due to the fact that the top of the page has been damaged. The conjecture of the editors [213] is now generally accepted and is, indeed, wholly justified. It is wrong to say, however, that the new text of ʿAbd al-Ǧabbār *proves* the correctness of the conjecture.[214] The fact that the introduction of the previous quotation (Mk 10,17 parr.) is the same as that of our passage (وقال له رجل) [215] should warn us to exercise some caution at this point: this may represent the Muslim author's free introduction of the Gospel passages.

(3) It is most interesting to read what T. W. Manson wrote, long before the discovery of Thomas, in his comments on Luke 12,13f.: 'The unknown person who appeals to Jesus is described by Luke as "one out of the multitude". No doubt it replaces a still more indefinite phrase, such as "a certain man".' [216] Apparently, Manson meant to say that ἐκ τοῦ ὄχλου was redactional in Luke's reproduction of the source material. I think he was definitely correct in making that assumption. Luke had to connect the isolated apophthegma (vss. 13-14) with the larger framework of ch. 12: vs. 1 τῶν μυριάδων τοῦ ὄχλου—vs. 54 ἔλεγεν δὲ καὶ τοῖς ὄχλοις. The speaker could not be one of the disciples (who are on the

---

[213] A. Guillaumont, a.o., *L'Évangile selon Thomas*, 40.
[214] So G. Quispel, *Het Evangelie van Thomas*, 92.
[215] Ed. ʿUthman, p. 113:8.
[216] T. W. Manson, *The Sayings of Jesus*, London (repr.) 1964 (= ²1949, = ¹1937), 271. Cf. W. Schrage, *Das Verhältnis*, 151; G. Quispel, *o.c.*, 92.

scene in vss. 1-12 and 22ff.) but must have belonged to the audience in the background, the crowd.

(4) It has been assumed that the Greek copy of Thomas must have contained the wording ἄνθρωπος or ἄνθρωπός τις.[217] It seems to me that the reading ἀνήρ or ἀνήρ τις might also be considered as a possible equivalent to ⲟⲩⲣⲱⲙⲉ.[218] The question now is whether this hypothetical reading ἄνθρωπος <τις> or ἀνήρ <τις> was a rendering of a pre- or at least non-Lucan tradition. The fact that both expressions are often regarded as *Semitisms* [219] seems to leave room for an affirmative answer to that question.[220] But is it really true that Luke wrote the better Greek form (τις) here, whereas Thomas retained the Semitic and consequently more original form (ἄνθρωπος, ἀνήρ) of the anecdote. Do we have conclusive evidence for the thesis that Thomas represents the original tradition?[221] I doubt it.

(5) Luke did not hesitate to use ἄνθρωπος [222] or ἀνήρ <τις> [223] in his writings. The expression ἄνθρωπός τις, which scarcely occurs in the more 'Semitic' Mark and Matthew, is found no less than seven times in the *Sondergut* of Luke.[224] Even where he was definitely not dependent on an Aramaic source, he made use of such expressions as ἄνθρωπός τις [225] and ἀνήρ τις.[226] If these expressions are Semitisms, they certainly belong to Luke's vocabulary. Is there really any reason to assume that Luke found ἄνθρωπός τις in his source and refused to adopt it in his rendering of the story for stylistic or linguistic reasons?

(6) Thomas and 'Abd al-Ǧabbār are not the only witnesses to the reading 'a man', for the Old Syriac text (Sy[s.c]) has ܓܒܪܐ ܚܕ

---

[217] Cf. R. Kasser, *o.c.*, 95; G. Quispel, *o.c.*, 92: 'In het Grieks moet er "anthroopos" ... gestaan hebben'.

[218] Cf. M. Wilmet, *Concordance du Nouveau Testament sahidique* II:2, Louvain 1958, 687f. ⲣⲱⲙⲉ = ἀνήρ, 148×; ⲣⲱⲙⲉ = ἄνθρωπος, 539×; we should notice the fact that ⲣⲱⲙⲉ might render the indefinite pronoun τις (so twice: Lk 7, 41; Mt 11, 25).

[219] G. Quispel, *loc. cit.*

[220] Some caution is necessary, because ἄνθρωπος sometimes occurs in the meaning 'someone' (cf. e.g. Epictetus, *The Discourses*, II, 13.1; III, 23.15); cf. F. Blass, A. Debrunner, *Grammatik*, par. 361.

[221] G. Quispel, *loc. cit.*

[222] Cf. Lk 2, 25; 4, 33; 6, 6; 20, 9 (+ τις?).

[223] ἀνήρ Lk (5, 12) 8, 41; 9, 38; 19, 2; 23, 50 and 8, 27 (+ τις).

[224] Lk 10, 30; 14, 2.16; 15, 11; 16, 1.19; 19, 12; 20, 9(?). Only 13, 23 has εἶπε δέ τις αὐτῷ (cf. 11, 1).

[225] Not only Acts 9, 33, but also 25, 16.

[226] Not only Acts 3, 2; 5, 1; 8, 9; 10, 1; 14, 8, but also 16, 9; 25, 14.

scl. 'one man', 'a man' instead of ܐܢܫ 'someone' (sy^p). Of course, it is possible to attribute their wording to the influence of the Western Aramaic wording of that hypothetical pre- or non-synoptic tradition that is supposed to have left its traces in Thomas and ʿAbd al-Ǧabbār. But there is not a single indication in the Old Syriac text of Luke 13,12f. that such a foreign tradition has influenced its wording. The same thing happened here as did in Mt 19,16, where Greek εἷς ('someone') was rendered with ܓܒܪܐ ܚܕ (Sy^{s.c}; Sy^p: ܐܢܫ). If any dependence is to be assumed, it would be more natural in my view to consider the possibility of a Syriac influence on Thomas and ʿAbd al-Ǧabbār.

(7) The Lucan τις may have been a mere reproduction of the wording in his source. The Aramaic tradition behind that source may have contained such words as חד (אחד), (א)נש or אנשא[227]. It was Luke who combined τις with the ὄχλος of ch.12: τις ἐκ τοῦ ὄχλου. The omission of the last three words in the Coptic and Arabic texts does not necessarily point to a pre-Lucan tradition, for it would be quite understandable for a narrator to omit these words if he were quoting the story detached from its original setting and did not intend to give historical information about the historical situation.[228]

(8) My conclusion, therefore, is that the evidence of Thomas and ʿAbd al-Ǧabbār cannot bear the burden of proof for the existence of a more original Aramaic tradition which deviates from the revised form of the story in Luke.

6.5. *Three different readings?*

(1) The last category of our *Collation* consists of only one instance (6:5.1) in which the three texts seem to differ from each other, namely when they describe the inheritance, although the Arabic and Coptic texts agree with each other in adding 'of my father' (6:4.3). The reading of the Arabic text was first assumed to be بركات ابي, lit. 'the blessings of my father', that is, the possessions or wealth of my father.[229] In ʿUthman's text, however, we are presented with a different wording, تركة ابي, which means 'de *nalatenschap*

---

[227] Cf. M. Black, *An Aramaic Approach to the Gospels and Acts*, Oxford ²1954, 248ff.; 250, n.2.
[228] Cf. also W. Schrage, *Das Verhältnis*, 152.
[229] Cf. S. Pines, *The Jewish Christians*, 13, n. 35: 'blessing'; G. Quispel, Belangrijke Ontdekking, II, 53: 'de rijkdom'; The Discussion, 86: 'wealth' *Het Evangelie van Thomas*, 91: 'de overvloedige bezittingen'.

van mijn vader' (which is synonym for 'erfenis', 'inheritance'), i.e., the things that my father has left behind. If the reading of ʿUthman is justified, it may be asked whether there is a real difference between Luke and the Arabic text at this point.

(2) As to the wording of Luke, κληρονομία, it may be said that it fits in well with the verb μερίζειν, since the combination of these words is usual both in biblical and profane Greek. There seems to be no conclusive reason for attributing to Luke an editorial correction in the material transmitted to him.[230]

(3) The text of Thomas, on the other hand, has all the features of a secondary development: there is a gnosticizing tendency in its wording.[231] Logion 61, which we have already discussed (par. 6:1.7), relates how Jesus speaks the mysterious words: [232]

> I am he who is from the Same,
> to me is given *from the things of my Father*

The last words (ⲉⲃⲟⲗ ϩⲛ̄ⲙⲁ ⲡⲁⲉⲓⲱⲧ, cf. ⲉⲃⲟⲗ ϩⲓⲧⲛ̄ ⲙ̄ⲡⲁⲉⲓⲱⲧ in Mt 11, 27//Lk, 10,22) are reminiscent of the Sahidic translation of ἐν τοῖς τοῦ πατρός μου in Luke 2,49 (ϩⲛ̄ ⲛⲁ ⲡⲁⲉⲓⲱⲧ), which is among the favourite texts of the Gnostics.[233] As we have seen, logion 61 sheds some light upon the idea of division and unity. The things of the Father cannot be divided, for they are the treasure of light. Any division of the things of the Father would result in darkness. There can be hardly any doubt that the author of Thomas replaced the ordinary word 'inheritance' by an expression that would be almost immediately clear to his readers.

(4) The addition, 'of my father', was therefore not a real addition, because it was required to define the neutral word 'things'. Quispel has made 'of my father' a test case for the common dependence of Thomas and ʿAbd al-Ǧabbār on some Aramaic source.[234] He was strengthened in that conviction through the reading of the Pepysian harmony ('ƿe heritage of his fader'), which in his view proves that the Diatessaron had been influenced by the same Ara-

---

[230] Ed. ʿUthman, 113:9.
[231] W. Schrage, *loc. cit.*: 'fraglos sekundär'; B. Gärtner, *The Theology*, 174f.
[232] Cf. A. Guillaumont, a.o., *L'Évangile selon Thomas*, 34 (Pl. 91:28-30: ⲁⲛⲟⲕ· ⲡⲉ ⲡⲉⲧϣⲟⲟⲡ· ⲉⲃⲟⲗ ϩⲙ̄ ⲡⲉⲧϣⲏϣ ⲁⲩϯ ⲛⲁⲉⲓ ⲉⲃⲟⲗ ϩⲛ̄ ⲛⲁ ⲡⲁⲉⲓⲱⲧ.
[233] W. Schrage, *loc. cit.*
[234] G. Quispel, *o.c.*, 91.

maic source.[235] It seems to me that the addition in this medieval text has nothing to do with the Diatessaron. The word 'hereditatem' standing alone could easily invite the addition of some defining word, e.g., 'onsen' (Liège Harmony), 'uncer' (Wessex Gospels). The author of the English harmony may have felt the need to define the inheritance as *patrimony*. The same may be true in the case of ʿAbd al-Ǧabbār's text. The somewhat neutral word كَرْ lit., 'what is left (behind)', 'inheritance' needs some explanation: that which is left behind by the father.

6.6. *Conclusion*

In this section I have dealt with the thesis of G. Quispel that the Gospel of Thomas was partly based on a Western Aramaic Gospel tradition current in Jewish-Christian circles. It was not my intention to try to disprove this thesis in general, but only to investigate the origins of one logion of that apocryphal Gospel. The question was, whether this particular saying was no more than a fixed point in the history of the Lucan *text* or whether it belonged to the sediment of a separate, pre- or non-canonical stream of *tradition*. Quispel defended the latter alternative. He made logion 72 the decisive evidence for his whole theory. In his view, the discovery of the Arabic document could prove that he was right in that, so that any other opinion was rendered out of date (par. 5:2.3). All I could do was to show some weak points in his argumentation. My research leads me to a different view, namely, that this logion presents us with the Gnostic version of Luke 12, 13-14, just as the Syro-Latin text presents us with the Marcionite version of that Lucan passage. The text of Luke was subservient to various aims. One might speak of dogmatical corrections of the text, but one ought not to say that the Gnostic author and Marcion deliberately perverted the text they knew and used. The way they understood the text was the only way in which the text became meaningful to them. This procedure is not restricted to heretics alone. St. Augustine, who seems above suspicion of heresy, should make that clear to us.

The Text of St. Augustine

7.1. *An African Western Text?*

The short form 'divider' is not restricted to the Coptic and

---
[235] G. Quispel, *o.c.*, 93.

Arabic documents mentioned; it occurs also in the writings of St. Augustine. This phenomenon, of course, did not escape Quispel's attention (par. 4: 5.2). He argues that the identity between Thomas and the Sahidic Gospel text does not imply any dependence of the former on the latter, which is a correct conclusion. But he continues: If it were necessary to assume such a dependence, St. Augustine should be said to have been influenced by the Sahidic Gospel as well, for this church father offers a similar reading, 'Who has appointed me a *divider* of the inheritance among you?'. According to Quispel, this cannot be true. And again, he is right in this conclusion. Thus, another explanation is required. Quispel's solution is that the Jewish-Christian tradition which has been assimilated by the Gospel of Thomas has influenced both the Coptic and African texts. St. Augustine is a witness to *another* Western Text which had its roots, directly or indirectly, in the archaic Jewish-Christian traditions.[236] I am afraid, however, that Quispel's admirable and intuitive scholarship has failed to perceive the real state of affairs here, and, therefore, that his conclusion may be wrong.

7.2. *The quotations of St. Augustine*

The passage to which Quispel referred [237] is not the only place at which Augustine deals with the text of Luke 12,13f. In no less than six of his sermons mention is made of the question of the dissatisfied heir and Jesus' answer. The interesting thing is that all these sermons date from the same period, i.e., from the time just before and after the *Collatio Carthaginiensis cum Donatistis* which took place in June, 411 A.D. The references are found in the following homilies:

(1) *Sermo de utilitate ieiunii* [238] which was most probably held at Carthage in Lent of the year 411. The sermon may have been delivered on May 14 of that year.[239]

(2) *Sermo (CCCLVIII) de pace et charitate*.[240] This sermon seems to have been preached shortly before the Collation, possibly at the end of May, 411.[241]

---

[236] G. Quispel, *Het Evangelie van Thomas*, 93.
[237] G. Quispel, *o.c.*, 139, n. 116: Sermo 359, 3.
[238] S. D. Ruegg, *De utilitate ieiunii*, in: *Aurelii Augustini Opera* XIII:2, Turnhout 1969, 225-241.
[239] S. D. Ruegg, *o.c.*, 227. The text of Luke is quoted on page 241.
[240] Ed. J. P. Migne, *P.L.* 39 (Paris 1845), 1586-1590, esp. 1587.
[241] A. Kunzelmann, Die Chronologie der Sermones des Hl. Augustinus, in: *Miscellanea Agostiniana* II, Roma 1931, 417-520, esp. 448; 514.518.

(3) *Sermo (CVII) de verbis Evangelii Lucae*, 'Dico vobis, abstinete ab omni avaritia' (Luc. xii.13 sq.).[242] The date must have been 411 A.D., in May or June, but before the Collation.[243]

(4) *Sermo (CCCLIX) in Eccles.* xxv.2, 'Concordia fratrum, etc.'.[244] The Collation was a thing of the recent past. We are now in the last months of 411 A.D.[245]

(5) *Sermo de ordinatione episcopi* (Sermo XXXII ex collectione Guelferbytana),[246] preached about the same time as was the foregoing sermon.[247]

(6) *Sermo (CCLXV) de ascensione Domini*.[248] This sermon was held on Ascension Day, May 23, in 412.[249]

In all these sermons the Lucan text has been adduced as an appeal for unity in the 'dialogue' with the Donatists. The strange thing is that neither before 411 nor after 412 the Lucan passage does occur in Augustine's sermons and writings.[250] It was used only during a very short period of the bishop's homiletical activity.

7.3. *The Form of the Quotations*

St. Augustine did not quote the text of Luke 12,13f. in the same form in the sermons just mentioned. Even though several editions of these sermons are not completely reliable, the variety of the forms of this text, sometimes even in one and the same sermon, makes it rather evident that Augustine did not stick strictly to the current Latin text. The six sermons present us with the following variations on Jesus' answer:

I. *Quis me constituit divisorem inter vos?*
   (3), 628:48f.

II. *Homo, quis me constituit divisorem inter vos?*
   (3), 628:38.

III. *O homo, quis me constituit divisorem hereditatis inter vos?*
   (4), 1592:20.

---

[242] Ed. J. P. Migne, *P.L.* 38 (Paris 1841), 627-632, esp. 628 (twice).
[243] A. Kunzelmann, *a.c.*, 449; 512.518.
[244] Ed. J. P. Migne, *P.L.* 39 (Paris 1845), 1590-1598, esp. 1592 and 1593.
[245] A. Kunzelmann, *a.c.*, 448, cf. 449; 514.518.
[246] G. Morin, Sancti Aurelii Augustini Sermones post Maurinos reperti, in: *Miscellanea Agostiniana* I, Roma 1930, 439-585, esp. 563-575.
[247] A. Kunzelmann, *a.c.*, 448f., 516.
[248] Ed. J. P. Migne, *P.L.* 38 (Paris 1841), 1218-1224, esp. 1224.
[249] A. Kunzelmann, *a.c.*, 449; 514.519.
[250] A. Kunzelmann, *a.c.*, 449.

IV. Dic, homo, quis me constituit divisorem hereditatis inter vos?
(1), 241:3; (4), 1593:7-8; (5), 574:6f.
V. Dic, homo, quis constituit me divisorem hereditatis inter vos?
(6), 1224:18f.
VI. Dic, homo, quis me constituit iudicem aut divisorem hereditatis inter vos? (2), 1587:4-6.

Is it possible to reconstruct the Gospel text used by St. Augustine? We cannot maintain on the basis of the last quotation alone that the text he used contained the current textual reading 'iudicem aut divisorem' (cf. *aur e f l q* Vulg). We do have to reckon with the possibility of a textual corruption either in the edition of his sermons which was at our disposal or in the copy underlying that edition. On the other hand, one should not a priori reject the possibility of St. Augustine's acquaintance with the longer text and his abbreviation of it in the other quotations.

7.4. *The 'Dividers of the inheritance'*

St. Augustine compares the Catholic church with the inheritance or possession, which according to Psalm 2,7f. shall be given to the Son.[252] This inheritance is quite different from ordinary heritages,[251] for it is to be described as 'love' and 'truth',[253] or as a heavenly inheritance consisting in the harmony of brothers.[254] One might even define it as 'Christ'[255] or 'God'.[256] But, at the same time, the Christians themselves are the inheritance of God which is to be given to the Son.[257] Concord is safely guarded in this inheritance,[258] for this possession that we inherit from the *living* Father [259] cannot be divided.[260] Why, then, should we *try* to divide it?[261] Why should we enter litigation over this common property?[262] Christians should

---

[251] Cf. (2), 1586:2; 1587:11f.; (4), 1593:42f.
[252] Cf. (1), 241:7 ('nec talis est hereditas nostra').
[253] Cf. (1), 241:14f. (John 14, 27); (4), 1593:32f.
[254] Cf. (4), 1593:28: 'concordia fratrum in caelesti hereditate'.
[255] Cf. (2), 1587:45f.; (3), 628:39f., 44f. (ref. to 1 Cor 1, 10ff.).
[256] Cf. (4), 1593:40: 'haereditas eorum Deus ipse est' (ref. to Ps 15, 5).
[257] Cf. (4), 1593:40ff.: 'Cuius sunt ipsi haereditas, ipse est vicissim eorum haereditas'.
[258] Cf. (4), 1593:45.
[259] Cf. (1), 241:31f.
[260] 'Dividi non potest', cf. (1), 240:41; 241:11f., 14f.; (4), 1591:12.
[261] Cf. (1), 241:11, 32.
[262] Cf. (2), 1586:37f.; (4), 1593:46.

be each other's brothers.[263] They have an inheritance, which is not to be divided but given to each other.[264] Every inheritance which is divided becomes smaller: one can no longer say '*our* inheritance', but 'this part is yours' or 'that part is mine'. There is nothing to be gained by division.[265]

Unfortunately, not all brothers share this sentiment. From the very beginning we are warned against division. Paul speaks of schismatic parties (1 Cor 1,10ff.) and early on Jude mentioned people who separate themselves (Jud 1,19). As a matter of fact, this came true in the movements of the Donatists. They were, indeed, the *dividers* ('divisores') who lacked charity, for Christian love cannot be achieved but in the unity of the church.[266] From the very beginning *dividers of the inheritance* ('divisores hereditatis') displeased our Lord Jesus Christ, as becomes evident in the story of the dissatisfied heir.[267]

7.5. *Jesus rejects division*

Jesus came to collect, not to divide.[268] This is what he meant when he mentioned those other sheep which were not of this fold and which he came to bring together, in order that there should be one flock and one shepherd (Jn 10,16).[269] The Lord who loved unity had come to unify; He hated division and therefore He did not want to become involved in the division that was asked for.[270] He did not want to be a *divider of the inheritance* ('noluit esse divisor hereditatis'). He had come to assemble the whole into unity, to bring *one* inheritance in all lands.[271] We should not fail to realize how bad those people are who want the One to be divided who did not want to be a divider: 'Who appointed me a divider among you'.[272]

---

[263] Cf. (1), 241:11 (frater), 37f. (fratres); (4), 1593:36, 38f.
[264] Cf. (4), 1593:38f.
[265] Cf. (1), 241:16ff. (16: 'divisio minorem facit').
[266] Cf. (6), 1223:57-59; cf. also 1224:1ff.
[267] Cf. (5), 573:32f.: 'Ab initio displicuerunt Domino nostro Jesu Christo divisores hereditatis'.
[268] Cf. (6), 1224:8f., 18 ('colligere veni, non dividere').
[269] Cf. (6), 1224:9ff.; (5), 574:3ff.
[270] Cf. (5), 574: resp. 5f., 3, 6, 2 (cf. (2), 1587:4).
[271] Cf. (5), 574:8-9.
[272] Cf. (3), 628:47-50: '... qui volunt esse divisum, qui noluit esse divisor ...', 42: (of Paul) ... nolebat esse divisor'; (2), 1587:45 (1 Cor 1, 12f.): 'divisus est Christus?'.

The attitude of Jesus in Luke 12,13f. is an example for all Christians. They would never think of saying with the dissatisfied heir, 'Domine, dic fratri meo, ut dividat hereditatem mecum', but instead intervene in favour of their brothers: 'Domine, dic fratri meo, ut teneat mecum hereditatem'.[273] The Catholic believer should say to the Donatist, 'I wish you to possess *with* me,[274] keep therefore the inheritance *with* me'.[275] Christians do not intervene against their brothers,[276] but invite them to a common possession of God's peace: 'Be brothers with us in the inheritance'.[277]

7.6. *The Judge*

It is beyond dispute that Luke 12,13f had great significance for St. Augustine in his 'dialogue' with the Donatist movement in the days of the *Collatio*. These schismatics appeared to him to be 'dividers of the inheritance'. All emphasis, therefore, is to be laid on Jesus' refusal to act as a divider. That is why he left out the words 'iudicem aut' so many times in his quotations. These words did not fit in well with the argument which he took from Jesus' answer. It seems to me that the rather stereotyped form in which he develops his argument again and again during the period of the *Collatio* might indicate that he worked out this particular exegesis with an eye to the three days talks with the Donatists. He may have written down this exegesis and may have used the notes in some of his sermons before and after these talks in June. The proof text, verse 14, seems to have taken on the paraphrased form:

Dic, homo, quis me constituit divisorem hereditatis inter vos?

This form contained two additions, namely, *Dic* (under influence of vs. 13) and *hereditatis* (which was the central word for his exegesis).[278] Moreover, there was an omission (*iudicem aut*) which

---

[273] This is found in several sermons (with small variations): (1), 241:9-10; (2), 1587:10-11 ('unitatem' loco 'hereditatem'); (4), 1594:16-18; (5), 575:22-24; (6), 1224:24ff.; cf. also En. II in Ps. 18 (*S. Aurelii Augustini Enarrationes in Psalmos*, C. C. Lat. xxxviii, Turnhout 1956, 109:20f).

[274] Cf. (2), 1586:44.

[275] Cf. (2), 1587:32f.

[276] Cf. (5), 575:24ff.

[277] Cf. (2), 1588:42ff., 45.

[278] It is not for nothing that the textual forms I and II (par. 7:3) do not contain the words 'dic' and 'hereditatis': both occur in the sermon which explicitly deals with the Gospel passage Luke 12, 13-21. Here he was guided both by his stereotyped exegesis and by the Gospel text with which he was acquainted.

resulted in all the stress being laid on Jesus' denial of being a *divider*. And so he forged his weapon against the dividers of the inheritance, to whom he has Christ pose his question with some impatience (*Dic, homo,* . . .).

In my view, this paraphrastic form was not identical to the text which Augustine read in his Gospel text. I do not base my conviction on the fact that the reading 'iudicem aut divisorem' occurs one time in his sermons, for that reading may be due to the industry of some editor or copyist (although it might then be asked why this zealot failed to correct the text in the other sermons). There are other indications that Augustine's text actually contained the word 'iudicem'.

In his sermon 'On the utility of Fasting' the church father quotes Lk 12,13f. ('. . . divisorem hereditatis . . .') and immediately declares: '. . . nolebat fieri *iudex* ad divisionem.[279] It seems to me that here Augustine unintentionally betrayed the fact that the true reading of his quotation contained the word *iudicem*. And when, in the same sermon, he exhorts his hearers with these words, 'nos autem, carissimi, non eum rerum talium *iudicem* requiramus',[280] it is again apparent that his text must have included the word *iudicem*.

In the sermon 'On Peace and Charity' he connects the idea of the court with the answer of Jesus, but he makes Jesus himself a judge: 'Quare ergo, fratres, de possessione litigamus, et non potius sanctas tabulas recitamus? Venisse opinemur nos ad iudicem: de possessione contentio est . . .'.[281] It is clear that Augustine has introduced Jesus as a judge here, because his text supplied him with the word *iudicem*. But precisely the fact that Jesus refused to be a *judge* in the sense of a *divider* makes him a judge who will deliver judgment against the dividers of the inheritance, which is the Catholic church.

The same is true for his sermon on Luke 12,13ff., where he repeatedly speaks of Jesus as a judge: . . . ipsa Domino interpellato et *iudicante* poscebat . . . sed iustum *iudicem* invenerat . . . Ille *iudex* hoc docturus erat . . . tanto *iudice* invento accedit . . . sed audiamus et *iudicantem* et docentem . . . advocatus est *iudex*

---

[279] Cf. (1), 241:5.
[280] Cf. (1), 241:6f.
[281] Cf. (2), 1586:36-39.

noster...².²⁸² Apart from two references in his sermon on Eccles 25,2,²⁸³ the notion of Jesus being a judge, precisely in refusing to be a divider, has wholly disappeared in his later sermons.

7.7. *The Text of St. Augustine*

My thesis is that Augustine was acquainted with the text current in his diocese and in his time, 'Homo, quis me constituit iudicem aut divisorem inter vos'. When he became involved in the Donatist struggles, however, the text of Luke 12,13f. suddenly took on supreme importance for him. When he faced the three days dialogue in June, 411 A.D., the fact that Jesus himself rejected any division of the *inheritance* became extremely meaningful: the schismatics could never refer to Jesus to justify their conduct, for Jesus had condemned such separatism. Circumstances caused him to transform the text at his disposal with a view to making it more decisive as a proof-text in the new historical context. It is not the Jewish Christians and their archaic traditions that stand behind the unexpected wording in Augustine's sermons, as Quispel was prepared to argue, but the church father himself, who in his concern for the unity of the church found support in these words of the Lord. There is no essential difference between the bishop and his heretic predecessors, Marcion and the author of the Gospel of Thomas. And all of them did what later commentators have done (be it without alteration of the text), namely, make the word of Jesus the exponent of their own *conditioned* view of the biblical message.

---

[282] Cf. (3), 628:9f.11.14.17.30; 629:4f.
[283] Cf. (4), 1592:15 ('quis talem iudicem inveniat'); 18 ('tanto iudice').

"AM I A JEW?"
JOHANNINE CHRISTIANITY AND JUDAISM

WAYNE A. MEEKS
Yale University

With the irony which is so characteristic of his style, the author of the Fourth Gospel has Pilate say at Jesus' trial, "Am I a Jew?" The absurd question does more than just add a touch of sarcasm to the portrayal of the prefect, for the scenes of the drama are so contrived that the reader is made to see Pilate scurrying back and forth between Jesus within the praetorium and "the Jews" outside. And despite his protests he is forced step by step to carry out the will of "the Jews." Just what does it mean to be "a Jew" in the Fourth Gospel? Could Pilate's question have been put in the mouth of the author himself? Or, for that matter, of his central character, Jesus? How Jewish was Johannine Christianity?

In the past half century scholarly opinion has swung—once again—from regarding the Fourth Gospel as the most hellenistic of the gospels to assessing it as the most Jewish. Practically speaking this means that when one wishes to illuminate some obscure passage in the Johannine writings by placing it in the history of traditions, one turns more frequently to Jewish sources from antiquity than to, say, the Greek doxographers or philosophers. Yet this does not mean that real consensus has been achieved on the question of the particular stream of development to which the Johannine symbolic language belonged, much less on the question of the specific historical milieu of the Johannine groups. For in the same half century our understanding of early "Judaism" and, to a lesser extent, of "Hellenism" has undergone extensive revision. Ideas which used to be identified as "hellenistic" came to be called "gnostic," [1] while later some of these were shown also

---

[1] E.g., the "Hellenists" in the title of B. W. Bacon's well known book on the Fourth Gospel were also called "gnostics" by Bacon, and the "salvation mysticism" which Hugo Odeberg saw in John, while the term is equivalent to the *Erlösungsmysterium* which Reitzenstein and Bousset took to be typical of "hellenistic piety," was also called "Jewish gnosticism" by him in a way that anticipated the mixture of terminology later applied to *merkabah* and *hekaloth* mysticism by G. Scholem.

to be "Jewish," in the sense that some Jews in Palestine believed them. And later writings that are indubitably "gnostic" turn out to be thoroughly permeated with notions that are, in terms of their origins and history, "Jewish." And when the Fourth Gospel itself speaks of "the Jews"—as it does more often than any other New Testament writing—it is not even absolutely clear what group it is referring to. Thus the term "Jewish" has multiple or ambiguous referents for us and also perhaps for the ancient author. And the complaint of Adolf Schlatter at the beginning of the century is still valid, that "das vierte Evangelium längst schon heimat- und namenlos hin und her geschoben wird und dabei zahlreiche Ausflüge in den Bereich der Phantasie unternommen worden sind. . ."[2]

I shall certainly not attempt in this essay to solve the problem of this Gospel's "home" or "name." Yet a summary of the present state of research in this area may be useful and seems an appropriate tribute to Morton Smith, who for years has insisted that the airtight compartments "Palestinian Judaism" and "Hellenism" which have been favorite utensils for many New Testament scholars were in fact useless sieves, since "Palestine in the first century was profoundly Hellenized."[3] On the other hand, I do not intend to provide a detailed bibliographical survey of recent research, since excellent bibliographies for Johannine studies are available.[4] Rather I shall try to sort out some of the different aspects of the question which are sometimes confused.

If it could be shown, as C. F. Burney argued in 1922,[5] that John was composed originally in Aramaic, then the *prima facie* case for locating it in a "Jewish" rather than a "Greek" milieu would be very strong. After two generations of scholars have worked on that question, however, it is now clear that no such demonstration is

---

[2] *Die Sprache und Heimat des vierten Evangelisten* (Gütersloh, 1902) reprinted in *Johannes und sein Evangelium*, ed. K. H. Rengstorf (Darmstadt, 1973) 28.

[3] M. Smith, "Palestinian Judaism in the First Century," in *Israel: Its Role in Civilization*, ed. M. Davis (New York, 1956) 71.

[4] Among the most useful are the section-by-section bibliographies in R. E. Brown, *The Gospel According to John* (Anchor Bible, 29, 29A; Garden City, 1966, 1970); see also E. Malatesta, *St. John's Gospel 1920-1965* (Analecta Biblica 32; Rome, 1967). I wish also to call attention to an incisive analysis of several present trends in Johannine scholarship by D. Moody Smith, "Johannine Christianity: Some Reflections on its Delineation," which the author kindly let me see in manuscript.

[5] *The Aramaic Origin of the Fourth Gospel* (Oxford, 1922).

possible.[6] The methodological principles laid down by E. C. Colwell in his refutation of Burney, Torrey, and Montgomery [7] have not been superceded, though numerous more recent comparisons of Johannine language with that of other bodies of literature have neglected the "adequate neutral control" on which he rightly insisted.[8] The Fourth Gospel as we know it is, as C. K. Barrett recently affirmed, "ein griechisches Buch." [9] Yet Barrett goes on to admit that it contains "einen durchdringenden semitischen Klang." The possibility that one or more of the sources used by the evangelist may have been composed in Aramaic remains open. As early as 1923 G. R. Driver pointed out that the "Aramaisms" were concentrated in the portions of the Johannine discourses that also showed some characteristics of Semitic poetic style.[10] Bultmann was persuaded that the *Redenquelle* he conjectured was in Aramaic,[11] and Black suggested that the discourses may have been based on free Greek paraphrases, "Targums" as he said, of an Aramaic sayings tradition, whether written or oral.[12] Unfortunately, while the quest for the narrative source(s), particularly for the miracle stories, of John has enjoyed a renascence of late,[13] skep-

---

[6] See the excellent survey by S. Brown, "From Burney to Black: The Fourth Gospel and the Aramaic Question," *CBQ* 26 (1964) 323-39.

[7] *The Greek of the Fourth Gospel* (Chicago, 1931).

[8] On the other hand, Colwell perhaps could be faulted for relying entirely on linguistic phenomena at the word and phrase level—which were the kinds of data most important in the works he was refuting. He does not discuss broader elements of style such as *parallelismus membrorum*, chiasm, chain-linking of sequential clauses by key words, etc.

[9] *Das Johannesevangelium und das Judentum* (Stuttgart, 1970) 60.

[10] In *The Jewish Guardian* (Jan. 5, 1923) cited by S. Brown, "From Burney to Black," 329.

[11] *Das Evangelium des Johannes* (KEK 2; 16th ed., Göttingen, 1959) 5; ET: *The Gospel of John*, trans. G. R. Beasley-Murray et al. (Philadelphia and Oxford, 1971) 18.

[12] *An Aramaic Approach to the Gospels and Acts* (3d ed.; Oxford and New York, 1967) 149-51. But see the critical reviews of the book as a whole by J. A. Fitzmyer, *CBQ* 30 (1968) 417-28 and M. Smith, *JBL* 90 (1971) 247-48.

[13] E. Haenchen, "Johanneische Probleme," "Probleme des johanneischen 'Prologs'" and parts of the other articles collected in *Gott und Mensch* (Tübingen, 1965) 78-156 and *Die Bibel und Wir* (Tübingen, 1968) 182-311; R. T. Fortna, *The Gospel of Signs* (SNTSMS, 11; Cambridge, 1969) and "Source and Redaction in the Fourth Gospel's Portrayal of Jesus' 'Signs'," *JBL* 89 (1970) 151-66; W. Nicol, *The Sēmeia in the Fourth Gospel* (NovTSup 32; Leiden, 1972. The latter two authors find traces of semitisms in their signs source, but none thinks the source itself to have been composed in a language other than Greek. See also W. Wilkens, *Zeichen und Werke* (AThANT 55; Zürich, 1969); the review of Wilkens by Fortna, *JBL* 89 (1970)

ticism about Bultmann's *Redenquelle* has led to a general neglect of the complicated question how that version of the sayings of Jesus which feeds into the Johannine discourses and perhaps later into distinctly gnostic speeches of Jesus first took shape and by what circle it was cultivated and handed on.[14] Hence, while it cannot be doubted that some elements of tradition that were originally formulated in a Semitic language are present in John, it has proved very difficult to identify them precisely or to specify the traditioning process by which just these elements came to the evangelist. The linguistic investigation of John at best confirms a Syro-Palestinian origin for part of the pre-Johannine traditions; it has helped little in locating the Johannine "school" itself.

These negative results of the linguistic investigation do not, to be sure, lay to rest the question formulated by Schlatter, for he never supposed that John or major parts of it were *written* in Aramaic, but only that its *Heimat* was Palestinian, its author bilingual, like many Palestinians equally at home with Greek or Aramaic. While the evidence Schlatter compiled to support that proposition was quite tendentious,[15] the inherent possibility of such a production

---

457-62; and the survey by J. M. Robinson in H. Koester and J. M. Robinson, *Trajectories through Early Christianity* (Philadelphia, 1971) 235-52.

[14] An important first step is J. M. Robinson, "*Logoi Sophōn*: On the Gattung of Q," in *Trajectories* 71-113. H. Koester (in "One Jesus and Four Primitive Gospels," reprinted in the same volume, 158-204) remarks that the "Johannine discourses occupy a crucial place in the development of the genre 'revelation' . . ." on its way to the characteristic gnostic re-revelations (197), but he does not attempt to elucidate the evolution from the sayings of Jesus (in the characteristic Johannine form) into the complex discourses. "The Jewish literary genre 'apocalypse' " seems to me not sufficiently precise for describing the earlier stage of the revelation genre. Among the few formcritical studies of specifically Johannine style elements K. Berger, *Die Amen-Worte Jesu* (BZNW 39; Berlin, 1970) and H. Leroy, *Rätsel und Missverständnis* (BBB 30; Bonn, 1968) deserve mention. J. Becker's source divisions in the Farewell Discourses ("Aufbau, Schichtung und theologiegeschichtliche Stellung des Gebetes in Joh 17," *ZNW* 60 (1969) 56-83; "Die Abschiedsreden Jesu im Johannesevangelium," *ZNW* 61 (1970) 215-46) and B. Lindars' analysis of the "editions" shed light on the latest stages of the discourse tradition and the Johannine redaction(s) of it, but not on its pre- or post-Johannine history.

[15] His challenge to "whoever doubts the results" to "attempt a commentary of this kind from Mekilta and Sifre to a genuinely Greek composition. . ." sounds like the kind of "neutral control" Colwell later insisted on, but in reverse: more pertinent is the question whether one could make a "commentary of this kind" on John from Greek sources—and that Colwell has done. The parallels adduced by Schlatter are of several different sorts, which are inadequately distinguished and of widely varying persuasiveness. E.g.,

in Palestine has increased with discoveries that have suggested that bilingualism and trilingualism were much more common than was formerly supposed.[16] Yet that observation must be balanced by the recollection that the use of Aramaic was by no means limited to Palestinian Jews.[17]—Burney in fact conjectured that his putative Aramaic original of John was produced in bilingual Antioch. Thus one cannot always posit a one-to-one correlation between original language of a tradition and even its geographical or cultural location, much less its ideological character. One might write of distinctively and thoroughly Jewish matters in Greek—as no less eminent a figure than Bar Kochba did.[18] But one might also say quite syncretistic things in Aramaic, as did members of the Qumran sect, the early Mandaeans, and perhaps the Dosithean sect of the Samaritans.[19] The point is that the linguistic data, even if they were less ambiguous than has so far been demonstrated, cannot alone solve the problem of the Johannine milieu.

Consequently most writers on the subject have been preoccupied with a broader question: Were the major ideas and symbols of Johannine Christianity derived from Judaism? An impressively broad consensus exists today that this question must be answered in the affirmative. If, nevertheless, confusion still reigns over at-

that the phrase "they spoke to one another" occurs both in John and in Tannaitic sources hardly makes this a Palestinian idiom—*elegon pros allēlous* is perfectly normal Greek and, while it *means* the same as *ʾamru zeh lazeh* it is certainly not *formally* similar. On the other hand, *natan nephesh* is a significant parallel to *psychēn tithēnai*.

[16] Morton Smith, "Aramaic Studies and the Study of the New Testament," *JBR* 26 (1958) 304-13; J. A. Fitzmyer, "The Language of Palestine in the First Century A.D.," *CBQ* 32 (1970) 501-31. Fitzmyer emphasizes the diversity of languages spoken. While he disagrees with Smith's contention that Greek was the most common language already in the first two centuries of our era, he grants that it was widespread and not restricted to urban centers or upper classes, but spoken "by farmers and craftsmen."

[17] Cf. Smith, "Aramaic Studies" 309.

[18] In one of the papyrus letters from Naḥal Ḥeber, Bar Kochba (if, as Lifshitz argues, *Soumaios* is the Greek equivalent of one of his nicknames) explains: "I am writing in Greek because I find no impetus [*hormē*] to write in Hebrew" (B. Lifshitz, "Papyrus grecs du désert de Juda," *Aegyptus* 42 [1962] 241, lines 11-15). The cave produced 15 letters from Bar Kochba, 4 in Hebrew, 9 in Aramaic, 2 in Greek (Y. Yadin, "More on the Letters of Bar Kochba," *BA* 24 [1961] 86-95).

[19] Smith's observation that the earliest examples of Palestinian Aramaic literature that have survived often conform to hellenistic literary or popular genres ("Aramaic Studies" 306) bears repeating, though one may debate one or another of his examples.

tempts to assign the Johannine writings a clear place in the history of religions, that is due more than to any other factor to failure to recognize the fateful ambiguity of the two dialectical terms, "Hellenism" and "Judaism." When those terms became, in the late nineteenth century, overarching categories in New Testament interpretation, "Hellenism" referred preeminently to modes of thinking and perceiving which were thought to be distinctive of classical Greek civilization, above all of Greek philosophy: more or less the "Geist des griechischen Denkens." "Greek" thought was rational, universalizing, metaphysical, abstract, and so on. "Jewish," in this kind of dialectic, meant concrete, particular, historical, dynamic, and the like. "Hellenistic Jewish" became a mediating category in the dialectic, requiring that *real* Judaism receive the further modification, "Palestinian." Of course every responsible historian knew from the outset that the picture was more complicated. The term "Hellenism" was in fact coined to *distinguish* the cultural epoch beginning with Alexander from the classical period of "hellenic" culture. Cultural historians have come more and more to use the term "Hellenism" to refer generally and neutrally to the *mixture* of western and eastern cultures which emerged in the Diadochean and Roman periods. "Hellenistic" thus comes to mean syncretic.[20] In the history of religions school in Europe, under the continued influence of the attempts to explain the evolution of early Christianity in dialectical fashion, Hellenism took on a rather special definition. A typical expression was Wilhelm Bousset's description of "hellenistic piety" as the soil in which the "Johannine piety" grew up.[21] It was, he said, a mystical piety characterized by the attempt to escape from the bonds of fate and the cosmic forces by union with a protective deity, through sacrament or pseudoscience. One must look to the mystery religions and astrology, and to the Greco-Egyptian speculations, Jewish and pagan, that depended on them, "outside the Old Testament and the genuinely Christian milieu," for parallels to Johannine mysticism.[22] In the dialectical model of Christianity's

---

[20] See for example the Introduction to H. Jonas, *The Gnostic Religion* (2d ed.; Boston, 1963) entitled "East and West in Hellenism."

[21] *Kyrios Christos* (1st ed., 1921; 5th ed., Göttingen, 1964) 154-83 (ET, Nashville and New York, 1970, 211-44).

[22] Though his interpretation of John differs significantly from Bousset's, yet it is striking that C. H. Dodd turns to the same sources for his description of "the higher religion of Hellenism" (a term he applies preeminently to

early development, inherited by Bousset from F. C. Baur in the modified form set forth by Wilhelm Heitmüller,[23] this "hellenistic piety" inevitably had as its opposite number the kind of religion and theology represented by "the Old Testament and the genuinely Christian milieu." Opponents of the history-of-religions interpretation of John were quite naturally tempted, therefore, to assume that Bousset and his successors—particularly Rudolf Bultmann, whose "gnostic redeemer myth" could be seen as a further refinement or alternative explanation of the "hellenistic piety"— could be refuted by showing that Johannine thought was Jewish, Palestinian, and in direct continuity with Old Testament thought. In this form even today the old antithesis Jewish vs. Hellenistic continues to exercise its simplistic influence, though a century's archaeological and literary discoveries have almost overwhelmed us with the incredible variety and fluidity of religious phenomena, including Judaism, in Greco-Roman culture.[24]

The discovery of the manuscripts around Qumran and the striking affinities of expression that many scholars have observed between these sectarian Jewish documents and the Johannine writings have lent an almost irresistable impetus to the drive to locate John safely in a Palestinian milieu.[25] As a result the danger of category

---

Hermeticism), which he sees as the principal "background" of the Fourth Gospel. See *The Interpretation of the Fourth Gospel* (Cambridge, 1953) Part I.

[23] "Zum Problem Paulus und Jesus," *ZNW* 13 (1912) 320-37; abridged ET in *The Writings of St. Paul*, ed. W. Meeks (New York, 1972) 308-19. The informed reader will see that I am greatly simplifying the history of research in this area, which needs a careful exposition from the viewpoint of the history of hermeneutics in the context of cultural history and, if possible, of the sociology of knowledge. For a model study of the beginning of modern biblical hermeneutics in the eighteenth and early nineteenth centuries, see now H. Frei, *The Eclipse of Biblical Narrative* (New Haven, 1974). For a survey, see the standard treatments by L. Salvatorelli, "From Locke to Reitzenstein," *HTR* 22 (1929) 263-369, and W. G. Kümmel, *The New Testament: The History of the Investigation of Its Problems*, trans. H. C. Kee (Nashville and New York, 1972).

[24] The fronts have shifted several times in the theological appropriation of the schema, whose roots lie apparently in the romantic theories of language that begin with Herder, but its continued power even in quite recent scholarship stems from the curious marriage of the romantic notion of *Volksgeist* with conservative theological viewpoints that attribute a unitary world view to the Bible as a whole. The most illuminating and devastating criticism of this ménage remains J. Barr, *The Semantics of Biblical Language* (Oxford, 1961) esp. chap. 2.

[25] The published studies of the relation between Johannine literature and Qumran texts are legion. See the careful review by H. Braun, *Qumran und*

mistakes has become quite acute, and we must carefully consider the plausibility of such forms of argument as, if Jewish then not Hellenistic; if Palestinian then not gnostic; and the like. Ambiguities lurk in the statements of even so careful a scholar as Raymond E. Brown, as when he says, "The critical import of the parallels between the Scrolls and John is that one can no longer insist that the abstract language spoken by Jesus in the Fourth Gospel *must* have been composed in the Greek world of the early second century A.D." [26] That is unexceptionable if "Hellenism" is taken in the first sense mentioned above: "Greek thought" is no longer the necessary or even a particularly likely context for the work of the fourth evangelist. "Hellenism" in the second sense, however, of a mystical, sacramental religion typical of Greco-Roman syncretism, is not excluded by this new evidence unless it can be shown that the Qumran Jews (and other Palestinian sects like them) were not in any way involved in that syncretism. Naturally the same is true for the special form of the latter postulated by Bultmann, for the fascination of the Mandaean texts for him was precisely that, used in conjunction with the Odes of Solomon and other evidence for a gnostic form or precursor of the Jewish wisdom speculation, they enabled him to escape the embarrassment of Bousset's schema, none of whose categories fit John. He did this by positing an early sectarian-Jewish gnosticism *in Palestine* and Syria,[27] and consequently, when he learned of the Qumran discoveries, found in them not a refutation of his thesis but further confirmation.[28]

By now, to be sure, it is apparent that Bultmann was mistaken in calling the Qumran group "gnostic," for the documents that have been uncovered so far give no hint of a "redeemer myth" of the sort that was essential to Bultmann's definition. Nevertheless, the Qumran evidence could not be taken to refute the hypothesis of a gnostic milieu for John unless it could be shown that the Essene

---

das Neue Testament (Tübingen, 1966) 1. 96-138, 290-326; 2. 118-44, and add, among the more recent literature, the fine collection of essays edited by J. H. Charlesworth, *John and Qumran* (London, 1972).

[26] "The Scrolls and the New Testament," *ExpT* 78 (1966-67) 23; reprinted in *John and Qumran* (see n. 25 above) 8.

[27] "Die Bedeutung der neuerschlossenen mandäischen und manichäischen Quellen für das Verständnis des Johannesevangeliums," reprinted in *Exegetica*, ed. E. Dinkler (Tübingen, 1967) 55-104.

[28] *Theology of the New Testament*, trans. K. Grobel (New York, 1951) 2. 13n.

documents explained the central features of Johannine ideology without remainder. That is not the case. Even the most ardent proponents of an Essene "background" for John admit that John differs in important respects from Qumran literature, most dramatically in the complete absence from the latter of anything approaching the myth of the descending and ascending Son of Man. Thus both John and the acknowledged gnostic texts differ from the Qumran texts in just that particular which they share with each other. Taken by themselves, then, the Qumran documents leave the question of the Johannine community's relation to gnosticism as unsettled as ever. For my own part, I am more and more persuaded that John did not "borrow" from either gnostics or Essenes. The Qumran documents are only one important source among many for recognizing the variety of syncretistic Jewish sects that existed in the first centuries of our era, whose beliefs were the fundamental raw material for the ideology of the variety of circles of emerging Christianity—including the peculiar Johannine circle and the groups that were later to be given the pejorative nickname "Gnostics" by their opponents in positions of ecclesiastical power. And the Johannine writings themselves are a key source for this development, because in them we see a Christian gnostic myth actually in the process of formation, as it were. The myth of Jesus in the Fourth Gospel is still Jewish in its roots, distinctively Christian in its form and function, and on the threshold of becoming gnostic in the sense used by the second century heresiologists. And it was all these things at once.

The nature of the Jewish roots from which the Johannine Jesus myth sprouted need to be more fully specified. First of all, the peculiarly ambivalent relation between the Johannine christology and the eschatological expectations of first-century Jews (and Samaritans) has attracted the attention of much recent scholarship. On the one hand, no other New Testament writer shows so precise an awareness of the variety and distinctiveness of the various eschatological titles and functions as does the fourth evangelist. Indeed, only the awakening brought about by the Qumran discoveries has enabled modern scholars to appreciate the careful differentiations represented, for example, in the catalogue of titles incorporated into chapter 1.[29] On the other hand, he shows a

---

[29] On this see Excursus III of R. Schnackenburg, *Das Johannesevangelium*, 1. Teil (Herders theologischer Kommentar zum NT, 4; Freiburg, 1975); ET:

sovereign freedom in the way he handles the titles. The contours of the Jewish expectations are so transformed by the peculiar christology of the Christian group that some aspects of the Johannine presentation become virtually a parody. The significance of these facts has been brilliantly explicated in two recent articles by Marinus de Jonge,[30] whose conclusions deserve careful attention. He shows that, while the evangelist "clearly wishes to confront Jesus' own statements about himself, or pronouncements of others concerning him, with current Jewish (and Samaritan) expectations,"[31] these are all bent to the purpose of his own literary scheme. "Representative people (disciples, ordinary people: the crowd, Jewish leaders, Samaritans) express representative beliefs and raise representative objections."[32] Further, they are "representative" not in the sense that they sum up typical beliefs of actual Jews in Jesus' time or even toward the end of the first century when the gospel was written, but in the sense that they represent the *Johannine* conception of the Jewish beliefs that are obstacles to Christian faith, in a form which can serve as foil to the gospel's refutation by irony. These formulations include views that are distinctly Christian, such as the notion that the Messiah is a miracle-worker (7:31)[33] and allude to conceptions that have evolved on both sides of the Christian-Jewish debate and which the evangelist finds inadequate, such as the belief that John the Baptist is Elijah who must reveal the hidden Messiah.[34] To put the matter sharply, with some risk of misunderstanding, the Fourth Gospel is most anti-Jewish just at the points it is most Jewish.

The Gospel According to St. John, Vol. 1 (New York and London, 1968). The point about the evangelist's awareness of Jewish eschatological diversity has been made most clearly by N. A. Dahl, e.g. in "The Johannine Church and History," in *Current Issues in New Testament Interpretation*, ed. W. Klassen and G. F. Snyder (New York, Evanston, and London, 1962) 129-30.

[30] "Jewish Expectations about the 'Messiah' according to the Fourth Gospel," *NTS* 19 (1972-73) 246-70, and "Jesus as Prophet and King in the Fourth Gospel," *Ephemerides theologicae lovanienses* 49 (1973) 160-77, the latter offering helpful additions and corrections to my own publications in this area. See also his earlier "Nicodemus and Jesus: Some Observations on Misunderstanding and Understanding in the Fourth Gospel," *BJRL* 53 (1971) 337-59, and "The Use of the Word *CHRISTOS* in the Johannine Epistles," in *Studies in John presented to Prof. Dr. J. N. Sevenster* (NovTSup 24; Leiden, 1970) 66-74.

[31] "Jewish Expectations" 247.
[32] Ibid. 248.
[33] Ibid. 258.
[34] As attested in the later Dialogue with Trypho by Justin (Ibid. 253-56).

While agreeing in the main with almost all of De Jonge's conclusions, I would emphasize more than he the extent to which the raw materials for the peculiar Johannine christology were available in Jewish traditions, particularly those concerning the Patriarchs and the Prophets, and above all those about Moses. For example, while I completely agree that "Jesus' kingship and his prophetic mission are both redefined in terms of the unique relationship between Son and Father" [35] and that the latter relationship as developed in John is a uniquely Christian theological production, yet I would insist that the striking parallels which exist in Jewish and Samaritan texts not be ignored. Those texts allow us to see that Moses was occasionally described as the "apostle" or agent of God so intimately related to God that he could bear the divine name, making visible to his disciples the inaccessible divinity, even the Image of God which was man's lost but ultimate good.[36] In Alexandrian tradition this notion was expressed in language with Stoic, Platonic, and Neo-Pythagorean overtones;[37] it is later attested in Samaritan and even in rabbinic literature in terms which differ only slightly. What John has done with this notion, as with so many others, is to force it to the breaking point of Jewish consciousness—at least of the Jews *he* had in mind. His use of Jewish tradition in this respect is a kind of *reductio ad absurdum*; the result in Jewish ears was blasphemy.

Very many of the things which have been said about the Johannine use of "messianic" titles and images can also be said of the Johannine use of Jewish scripture. C. K. Barrett will probably be proven correct in the long run when he says that the most important aspect of the Qumran discoveries for Johannine studies is the *pesharim*, the biblical commentaries.[38] Certainly the publication of these examples of actualizing exegesis, so similar to ways in which several New Testament writers used scripture, have stimulated intense interest in comparative study of the variety of Jewish and early Christian (and Samaritan) modes of interpreta-

---

[35] "Jesus as Prophet and King" 162. My failure to make this sufficiently clear is De Jonge's principal criticism of my book, *The Prophet-King* (NovTSup 14; Leiden, 1967).

[36] See my "Moses as God and King," in *Religions in Antiquity, Essays in Memory of Erwin Ramsdell Goodenough*, ed. J. Neusner (Leiden, 1968) 354-71.

[37] Compare, for example, Philo, *Mos.* 1.156-59 with Philostratus, *VAp.* 8.7.

[38] *Das Johannesevangelium und das Judentum* 58.

tion.[39] This interest was further enhanced by recent enthusiasm for study of the Palestinian Targums, aroused in part by such discoveries as Codex Neofiti I and the Job Targum from Qumran Cave 11, coming on the heels of the earlier publications of Cairo Geniza fragments by Paul Kahle.[40] Since formula-quotations from the Old

---

[39] The programmatic essays by Renée Bloch have had very great influence despite her untimely death: "Note méthodologique pour l'étude de la littéture rabbinique," *RScR* 43 (1955) 194-227; "Midrash," in *Dictionnaire de la Bible, Supplement* 5 (1957) cols. 1263-81. G. Vermes begins with Bloch's proposals in his fundamental work, *Scripture and Tradition in Israel* (SPB 4; Leiden, 1961). In England C. H. Dodd's *According to the Scriptures* (New York, 1953) and D. Daube's *The New Testament and Rabbinic Judaism* (London, 1956) represented an independent interest in comparison of aggadic traditions that far antedated the Qumran discoveries. The fruitfulness of this approach is visible in the Johannine commentaries by Dodd and C. K. Barrett, and especially in B. Lindars, *New Testament Apologetic* (London, 1961). Scandinavian NT scholars had also long been interested in this method for tracing the history of traditions, which was brought to the United States by K. Stendahl (*The School of St. Matthew* [Lund, 1954; 2d ed. Philadelphia, 1968]) and by N. A. Dahl. Dahl's quite original perceptions in this area have unfortunately become known beyond the circle of his students and colleagues only in scattered articles, including "Christ, Creation and the Church," in *The Background of the New Testament and Its Eschatology*, ed. D. Daube and W. D. Davies (Cambridge, 1956) 422-43; "Kristus, jødene og verden etter Johannesevangeliet," *NTT* 60 (1959) 189-203; "The Johannine Church and History" (above, n. 29); "Manndraperen og hans far (Joh 8:44)," *NTT* 64 (1963) 129-62; "Der Erstgeborene Satans und der Vater des Teufels (Polyk 7.1 und Joh 8.44)," in *Apophoreta: Festschrift für Ernst Haenchen*, ed. W. Eltester (Berlin, 1964) 70-84; "The Atonement—an Adequate Reward for the Akedah? (Ro 8:32)," in *Neotestamentica et Semitica; Essays in Honor of Matthew Black*, ed. E E. Ellis and M. Wilcox (Edinburgh, 1969) 15-29; "Widersprüche in der Bibel, ein altes hermeneutisches Problem," *Studia Theologica* 25 (1971) 1-19. He has inspired a number of dissertations using these techniques by students at Yale, where until recently they were also nourished by the seminar on midrash of Judah Goldin, now at the University of Pennsylvania. (See dissertations by D. Hay, F. O. Francis, J. P. Sampley, D. Smith, W. Meeks, D. Juel.) For a survey of recent work in this area, see M. P. Miller, "Targum, Midrash and the Use of the Old Testament in the New Testament," *JSJ* 2 (1972) 29-82; the brief introduction by J. A. Sanders to the ET of R. Le Déaut, "Apropos a Definition of Midrash," *Interpretation* 25 (1971) 259-61; and D. M. Smith, "The Use of the Old Testament in the New," in *The Use of the Old Testament in the New and Other Essays: Studies in Honor of William Franklin Stinespring* (Durham, N. C., 1972) 3-65.

[40] Besides the survey by M. P. Miller cited in the previous note, see especially R. Le Déaut, *Liturgie juive et Nouveau Testament* (Scripta pontificii instituti biblici 115; Rome, 1965); *Introduction à la littérature targumique* (Rome, 1966); *La nuit pascale* (Rome, 1963); P. Nickels, *Targum and New Testament: A Bibliography Together with a New Testament Index* (Rome, 1967); M. McNamara, *The New Testament and the Palestinian Targum to the Pentateuch* (Rome, 1966).

Testament are very prominent in the Fourth Gospel,[41] it came in for its share of attention, both in general works on comparative exegesis and in specialized articles and monographs on midrash-like passages in John. These have shown that there is in numerous passages in John an expository structure linked to one or more scriptural texts,[42] and that these share elements of formal structure and aggadic motifs with both rabbinic midrash and Alexandrian allegorical interpretations.[43] These midrash-like elements, moreover, seem to be integral both to major portions of the discourse material in its penultimate stage, that is, the form of the sayings of Jesus which, already distinctly "Johannine," was used by the evangelist, and to the literary work of the evangelist himself.[44] There can no longer be any question then that the use of and appeal to the Jewish scriptures is an essential and theologically significant characteristic of John. One must nevertheless be wary about further conclusions to be drawn from that fact. The same general statement could be made, for example, of several of the Nag Hammadi gnostic tracts. And, while kinship can be shown both with the Qumran *pesharim* and with rabbinic midrashim, some of which are even found in collections of Palestinian origin, Borgen's striking parallels between rabbinic and Philonic passages show how precarious is any attempt to say what *must* have been Palestinian. Further, while these studies appear to vindicate those who have insisted that Johannine Christianity stands in continuity with Old Testament religion, one must remember that it is not the traditions of ancient Israel as such, and certainly not our modern historical understanding of the Old Testament texts that is appropriated by John, but the scriptures seen through two powerful controlling perspectives: 1) the exegetical traditions of Judaism down to the time of John and 2) the Christian and the specifically Johannine modification of these

---

[41] See E. D. Freed, *Old Testament Quotations in the Gospel of John* (NovTSup 11; Leiden, 1965); cf. Meeks, *Prophet-King* 288-91.

[42] Or to a saying of Jesus, a point of considerable importance for understanding the "Johannine school." See *Prophet-King* 289 and "The Man from Heaven in Johannine Sectarianism," *JBL* 91 (1972) 58, n. 50.

[43] This has been shown most thoroughly and forcefully by P. Borgen, *Bread from Heaven: An Exegetical Study of the Concept of Manna in the Gospel of John and the Writings of Philo* (NovTSup 10; Leiden, 1965).

[44] Cf. Freed, *OT Quotations* 129: "... in no other writer are the O. T. Quotations so carefully woven into the context and the whole plan of composition as in Jn."

traditions. Here, too, John uses Jewish exegesis against the Jews.[45] Finally, there continues to be great uncertainty and excessive carelessness in the dating of Jewish and Samaritan traditions and a curious reluctance to expect the same kind of techniques of synoptic studies, formal analysis, and the history of traditions and of redaction to be applied to rabbinic sources as are taken for granted in the study of the New Testament.[46] There seems to be an irrational and unconscious assumption among many New Testament scholars that anything Jewish is *old*. Critics who have vigorously rejected the use of Mandaean texts for reconstruction of pre-Johannine gnostic traditions because these texts date in written form from the fifth, sixth, and seventh centuries or later, have themselves not infrequently appealed to Jewish traditions found only in the Babylonian Talmud or in midrashim not redacted before the middle ages. Here, too, there are no shortcuts to sound historiography.

Several times in the preceeding discussion the words "and Samaritan" appear, usually in parentheses. The style accurately represents the use of Samaritan evidence in New Testament studies. In his article on Palestinian Aramaic in 1956, Morton Smith called the neglect of Samaritan sources by New Testament scholars "a scandal."[47] That challenge, together with the remarks by John Bowman on "The Fourth Gospel and the Samaritans,"[48] convinced me in 1962 that anyone exploring traditions that depicted Moses as prophet and king would have to take account of the surviving Samaritan literature. I quickly found that the scandal had a simple explanation: the state of Samaritan studies was so primitive that one ventured into the morass at one's own risk.[49] Today the situation, while still far from ideal, is much improved, because

---

[45] Cf. Dahl, "Johannine Church and History," 130-36.

[46] I need only mention the remarkable impact which the recent works of J. Neusner, including especially *The Rabbinic Traditions about the Pharisees before 70* (Leiden, 1971) and *Eliezer ben Hyrcanus: The Tradition and the Man* (Leiden, 1973), have had in this field. On questions of method see, besides the numerous articles by Neusner, the excellent discussion in W. S. Towner, *The Rabbinic Enumeration of Scriptural Examples* (SPB 22; Leiden, 1973) 14-58 and "Form-Criticism of Rabbinic Literature," *JJS* 24 (1973) 101-18.

[47] "Aramaic Studies" (see n. 16 above) 307.

[48] Part of his "Samaritan Studies," *BJRL* 40 (1958) 298-308; cf. *Samaritanische Probleme* (Stuttgart, 1967) 53-76.

[49] The results of my cautious sortie are found in Chap. 5 of *Prophet-King*: "Moses as King and Prophet in Samaritan Sources."

of the work of students of the Oriental Studies program at the University of Leeds, first under Bowman and then, until recently, under John Macdonald, and the textual and linguistic work by Z. Ben-Haim and R. Macuch. [50] Most important for New Testament scholars, the history of early Samaritan traditions has at last been given a sound foundation by H. G. Kippenberg.[51] Though his reconstruction of the origins of the Dosithean sect and his argument for the anti-Dosithean nature of the polemic in Marqah and his immediate predecessors, which I find convincing in the main, require some modification of my own assessment of the early Samaritan traditions, by and large my conclusions about the role of those traditions in the shaping of the Johannine Christology are reinforced.[52] But that role must not be exaggerated, as some recent studies have done.[53] The Fourth Gospel itself does not give the impression that the Samaritans were a dominant factor in the

---

[50] Z. Ben-Ḥayyim, *The Literary and Oral Tradition of Hebrew and Aramaic amongst the Samaritans* [Heb. with Eng. prefaces] 3 vols. (The Academy of the Hebrew Language, Texts and Studies 1, 2, 3, 6; Jerusalem, 1957-67); R. Macuch, *Grammatik des samaritanischen Hebräisch* (Berlin, 1969).

[51] *Garizim und Synagoge* (RGVV 30; Berlin, 1971). See also J. D. Purvis, *The Samaritan Pentateuch and the Origin of the Samaritan Sect* (Cambridge, Mass., 1968). For an example of the way the history of traditions may be developed by using together Jewish, Samaritan, and Christian materials, see M. Collins, "The Hidden Vessels in Samaritan Traditions," *JSJ* 3 (1973) 97-116.

[52] De Jonge criticizes Kippenberg for confusing *Begriffsgeschichte* with *Traditionsgeschichte*; the development of Samaritan ideology, he suggests, may have been much more diverse and less sequential than Kippenberg supposes ("Jewish Expectations" 269). The point is well taken, but Kippenberg's work remains a landmark. I cannot enter here into debate on the minor points on which I disagree with particular interpretations, such as the question whether *Memar Marqah* may attest belief in a final assumption of Moses, which K. denies. He does not discuss the passages in which I find that belief presupposed (*Prophet-King* 244-46; Kippenberg 320).

[53] Particularly G. W. Buchanan, "The Samaritan Origin of the Gospel of John," in *Religions in Antiquity: Essays in Memory of Erwin Ramsdell Goodenough*, ed. J. Neusner (Leiden, 1968) 148-75. Although he offers many illuminating insights, his flat statement "that the Gospel attributed to John came from the Samaritan Christian Church" (175) is an aberration. E. D. Freed, "Samaritan Influence in the Gospel of John," *CBQ* 30 (1968) 580-87, also adds little to the discussion, but his insight that the name Ephraim in 11:54 may have had particular relevance to Samaritans and thus may support Bowman's suggestion that the Johannine group saw itself as a reconstituted Israel, reuniting the North and the South, bears examination. For a good survey of recent scholarship linking Samaritan and NT studies, see C. H. H. Scobie, "The Origins and Development of Samaritan Christianity," *NTS* 19 (1973) 390-414.

composition of the Johannine group. In the geographical and dramatic symbolism of the book, they have a place parallel but secondary to the "Galileans."[54] Further, the author of the gospel shows no sensitivity to specifically Samaritan concerns and terminology. To call the Prophet like Moses "Messiah" (4:25) is quite un-Samaritan,[55] and while the very great reserve about specifically *Davidic* connections of the Messiah in the Fourth Gospel[56] would be attractive to Samaritans, the extensive use of the prophetic writings of Judaism[57] would not be. Still, the puzzling dialogue between Jesus and his disciples in 4:31-38 probably does hint at a Christian mission in Samaria which had been important in the birth of the Johannine movement. The relation between that mission and the description of the origin of Samaritan Christianity in the book of Acts has not yet been satisfactorily clarified, despite the ingenious, but largely speculative, suggestions by Benjamin Bacon and, more recently, Oscar Cullmann.[58] It may be that Kippenberg's work has provided the basis for a more systematic investigation of the question.

Reviewing the attempts to locate the milieu of the Johannine writings, one is astonished how frequently the attempt has been made to settle issues by mere comparisons of key words, particular metaphors, and discrete concepts between these writings and other documents. Rarely has anyone tried to describe what an anthropologist might call the "system of symbols" involved, and still less often its probable function. To a certain extent the unusual attention which has been given to the myth of Jesus' descent and

---

[54] See W. Meeks, "Galilee and Judea in the Fourth Gospel," *JBL* 85 (1966) 159-69.

[55] Kippenberg (303) finds no use of the term "anointed" in an eschatological sense before the sixteenth century.

[56] This was one of the major problems addressed by *Prophet-King*, which I apparently failed to make clear, since no reviewer before Scobie (n. 50 above) noticed it.

[57] Cf. F. W. Young, "Jesus the Prophet: A Re-Examination," *JBL* 68 (1949) 285-99 and "A Study of the Relation of Isaiah to the Fourth Gospel," *ZNW* 46 (1955) 215-33; Dahl, "Johannine Church and History," 130-36.

[58] B. W. Bacon, *The Gospel of the Hellenists*, ed. C. H. Kraeling (New York, 1933), esp. Chap. IX; O. Cullmann, "The Significance of the Qumran Texts for Research into the Beginnings of Christianity," in *The Scrolls and the New Testament*, ed. K. Stendahl (London, 1958) 18-32; "L'Opposition contre le temple de Jerusalem, motif commun de la théologie johannique et du monde ambiant," *NTS* 5 (1958-59) 157-73; "Samaria and the Origins of the Christian Mission" in his *The Early Church* (London, 1956) 185-92.

ascent is an exception, for it has long been recognized that the dynamic structure of the myth itself is more important in identifying Jesus than the particular titles and metaphors attached to him. Since the independent and almost simultaneous studies by J. R. Harris and Rudolf Bultmann of the Fourth Gospel's Prologue,[59] it has been widely acknowledged that the dominant parent of this myth was the Jewish speculation about Wisdom. Several recent monographs and innumerable articles have been devoted to the evolution of the Wisdom myth and its use in christology and in the portrayal of various gnostic revealers.[60] Despite this attention, the form and the Sitz im Leben of the myth as it came to the author of the Fourth Gospel have yet to be fully clarified. It is obvious that the myth was adapted to christology extremely early, since the adaptation is pre-Pauline, but it is used in somewhat different ways by various New Testament authors. Further, it is important to note here once again that it is impossible to play off Jewish use against gnostic use as if the two were mutually exclusive. With the publication of the Nag Hammadi documents it becomes more and more evident that the Sophia speculations were exceedingly important in the evolution of gnostic myth. Key questions remaining to be answered include the way in which the female imagery of Sophia-Hochma [61] was related to the masculine imagery of the Logos. But the most pressing issue is to discover how the myth was put to work by the Johannine Christians—what aspects of their history made this form of the myth appropriate and how did its use help to form their group life and their relationship to other groups in the larger society? [62]

[59] J. R. Harris, *The Origin of the Prologue to St. John's Gospel* (Cambridge, 1917); R. Bultmann, "Der religionsgeschichtliche Hintergrund des Prologs zum Johannes-Evangelium," in *Eucharisterion: Festschrift für H. Gunkel* (FRLANT 19/2; Göttingen, 1921) 3-26 (reprinted in *Exegetica* 10-35).

[60] F. Christ, *Jesus Sophia: Die Sophia-Christologie bei den Synoptikern* (AThANT 57; Zürich, 1970); M. J. Suggs, *Wisdom, Christology, and Law in Matthew's Gospel* (Cambridge, Mass., 1970); R. G. Hamerton-Kelly, *Pre-Existence, Wisdom, and the Son of Man* (SNTSMS 21; Cambridge and New York, 1973); Schnackenburg, Commentary, Excursus I; U. Wilckens, "*Sophia, sophos, sophizō*," *TDNT* 7 (Grand Rapids, 1971) 465-528, and *Weisheit und Torheit* (BHT 26; Tübingen, 1959) Part II; G. W. MacRae, "The Jewish Background of the Gnostic Sophia Myth," *NovT* 12 (1970) 86-101.

[61] See for example H. Conzelmann, "Die Mutter der Weisheit," in *Zeit und Geschichte: Dankesgabe an Rudolf Bultmann*, ed. E. Dinkler (Tübingen, 1964) 225-34.

[62] I tried an experiment in this direction in "The Man from Heaven in Johannine Sectarianism," *JBL* 91 (1972) 44-72. The great difficulty in

Some progress has been made in identifying the function of the Fourth Gospel as a whole, and perhaps of its immediate sources, in the interaction between the Johannine Christians and a Jewish community. Earlier several scholars argued with some force that John was written as a missionary tract addressed primarily to Jews.[63] Today, however, there is a growing consensus that the form of the book would make it quite unsuited for that purpose. It was rather written for intra-Christian use, to strengthen the faith of the church.[64]

If that is the case, though, why are "the Jews" so prominent in the book? The term *hoi Ioudaioi* occurs 67 times in John, the singular four times; the singular occurs not at all in the Synoptics, the plural only four times apart from the phrase "King of the Jews," which is found five times in Mark and parallels and once in Matt 2:2 (this phrase occurs six times in John, all in the passion narrative, as in Mark).[65] Further, apart from the King of the Jews title, which, while lodged in the passion narrative from its earliest stage, is not unimportant for the evangelist, most if not all occurrences of *hoi Ioudaioi* in John are attributable to the evangelist. Five are in the stereotyped expression, "a festival (the passover, tabernacles) of the Jews,"[66] and two serve a similar purpose,

controlling such efforts, of course, lies in our lack of information about the actual social forms of the earliest communities. A working group of the American Academy of Religion and the Society of Biblical Literature, chaired by Leander E. Keck and myself, began in 1973 a five-year project to explore ways of describing "the social world of early Christianity," focusing initially on Syrian Antioch.

[63] The classic work advocating this position was K. Bornhäuser, *Das Johannesevangelium: Eine Missionsschrift für Israel* (Gütersloh, 1928). Of more recent literature supporting this viewpoint, the articles by W. C. van Unnik, "The Purpose of St. John's Gospel," in *Studia Evangelica I*, ed. K. Aland et al. (Berlin, 1959) 382-411, and J. A. T. Robinson, "The Destination and Purpose of St. John's Gospel," *NTS* 6 (1959-60) 117-31 (reprinted in *Twelve New Testament Studies* [London, 1962] 107-25) have had the widest influence.

[64] For example, C. K. Barrett, *The Gospel According to St John* (London, 1955) 21 and his much stronger statement, refuting Van Unnik, in *Das Johannesevangelium und das Judentum* 22-23; E. Grässer, "Die antijüdische Polemik im Johannesevangelium," *NTS* 11 (1964) 74-90, esp. 82-83; Brown, Commentary, LXXVIII; Schnackenburg, Commentary (ET), 1.153-72, esp. 154, n.1 and 165-67; De Jonge, "Jewish Expectations," 263-66; Meeks, "Man from Heaven," 67-72.

[65] Cf. C. J. Cuming, "The Jews in the Fourth Gospel," *ExpT* 60 (1948-49) 290-92; Schnackenburg, Commentary, 1.165; Nicol 23 (but the number printed for the rest of the NT in Nicol's statistics is obviously a mistake).

[66] 2:13; 5:1; 6:4; 7:2; 11:55; compare 10:22 where Hannukah (*ta engkainia*) is not so designated but rather "in Jerusalem."

"purification of the Jews" (2:6) and "for Jews do not associate with [or, use utensils in common with] Samaritans" (4:9). These notes are commonly taken to indicate the distance of the author from Judaism, since only an outsider would presumably speak thus of Jewish customs. That presumption is shaken somewhat by the recent discovery that Bar Kochba (or someone very close to him) could speak in just this fashion when writing an order for delivery of lulabs and ethrogs for Sukkoth![67] Still, it is undeniable that in the Fourth Gospel "the Jews" is generally used in an alien, even hostile sense, particularly in the notes, evidently by the hand of the evangelist, that "the Jews persecuted Jesus" or "sought to kill him,"[68] and in the repeated phrase, "because of the fear of the Jews."[69] The Jesus of the Fourth Gospel is also distant from "the Jews," even though (or just because) they are "his own" who reject him, and even though what Pilate "has written" stands ineffaceably, that he is "King of the Jews." The fact that he is naturally seen by a Samaritan as "a Jew" (4:9; cf. vss. 20-22) does not alter this distance; by Jews he can also be called "a Samaritan" (8:48), and they reject suggestions that he may be the Messiah or the Prophet on grounds that he is a Galilean (7:40-52).

As a matter of fact, no Galilean is ever called *Ioudaios* in John, except perhaps in chap. 6, depending on the way one solves the *aporiae* between that chapter and its context. It is a Galilean who first confesses Jesus "King of Israel," after being designated himself "a real Israelite" (1:47, 49), thus providing preliminary fulfillment of the Baptist's mission, "that he should be revealed to Israel" (1:31), while a Jew who takes Jesus' side may be sarcastically asked if he is "a Galilean" (7:52). Because of this sharp division between Galileans (and Samaritans) on one hand and

---

[67] In the Greek papyrus letter to Jonathan bar Baʿayan and Masabbala (above, n. 18) Soumaios, probably a nickname of Bar Kochba, orders these lieutenants to furnish "branches" (Lifshitz takes the rare word to refer to the *lulab*; Fitzmyer thinks it might refer to "beams" for constructing the *sukkot*) and "citrons" for the [*k*]*itreiabolēn Ioudaiōn*. There is no doubt about the identity of the festival (cf. the Hebrew letter on the same subject which speaks of "palm branches and citrons ... willows and myrtle," Yadin, "More on the Letters," 90) even though the term "citron festival" (lit., "citron-throwing") is otherwise unattested. Lifshitz's explanation that it translates *neṭilat lulab* does not tell us how the "principal ritual action" of shaking the *lulab* got transferred to the citrons.

[68] 5:16, 18; 7:1; 10:31; 11:8.

[69] 7:13 (in apparent contradiction to vs. 11); 9:22; 19:30; 20:19; but see 12:42 *dia tous Pharisaious*.

Ioudaioi on the other, the suggestion has been made that the latter term is primarily geographical and should be translated "Judeans" rather than "Jews" in most of the Johannine occurrences.[70] The suggestion has great plausibility in view of passages like 7:1, where we read that Jesus stayed in Galilee, "for he did not want to go about in *Judea* because the *Ioudaioi* were seeking to kill him," and similar notes in 11:7 and 54. On the other hand, there are numerous passages already mentioned in which the term must designate an organized religious community, with its "festivals" and special customs, its "rulers" and "high priests," centered in Jerusalem. And in perhaps the majority of the occurences one would be hard put to choose between the two. Yet no choice may be necessary, for ancient authors in the age of syncretism tend to identify a cultic community either by its principal deity (the worshippers of Isis, the servants of the God of Heaven) or by its place of origin (the Phrygian cult, the Syrian goddess). When pagan authors speak of *Ioudaioi*, as they usually do when referring to the people we call Jews,[71] the term denotes the visible, recognizable group with their more or less well-known customs, who have their origin in Judea but preserve what we would call their "ethnic identity" in the diaspora. What remains important to note is that the author of the Fourth Gospel maintains a careful geographical and religious differentiation between Judeans, Galileans, and Samaritans, but very little differentiation *within* any of these groups.[72]

It seems clear that at the time of composition of the Gospel the Johannine community is separate from "the Jews" and no longer expects "Jews" to convert. The Johannine letters show no sign of any further direct involvement with Judaism.[73] A good case can be made, as Bultmann has shown,[74] for regarding "the Jews" as a cipher for "the disbelieving world." Since First John can apply to Christian deviants the same kind of language used in the Gospel for "the Jews,"[75] one might even go further and suppose that

---

[70] Cuming (see n. 65 above) passim.

[71] J. Juster, *Les Juifs dans l'empire romaine* (Paris, 1914; reprinted New York, n.d.) 1.172-79.

[72] Thus "Pharisees" are the only named Jewish sect, and the term is virtually interchangeable with *Ioudaioi*.

[73] *Pace* J. A. T. Robinson, "The Destination and Purpose of the Johannine Epistles," *NTS* 7 (1960-61) 56-65 (*Twelve New Testament Studies* 126-38).

[74] *Das Evangelium des Johannes* 59; ET 86.

[75] 1 John 3:12; John 8:44; see J. L. Houlden, *A Commentary on the Johannine Epistles* (Black NT Commentaries; London, 1973) 95.

"the Jews" refers not to actual Jews at all, but to Christians whose faith is wanting in general [76] or specifically to "Jewish-Christians."[77] That is less certain; the issue turns on the way one interprets those passages in John which say that (some of) the Jews believed in Jesus: 2:23; 8:30; 11:45; 12:11, 42 ("many of the rulers"). All but one of these are explicitly said to be because of "signs" which Jesus had done. In 2:23; and 8:30 this faith is quickly unmasked as lacking understanding and persistence (*menein*) and therefore containing the potential of reverting to a demonic opposite, rejection and hatred (8:31-59). The result in 11:45-54 is ambiguous: some believe, others join the plot against Jesus. In 12:11 there is no immediate negation of the faith of those who are said to believe because of Lazarus; indeed this verse could be translated, "Many *left the Jews* and believed in Jesus." Are these passages cryptic allusions to a Jewish-Christian group rejected by the author, or warnings against a certain theological position he rejects, or are they reflections of the actual history of the Johannine community? Was there an earlier stage at which the Johannine groups were still closely associated with the synagogue, engaged in both active mission and active polemic among the Jews, so that the trauma of the ultimate rupture from the synagogue and the failure, in the main, of the mission left an indelible mark in the primary symbols of the group's identity? The last seems to me indubitable, and the reconstruction of that stage by J. Louis Martyn has, in its main outline, won wide acceptance.[78]

Martyn has also taken the most plausible first step in seeking to correlate the stages of redaction of the gospel with stages in the history of the Johannine community.[79] Beginning with the working hypothesis that R.T. Fortna's reconstruction of a unitary narrative

---

[76] Cf. Grässer (n. 64 above).

[77] E.g. C. H. Dodd, *Historical Tradition in the Fourth Gospel* (Cambridge, 1963) 330-32; B. Schein, *Our Father Abraham* (Yale Dissertation; Ann Arbor, Mich. [microfilm], 1972) Chap. IV.

[78] *History and Theology in the Fourth Gospel* (New York, 1968); see the reviews by D. M. Smith, *Interpretation* 23 (1969) 220-23; R. E. Brown, *USQR* 23 (1968) 392-94; T. A. Burkill, *JBL* 87 (1968) 439-42; R. A. Kysar, *Dialogue* 8 (1969) 70-72; W. A. Beardslee, *Religion in Life* 38 (1969) 150; R. Schnackenburg, "Zur Herkunft des Johannesevangeliums," *BZ* 14 (1970) 7-9; J. Beutler, *Martyria* (Frankfurter Theologische Studien 10; Frankfurt a/M, 1972) 345.

[79] "Source Criticism and Religionsgeschichte in the Fourth Gospel," in *Jesus and Man's Hope*, vol. 1 (Pittsburgh, 1971) 247-73.

source, including not only all the Johannine "signs" but also the passion narrative,[80] is substantially correct, he tries to locate in the redactional history the occasion for the construction of the "two-level dramas" that he has found in chapters 5 and 9 (*History and Theology*) and for the commandeering of the Moses traditions for an agressive christology which I sought to document in *The Prophet-King*. The "Signs Gospel," he reasons, was a missionary tract, and must have been used at a time when the Johannine community was in close contact, even overlapping with a Jewish community, so that the *"theios anēr* christology" which, with Fortna, he takes to be the main interest of the Signs Gospel, could still be expected to persuade some Jews to "believe that Jesus is the Christ" (20:31). After the Signs Gospel was written, however, the Johannine community experienced, Martyn believes, a strong counter challenge from the Jewish community, including at least (1) an insistence that the christological claims be defended by careful midrashic proof, (2) the claim that Moses, who had ascended to heaven and brought down the heavenly secrets, rendered the Christian *theios anēr*-Christ superfluous and (3) the accusation that the Christians are ditheists.[81] The completed form of the Fourth Gospel was occasioned in large measure by the necessity of responding to these (and perhaps other) challenges.

Space will not permit a full discussion of these fascinating proposals. It is doubtful that all parts of the outline will withstand detailed critical appraisal, but it is precisely the specificity of the scenario, which makes it vulnerable to various objections, that also makes it a prolific working hypothesis. The weakest point, however, is just the starting point: the attempt to reconstruct a single, unitary *narrative* source independently of form and redaction-critical study of the *discourse* material. Thus neither the extraordinary scope nor its supposed theological and missionary implications are convincing.[82] I have to agree with Barnabas Lindars' criticism of Fortna and other recent source critics, and especially

---

[80] *The Gospel of Signs* (n. 13 above).

[81] "Source Criticism," 254-56.

[82] Nicol's *Quellenscheidung* (n. 13 above) is somewhat more persuasive than Fortna's reconstruction just because it is more modest. Yet Nicol is so determined to show that there is nothing "hellenistic" about the signs source that he falls into an incredibly wooden and confused use of the categories "hellenistic" and "Jewish." Consequently the second chapter is an anachronism in research today.

with his keen observation that narrative and discourse cannot be rigidly separated in John, as the Lazarus story most clearly shows, since it is almost entirely dialogue, though its presumed *Vorlage* is universally counted as one of the "signs." [83] Lindars is likely right that, instead of a single source, *all* of which was used by the evangelist, there was "a mass of unrelated traditions or .... several short collections" or both.[84] He thinks it can be shown that the evangelist used bits of "sayings" tradition and built them up into discourses in much the same way that he used "semeia" stories and built *them* up into discourses or explanations.[85] His discussion of the "literary craftsmanship" of the evangelist and his proposal reconstructing "two editions" of the complete gospel[86] also will repay careful consideration. If the literary sensitivities of Lindars can somehow be brought together with the historical instincts of Martyn, the "Johannine puzzle" may yet have hope of solution.[87]

Morton Smith has pioneered in trying to persuade biblical scholars that "Palestinian-Jewish" and "Hellenistic" are not terms denoting separate planets. The history of research on the Johannine writings amply vindicates his insistence on this point and shows the continuing mischief which is worked when such categories are permitted to substitute for careful assessment of all sorts of available evidence and a genuinely historical imagination. The Fourth Gospel is indeed one of the most Jewish of the early Christian writings, even as it develops one of the most vehement anti-Jewish polemics in the first century. At the same time it reveals some of the diversity of Judaism in the first century, a diversity still scarcely acknowledged, and shows some of the torment that was experienced on both sides as Christian groups were wrenched from their Jewish (and Samaritan) matrix.

---

[83] *Behind the Fourth Gospel* (London, 1971) 41-42.
[84] Ibid. 38.
[85] Ibid. 24-26.
[86] Ibid., Chaps. 3 and 4; cf. his commentary in the New Century Bible series (London, 1972) 46-54 and on particular passages. There are many parallels between the general stages which Lindars distinguishes in the formation of the pre-Johannine and Johannine tradition and the five stages posited by R. E. Brown in his Anchor Bible commentary, though they differ in detail.
[87] I have profited greatly from a careful survey of Johannine *Redaktionsgeschichte* by R. Kysar, which Prof. Kysar kindly let me see in draft form. It will appear as Chap. 2 of his forthcoming book, an introduction to current scholarship on the Fourth Gospel.

ABBREVIATIONS

AThANT	Abhandlungen zur Theologie des Alten und Neuen Testaments
BA	*The Biblical Archaeologist*
BBB	Bonner Biblische Beiträge
BHT	Beiträge zur historischen Theologie
BJRL	*Bulletin of the John Rylands Library*
BZ	*Biblische Zeitschrift*
BZNW	Beihefte zur *Zeitschrift für die neutestamentliche Wissenschaft*
CBQ	*Catholic Biblical Quarterly*
ExpT	*Expository Times*
FRLANT	Forschungen zur Religion und Literatur des Alten und Neuen Testaments
JBL	*Journal of Biblical Literature*
JBR	*Journal of Bible and Religion*
JJS	*Journal of Jewish Studies*
JSJ	*Journal for the Study of Judaism*
KEK	Kritisch-exegetischer Kommentar über das Neue Testament (Meyer)
NovT	*Novum Testamentum*
NovTSup	*Novum Testamentum*, Supplements
NTS	*New Testament Studies*
NTT	*Norsk Teologisk Tidsskrift*
RGVV	Religionsgeschichtliche Versuche und Vorarbeiten
RScR	*Recherches de Science Religieuse*
SNTSMS	Monograph Series of the Studiorum Novi Testamenti Societas
SPB	Studia Post-Biblica
TDNT	*Theological Dictionary of the New Testament*
USQR	*Union Seminary Quarterly Review*
ZNW	*Zeitschrift für die neutestamentliche Wissenschaft*

ADDENDA

The article by D. M. Smith mentioned in n.4 will appear in *NTS* 21 (1974-75). To the literature cited in n.53 add the important essay by J. D. Purvis, "The Fourth Gospel and the Samaritans," to appear soon in *NovT*.

The dissertation by M. C. White, "The Identity and Function of the Jews and Related Terms in the Fourth Gospel" (Emory, 1972), to which I gained access only after this essay had gone to the printer, contains a good survey of pertinent literature and a careful but rather mechanical sorting of the usage in John. He fails to persuade me of his thesis that John is a "patchwork gospel," without consistency or unity.

THE KINSHIP OF JOHN AND ACTS

PIERSON PARKER
The General Theological Seminary

John is a gospel. Acts is not. Acts resembles the Third Gospel in language and style, and the words about "the former treatise" (Acts 1:1) fit Luke as they do no other book. And yet, in their reflections of early Christian thought, and supremely in what they say about Jesus, *John and Acts are closer to each other* than either of them is to Luke's Gospel. Their agreements together against Matthew and Mark are stronger still. That is to say, for all their differences of language and of topic, John and Acts are akin.

How the kinship came about, I shall try to guess toward the end of this study. Whatever be thought of that guess, however, the agreements themselves are inescapable.[1]

1. *Agreements about Jesus' career*

John 1:20 and 3:28 and Acts 13:25 all quote the Baptist as expressly denying his Messiahship. Both books have him say οὐκ εἰμὶ ἐγώ. No such flat denial is recorded anywhere else in the New Testament, not even at Luke 3:15 where, as in John-Acts, the people wonder who he is. Then consider:

John 1:27. ὁ ὀπίσω μου	Acts 13:25. ἔρχεται
ἐρχόμενος	μετ' ἐμέ
οὗ οὐκ εἰμὶ ἄξιος	οὗ οὐκ εἰμὶ ἄξιος
ἵνα λύσω αὐτοῦ τον ἱμάντα	τὸ ὑπόδημα (sing.)
τοῦ ὑποδήματος (sing.)	τῶν ποδῶν λῦσαι.

Neither Matt 3:11, Mark 1:7 nor Luke 3:16 is as close to John-Acts, here, as they are to each other.

Acts is interested almost exclusively in Jesus' *Judean* ministry.[2]

---

[1] Part of what follows was touched on in three earlier articles: "The 'Former Treatise' and the Date of Acts," *JBL*, LXXXIV (1965), 52-58; "Mark, Acts, and Galilean Christianity," *NTS*, 16 (1969-70), 295-304; "When Acts Sides with John," *Understanding the Sacred Text*, J. Reumann, ed. (Valley Forge: Judson, 1972), 203-215.

[2] Acts 1:3-9; 2:14, 22; 3:11f., 26; 4:5, 8, 10f.; 10:36-39.

John similarly devotes more than four-fifths of its narrative to Judea and the south.[3] These, incidentally, are the only New Testament books that mention Solomon's Porch (John 10:53; Acts 3:11; 5:12).

In both John and Acts, Jesus commands his followers to minister in Samaria (John 4:35-38; Acts 1:8). Not only does he never do that in the Synoptics: Matt 10:5 actually forbids such work! The words Σαμαρείτης, Σαμαρεῖτις, Σαμαρία together occur in John 9 times, Acts 8, but in Luke only 4, Matthew 1, rest of New Testament 0.

According to John and Acts, Jesus got his first disciples in Judea, while the Baptist was active, and apparently under his aegis (John 1:34-43ff.; Acts 1:21f.). Yet Matt 4:12-22 and Mark 1:14-20 say that Jesus secured his first disciples in Galilee, after the Baptist was imprisoned. On this point Luke's Gospel is vague: Peter gets a kind of call at the Sea of Galilee (5:10) but he is already a follower at 4:38f. Luke's only allusion to the Baptist's jailing is at 3:20, i.e., *before* it records Jesus' baptism; and it does not mention the Baptist in connection with that event (3:21ff.). As if to underscore their divergence here, John and Acts add that the inner band of disciples was with Jesus *from the beginning* (John 15:27; Acts 1:21). Luke 1:2 has ἀπ᾽ ἀρχῆς, but it is not clear whether that applies to the inner circle or to a larger group. Matthew and Mark lack the phrase entirely.

Some individual disciples are treated in similar ways in John and Acts. Both books name the other Judas (John 14:22; Acts 1:13); so does Luke 6:16, but not Matthew or Mark. Is the Philip of Acts 8 the "deacon" of 6:5,[4] or the apostle of 1:13? True, Peter and John follow up Philip's work (8:14-25) as though this Philip were a subordinate. On the other hand, the mission of 8:5-25 is to Samaritans who speak Aramaic, whereas the Philip of 6:5, 21:8 was appointed to work among speakers of Greek. Furthermore it was precisely the apostles who, Jesus had said, were to work in Samaria (Acts 1:8). *If* the Philip of Acts 8 is the apostle, he is named in Acts 15 times, John 12, and plays an outstanding role in both books. Yet Matthew-Mark-Luke merely list him among

---

[3] John 1:6-9, 15, 19-51; 2:13 - 4:3a; 5:1-47; 7:10 - 20:31 — 665 verses out of 816.

[4] Although no one is called "deacon" in Acts 6:2ff., the passage is commonly used in ordinations to the diaconate.

the Twelve (Matt. 10:13; Mark 3:8; 6:14) and otherwise totally ignore him. John treats Peter's denial much more leniently than the Synoptists do: Peter is willing to die for Jesus (John 13:37). The story of the denial is interrrupted by an interlude (18:19-24). At no point does Peter swear, or curse, or deny that he knows Jesus (cf. Matt 26:74; Mark 14:71; Luke 22:57). He just insists that he was not with the group in the garden (John 18:17, 25-27)—a lie, but an understandable one if he had attacked an officer! Acts knows nothing of the incident at all; and there Peter is able, with no apparent qualms, to accuse *others* of denying Jesus, using the very same verb ἀρνέομαι (Acts 3:13f.). John and Acts say that Peter ate with Jesus after the resurrection (John 21:11-22; Acts 10:41). Yet Peter is evidently absent from the meals of Luke 24, and nobody eats in Matt 28 or Mark 16:1-8.

In describing Jesus' mighty works, John and Acts say δι' αὐτοῦ (John 1:3, 7, 10; 3:17; Acts 2:22; 3:16). No other gospel has the phrase. John and Acts call Jesus' miracles "signs." [5] The Synoptics never do. Indeed Mark 8:11f. roundly condemns the notion that Jesus might perform signs, and Mark 13:4, 22 gives the word σημεῖα a frightening sense. Jesus' wonders proved, say John and Acts, that God was with him (John 3:2; 9:16; Acts 2:22; 10:38). People believed in him *because* they saw these works.[6] Contrast Matt 15:32 and 27:42! Perhaps, then, ἀνοίγειν ὀφθαλμούς has not just physical but theological overtones. It occurs in John 9 times, Acts 3, but Matthew 2, rest of New Testament 0.

The Pharisees as a group appear in better light in John and Acts than in the Synoptics. They are perplexed and bewildered, but they are not fiends; and opposition to Jesus and his people comes far more from the Temple leadership. In this opposition, a major part is taken by Annas (John 18:13, 24; Acts 4:6). Yet, while Annas is named at Luke 3:2, he does nothing whatever in that Gospel; and Matthew and Mark never mention him. In John and Acts opponents are bent on punishing Jesus' followers, out of fear lest these lead the populace astray.[7] For both authors, Isa 6:10 prophesied the rejection of Jesus by his countrymen (John 12:40; Acts 28:27). This *might* be reflected at Luke 19:42, but

---

[5] Acts 2:22; John 2:11, 23; 3:2; 4:54; 6:2, 4, 26; 7:31; 9:16; 11:47; 12:18, 37; 20:30.

[6] Acts 8:13; 13:12; 17:13, 34; John 1:50; 4:48, 53; 6:30; 10:37f.; 11:45; 20:8, 25, 29, 31; also the allusions to "signs," n. 5 above.

[7] John 7:12, 47; 16:2; Acts 4:17f., 21, 29. Cf. *Clem. Rec.* I.62.1.

elsewhere the Synoptists all cite Isa 6:10 to explain not his rejection but his use of parables (Matt 13:14f.; Mark 4:12; Luke 8:10).

Judas' death, say John and Acts, was in fulfilment of Scripture.[8] Perhaps Matt 27:9 links Jeremiah and Zechariah to that death, though far more likely the allusion is only to the place of burial. The other Synoptists do not mention the event.

John 19:27 and Acts 1:14 indicate that, after the crucifixion, Jesus' mother dwelt in or near Jerusalem. No Synoptist says that. In fact Matthew-Mark-Luke show no interest at all in what became of her, their last notice of her being at the rejection in Nazareth (Matt 13:55; Mark 6:3) or at Jesus' refusal to see her (Luke 8:20).[9]

John and Acts hold that Jesus' resurrection was foretold in Scripture.[10] Luke 24:26f. does not quite say this, and the idea is absent from Mark and, strangely enough, from Matthew. Unlike the first three Gospels, John and Acts both say that there were many resurrection appearances, over a considerable period of time (John 20:19-21:1; Acts 1:3; 13:31). Jesus was seen not by everybody but by a chosen few (John 14:19, 22; Acts 10:40f.). Acts puts *all* the resurrection appearances in Judea (1:2-13; 3:1-26; 10:34-41ff.; 13:30f.). So does John, except for one incident in the appendix. Luke 24 too is confined to Judea, but it records events of only one day. Mark, in contrast, contemplates Galilean appearances exclusively (14:27f.; 16:6f.) and Matt 28:9-20 makes Galilee the chief resurrection setting. Note also John's and Acts' use of the verb ἀνιστάναι. In Acts, *God raised up* Jesus from the dead (2:24-32; 13:32, 34; 17:31). In John, *Jesus will raise up* others from the dead (6:39f., 44, 54). No other New Testament book employs ἀνιστάναι, transitive, in this way, and Luke's Gospel does not have it at all.

John 20:17 and Acts 1:6-11 tell of Jesus' ascension. Yet Matthew and Mark never mention it. Perhaps Luke 9:51 does (ἀνάλημψις) or Luke 24:51b (ἀναφέρετο εἰς τὸν οὐρανόν), but the former is ambiguous, the latter is textually doubtful, and both are uncon-

---

[8] John 17:12, 20; Acts 1:20. Possibly they had Psalm 109:8 in mind.

[9] The descriptions of "Mary the mother of . . . ," Matt 27:56, Mark 15:41, 47 and Mark 16:1, resemble those of Jesus' mother at Matt 13:55, Mark 6:3, but Matthew and Mark do not notice it. If she is among the women of Luke 8:3 or 23:49, 55, Luke does not say so.

[10] John 20:9; Acts 2:25-31; 13:29-35; 17:2f.; 26:2f.

scionably cursory for so enthralling an event. Then consider:

> Acts 7:56. Behold, I see the heavens opened, and the son of man standing at the right hand of God.
> John 1:51. You will see the heaven opened, and the angels of God ascending and descending upon the son of man.
> John 3:13. No one has ascended up to heaven, except the one who came down from heaven, namely the son of man [who is in heaven].[11]
> John 6:62. What if you see the son of man ascend where he was before?

All these passages diverge from Synoptic usage. Matthew-Mark-Luke say that the son of man *will come* on clouds in the future,[12] or *will sit* in judgment here on earth.[13] Perhaps Luke 12:8f. *foresees* the son of man in heaven. No Synoptic matches the John-Acts imagery of the son of man now risen, now ascended, now in heaven.[14]

2. *Agreements about Jesus' message*

Acts quotes few of Jesus' words, and almost none from before his death (20:35?). However, Acts voices many ideas which *according to the Fourth Evangelist* came from Jesus himself. For example, John's only discussion of the Kingdom of God is in a discourse on the Holy Spirit (3:3, 5, 8). In Acts *every* mention of the Kingdom is in a context that tells of the impact of the Spirit: in Jerusalem (1:3, 5), Samaria (8:12, 15), Iconium (13:52; 14:22), Ephesus (9:6, 8), Miletus (20:23, 25), Rome (28:23, 25, 31). The only Synoptic passages at all comparable are Matt 10:7, 12 and Luke 4:14, 43, and there the relation, if any, is much more remote. Matt 5:3 even says that the Kingdom belongs to the *poor* in spirit; whatever πνεῦμα means there, it could hardly have been so used had there been any thought of linking Kingdom and Spirit as John and Acts seem to do.

Indeed, whereas Synoptic teaching about the Spirit is scanty, in John-Acts it is well developed. Compare, e.g., John's story of Nicodemus with Acts' story of Pentecost:

---

[11] Ὁ ὢν ἐν τῷ οὐρανῷ is absent from Alexandrian MSS, but appears in Caesarean, and in most versions and patristic citations.
[12] E.g. Matt 24:30; 26:64; Mark 13:26; 14:62; Luke 21:27.
[13] E.g. Matt 16:27; 25:31ff.; Mark 8:38; Luke 9:26; 17:30.
[14] Luke 24:7 is post-resurrectional, but merely recalls a pre-resurrectional saying. Actually the nearest equivalents to John-Acts, here, are Rev. 1:13, 14:14 which describe the heavenly Christ as "like a" (not "the") son of man.

John 3:8, 11f. The *wind* blows where it will, and you hear the *sound* of it, but do not know whence it *comes*, and whither it goes. So is every one who is born of *the Spirit* ... We *speak* what we know and bear witness of what we have seen; and you do not receive our witness ... How shall you believe if I tell you heavenly things?

Acts 2:2-4, 6, 12f. Suddenly there *came* from heaven a *sound* as of the rushing of a mighty *wind* ... And they were all filled with *the Holy Spirit*, and began to *speak* ... as the Spirit gave them utterance ... And when this sound was heard, the crowd were all amazed and were perplexed, saying to one another, What does this mean?

If, as I have suggested elsewhere, John 4 was a later insertion,[15] then the unnamed feast that followed Nicodemus' visit (John 5:1) was itself a Pentecost. Further, John and Acts, but not the Synoptics, tell how the Spirit comes after Christ has completed his ministry (John 7:39; Acts 1:5, 8),[16] at Christ's behest (John 16:7, 14; Acts 2:33), and creates the apostolic witness (John 15:26f.; Acts 6:3; 15:8).

John and Acts share a host of other concepts which, in John, are attributed to Jesus.[17] In the New Testament, only Jesus and Peter speak of "the gift (δωρεά) of God" (John 4:10; Acts 8:20). John and Acts have much on speaking boldly or openly—usually παρρησίᾳ in John, μετὰ παρρησίας in Acts.[18] The idea occurs once in Mark (8:32), nowhere in Matthew or Luke. Of the New Testament historical books, only John and Acts refer to the "seed of Abraham," "seed of David;" these are their only uses of σπέρμα. and in both, "seed of Abraham" always means Israel, "seed of David" always means Christ.[19] (The same distinction holds throughout the Epistles, except at Heb 2:16 which is obscure, and Gal 3:16 where the "seed of Abraham" is Christ.) At John 10:12, Jesus predicts that wolves will come among the sheep to scatter and destroy them; Paul makes a like prediction at Acts 20:29. At John 10:34f. Jesus applies Psalm 82:6 to Judaism, and uses the plural θεοί, while Acts uses the same plural in reference to apostate

---

[15] "Two Editions of John," *JBL*, LXXV (1956), 303-314.

[16] But John may intend to date this coming on the night after the resurrection (20:22f.), or even at the crucifixion (19:30) when Jesus said "Τετέλεσται," and thereupon παρέδωκε τὸ πνεῦμα.

[17] Items in this paragraph are given in the order of their first appearance in John.

[18] John 7:13, 26; 10:24; 11:14; 16:25, 29; 18:20; Acts 2:29; 4:13, 29, 31; 28:31.

[19] John 7:42; 8:33, 37; Acts 3:25; 7:5, 6; 13:23.

and pagan ideas (7:40; 14:11; 19:26); no Synoptist uses it at all. The δόξα θεοῦ (John 11:4, 40; 12:43; Acts 7:55) is never mentioned in Matthew-Mark-Luke. At John 16:33, Jesus says to the disciples, "In the world you have tribulation; but θαρσεῖτε, I have overcome the world." At Acts 23:11 he tells Paul, "Θάρσει, for as you have testified about me at Jerusalem, so you must bear witness also at Rome." Θάρσειν does not occur in Luke. In Matthew and Mark it relates only to healings.

Although John and Acts have far less eschatology than have Matthew-Mark-Luke, they agree closely in what they do say. They are the only historical books in the New Testament to declare, unequivocally, that Jesus will return (John 14:3; 21:22f.; Acts 1:11). There will be a general resurrection of both righteous and unrighteous.[20] God appointed Christ to judge the world.[21] Christ *has come* as Judge (John 5:27; 9:39; Acts 10:42). So Acts, quoting Joel 3:1, seems to think the present moment is "the Last Day" (Acts 2:17). John is the only other New Testament historical book to mention "the Last Day", though, unlike Acts, it gives no hint of when that day is to be.[22]

As to Jesus' personal claim, in John he calls himself the Light for the world; and the figure recurs time and again in this Gospel.[23] In Acts' accounts of Paul's conversion, Jesus is always associated with light (Acts 9:25; 22:6-11; 26:13), and elsewhere he, or his gospel, is called light for the world (13:47; 26:18, 23). Yet in the Synoptics, the idea appears only at Luke 2:32, an echo of Isa 42:6, 49:6. Only in John and Acts does any one but Jesus speak the phrase "the son of man" (John 12:34, Acts 7:56). In John, Jesus explicitly calls himself the Messiah (4:25f.; cf. 9:35-37) and the author's own purpose, he declares, is to establish that claim (20:31). In Acts, that is the purpose of Christian missionaries in the synagogues (9:20; 18:5, 18). Οὗτός ἐστιν ὁ Χριστός (John 4:29; 7:26, 41; Acts 9:22). And both John and Acts link this insistence to the resurrection (John 20:31; Acts 13:32f.; 17:2f.).

3. *Agreements in the author's own viewpoints*

Some items of their common Christology seem less closely related, in John, to Jesus' own words. Only in John and Acts do

---

[20] John 5:28f.; 6:39f.; 11:24; Acts 23:6; 24:15.
[21] John 5:22, 30; 8:15f.; Acts 17:31; but cf. John 3:17.
[22] John 6:39f., 44, 54; 7:37; 11:24; 12:48. Cf. James 5:3; II Peter 3:3; II Tim 3:1.

human beings call Jesus "Savior" (John 4:32; Acts 5:31; 13:23). At Luke 2:11 angels do so, but at Luke 1:47 the Savior is God. Matthew and Mark do not use the term. John 1:29, 36 calls Jesus the ἀμνός, as does Acts 8:32 in a quotation from Isa 53:7. No other New Testament book does this.[24] John and Acts both discuss popular expectations of The Prophet. At John 1:21, the Baptist is not The Prophet. At John 6:14 and 7:40, crowds think that The Prophet is Jesus. At Acts 3:22, 7:37 it *is* Jesus. Even the Johannine Logos might have counterparts in Acts:

> Acts 10:36. He sent *the Word* (τὸν λόγον) to the sons of Israel. (Cf. John 1:11).
> Acts 13:26. To us [Jews] *the Word* of this salvation was sent. (Cf. John 1:14).
> Acts 13:48. They glorified *the Word* of God. (Cf. John 1:14).
> Acts 20:38. ... to God and to *the Word* of his grace. (Cf. John 1:16f.).

This correspondence, however, cannot safely be pressed.

John and Acts use the verb πιστεύειν far more often than the Synoptics do: John 93 times, Acts 39, Matthew 11, Mark 10, Luke 9. In the first three Gospels πιστεύειν *always* means the cast of mind that makes miracles possible. In John-Acts it *never* means that; instead it refers nearly always to believing in Christ.[25] Again, the words μαρτυρεῖν, μαρτυρεῖσθαι, μαρτυρία, μαρτύριον, μάρτυς together occur in Acts 31 times, John 48 (μαρτυρεῖν and μαρτυρία only), but Luke 8, Mark 7, Matthew 6.

Next, John and Acts take remarkably similar attitudes toward Judaism and the Jewish Law. Consider, e.g., these expressions:

	John	Acts	Matthew	Mark	Luke	Other NT
"the Jews"	64	50	4	6	5	5
"Jews," no art.	3	20	1	0	0	10
"Jew," sing.	4	10	0	0	0	11
	71	80	5	6	5	26

---

[23] John 8:12; 9:5; cf. 1:4f., 9; 3:19-21; 11:9f.; 12:35f., 46.

[24] I Peter 1:19 says he was *like* a lamb. Revelation has a different word, ἀρνίον.

[25] Similarly with the noun πίστις which John lacks: In the Synoptics it almost always denotes the power to bring about miracles. Of a score of occurrences in Acts, only two have that meaning (3:16; 4:9f.), the rest referring to deep religiousness, and commitment to Christ and his movement.

John and Acts each speak of "Jews" (plural) more than twice as often as all the rest of the New Testament combined. Because of this persistent usage it is sometimes supposed that the Johannine author must have been gentile, even anti-Semitic. Yet Paul, a Jew and proud of it, used the expression;[26] so did the author of Rev 2:9, 3:9; and so, says Acts, did Peter. These expressions show not anti-Jewishness, but intense *interest* in Judaism—or else in Judea, since Ἰουδαῖος can mean "Judean." The interest in Judaism is demonstrated in many other ways. Of the New Testament historical books, *only John and Acts*

—use the word "Israelite."[27]
—refer explicitly to Jewish ἔθος.[28]
—refer to Shechem, and to Gen 33:19 and Jos 24:32 (John 4:5; Acts 7:16).
—mention Joseph the son of Jacob (John 4:5; Acts 7:9, 13, 14, 18).
—use the noun περιτομή (John 7:22f.; Acts 8:8; 10:45; 11:2).
—use the verb περιτέμνειν in reference to general circumcision of children and adults.[29]
—say that Moses gave the Jews circumcision (John 7:22; Acts 7:8; cf. Gen. 17:10-13).
—mention punishment by stoning (λιθάζειν).[30]

Similar, too, are John's and Acts' stances with regard to the surrounding culture. Only here do we meet the figure of the βασιλικός (John 4:46, 49; Acts 12:20). Of New Testament books, only these two mention the Greek language (John 19:20; Acts 21:27).[31] These are the only New Testament historical books to speak of Ἕλληνες.[32] John's Greeks appear, however, to be proselytes or else Greek-speaking Jews, for they live in the Diaspora (7:35) and

---

[26] I Cor 9:20; Gal 2:13; I Thess 2:14; plus 10 instances without the article, and 13 of Ἰουδαῖος singular. The Thessalonian passage is more vitriolic than anything in the Fourth Gospel.

[27] Singular at John 1:48; plural at Acts 2:22; 3:12; 5:35; 13:16; 21:28.

[28] John 19:40; Acts 26:3. Elsewhere Luke's Gospel, like Acts, has ἔθη, where Jewish ἔθη are plainly meant: Luke 1:9; 2:42; Acts 6:14; 15:1; 21:21; 28:17.

[29] John 7:22; Acts 7:8; 15:1, 5; 16:3; 21:21. Luke's Gospel has it only for John the Baptist and Jesus (1:59; 2:21). Matthew and Mark do not have it at all.

[30] John 10:31-33; 11:8; Acts 5:26; 7:59; 14:19. The only other New Testament allusions to stoning are at [John 8:5, 7], II Cor 11:25, Heb 11:37.

[31] Unless we read γράμμασιν ἑλληνικοῖς at Luke 23:38.

[32] Masculine plural; see John 7:35; 12:20; Acts 14:1; 16:1, 3; 17:4; 18:4; 19:10, 17; 20:21; 21:28. One female Ἑλληνίς does appear at Mark 7:26.

come to Jerusalem to worship at the feast (12:20). Only John and Acts have the word 'Ρωμαῖος.[33] Soldiers (στρατιῶται) appear in Acts 13 times, John 6 (all in chapter 19), but in Matthew only 3, Luke 2, Mark 1.

The topics so far considered involve a *vocabulary* which John and Acts share, to the exclusion or near exclusion of the first three Gospels: ἀμνός, ἀνιστάναι transitive, ἀνοίγειν ὀφθαλμούς, ἀπ' ἀρχῆς, βασιλικός, δι' αὐτοῦ, δόξα θεοῦ, δωρεά τοῦ θεοῦ, ἔθος of Judaism, Ἕλληνες, Ἑλληνηστί, ἐσχάτη ἡμέρα, θεοί plural, Ἰουδαῖος singular, Ἰουδαῖοι plural, Ἰσραηλείτης, λιθάζειν, μάρτυς and derivatives, οὐκ εἰμὶ ἐγώ, περιτέμνειν and περιτομή, πιστεύειν in Jesus, Ῥωμαῖος, Σαμαρία and derivatives, σπέρμα Ἀβρααμ, σπέρμα Δαυείδ, στρατιῶται, σωτήρ, ὑπόδημα singular.

Also the following occur in John and Acts but never in Matthew, Mark or Luke. Those starred do not appear anywhere else in the New Testament: ἁγνίζειν, ἀκούειν + παρά, ἄλλεσθαι, *ἄν τις, ἄνω, γογγυσμός, δεκαπέντε, δέκατος, διατρίβειν, *ἐὰν μή τις, *εἴπας participle, ἑλκύειν, ἐντολή.... ἵνα, *ἐξέρχεσθαι καὶ εἰσέρχεσθαι, *ἐπιλέγεσθαι, ἐρῶ with personal accusative, ἐχθές, ζῆλος, ζήτησις, *ζωννύναι, κἄν with indicative, λαμβάνειν ἐκ, λούειν, μαίνομαι, μάχομαι, *μένειν ἐπί + accusative, *νεύειν, *ὁμοῦ, *οὕτως .... ὥστε, *παρ' αὐτοῖς, περιϊστάναι, πιάζειν, σημαίνειν, σύρω, *σχοινίον, τύπος, ψύχος.

4. *Parallel stories*

Finally, many stories about *the young Church in Acts* resemble stories about *Jesus in John*.

In John, Jesus goes from Jerusalem (2:13ff.) through Judea (3:22ff.) into Samaria (4:4ff.). In Acts 2-8 the Apostles make a like progress; and the order, Jerusalem-Judea-Samaria, is explicitly asserted at Acts 1:8; 8:2.[34] In both series, the sojourns in Jerusalem involve signs and wonders, but also opposition from Temple authorities. In both, the missions to Samaria are highly successful.

At John 7:15, Jesus' opponents think him unlettered and unlearned. At Acts 4:13, the apostles' opponents find them unlettered and ignorant.

---

[33] John 11:28; Acts 2:10; 16:21, 39f.; 22:25-27, 29; 23:27; 25:16; 28:17.
[34] John 3:22 says that Jesus went from Jerusalem εἰς τὴν Ἰουδαίαν γῆν. This is sometimes attributed to carelessness or ignorance, for Jerusalem is *in* Judea. Since Acts makes a like division, however, it is probably *we* who are ignorant of ancient ways of describing the country.

At John 7:50f., Nicodemus, a Pharisee and member of the Sanhedrin, warns that body against hasty condemnation of Jesus. At Acts 5:34ff., Gamaliel, a Pharisee and member of the Sanhedrin, warns that body against hasty condemnation of Jesus' followers.[35]

At John 4:53, a nobleman "and all his house" believe. At Acts 11:14, a centurion "and all his house" receive the Holy Spirit. At Acts 16:14f., Lydia "and all her house" are converted. At Acts 16:31 it is the Philippian jailer "and all his house." The only thing remotely like this in the Synoptics is Luke 19:9, "Salvation has come to this house"—which is much less sweeping.

In John 9 a beggar, blind from birth, is healed, to the consternation of the Jewish authorities. In Acts 3 a beggar, lame from birth, is healed, to the consternation of the Jewish authorities. In each case the healed man later shows up in the Temple, and

| *John* 9:8 ... the neighbors and those who watched him previously when he was a beggar said, "Is not this he who sat ... ?" | *Acts* 3:9f. ... all the people recognized him as the one who sat begging ... and they were filled with wonder.. |

At John 11:46-51, Caiaphas and others of the Sanhedrin meet and are in a quandary. At Acts 4:5-17, Caiaphas and others of the Sanhedrin meet and are in a quandary. They say:

John 11:47f. What do we do?	*Acts* 4:16f. What shall we do to these men?
For this man does many signs.	For it is manifest to all ... that a notable miracle has indeed been wrought through them
If we let them alone thus, all the people will believe in him ... It is expedient for you that one man should die for the people.	... But that it spread no further among the people, let us threaten them.

At John 18:18, they "made a fire of coals, for it was cold (ψῦχος)." At Acts 28:2, they "kindled a fire .... because of the cold (ψῦχος)." These are the only places in the New Testament where the weather gets ψῦχος.

At John 18:22f., Jesus gets slapped for insulting the high priest

---

[35] *Clem. Rec.* I.65.1ff. makes Gamaliel, like Nicodemus, a secret convert. Cf. John 12:42; also *Act. Pil.* 5.

Annas. At Acts 23:2-5, Paul gets slapped for insulting the high priest Annas. The coincidence is the more notable because, to judge from non-Christian information, Annas had long since been officially replaced by Caiaphas.[36]

At John 18:31, Pilate tells the Jews that it is a matter for *their* law, not for a Roman tribunal. At Acts 18:15, Gallio tells the Jews that it is a matter for *their* law, not for a Roman tribunal.

At Acts 17:5-8, "the Jews" stir up a mob, set the city in an uproar, try to bring Jesus' followers out to the crowd, drag one of them before the city tribunal, accuse him and his companions of upsetting the people. The story is strongly reminiscent of Jesus' trial before Pilate, in John 18:28-19:15, right down to the accusation that Jesus sought to replace Caesar (John 19:12, 15; Acts 17:7).

5. *Some common omissions*

Most of what the Synoptic Gospels say is peculiar to those three books, so it would be bootless to list everything in Matthew-Mark-Luke that is absent from John and Acts. However, some Synoptic themes are pressed so constantly, so emphatically, that it is worthy of note when John and Acts ignore them. This is especially the case when a theme ought, one would think, to have served John's and Acts' purposes admirably.

Jesus' family. John and Acts know that Jesus had brethren but, unlike the Synoptics, they fail to name most of them.[37] Neither John nor Acts (nor Luke) says that he had sisters. Cf. Matt 12:50; 13:56; Mark 2:32ff.; 6:3.

Galilee. The Synoptists concentrate on a Galilean ministry (Matt 4:12-18:35; Mark 1:14-9:50; Luke 4:14-9:50).[38] The Twelve are commissioned to work there (Mark 6:6ff.; cf. Matt 10:5ff.; Luke 9:1ff.). The Fourth Gospel recalls no such commission, and less than one-sixth of it is allotted to Galilee. Acts barely mentions Jesus "beginning from Galilee," shows no interest in the Christian

---

[36] Cf. Josephus, *Ant.* XVIII.ii.1.

[37] John 2:12; 7:3, 5, 10; (20:17?); Acts 1:14. The James of Acts 12:17; 15:13; 21:18 is presumably Jesus' brother (cf. Gal 1:19; 2:9) though Acts does not say so. Contrast Matt 12:46-49; 13:55; (28:10); Mark 3:31-34; Luke 8:19-21.

[38] In Luke 9:51-18:34, geographical settings are notoriously vague; but much of that section, too, parallels materials that Matthew and Mark locate in Galilee: Luke 9:57-62; 10:13-16, 21-23; 11:1-26, 29-36; 12:1-12, 22-34, 49-59; 13:18-30; 14:25-35; 16:14-18.

movement there, names no other northern sites of Jesus' work (cf. 9:31; 10:37; 13:31). At Acts 1:8, in fact, Jesus commands the apostles to "be my witnesses in Jerusalem, and all Judea and Samaria, and to the uttermost part of the earth," with not a word for Galilee.

Place names. Not just Acts, but John too, ignore northern places like Caesarea Philippi, the Decapolis, Gadara, Gennesaret, Gerasa. They are equally oblivious of some southern spots: Jericho, Bethphage, Gethsemane. Yet all those places, north and south, are crucial for the Synoptic story. Nor do John-Acts name τὸ ὄρος τῶν ἐλαιῶν. (Acts 1:12 has ἀπὸ ὄρους τοῦ καλουμένου ἐλαιῶνος, which is not the same thing, and which does not appear elsewhere in the New Testament.)

The local scene. Camels are mentioned often in the Synoptics, especially Matthew, but never in John or Acts. The plural σάββατα is applied to a single sabbath, in Matthew 5 times, Mark 5, Luke 4; but Acts has the word only at 17:27 where three successive sabbaths are meant, and John does not use it at all. John and Acts never allude to tax collectors and their work; yet τελώνης and τελώνιον together appear 11 times in Luke, 9 in Matthew, 4 in Mark.

John the Baptist. Despite their intense interest in John the Baptist, neither the Fourth Gospel not Acts recalls Jesus' baptism. They do not call John βαπτιστής, though Matthew does so 7 times, Mark 2, Luke 3. In the Fourth Gospel and Acts, the Baptist does not refer to the Coming One as "he who is mightier than I;" [39] contrast Matt 3:1; Mark 1:8; Luke 3:16.

Elijah. Matt 11:14 and 17:10-12 assert positively that John the Baptist is Elijah *redivivus*, and the same idea is implied at Mark 9:12 and Luke 1:17. Yet the idea is ignored in Acts and is flatly rejected at John 1:21, 25. Further, the very name Elijah occurs nowhere else in John, and never in Acts, whereas Matthew has it 9 times, Mark 9, Luke 8.

The transfiguration is a, one might almost say *the*, major turning point in Jesus' career as the Synoptists portray it (Matt 17:1-8; Mark 9:2-9; Luke 9:28-36). John and Acts do not mention it.

Last Supper. Neither John nor Acts recalls the institution of the Eucharist at the last supper. John does record meals in or near

---

[39] The omission is particularly surprising at John 1:33; 3:5; 3:28-30; 4:1f.; 16:7; and at Acts 13:25.

Jerusalem (12:2-8; 13:2-30ff.) but it says nothing of what was eaten or its significance.[40] Acts has many meals (2:42, 46; 10:40f.; 20:7-11; 27:33-38) but connects none of them either to Passover or to any word or deed of Jesus.

Jesus' trial. Neither John nor Acts dates the trial on the Passover. Neither recalls a hearing before the Sanhedrin.[41] John and Acts both say that people *asked* Pilate to release some one other than Jesus (John 18:39f.; Acts 3:14) but neither of them says that Pilate did so! John calls that other prisoner a λῃστής, Acts an ἄνδρα φονέα, but neither of them says that he had actually engaged in insurrection. Contrast Mark 15:7; Luke 23:19.

The crucifixion. The Synoptics say that Jesus was crucified along with λῃσταί (Matt 27:38; Mark 15:27; Luke 23:32) but there is no such suggestion in John or Acts—not even at John 19:18. The Synoptists report fearful prodigies attending the crucifixion: darkness (Matt 27:45; Mark 15:33; Luke 23:44f.);[42] the Temple veil rent lengthwise (Matt 27:51; Mark 15:58; Luke 23:45); earthquake, bursting tombs, corpses walking in the Holy City (Matt 27:51-54). John and Acts know nothing of all this.

The resurrection. According to the Synoptics, Jesus often foretold his resurrection. Matthew which, strangely, does not find that resurrection predicted in Scripture, has the largest number of predictions from Jesus himself, though Mark runs a close second.[43] Luke at one point bases the resurrection on Scripture (24:26f., 32) and it reports far fewer of Jesus' own forecasts (9:22; 18:33; [24:7 = 9:22]). In contrast, Acts and John make much of the Old Testament basis, while giving no positive predictions from Jesus at all.[44] This is the more surprising in the Fourth Gospel,

---

[40] Contrast the meals in Galilee, John 2:1-12; 6:3-15; 21:4-13. These all involve supernaturally provided, lavishly excessive supplies of food and drink.

[41] Contrast Matt 26:57ff.; Mark 14:53ff.; also Luke 22:66ff. Luke at least has no *night* meeting of the Sanhedrin, Luke 22:54f., 63f. being informal and rather like John 18:12f., 22f.

[42] In the best MSS, Luke 23:45 reads τοῦ ἡλίου ἐκλίποντος. Taken literally, this would be impossible during or near the full moon of Passover.

[43] Matt 12:40; 16:21; 17:9, 23; 20:19; 26:32; 27:63; 28:6; Mark 8:31; 9:9f., 31; 10:34; 14:28; 16:7.

[44] John 2:19-23 gives an obscure saying which *the author* takes to be a resurrection forecast. Jesus himself, however, does not say it is. Neither do the authors of Matt 26:61 or Mark 14:58 when alluding to a somewhat similar saying.

which everywhere emphasizes Jesus' clairvoyance, and still more his knowledge of the future.[45]

As is seen from the last item, John and Acts not only ignore important aspects of Jesus' *career* as the Synoptists record it. They are likewise oblivious to some of his most emphatic and most cherished *teachings*.

Forgiveness. John and Acts say little about forgiveness. The verb ἀφιέναι occurs in Matthew 47 times, Mark 38, Luke 32; but in John 14, Acts 3.

Wealth. In Matthew and Mark, and even more in Luke, Jesus talks about wealth and its evils. The words πλούσιος, πλουτέω, πλοῦτος together occur 14 times in Luke, 4 in Matthew, 3 in Mark.[46] John and Acts use none of these words, and carry no warnings against riches, even though some of their characters are obviously persons of means.

Adultery. The words μοιχαλίς, μοιχᾶσθαι, μοιχεύειν, μοιχός appear in Matthew 12 times, Mark 5, Luke 4, other New Testament 12. Except for the spurious John 7:53-8:11, John and Acts do not mention the subject of adultery.

Food laws. No one would suspect, from John or Acts, that Jesus ever set aside any dietary laws. On the contrary, Peter at Acts 10:14 has never heard of such a thing; and despite Peter's vision (10:10-16; 11:5-10) the Jerusalem apostles retain food prohibitions for gentile converts (15:29; 21:25).[47] Yet Mark 7:19 has it that Jesus declared *all* foods "clean." (Cf. Matt 15:10-20; Rom 14:14.) Here, as so often elsewhere, the Third Gospel seems to equivocate. It has nothing resembling the Acts prohibitions. Yet in using Mark, it skips *every* passage that would modify or abrogate a Mosaic ordinance: Mark 2:27; 7:1-23, (28f.); 10:2-12; 12:31b-34.

Hypocrites. Ready as they are to denounce enemies of Jesus, and enemies of his band, John and Acts have not a word about hypocrites or hypocrisy. Yet in the Synoptics, espedially Matthew, that is *the* sin against which Jesus inveighs most heavily. Ὑποκριτής

---

[45] The passages are far too many to list in detail. Instances of clairvoyance appear in chs. 1, 2, 4, 6, 11, 13, 20; of foreknowledge in every single chapter.

[46] Rest of New Testament 41. The epistles have also πλουτίζειν and πλουσίως.

[47] At John 4:8, 31-34, Jesus refuses Samarian food, thus *perhaps* showing more strictness than his disciples about dietary ordinances. But if so, what did he eat during the next two days?

and ὑπόκρισις together occur 15 times in Matthew, 4 in Luke, 2 in Mark.

The fate of Israel. The Synoptics contain many forecasts of Jerusalem's doom. Some are ambiguous, others unmistakable.[48] Those in Luke are especially vivid, often reading like *vaticinia ex eventu.*[49] Yet Acts has not the slightest foreshadowing of the city's fate. In John, the only possible allusion is 4:21ff.:

> "The hour is coming when neither in this mountain nor in Jerusalem will you worship the Father.... The hour is coming *and now is,* when the true worshippers will worship the Father in spirit and in truth, for such the Father seeks to worship him."

Actually that no more predicts the fall of Jerusalem than of Mount Gerizim. It is a theological statement, with near equivalents in the words of Stephen and of Paul (Acts 7:48-50; 10:24f.).

Woes. There are no "woes" in John or in Acts, and neither of them uses the word οὐαί. Matthew has it 13 times, Mark 2, Luke 14, rest of New Testament 11.

Leaven. Of the New Testament historical books, only John and Acts have no word about leaven. *Un*leavened bread is mentioned at Acts 12:3; 20:6; but even that is ignored in John, despite its constant references to the Passover.[50]

Use of parables. The Synoptics make Jesus' parables both rich, and fundamental to his proclamation. With the possible exception of John 16:21f., John and Acts recall no parables, and neither of them uses the word παραβολή.

Christology. Finally, John and Acts are alike in disregarding important facets of Synoptic Christology. For example, while they speak of the "seed" of David, neither of them ever calls Jesus David's son. Yet in Matthew he is 10 times so designated, 3 being in direct address; in Mark, and also in Luke, he is 4 times called "son of David," 2 being in direct address. Again, although John and Acts both expect fierce "wolves" to come among Christ's flock (John 10:12; Acts 20:19), neither of them predicts the coming of false Messiahs. The Synoptists do (Matt 24:4, 5, 24; Mark 13:5, 6, 28; Luke 21:8).

---

[48] Cf. Matt 21:40-43; 22:7; 23:35-39; 24:6f., 15-22, 34; Mark 12:9f.; 13:7f., 14-20, 30.
[49] Luke 11:50f.; 13:34f.; (17:31); 19:27, 41-44; 20:15f.; 21:9f., 20-24, 32.
[50] John 2:13, 23; 6:4; 11:55; 12:1; 13:1; 18:28; 19:14.

6. Inferences

Thus at some 100 points John and Acts share material that Matthew, Mark and Luke either lack entirely or give very little weight to. Conversely, we looked at about 50 items which the Synoptists regard as of paramount importance, but which John and Acts totally or almost totally ignore. This second group is inevitably incomplete and could easily have been extended. Both groups run the gamut from single words and usages to full narratives, Christological concepts, and cultural attitudes.

Often the gap is about equally wide from Matthew, from Mark, and from Luke. At times, however, John-Acts diverge *further* from one Synoptic than from the other two; at other times the separation from one is *narrower* than from the other two. Of the approximately 150 items above examined, John and Acts stand *farthest* from:

Matthew	Mark	Luke	
3 times	3 times	1 time	regarding Jesus' career,
—	1 time	—	regarding Jesus' message,
—	1 time	2 times	in their own viewpoints,
13 times	1 time	4 times	in ignoring important Synoptic items.

Conversely, they stand *least far* from:

Matthew	Mark	Luke	
2 times	—	13 times	on Jesus' career,
—	1 time	1 time	on Jesus' message,
—	—	1 time	in their own viewpoints,
1 time	6 times	12 times	in ignoring important Synoptic items.

Counts like these are bound to be inexact, and estimates by others would doubtless vary here and there. No variation is likely, however, to change the over-all result. John and Acts stand together at wide remove from Luke, wider from Mark, widest of all from Matthew.

Now among the common John-Acts expressions noticed above—expressions rare or absent elsewhere in the New Testament—we find a number of syntactical forms: ἀκούειν παρά, ἀπ' ἀρχῆς, ἄν τις, ἄνω, δι'αὐτοῦ, ἐὰν μή τις, εἴπας participle, ἐντολὴ ἵνα, ἐξέρχεσθαι καὶ εἰσέρχεσθαι, ἐρῶ with personal accusative, κἄν with indicative, λαμβάνειν ἐκ, μένειν ἐπί with accusative, ὁμοῦ, οὐκ εἰμὶ ἐγώ, οὕτως .... ὥστε, παρ' αὐτοῖς. It is just possible, then, that part of their common material reached these authors in fixed or even written form. Yet it cannot have been a large part. Even in John and Acts most of these expressions are fairly infrequent. The real literary affinities of Acts are with the Gospel of Luke.

The chief links between John and Acts lie evidently in the realm of *concepts*, or common background and inherited attitudes. For example, these two books are almost *anti*-Galilean. They take almost no interest in Elijah, the great prophet of the north. Indeed, they say little at all about areas north of Samaria.

In contrast, both books are deeply concerned about Judea. Jesus, they imply, got his first disciples there. Judea was, for them, the chief scene of Jesus' work. There, too, he appeared after his resurrection. There his mother and brethren remained.

John and Acts are interested in Samaria too. Jesus commanded his followers to labor there. Each book makes Samaria the site of an unusually effective ministry.

They are aware of the Roman yoke. They speak of the Greek language, and of Roman people, and particularly of Caesar and his soldiers.

Supremely they are conscious of Judaism; and each author writes as though he stood within it. Words like "Jew", "Israelite," "seed of Abraham" fall steadily from their pens. If circumcision posed more problems for the author of Acts than for John, neither book hints that Jesus set aide either it or any Mossaic requirement. And they write of the gifts of God, and the glory of God, and of Israel, and of Joseph.

In short, *John and Acts evidently reflect that form of Jewish Christianity that was known and practised in the Roman province of Judea.*

This was a Christianity which honored John the Baptist, but refused to call him "Baptist" or to link him to Elijah. It ignored, or did not know, the tradition that John baptized Jesus. And John, it taught, explicitly denied his own Messiahship.

Among Jesus' disciples, the chief concern of this Christianity was with Peter and his outstanding leadership. It knew of a second Judas, and of one Philip who played a leading role. It believed that there lay, upon all the disciples, a commission to *witness* to the risen Christ who had appeared to a chosen few.

Apparently this Christianity knew little or nothing of Jesus' parables; or that the spoke about wealth, or adultery, or hypocrisy, or forgiveness; or that he foretold his own resurrection—though it proclaimed that resurrection itself.

Indeed, this Christianity had a view of Christ in many ways "higher" than was preached in the north. Jesus is, positively, the Messiah. That is the burden of the Christian message. Belief means, supremely, belief in him. He is the seed of David. He is Light, and Lamb, and Savior to Israel. Through him God worked miracles, signs that convincingly demonstrated his claim. Another proof is Scripture, which foretold his rejection and death and rising again. The very phrase "the son of man" designates this risen and ascended One. This Christianity's thoughts of the future, even in their scantiness, underscore its Christology. Jesus is Judge. He ushers in the Last Day. He, himself, will return.

He, too, is the One who instigates the Spirit's coming. The impact of the Spirit is linked to Pentecost, but also to baptism, and to the Kingdom of God. The Spirit, too, empowers and makes possible the witness of this Christianity's apostles.

A FOREWORD TO THE STUDY OF THE SPEECHES IN ACTS*

MAX WILCOX
University College of North Wales, Bangor

Our estimate of Acts as a whole is closely related to the view we take of the origin and nature of the speeches which form such a striking, indeed distinctive, feature of the book. At one time they were regarded as valuable sources for the reconstruction of the thought and teaching of the Primitive Church, and with certain modifications this position still has its supporters today. However, the overwhelming tendency in recent years has been to see the speeches as to all intents and purposes due to Luke's hand, although it is not unusual to concede that the writer may have had access to older material in places. The pioneer of this theory seems to have been J. G. Eichhorn, in 1810,[1] who drew attention to the apparent parallel with the use of speeches by Thucydides in his *Peloponnesian War*. It was subjected to careful criticism in 1873 by Martin Kähler in a detailed study which not only appears to have received rather too little attention, but which also in many ways strikingly anticipates modern redaction critical work.[2] We shall have cause to refer to his contribution more fully later. Yet another earlier writer who advanced the theory was Paul Wendland, in his classic *Die urchristlichen Literaturformen*,[3] where the contemporary debate about Luke as a "primitive Catholic" (*frühkatholisch*) writer who looks back on the stories he tells from a standpoint far beyond that of the Apostolic period is clearly foreshadowed. But the present vogue of the view we are discussing is more directly due to the studies of H. J. Cadbury[4] and Martin Dibe-

---

* The original draft of this essay was read as a paper at a Colloquium, held in the Department of Religious Studies, Brown University, Providence, Rhode Island, U.S.A., on April 30th, 1971.

[1] In his *Einleitung in das Neue Testament*, 5 vols. (1804-27), Vol. 2 (1810). (Not available to the writer.)

[2] 'Die Reden des Petrus in der Apostelgeschichte', *TStKr* 46 (1873), 492-536.

[3] Tübingen (1912) (2. u. 3. Aufl.), HNT I, 3, pp. 314-335.

[4] *The Making of Luke-Acts*, New York (1927), pp. 184ff.; *The Beginnings of Christianity*, I (ed. F. J. Foakes Jackson and Kirsopp Lake), Vol. 5 (London, 1933), pp. 402-427, etc. (cited hereafter as *Beginnings*, I).

lius.⁵ However it is not our intention here to attempt a full-scale review of the history of the question, but rather to limit ourselves to consideration of the main issues involved.⁶

The earlier phase of the discussion concerned two basic questions: (a) the historical reliability of Acts (or of its sources), and (b) the mode of its composition. In this debate Cadbury, appealing to the custom of ancient historians, notably Thucydides, saw the speeches of Acts as contrived deliberately by the author; he concluded that although they were 'devoid of historical basis in genuine tradition', they nevertheless were evidence of 'the simple theological outlook conceived to have been original by at least one Christian of the obscure period at which Acts was written'.⁷ We see at once the underlying assumption that Luke was an historian, yet it is by no means clear that this is the only view possible. Indeed Wendland had already queried it in 1912, and suggested that Acts was not so much a true piece of historical writing as something in between history and epic, rather like the Books of the Maccabees: 'Acts finds its real continuation in the stories of the martyrs and saints, the heroes of the later period of the Church'.⁸ On a somewhat different line, Dibelius argued that when everything was considered, the differences between Luke's work and that of ancient historians lay in the fact that he was essentially 'not an historian but a preacher'.⁹ This leads us to our last comment here. Over the years Luke has been cast in a number of roles—historian, biographer, apologist, writer, preacher, and in more recent times, theologian.¹⁰ In fact Paul Schubert asserted that he was 'one of the most theo-

---

⁵ 'Die Reden der Apostelgeschichte und die antike Geschichtsschreibung', *SAH*, phil.-hist. Kl. 1949, Abh. 1 (Heidelberg, 1949). The paper was originally given in 1944. Reprinted in *Aufsätze zur Apostelgeschichte*, hrsg. Heinrich Greeven, Göttingen, 1951 (2. Aufl. 1953), pp. 120-162 = ET *Studies in the Acts of the Apostles*, London, 1956, pp. 138-185.

⁶ For further detail on the history of the question, see J. Dupont, *Les sources du Livre des Actes*, Bruges, 1960, and Ulrich Wilckens, *Die Missionsreden der Apostelgeschichte*, Neukirchen-Vluyn, 1961 (2. Aufl. 1963).

⁷ *Beginnings*, I, 5, pp. 426-427.

⁸ *op. cit.*, p. 325 (translation mine).

⁹ *Studies*, p. 183 (= *Aufsätze*, p. 157).

¹⁰ Cf. C. K. Barrett, *Luke the Historian in Recent Study*, London, 1961; B. S. Easton, 'The Purpose of Acts', in *Early Christianity: the Purpose of Acts and other Papers*, ed. F. C. Grant, London, 1955; Hans Conzelmann, *Die Mitte der Zeit*, Tübingen, 1953 (2. Aufl. 1957), ET *The Theology of St. Luke*, London & New York, 1960; J. C. O'Neill, *The Theology of Acts in its Historical Setting*, London, 1961, 2nd. ed. 1970.

logically minded among the New Testament authors...' [11]—a far cry from Cadbury's assessment of the matter cited above. It is plain that the time is due for some kind of reappraisal of the whole question.

The aim of the present study is a relatively modest one. It is to sift out the basic problems which underlie the whole discussion of the nature and origin of the speeches in Acts, to discover how best to seek a reliable, meaningful, and coherent solution to the question. It is thus primarily a study in method.

I

Let us begin, then, with the question, how far the speeches are Lukan compositions and how far they incorporate earlier material: or, to put it another way, to what extent Luke was not merely a compiler or editor but an author in his own right —leaving aside for now consideration of just what kind of author he might have been.

Unfortunately Luke himself is very reticent about the degree of his own involvement. Nevertheless, if we make the common assumption that the Third Gospel and the Acts are by the same person, it seems clear enough that the writer did not see his role as restricted to that of a mere compiler: in Lk 1:1-4 he tells us (i) that others had already set out to commit the tradition concerning Jesus to writing, (ii) that he himself now proposed to do likewise, albeit making a thorough job of it, and (iii) that his immediate aim was to enable "Theophilos' (whoever he may have been) to appreciate the certainty of the matters in which he had been instructed. We are not told whether he made use of written material, but simply that it was in existence. Nor do we gain any hint of the manner in which he might have utilized it in his work, if in fact he had chosen to do so, apart from the rather broad comment that his account was to be 'meticulous' (ἀκριβῶς). For this we are left to make such inferences as we dare from a comparative study of the parallels with, and deviations from, other Gospels, and to a certain extent, material found elsewhere in the NT.[12] In this

---

[11] 'The Structure and Significance of Luke 24', in *Neutestamentliche Studien für Rudolf Bultmann zu seinem 70. Geburtstag*, Berlin, 1954, (BZNW, 21), pp. 165-186. P. 171.

[12] See especially H. J. Cadbury, *The Style and Literary Method of Luke*, Cambridge, Mass., 1920 (Rp. New York, 1969), Harvard Theological Studies, 6, and *The Making of Luke-Acts*. Apart from comparison with the Gospels

connection Paul Schubert, commenting on Lk 1:1-4, observed:

> "'Following all things with keen interest' and 'writing an orderly account' meant for him but one thing, to collect and select traditional material and bits of information and to base on them an account that would make sense, the sense which his own understanding of the Christian faith (ὁδός) made."[13]

Schubert then sees Luke not as a mere editor or compiler, but as a fully-fledged author. If, however, we leave aside till later consideration of what is meant by Luke's 'own understanding of the Christian faith' as a factor in the composition of the Gospel, and turn instead to the question of his use of 'traditional material and bits of information', two important points emerge. (1) Continued study of the Gospels has led to some radical re-thinking about what is meant by a 'source'. This is one result of form and redaction criticism. Thus the older, 'monolithic' conception of the 'source(s)' of the (Synoptic) Gospels will not do. Accordingly Luke, in shaping his Gospel, may have had less regard for such compilations or accounts as were already to hand than for the actual elements of traditional material which they sought to enshrine. By way of illustration we may recall that outside the Passion Narratives, it is in the actual Sayings of Jesus themselves that the most convincing agreements between the various Gospels are to be found. Setting, order and context can change, but the Sayings retain a surprisingly high degree of fixity both of form and of content.[14] (2) In the case of Acts evaluation of the matter is obviously hampered by the total absence of any kind of parallel account: we lack the advantages of a 'synoptic' situation, except to the limited degree that some parts of Acts do have material if not verbal parallels with certain passages in the Pauline letters, and occasionally elsewhere.[15] Nevertheless it seems reasonable to suppose that if Luke did in fact have at his disposal for Acts some kind of traditional material, written or oral, he may well have treated

---

we have several notorious problems, such as the inversion of the order of the uprisings of Judas the Galilean and of Theudas (Gamaliel's speech, Ac 5, 35ff.), the problem of reconciling Acts and Galatians, etc.

[13] *loc. cit.*, p. 171.

[14] This fact is acknowledged by Cadbury, cf. *Beginnings*, I, 5, p. 416; *The Making of Luke-Acts*, p. 188 (Luke takes over the Jesus-Sayings material from earlier sources and gives it to us 'with only slight change of wording'). Cf. especially, such passages as Matt 19:28b//Lk 22:30.

[15] Of particular interest in this connection is Ac 1:15-26 (cf. Matt 27:3-10). See below, pp. 222-223.

it in a way similar to his handling of the Jesus-tradition in his Gospel.[16]

This brings us to our next problem: how far the manner in which Luke used the traditional material preserved also in Mark and/or Matthew constitutes a valid model for his employment of some such material in Acts. With this goes the related question, how far such material was in fact available for Acts.

These matters have received rather less attention than is their due. Thus Haenchen largely discounts the possibility that Luke may have had any extensive material to hand for Acts which he could have treated as, for example, his Gospel sources: 'there just were no "histories of the Apostles" ' which he could have so used.[17] What he is entitled to say, however, is no more than that if there were such, they are no longer extant as separate entities. Nor is it correct to assume that because the Apostles and their fellow-workers did not proclaim their own words and deeds but those of Jesus, no tradition like that preserved in the Synoptic Gospels concerning Jesus had formed about Paul and the Apostles.[18] Here Dibelius was far more careful: he even looked to the possibility that the primitive Church may have preserved—'probably in the form of stories'—accounts of incidents of significance in its earlier history; these would have served 'as a perpetual reminder to them of the reason for their existence.'[19] It has further been argued that Acts is in a different class as literature from the Third Gospel, and that as a result it is not valid to use Luke's methods in the Gospel as a model for literary analysis of Acts.[20] Moreover, Luke was bound by the precedent of Gospel-form in the one case, whereas

---

[16] After all, we do not have parallels to all of the material in Luke's Gospel. What are we to say about the way he may have treated the special-material? Further, may it not be that the Baptist-Sayings were also preserved with care?

[17] *Die Apostelgeschichte*, Göttingen, 5. Aufl. 1965, p. 73, = ET, *The Acts of the Apostles*, Oxford, 1971, p. 82.

[18] Haenchen, *op. cit.*, p. 73 = ET, p. 82.

[19] *Studies*, p. 124 (= *Aufsätze*, p. 109). Of particular interest is his later comment that in assessing the circumstances of early Christianity 'we must keep to the principle that individual elements of tradition, such as the story of Ananias and the note about Barnabas, are older tradition and therefore more reliable than what the author added, namely the narrative-summary' (*Studies*, p. 128, = *Aufsätze*, 112-113).

[20] Cf. Dibelius, *Studies*, p. 4 (= *Aufsätze*, p. 12); p. 146 (= *Aufsätze*, pp. 126-127); p. 195 (= *Aufsätze*, pp. 165-166).

in the other he was not.[21] Or it may be objected that in any event Luke would not have been so conservative in his treatment of information about the Apostles and the early Church as he seems to have been in dealing with the Jesus-tradition: he may well have handled them in a 'freer way'.[22]

A more fundamental objection is that appeal to Luke's literary procedures in the Gospel is doomed to fail from the outset, regardless of whether he may have had some kind of source material available for Acts, since the degree of liberty which he shows towards his sources is so great that no sure decision could be made either way. So Jacques Dupont, developing a line foreshadowed by Cadbury.[23] This brings us rather near to the heart of the matter, for if Luke has indeed proceeded as Dupont claims, that is, if he was not content to transcribe his sources but recomposed them in his own language and style, how should we ever determine the issue at all?[24] There is a hidden assumption here, however, that all has been rewritten smoothly and without hiatus or seam. But in fact unevennesses and inner difficulties do remain in the speech-material and must be explained. That is, purely linguistic and stylistic criteria are not enough. Is it then possible after all to distinguish between Lukan composition and Lukan redaction in the speeches of Acts? Let us return briefly to discussion of the Synoptic model.

We begin by recalling that where Luke and Mark run parallel, the Lukan account is frequently quite thickly strewn with marks of Luke's favourite style and diction. Moreover, in a significant number of places these replace—so to speak—their Markan equivalents. The phenomenon was noted long ago by Cadbury, and may be readily confirmed by consulting a synopsis.[25] Now if such

---

[21] Ibid., p. 124 (= *Aufsätze*, p. 109): 'The *new style* is conditioned by the *new task*'.
[22] Cf. Cadbury, *Beginnings*, I, 5, pp. 416-417.
[23] Dupont, *Les sources du Livre des Actes*, p. 85.
[24] Ibid., pp. 159-160.
[25] Cadbury, *The Style and Literary Method of Luke*, p. 73ff. Several examples of the addition of Lukan favourite words and phrases in these parallels may be given: p. 154-155, the Lukan καλούμενος is 'inserted' into the form preserved in Mark; p. 155, a similar use of ὀνόματι; p. 199, for the Markan εὐθύς we find the Lukan παραχρῆμα. But despite changes of this and related kinds, Cadbury is still able to say that 'the words of Jesus themselves, the *verba ipsissima*, whether reported by Mark or found in the source designated as Q, have rarely been retouched by the author of the third Gospel to give them a wider scope or application.' (p. 124). Cf. also Dupont, *Les sources*, p. 85.

phenomena were found in a speech in Acts they would be held by many to indicate Lukan composition; in the case of the Gospel, however, we see that what is before us is more probably Lukan *redaction*: may not the same apply in the case of the speeches in Acts? Again, in Lk 1-2 it is well known that the style departs quite radically from most of the rest of Luke-Acts (with the possible exception of parts of Ac 3 and 4).[26] But this deviation is nevertheless often passed off as simply due to the fact that Luke has changed his style.[27] The danger of circularity in the argument is plain. True, a change of style does not in itself compel the assumption of source, although it would be consistent with it. Conversely, the presence of Lukan style and diction—and in some profusion—in passages of Luke where Mark is available for comparison is not usually held to exclude use of sources: Luke, we are told, has edited or revised what he found in Mark.[28] Why should the matter be otherwise where no parallel text is to hand (e.g., in Acts or special-Luke)?

Next, comparison of Luke with Mark and Matthew leads to the observation we mentioned earlier, that apart from the Passion Narrative it is in the Sayings of Jesus that the most compelling verbal agreements are to be found.[29] That is, whereas the narrative and framework material in which a Jesus-saying is embedded may well have undergone quite radical revision, the evangelist seems to have been rather more reluctant to alter so severely the words of the Master himself. This is all the more striking where the setting is quite different in one Gospel from another, but the saying itself virtually constant. Perhaps the real link behind the Gospels is to be sought in basic collections of Jesus-sayings? Be that as it may, it is clear that there were limits to which Luke for one was prepared to go in editing his material. That is, not only is Lukan revision 'uneven' in the Gospel, it is in a sense 'selective': may not the same be true in Acts?

If we take these two lines of thought together, we see that for the Third Gospel, (i) style serves to indicate redaction rather than source, and (ii) some elements of tradition seem, so to speak, 'more resistant' to redaction than others. It is suggested that this

---

[26] See the discussion in the writer's *The Semitisms of Acts*, Oxford, 1965, pp. 65ff.
[27] So Cadbury, *Beginnings*, I, 5, pp. 416-420.
[28] This is the basis of most comparative study of Luke and Mark.
[29] See above, note 25.

may provide a useful clue to the understanding of the problem of the speeches in Acts.

Now, if for the sake of the argument we were to assume that the speeches in Acts were in fact wholly Lukan compositions (whether or not they involved earlier material), it would surely be natural to expect them to fit their contexts. If, for example, Luke's model was the Thucydidean one, the speeches ought to represent at the least what the writer thought the speakers in each case would most probably have said, and in any case they should adhere as closely as possible to the general sense of what was actually spoken.[30] True, Luke may not have regarded himself as an historian, and he may not have followed the Thucydidean pattern: but it is still reasonable to expect a deliberately contrived speech to fit its context, and not look as though it was pasted in afterwards. But it is well known that in a number of cases this is simply not so: certain speeches seem awkward in their contexts—that of Stephen is quite notorious in this regard, as Foakes Jackson showed long ago.[31] Nor is it enough to argue, with Dibelius and Evans, that although the speeches in question do not fit their contexts they nevertheless fit the theme of the book as a whole rather than the specific occasions to which they are presently attached.[32] Apart from the rather subjective idea of 'the theme of the book as a whole' there is a further problem: it is not just that the speeches are difficult in their contexts in terms of their actual content, they are also—more importantly—in certain cases attached to those contexts by the most artificial of links. We have already noted the example of the speech of Stephen as a glaring one. It seems scarcely relevant to its context, comes out of it easily and the resultant text runs if anything more smoothly. In cold terms this suggests that the links between the speech and its present context are redactional rather than traditional. If we still hold that the speeches are wholly Lukan compositions, we would seem compelled to argue (a) that in certain cases at least, the author

---

[30] Thucydides, *Peloponnesian War*, 1:22.
[31] 'Stephen's Speech in Acts', *JBL* 49 (1930), 283-286.
[32] C. F. Evans, 'The Kerygma', *JTS* N.S. 7 (1956), 25-41, Cf. Dibelius, *Studies*, pp. 174-175 (= *Aufsätze*, p. 150). The point was raised long ago by Paul Wendland, *op. cit.*, pp. 331ff.: the author of Acts proceeds somewhat as does the Fourth Evangelist in the shaping of the speeches, and like him he makes little show of individualizing, frequently does not suit the speeches to their situation, but uses them as means of expressing his own religious views.

composed them independently of his narrative and after its completion, and then (b) that he subsequently inserted them into it, but was apparently either not prepared or perhaps unable to revise the whole sufficiently to eliminate the resultant seams. There are indeed some writers who think that Acts contains signs that its author for some reason or other had not finished revising it. Nevertheless to hold that the speeches or some of them were written by Luke and inserted into Acts at a later stage in its composition seems in many ways a theory of last resort. Would it not be simpler to argue that Luke may have needed to adapt to his story certain pieces of material which did not readily fit into it but which for some reason or other he did not feel prepared to abandon? We have seen already that in the Gospel he does not treat all his material in the same way, but shows a rather more conservative attitude towards the Jesus-sayings: is the problem here in the speeches possibly due to a similar conservatism with other early traditional material? If clear indications of the presence or use of earlier material could be detected in even a few of the offending speeches, we might well be taken a step further towards solving this problem.

To sum up, then, we have found one clue for our enquiry, namely, the fact that the links between certain of the speeches and their contexts appear to be redactional rather than traditional. This poses rather sharply the question of the manner in which the book was composed. But it is now time to look at another problem: what of the speeches themselves—are they unitary wholes or do not similar issues of tradition versus redaction appear within them too? Are they perhaps artificial attempts by the author of Acts to incorporate into his work elements of pre-existing traditional material? If so, in which direction does the composition-process run? That is, have bits of tradition been worked up into speeches and inserted into a basic narrative framework, or has the procedure perhaps been the reverse—with the narrative and the speeches being developed out of such material?

II

It has often been claimed that the speeches display a certain uniformity of structure and a tendency to complement one another.[33] Thus 'one passage in Acts often explains the line of argu-

---
[33] So, for example, Cadbury, *Beginnings*, I, 5, pp. 407-410; esp. p. 409.

ment which the very terseness of a speech elsewhere makes obscure through omission' (Cadbury).[34] Or again, even after allowance has been made for differences in content, the speeches reveal 'a *far reaching identity of structure*' (Eduard Schweizer).[35] Other examples might be cited. Hence it is argued that the speeches are Luke's work (despite the possible use of earlier material in places), and their purpose is to interpret the book at certain vital turning-points in its plot. Accordingly they reflect the outlook of the author rather than that of the speakers they purport to represent. A natural next step is to see them as evidence for Luke's own theology, rather than that of the Primitive Church. Thus, for example, the portrait of Paul which we gain through the speeches attributed to him in Acts differs so markedly from that presented to us in his own letters.[36] The book breathes the spirit of a later age, that of the emergent catholic church.[37]

This is not the whole story, however. In the first place, scholars are by no means agreed that Luke's theology—if that is really what the speeches give us—is that of primitive Catholicism. In particular, Hans Conzelmann has warned that while Justin, and indeed Ignatius and I Clement also, may rightly be claimed as 'early catholic', the essential marks of early catholicism 'are lacking in Luke or can be found only as initial traces'; Luke, especially in his Christology, far from being 'early catholic' and hence 'post-Pauline' in his thought, is working with 'pre-Pauline motifs and formulas'.[38] Likewise, Philipp Vielhauer has argued that although Luke's portrait of Paul is late, his Christology is nearer to that of the earliest Church.[39] He made this inference, however, on the assumption that the similarity of the speech of Paul in Ac 13 to those of Peter in the first part of Acts was due to the use by Luke of pre-formed material. He was thus aware of the operation of more than one factor in the creation of the speeches, that is, not only Lukan composition but also primitive, non-Lukan material. Far

---

[34] Ibid., p. 407.
[35] 'Concerning the Speeches in Acts', in *Studies in Luke-Acts*, ed. L. E. Keck and J. L. Martyn, London, 1968, pp. 208-216; p. 210. (The book is hereinafter referred to as *SLA*.)
[36] So Philipp Vielhauer, 'On the "Paulinism" of Acts', in *SLA*, pp. 33-50.
[37] Vielhauer, *l.c.*, p. 49.
[38] 'Luke's Place in the Development of Early Christianity', in *SLA*, pp. 298-316; here, pp. 304, 308. Similarly, Vielhauer, *SLA*, pp. 44-45.
[39] *l.c.*, p. 45.

from the speeches being homogeneous, attention is drawn to different strains within them.

This point has been taken up by J. A. T. Robinson and C. F. D. Moule. Robinson argued that the theology of the apostolic preaching as represented in the early speeches of Acts was not homogeneous: in Ac 3—and with 'reflections' in Ac 7—we have 'an extremely primitive Christology', essentially of the form, ' "We know who the Messiah will be" ', although it does not yet see the death and resurrection of Jesus as the event by which God inaugurates his Kingdom and reveals Jesus as Messiah.[40] Moule takes this a stage further and claims that it is 'flying in the teeth of the evidence' to maintain that Luke has imposed his own mentality uniformly upon the material: he has either tried to imitate various differing viewpoints, or has been controlled by sources, regardless of the extent to which he may have edited and shaped them.[41]

This last point was strikingly anticipated by Martin Kähler in the article mentioned at the beginning of this paper. In a discussion of the speech in Ac 3 (Peter), he pointed out how completely it belonged within the sphere of a really Jewish Christianity; it lived and moved so fully within the thoughtpattern of a Jew who believed in the Messiah and expected the imminent restoration of the Kingdom to Israel, that we should have to assume in any case a masterly imitation or a level of historical objectivity on the part of the 'inventor' such as is scarcely to be found.[42]

The whole question of the supposed uniformity of the speeches is thus thrown once more into the melting-pot. If the speeches were wholly the creations of Luke, we might well expect them to reflect *his* theology (unless, of course, we take refuge in the view that he is trying to imitate various viewpoints). If, on the other hand, he is working with some form of primitive tradition, it is open to us to ask whether the reverse may not have taken place— that is, whether the tradition may not have shaped the theology, rather than the theology the present form of the speeches. This would further be consistent with the presence of different strains within the speeches, and also with the fact that there are notorious

---

[40] 'The Most Primitive Christology of All?', *JTS* N.S. 7 (1956), 177-189, reprinted in *Twelve New Testament Studies*, London, 1962 (SBT, 34), pp. 139-153; p. 151.
[41] 'The Christology of Acts', in *SLA*, pp. 159-185; p. 182.
[42] 'Die Reden des Petrus ... ', *TStKr* 46 (1873), p. 516.

difficulties inherent in some of them.[43] We should not need to postulate the use of an extensive source or sources such as was proposed, for example, by Torrey;[44] rather, we might well find here clues to detection of different stages in the history of the transmission of the material, clues which survived because of a certain reluctance on the part of the author of Acts to smoothe out all the difficulties in his material. One may recall his restraint with the Jesus-Sayings.

Here it is appropriate to return to the article by Kähler. He acutely observed that although the speeches in Acts were in part very close indeed in language to the style of the author, this did not compel us to discount our initial impression of their authenticity.[45] The case was similar with the Sayings of Jesus: their basic character was still discernible through the varied treatment given to them by the three Synoptists, despite the hopelessness of attempting to determine with certainty just exactly what was said. We might not be persuaded by his proposal to compare the speeches of Peter in Acts with the teaching found in the letters which bear Peter's name, but the principle of seeking some external point of reference was surely right and fundamental. Kähler's aim was thus to sift out those elements in the speeches which might be traceable to the author of Acts, and then to examine the remaining parts where material foreign to Lukan style and diction appeared, so as to determine the limits of what we should today term 'tradition' and 'redaction'.

In the process of applying the criterion of 'Lukan style' Kähler noted several important facts:

(i) The speeches are not uniform in type: even length varies, but more seriously, whereas one speech may contain much non-Lukan material, another may not, but may be little more than a secondary development of material found elsewhere in Acts.[46]

(ii) In particular, in the more independently given speeches Luke's pen is detectable only in the redaction.[47]

(iii) In certain places the author may have had available a

---

[43] A useful summary of some of these is to be found in Wendland, *op. cit.*, pp. 315-317.
[44] *The Composition and Date of Acts*, Cambridge, Mass., 1916, (Harvard Theological Studies, 1).
[45] *l.c.*, p. 493.
[46] *l.c.*, pp. 531, 532, etc.
[47] Ibid., p. 532.

source or sources, which he revised with restraint; such material, however, most probably lay before him already in Greek translation.[48]

He thus strikingly anticipated the modern situation and looked for several stages in the development of the speeches. We might depict them as follows: (a) an Aramaic (or Hebrew?) stage, (b) a Greek stage embodying that material in whole or in part, and (c) Luke's reworking of it in the light of his own understanding of it.[49]

On this analysis, then, it would be open to us to ask whether the speech-form in Acts might not in fact be a Lukan device for incorporating into his work pieces of primitive Christian tradition. Such a theory would have the further advantage of helping to explain at once the apparent inner kinship between certain of the speeches and the signs that some of them at least rest upon or embody primitive material.

So far, however, we have still been speaking as though in some sense at least, the speeches were 'inserted' into a pre-existing narrative. Ulrich Wilckens, in his book on the so-called 'missionary speeches' in Acts, repeatedly speaks of the critical problem of determining whether the speeches *in their entirety* have been inserted into a ready-made narrative framework, and he comes up with a negative verdict.[50] It is pertinent, nevertheless, to ask just what would be left in Acts—especially in the first half—if we were to omit the speeches altogether. Consider, for example, the vagueness of the connecting links at Ac 1:15, 3:1, 5:1, 6:1, 8:1, etc. Have we in fact any more evidence for a pre-existing framework here in Acts than we have in the Gospels, or may not this assumption really belong with the lumber attaching to the old approach to the Gospels which saw them as basically histories or biographies of Jesus? In the earlier part of Acts at least, have we much more than collections of stories, not always too well understood by the author himself,[51] rather loosely put together on the whole, and giving an impression of historical writing by

---

[48] Ibid., pp. 535-536.

[49] Ibid., p. 535, 506, etc. This short summary is ours, and is inferred from Kähler's work, but is not explicitly stated by him in quite these terms.

[50] *Die Missionsreden der Apostelgeschichte*, p. 71. He does, however, allow that they may rest ultimately in whole or in part on pre-formed tradition.

[51] Cf. Ac 2:1ff., where the phenomenon of glossolalia is either misunderstood or misrepresented.

the simple fact that they follow one another in the book?[52] We do not, of course, deny that there are more logical links at places, e.g., Ac 8:2 (the 'scattering' of Church members after the stoning of Stephen), and the words of Ac 8:4 which take up this theme and use it as a peg on which to hang the Philip-story (Ac 8:5-40). But is it not still valid to ask whether such links are traditional (not to say historical) or redactional? With regard to the later part of Acts, the Pauline section, Philipp Vielhauer rightly observes that it was just this section to which Luke 'was most required to give form, for apart from the so-called itinerary, which provides the skeleton for 13:1-14:28; 15:35-21:6, it does not seem possible to demonstrate a source..'[53] Perhaps, then we are on a false trail when we ask whether the speeches were inserted into their framework; it may well be the framework, rather than the speeches, that is secondary.

Here a further question arises. Wilckens and others have argued that the speeches in Acts have a special importance for the understanding of the work, in that they have been placed at vital turning-points in the history of the primitive Church, as Luke portrayed it.[54] But if it could be shown that some of them at least embodied pre-Lukan material stemming from the Aramaic-speaking Church, it might be worth asking whether the process had not been the reverse: that is, might not the narrative have been composed out of, and in the light of, such traditional material as is incorporated in the speeches. Such a view might also explain the disturbances in the chronology of Acts [55] and the notorious difficulty of reconciling parts of it with other sections of the New Testament. One is reminded of Martin Noth's suggestion that in Ezra-Nehemiah, a distinctly odd piece of chronology alongside apparent citation of Aramaic documents is to be explained thus: the documents were primary, and the error entered through the Chronicler having failed to realize their order—he was thinking of another Darius and another Artaxerxes.[56] In the case of Acts this does not involve

---

[52] Dibelius also noted this; cf. *Studies*, pp. 106, 107 (= *Aufsätze*, pp. 94, 95).
[53] *SLA*, p. 33.
[54] Wilckens, *Die Missionsreden*, p. 71, 100, etc.
[55] For example, the apparent inversion of the order of the revolts of Judas the Galilean and Theudas, Ac 5:36-37. Or the notorious difficulties in relating Acts and Galatians, etc.
[56] *Überlieferungsgeschichtliche Studien*, I, Halle (Saale), 1943, pp. 152-153.

us in holding that it repeats word for word several blocks of already written source-material, but rather that at certain places it gives the impression of being *based* on traditional material, and in some of them at least of transmitting it rather faithfully.

Our problem now is the positive one of developing a method of approach which may lead to some kind of objective solution of the problems raised above.

III

First, there is the criterion of language and style. Here we have already seen above how the presence or absence of Lukan characteristics is more indicative of redaction than of origin.[57] More important is 'non-Lukan' style or language, and if we are seeking marks of a link with the Aramaic-speaking Church, then the location and evaluation of the Semitisms in Acts must be of the highest importance. The writer has already dealt with this subject at length elsewhere, and there is no need (nor indeed space) to go over the matter in detail here.[58] But one example from that work should perhaps be mentioned in the present context. In Ac 13:22, after the opening words 'I found David' (Εὗρον Δαυειδ, Ps 88 (89):21) we find the quotation 'a man after my (own) heart' (ἄνδρα κατὰ τὴν καρδίαν μου cf. 1 Kgd 13:14, ἄνθρωπον κατὰ τὴν καρδίαν αὐτοῦ = MT), followed by the words 'who will do all my wishes' (ὃς ποιήσει πάντα τὰ θελήματά μου.). Now let us observe: (i) the part cited from 1 Sa 13:14 = 1 Kgd 13:14 differs slightly from the LXX form as we have it, although the deviation would not require a text different from the MT; (ii) the second part, which for the moment we have left unidentified, has usually in the past been referred to Isa 44:28 (Πάντα τὰ θελήματά μου ποιήσει). However, the Targum to the Prophets reads at 1 Sa 13:14 גבר עביד רעותיה, which may be read either, 'a man (who) does his wish', or 'a man (who) does his wishes', depending upon how we vocalize the last word.[59] Here then we have set down side by side two different— and as it happens—alternative readings from the same verse of Scripture. True, J. A. Emerton has tried to counter by saying that despite the differences between Acts and the LXX, 'a resemblance in wording remains, and it is difficult to deny the dependence of

---

[57] See above, p. 212.
[58] *The Semitisms of Acts*, Oxford, 1965.
[59] Ibid., pp. 21-24.

the former on the latter'.⁶⁰ Well, apart from the 'ἄνδρα' and the words in the second line, agreeing with the Targum *against* both MT and LXX. But after all, it is hard to think how else an original כלבבו might have been rendered into Greek, if not by κατὰ τὴν καρδίαν (αὐτοῦ). He finds a further difficulty in 'why a single Hebrew phrase should appear in two different renderings in the same quotation in Acts...' ⁶¹ This, of course, is just the precise point at issue. Short of Luke having had a most incredible memory, capable of remembering accidentally such combinations from various versions of the Scriptures, the simplest explanation would surely be to see the origin of the present quotation in a piece of source-material originally in Aramaic and Hebrew: first the Hebrew form, then the Aramaic (Targumic) form is given. We are reminded of the way in which several of the MSS. of the Palestinian Pentateuch Targum do just this: they cite the opening words of a verse in Hebrew, and then follow them by the Targum. Related phenomena can be attested in other early Jewish material.⁶² That is, not only is Emerton's objection no real objection, it is in fact one of the keys to the fact that what we have before us is very probably rooted in primitive tradition going back to the Aramaic stage of the Church. The fact that Luke does not seem to have accommodated it to the LXX may suggest no more than that he either acted conservatively with it, or simply did not recognize it as from the Targum, as by the time he got it the material was already in Greek form anyway.

Secondly, there is the criterion of appropriateness to a primitive Jewish-Christian setting. This is, of course, very risky ground, as it is difficult to determine with any real certainty what was and what was not actual practice in the First Century A.D. However, haggadic procedures and at times examples of rules of interpretation such as those of Hillel do appear in the Gospels, and also in the Pauline Letters: ⁶³ it would not be unreasonable to look for them also in Acts—even if to do so, we must put aside once and for

---

⁶⁰ In a review of *The Semitisms of Acts, JSSt* 13 (1968), 282-297; p. 287.
⁶¹ *l.c.*, p. 287.
⁶² The use is quite regular in Codex Neofiti and in the Geniza fragments published by Paul Kahle in his *Masoreten des Westens*, II, Stuttgart, 1930.
⁶³ There is not space to go into details here, but we may refer to the interesting article by J. Jeremias, 'Paulus als Hillelit', in *Neotestamentica et Semitica: Studies in Honour of Matthew Black*, ed. E. E. Ellis and Max Wilcox, Edinburgh, 1969, pp. 88-94.

all any built-in prejudice against the possibility of a 'Hellenist' such as Luke transmitting such material. We shall have cause in a moment to look at one possible example of early (pre-Lukan) haggadic material in Luke,[64] but for the moment let us mention briefly the attempts by J. W. Doeve and J. W. Bowker to trace Jewish patterns in some of the speech-material in Acts.[65] In particular Bowker has argued that in certain speeches of Acts we seem to have traces of synagogal preaching-forms; of special interest is his claim that the two passages in Paul's speech in the synagogue at Pisidian Antioch which appear to be linked there —viz., 1 Sa 13:14 (which we have just discussed above) and 2 Sa 7:6-16—actually contain a verbal tally in the Hebrew text: ועתה ... לנגיד עמו and להיות נגיד עמי ... ועתה ('and now ... for a leader over his (my) people').[66] This fact—if it really has the significance Bowker sees in it—would further suggest that Luke's apparent unawareness of its role was probably due to the material being already in Greek as it lay before him. Certainly Luke can hardly have 'invented' it.

Thirdly, there are some places where objective comparison is possible between Acts and other New Testament writings. Here of first importance for our present enquiry is Ac 1:15-26, the Judas-tradition, with its near parallel in Matt 27:3-10. This has long been a difficult passage, and in many ways it seems that it was so to Luke also. In a recent article on the subject, the writer drew attention to the presence within it of a piece of material which appears to reflect closely an element of early Jewish tradition preserved in some of the Palestinian Targumim to Gen 44:18, in a quite extensive haggadah.[67] The material, as we know, forms part in Acts of a speech by Peter, and it would appear from the analysis in the article mentioned that Ac 1:18-19 (perhaps more correctly, vv. 17-19) formed part of a chunk of pre-Lukan scriptural exegesis related to that preserved in Pal.Tgg. Gen 44:18. In Acts it is used to deal with the defection of Judas and his replacement by Matthias, a man whose name is not thereafter mentioned. Although this piece of material, Ac 1:(17)18-19, has sometimes

---

[64] See below, pp. 222-223.
[65] J. W. Doeve, *Jewish Hermeneutics in the Synoptic Gospels and Acts*, Assen, 1953; J. W. Bowker, 'Speeches in Acts: a study in Proem and Yelammedenu Form', *NTS* 14 (1967-68), 96-111.
[66] *l.c.*, p. 103.
[67] 'The Judas-Tradition in Acts i, 15-26', *NTS* 19 (1972-73), 438-452.

A FOREWORD TO THE STUDY OF THE SPEECHES IN ACTS 223

been thought to be an 'insertion' into the speech, the evidence now suggests that the reverse is true: that the speech itself was probably woven around this element of the tradition. Its place in the Aramaic stage of the tradition is indicated by the quotation in vs. 17, not previously identified; by the 'haggadah' on it in vv. 18.19b, where there appears to be a play on the Aramaic words חלק and חקל behind the present text; and by other peculiarly Palestinian traits (for example, the stress on the 'Twelve'). Like the material referred to in Ac 13:22 above, however, this originally Aramaic and Jewish nature escaped Luke, as the text was probably already in Greek when it reached him.[68] He therefore recast it in a quite new form, and added to it the Psalm-quotations in vs. 20 to make new sense of it. We thus see a speech developing out of pre-existing tradition of Aramaic origin.

Fourthly—one hesitates to write 'lastly'—there is the case where there are no known parallels of a direct nature, but there are some 'material' parallels in a general way elsewhere in the New Testament. An example is Ac 2:1ff., where the phenomenon known to us from the Paulines as glossolalia, 'speaking with tongues', is interpreted by Luke as a language-miracle. Of immediate importance to us here, however, is that when Peter speaks in this section (vs.15), the words attributed to him show that glossolalia, and not a language-miracle, is what is involved. Thus the words put into Peter's mouth conflict with the Lukan interpretation of the event. This must surely heighten the possibility that the words attributed to Peter here, whether or not they are his, nevertheless have a greater claim to antiquity than scholars such as Cadbury and others might have been prepared to allow.[69]

It remains, then, to sum up. What is striking about the four examples above is that they all suggest that Luke started with material of a primitive nature, some of it at least with roots back in the Aramaic stage of the tradition. On the other hand, the evidence so far as it goes seems to indicate that such material was already in Greek when it came to Luke. At certain points its Greek garb has masked features which might have been more obvious in Aramaic—word-plays, haggadic material, kinship with Jewish traditions preserved in the Targumim, etc.; at others, Luke seems to have given it a new meaning. But even so, despite the difficulties

---
[68] Ibid., p. 452.
[69] Ibid., p. 443.

which have resulted for him and his readers, he has treated it rather conservatively. It therefore appears to have had a somewhat higher status for him at least than is commonly assumed. This alone would seem to demand that we clear our minds once and for all of the assumption that a quest for pre-Lukan material in the speeches is a wholly vain pursuit because 'no tradition corresponding to the Synoptic had formed with reference to Paul and the Apostles'.[70] Rather, our enquiry, though limited in scope, would suggest that Acts arose out of the need to preserve and make sense of certain basic elements of traditional material; they were not pasted in, so to speak, afterwards, but were of the very essence of the venture, even though the use to which the author of Acts put them was at times different from that which they originally had.

A second point should now be made. Whereas much of the work on the speeches in Acts since Cadbury and Dibelius has concerned itself with discussion and evaluation of the Lukan factor in their composition, this enterprise was in danger of becoming 'circular': what was needed was an objective method of determining the existence and extent of non-Lukan material within the speeches, so that the author's methods of composition could be examined. This then rightly raised the question of what criteria, if any, could be developed to unearth and evaluate that pre-Lukan material.

We thus come to the criteria themselves. In what has been said above we listed four of them, and doubtless the number could be increased, but these are those we have so far found useful:

(a) Language and style, especially Semitism. This is the more convincing if it can be shown that Luke does not appear to have understood the forms in question himself.

(b) Appropriateness to a Jewish-Christian setting. Here the presence of certain thought-forms and modes of expression (e.g., haggadic procedures and other features known to be at home within a Jewish setting, but not proven to be so within a Hellenistic one) are examined and evaluated.

(c) Objective comparison with such elements as may have parallels elsewhere in the N.T., to elucidate their tradition-history.

---

[70] Haenchen, *op. cit.* p. 73 (= ET, p. 82).

(d) Apparent inconsistencies of interpretation of detail within a speech and its context, like the glossolalia/language-miracle problem in Ac 2.

What of the scope of such material? Here one important fact ought not to be overlooked. When we do locate signs of pre-Lukan material, we should be careful not only to avoid over-valuing it but also to remember that what we have found may be but 'the tip of the iceberg', so to speak. This is especially so with Semitisms of language and style, for it is well known that persons who are familiar with several languages not infrequently betray that fact only by the occasional slip; to hold that for Semitism to be present, whole tracts of material must be riddled with slips and deviant idioms is to confuse translation with literal translation. It is of course true that apparently isolated Semitisms do not *prove* that a whole section has had a Semitic origin, but they ought to warn us not to dismiss the possibility too hastily.

When we have thus examined the question of the nature and scope of the non-Lukan material in the speeches, we shall be in a better position to see how the author went about his work. In particular, we shall be better placed to determine whether the theology of the speeches is due to Luke, or whether here too his work may have been controlled to some extent at least by his material.

L'HYMNE CHRISTOLOGIQUE DE Col 1,15-20

Jugement critique sur l'état des recherches

PIERRE BENOIT, O.P.
École Biblique, Jérusalem

Le riche et beau passage de l'épître aux Colossiens, 1,15-20, a été depuis plus d'un siècle l'objet d'un intérêt critique qui ne s'est pas relâché dans les dernières décades. Sa structure littéraire, son contenu doctrinal, ses sources, autant de problèmes qui ont été et qui restent chaudement discutés.[1] Il serait difficile de reprendre tout cela dans un article nécessairement court. Mon propos est de résumer et d'apprécier le résultat de ces discussions, notamment en ce qui concerne la structure littéraire et l'origine du morceau. Le contenu doctrinal, qui commande si fortement la structure, sera nécessairement considéré, et aussi le ou les milieux de pensée où cette doctrine plonge ses racines, mais sans qu'il soit possible de poursuivre à fond l'examen critique des influences postulées. Aussi bien ne sera-ce pas nécessaire si l'on arrive à conclure que le passage s'explique au mieux par le génie de Paul lui-même, comme un aboutissement de sa pensée théologique, développée au cours des épîtres antérieures et cristallisée ici de façon nouvelle par réaction contre des spéculations rencontrées à Colosses.

I. — Avant d'examiner les structures qu'on a voulu imposer à ce morceau, les amputations ou les transpositions qu'on lui a infligées, il ne sera pas mauvais de le considérer d'abord tout simplement tel qu'il se présente, le laissant parler par lui-même, afin d'entendre d'abord sa propre justification et de ne le corriger que si cela est nécessaire.

Ce premier regard fait sauter aux yeux des parallélismes de mots ou d'expressions, des correspondances de langage ou de pensée, des reprises, des progressions, qui sont manifestement voulues et

---

[1] On trouvera à la fin de cet article une Bibliographie, à laquelle renvoient mes références en indiquant simplement le nom de l'auteur (avec la précision de tel ou tel ouvrage s'il en a écrit plusieurs), et à l'occasion la page ou les pages citées. — Parmi ces travaux, plusieurs offrent d'utiles revues de la marche de la recherche: ainsi ceux de B. Rigaux, de W. Schmauch, et surtout de H. J. Gabathuler.

qui doivent être reconnues si l'on veut bien apprécier les intentions de l'auteur.

On remarque d'abord les deux ὅς ἐστιν, aux vv. 15 et 18b, qui sont chacun suivis de deux termes accouplés se correspondant d'un verset à l'autre, d'une part εἰκών et πρωτότοκος (v.15), d'autre part ἀρχή et πρωτότοκος (v. 18). Autre parallèle, dans les deux cas l'énoncé est suivi par une justification commençant de la même manière: ὅτι ἐν αὐτῷ. Un troisième parallélisme s'impose: les deux débuts de propositions identiques, καὶ αὐτός, qui se correspondent manifestement et qui font des vv. 17 et 18a une petite cellule littéraire au centre du tableau, entre les deux propositions relatives.

La première impression qui se dégage de ces observations est celle d'un diptyque qui soutient littérairement l'exposé de deux thèmes mis en parallèle: vv. 15-17 la primauté du Christ dans l'ordre de la création; vv. 18-20 la primauté du Christ dans l'ordre du salut.

Mais, avant d'approfondir ce parallélisme doctrinal, il nous faut poursuivre le relevé purement formel des correspondances littéraires. Outre les charnières qui introduisent les propositions, on relève encore en cours de phrases des reprises verbales également intentionnelles. Dans chacune des deux propositions commençant par ὅτι ἐν αὐτῷ, on a les trois formules ἐν αὐτῷ, δι'αὐτοῦ, εἰς αὐτόν énoncées dans le même ordre: au v. 16 d'une part, aux vv. 19-20 d'autre part. Et on a aussi, deux fois, le couple ἐν τοῖς οὐρανοῖς et ἐπὶ τῆς γῆς: d'abord au v.16, et en ordre inverse au v. 20.

Ce n'est pas tout. Dans le premier panneau du diptyque, on remarque la triple occurence de τὰ πάντα, deux fois au v. 16, une fois au v. 17; et aussi le développement d'une même idée par les trois verbes qui se correspondent en se reprenant: l'aoriste ἐκτίσθη (acte de la création), le parfait ἔκτισται (la création considérée dans son effet qui dure), le parfait συνέστηκεν (résultat de la création: la subsistance dans l'être).

Un autre fait encore: la répétition constante du pronom αὐτός, qui apparaît douze fois (onze, si l'on adopte avec certains manuscrits l'omission de δι' αὐτοῦ au v. 20). Ce "lui" sans cesse repris se rattache au relatif ὅς du v. 15, qui lui-même s'accroche au ἐν ᾧ du v. 14. Un même et identique personnage est en cause tout au long du diptyque: celui des vv. 13-14, à savoir "le Fils bien-aimé (du Père), en qui nous avons la rédemption, la rémission des péchés". Le texte ne parle explicitement ni du Logos ou de la Sagesse, ni du Verbe "préexistant" ou "incarné". Cette distinction fréquente chez les exégètes ou les théologiens lui est étrangère. C'est la même et unique personne, Jésus Christ, à la fois éternel et temporel, céleste et terrestre, divin et humain, qui est tout entier, indivisible, sous les ὅς et les αὐτός du diptyque. Cette observation est importante et devrait dissiper un faux dilemme qui a mené à bien des impasses.[2]

Dernière observation d'ordre littéraire. Le v. 17 est fortement rattaché à tout ce qui précède: d'un côté, par τὰ πάντα, ἐν αὐτῷ et συνέστηκεν qui reprennent des expressions identiques ou analogues du v. 16, ainsi qu'il a été dit plus haut; de l'autre, par le πρὸ πάντων qui reprend le πρωτότοκος πάσης κτίσεως du v. 15. Mais nous avons noté aussi que, par son début καὶ αὐτός, ce v. 17 est mis en parallèle avec le v. 18a, qui a le même début. Or ce v. 18a, sinon par ses mots du moins par sa pensée, se rattache à ce qui suit. D'après le texte actuel, auquel nous nous en tenons volontairement pour le moment, ce n'est plus dans l'ordre de la création mais dans l'ordre du salut (nouvelle création) que le Christ est "Tête du Corps, de l'Eglise". On est donc amené, ainsi que je l'ai déjà suggéré plus haut, à voir en 17-18a une sorte de tristique intermédiaire qui relie entre eux les deux panneaux du diptyque tout en les distinguant: le v. 17 conclut le premier panneau en redisant la priorité temporelle et la causalité première du Christ dans l'ordre de la création; le v. 18a amorce le deuxième panneau en annonçant la primauté du Christ par rapport à son Corps, l'Eglise, c'est-à-dire dans l'ordre du salut. Joints l'un à l'autre par la répétition de la même formule καὶ αὐτός, ces deux versets jouent en somme le rôle d'une charnière qui distingue mais aussi rattache l'une à l'autre les deux parties de l'ensemble.

C'est ce que j'ai voulu exprimer par la disposition typographique que j'ai adoptée — sans pouvoir alors la justifier — dès la première édition (1949) de mon fascicule de la "Bible de Jérusalem" consacré aux épîtres de la Captivité.[3] Disposition que je reproduis ici en grec, en ajoutant des lettres qui divisent intérieurement les versets et seront des repères commodes pour la discussion qui va suivre.[4]

---

[2] Voir P. Benoit, "Préexistence et Incarnation", *RB* 77 (1970) 5-29 à la page 15.

[3] La mise en pages de ce fascicule, où le v. 17 commence le haut d'une page nouvelle, ne m'a malheureusement pas permis de faire sentir un interligne entre 16 et 17 comme je l'ai fait entre 18a et 18b.

[4] Ces lettres ne prétendent pas soutenir une division formelle de la structure; elles ne veulent que servir matériellement à décrire et à discuter les découpages des critiques.

15 *a* ὅς ἐστιν εἰκὼν τοῦ θεοῦ τοῦ ἀοράτου
    b πρωτότοκος πάσης κτίσεως
16   *a* ὅτι ἐν αὐτῷ ἐκτίσθη τὰ πάντα
        b ἐν τοῖς οὐρανοῖς καὶ ἐπὶ τῆς γῆς
        c τὰ ὁρατὰ καὶ τὰ ἀόρατα
        d εἴτε θρόνοι εἴτε κυριότητες
        e εἴτε ἀρχαὶ εἴτε ἐξουσίαι
     f τὰ πάντα δι' 'αὐτοῦ καὶ εἰς αὐτὸν ἔκτισται

17 *a* καὶ αὐτός ἐστιν πρὸ πάντων
    b καὶ τὰ πάντα ἐν αὐτῷ συνέστηκεν

18 *a* καὶ αὐτός ἐστιν ἡ κεφαλὴ τοῦ σώματος τῆς ἐκκλησίας

 b ὅς ἐστιν ἀρχή
      πρωτότοκος ἐκ τῶν νεκρῶν
        c ἵνα γένηται ἐν πᾶσιν αὐτὸς πρωτεύων
19   ὅτι ἐν αὐτῷ εὐδόκησεν πᾶν τὸ πλήρωμα κατοικῆσαι
20   *a* καὶ δι' αὐτοῦ ἀποκαταλλάξαι τὰ πάντα εἰς αὐτόν
        b εἰρηνοποιήσας διὰ τοῦ αἵματος τοῦ σταυροῦ αὐτοῦ δι' αὐτοῦ
        c εἴτε τὰ ἐπὶ τῆς γῆς εἴτε τὰ ἐν τοῖς οὐρανοῖς

L'analyse qui vient d'être esquissée rend compte de la plupart des termes et de leur place, mais il en reste quelques-uns qui semblent échapper au parallélisme. Ce sont, par exemple, en 16c-e les mots τὰ ὁρατὰ καὶ τὰ ἀόρατα, εἴτε θρόνοι εἴτε κυριότητες εἴτε ἀρχαὶ εἴτε ἐξουσίαι qui allongent et surchargent la première proposition ὅτι ἐν αὐτῷ (16a-b) et qui n'ont pas de correspondant en 20c. C'est encore la proposition finale 18c: ἵνα γένηται ἐν πᾶσιν αὐτὸς πρωτεύων qui vient s'insérer entre ὅς ἐστιν ... ἐκ τῶν νεκρῶν de 18b et ὅτι ἐν αὐτῷ κτλ. de 19, alors qu'il n'y avait rien de semblable entre ὅς ἐστιν ... πάσης κτίσεως de 15a-b et ὅτι ἐν αὐτῷ κτλ. de 16a. En dehors des questions de parallélisme, d'autres anomalies littéraires inquiètent l'exégète. En 20b l'expression redoublée διὰ τοῦ αἵματος τοῦ σταυροῦ αὐτοῦ δι' αὐτοῦ donne l'impression d'une surcharge. De même, en 18a le génitif τῆς ἐκκλησίας, dont le rattachement au génitif τοῦ σώματος n'est pas clair. Si des considérations doctrinales viennent s'ajouter à ces difficultés littéraires, on comprend que des exégètes concluent dans ces divers cas à des additions ou gloses qui ont surchargé un texte primitif. Nous examinerons bientôt ces hypothèses.

Auparavant, il nous faut conclure notre premier examen du texte en appréciant son genre littéraire. Bien des désignations ont été proposées. La plupart des auteurs parlent d'un "hymne". L'expression n'est pas mauvaise si on la prend en un sens large, entendant par là un morceau de style poétique, d'un rythme calculé des mots et de la pensée, sans exiger la rigueur dans la quantité des pieds, le nombre des syllabes, ou l'assonance des rimes, qui caractérisent normalement les hymnes proprement dits, anciens et modernes. L'équilibre des formules que nous venons de constater permet d'appeler cette pièce un "hymne" au sens large.

Peut-on préciser davantage, en découvrant son intention? Norden 253 a parlé à son sujet de "Doxologie". Sans doute ce passage vient-il dans un contexte de prière de la part de Paul (v. 9) et d'action de grâces qu'il conseille à ses lecteurs (v. 12 εὐχαριστοῦντες); sans doute aussi cet énoncé de la primauté du Christ tourne-t-il en définitive à sa gloire et à celle de son Père. On ne trouve cependant pas à l'intérieur de l'hymne les expressions littéraires de la prière ou de la doxologie. C'est un énoncé, une affirmation: ὅς ἐστιν ... ὅς ἐστιν. Faut-il l'appeler "dogmatique" avec Joh. Weiss?[5] N'en déplaise à Gabathuler 24, l'expression est assez juste, pourvu qu'on ne mette pas dans ce mot la raideur théorique et spéculative d'une époque plus récente. Il s'agit bien ici d'une proclamation doctrinale. Dirons-nous "confession de foi"[6] ou "profession de foi"?[7] Assurément la foi est à la base des affirmations ici prononcées. Mais il y a ici plus que la foi fondamentale du kérygme, telle qu'on la trouve, par exemple, à la base des vv. 13-14. Il y a déjà une élaboration théologique, et de haut vol, qui repense la personne du Christ et son oeuvre de salut dans le cadre du Cosmos. Vraiment, on entend ici une proclamation doctrinale, un enseignement d'autorité, revêtu de solennité par une forme littéraire soignée, de caractère hymnique. Faut-il l'appeler "liturgique"? J'en doute, si l'on songe à une occasion liturgique bien précise, telle que le Baptême[8] ou l'Eucharistie.[9] Car rien dans le texte de l'hymne ne suggère une allusion particulière à ces sacrements. Mais si l'on veut dire seulement que cet énoncé solennel

---

[5] *Die Anfänge des Dogmas.* Tübingen 1909 45s.
[6] Vawter 69: "confessional poetry", comme Phil 2, 6-11; 1 Tim 3, 16; Heb 1, 3; 1 Pet 2, 22-25; 3, 18s, 22: "all confessional acclamations of the homology type".
[7] Masson RThPh 142.
[8] En ce sens Käsemann (pour l'état christianisé de l'hymne gnostique primitif qu'il postule), Eckart, Conzelmann, Jervell 201s, Vawter.
[9] En ce sens Bornkamm, Dahl, Robinson.

de la primauté du Christ revêt une forme qui l'adapte bien à une proclamation dans l'assemblée ecclésiale, alors la qualification de "liturgique" peut convenir.

Une autre épithète a encore été proposée: celle de "polémique". Elle semble exacte, de façon indirecte, non de façon directe. Le style de cette pièce ne présente rien, en effet, de ce que comporte normalement l'attaque ou la réfutation d'opinions adverses; qu'on la compare à 2,4-23. Elle se tient volontairement sur le plan des affirmations positives, sereines, catégoriques. Mais on devine sans peine que ces affirmations prennent tacitement le contre-pied d'affirmations contraires, et c'est en cela que l'hymne a une valeur polémique. S'il proclame que le Christ est premier en tout, c'est en contraste avec des rivaux, les Puissances célestes que certains Colossiens sont en passe de placer à côté de lui ou au-dessus de lui. L'auteur de Col. s'est-il contenté de citer pour cela un hymne qui avait été composé pour une autre occasion, mais qu'il trouvait convenable à son propos, quitte à l'adapter quelque peu ? ou bien a-t-il composé cet hymne tout exprès pour la circonstance ? Je penche pour cette dernière hypothèse, mais je ne pourrai la justifier qu'après avoir discuté plus loin le problème de l'origine et des sources.

II. — Pour le moment, il nous faut passer à l'examen des structures littéraires qui ont été proposées pour cet hymne.

Nous devons dès l'abord rejeter, avec l'ensemble des commentateurs, les tentatives qui ont été faites d'imposer à ce morceau la rigueur d'une strophique exacte. Ainsi celle de Lohmeyer. Il discerne deux strophes de sept stiques, précédées chacune d'une introduction de trois stiques. Voici le schéma de sa restitution:

Introduction à la première strophe: 13a/13b/14
Première strophe: 15a/15b/16a/16b/16c/16d/16e
Introduction à la deuxième strophe: 16f/17a/17b
Deuxième strophe: 18a/18b/18c/19/20a (s'arrêtant à τὰ πάντα)/ 20b (commençant à εἰς αὐτόν et s'arrêtant à τοῦ σταυροῦ αὐτοῦ)/20c (commençant à δι' αὐτοῦ).

Une première observation à faire concerne l'incorporation à l'hymne des vv. 13-14. Lohmeyer n'est d'ailleurs pas le premier, et n'est pas resté le seul, à intégrer plus ou moins à l'hymne les versets qui précèdent le v. 15. Norden incorporait à son analyse les vv. 12-14. Käsemann voit dans 13-14 l'introduction liturgique ajoutée à un hymne primitive pré-chrétien, d'origine gnostique, pour l'adapter à une liturgie baptismale. Schille fait de 12-14 l'"Introïtus" de l'"Erlöserlied" chrétien (qui reprend un "Initiationslied" non-chrétien). Eckart remonte jusqu'au v. 9, voyant en 9-12 une parénèse introductive et en 13-14 la confession de louange des baptisés précédant l'hymne christologique (15-20 remaniement chrétien d'un hymne non-chrétien), que suit l'épiclèse prononcée par celui qui baptise (21-23). D'autres auteurs [10] encore maintiennent un lien étroit des vv. (12)13-14 avec les vv. 15-20, tout en l'expliquant de diverses manières: introduction appartenant de façon organique à l'hymne primitif reçu par l'auteur de Col. (Bornkamm 196s, Stanley 202s,[11] Kehl 36s, 50s, 162s) ou composé par lui (Larsson 189); introduction ajoutée à l'hymne avant son insertion dans Col. (Vawter 68) ou au moment de son insertion (Lähnemann 35). Il ne manque pourtant pas de critiques qui résistent à cette extension et qui, soulignant la rupture de style entre 14 et 15, préfèrent limiter l'hymne aux vv. 15-20: ainsi Masson, Hegermann, Conzelmann, Lamarche, Feuillet, Gabathuler, Deichgräber.[12]

Quoi qu'il en soit des interprétations liturgiques, il semble préférable, pour l'analyse de la structure littéraire qui nous occupe, de s'en tenir aux vv. 15-20. Ils représentent un tout structuré qui tranche sur le contexte et s'en détache aisément. Ce qui précède et ce qui suit est d'un autre style. Même si l'on voit, avec raison, en 12-14 une modulation qui introduit l'hymne de 15-20, il ne convient pas de mélanger la forme littéraire plus prosaïque de ces versets avec la forme bien rythmée du morceau qui suit.

Pour en revenir au cas particulier de la structure proposée par

---

[10] Sur la variété des hypothèses, voir entre autres Kehl 28-30.

[11] Cf. aussi D. Stanley, "Carmenque Christo quasi Deo dicere...", *CBQ* 20 (1958) 173-191 à la page 187.

[12] Notons pour mémoire l'étrange reconstruction de Schattenmann 18, selon qui on devrait restituer deux hymnes: un "Logoshymnus" (12 + 15-18a) et un "Christushymnus" (13-14 + 18b-20). — J'avoue n'être pas convaincu non plus par la structure de "simmetria totale concentrica" de Giavini: X (16b-e) plaçant au centre les sujets sur lesquels s'exerce la primauté du Christ Créateur (A: 16a et A': 16f-17ab) et du Christ Rédempteur (C: 12-14 et C': 19-20ab), les prérogatives du Christ étant énoncées en B: 15.18a et B': 18b, et X': 20c figurant à la fin comme reprise finale du "centro focale" 16b-e.

Lohmeyer, il saute aux yeux que sa première "introduction" (13-14) n'a pas avec sa première strophe (15-16e) les mêmes attaches littéraires que sa deuxième introduction (16f-17) a avec le contexte intérieur de l'hymne. Chose plus grave, les attaches littéraires de cette deuxième introduction (16f-17) sont avec la première strophe (15-16e) et non avec la deuxième (18-20) qu'elle est censée introduire! En effet, nous l'avons vu, 16f-17 sont la conclusion de ce qui précède; c'est donc faire violence au texte, forme et fond, que d'y voir l'introduction de ce qui suit. Si l'on ajoute à cela que les stiques de la deuxième strophe de Lohmeyer sont d'une longueur disproportionnée à la longueur des stiques de la première strophe; que εἰκών et πρωτότοκος sont répartis par lui sur deux stiques de la première strophe, alors que ἀρχή et πρωτότοκος figurent dans un même stique de la deuxième; que détacher εἰς αὐτόν de ἀποκαταλλάξαι (20a) pour le rattacher à εἰρηνοποιήσας (20b) accule à un contresens; qu'on ne peut davantage séparer δι' αὐτοῦ de ce qui le précède (20b) pour l'associer à ce qui suit (20c), on conviendra que la structure proposée par Lohmeyer est artificielle et brutalise le texte. De fait, nul ne l'a adoptée.

D'une forme toute différente et fondée sur des considérations tout autres, la structure élaborée par Charles Masson n'est pas plus vraisemblable. Elle répartit le texte en cinq strophes de quatre stiques chacune, dont voici le schéma:

I. 15a/15b/16a/16b
II. 16c/16d/16e/16f
III. 17a/17b/18b/18c (18a est supprimé)
IV. 19a^1/19a^2/20a^1/20a^2 (chacun de ces stiques étant coupé en deux)
V. 20b^1 εἰρηνοποιήσας/20b^2 διὰ τοῦ αἵματος τοῦ σταυροῦ αὐτοῦ/ 20b^3 δι' 'αὐτοῦ et 20c^1 εἴτε τὰ ἐπὶ τῆς γῆς/20c^2 εἴτε τὰ ἐν τοῖς οὐρανοῖς.

Une telle restitution prête à maintes objections. Plusieurs des strophes sont mal équilibrées, la cinquième en particulier, où εἰρηνοποιήσας doit constituer à lui seul un stique, et où δι' αὐτοῦ est séparé de ce qui précède pour être joint à εἴτε τὰ ἐπὶ τῆς γῆς, ce qui compromet le parallélisme de ces derniers mots avec εἴτε τὰ ἐν τοῖς οὐρανοῖς. Quant à la strophe III, il ne suffit pas de l'appeler "charnière" pour légitimer l'association étrange de 17 qui conclut ce qui précède et de 18b-c qui est le début essentiel de ce qui suit.[13]

Les raisons invoquées par Masson en faveur de sa structure la compromettent plus qu'elles ne la justifient. Ce sont des comptes de syllabes et des assonances qui règlent, à son avis, cette étrange poésie: le mot long εἰρηνοποιήσας aurait été choisi pour avoir six syllabes comme le stique précédent (τὰ πάντα εἰς αὐτόν). Ce mot aurait encore l'avantage d'offrir par sa première syllabe — ει — une assonance avec la syllabe initiale du dernier vers de la cinquième strophe et de l'hymne (εἴτε). Au v. 19 τῆς θεότητος aurait été omis ici après πᾶν τὸ πλήρωμα (voir 2,9) pour ne pas avoir un vers de quatorze syllabes "qui eût été sans parallèle dans l'hymne". On sera difficilement convaincu par de tels arguments. En fait les "vers" de la restitution proposée sont de longueurs fort inégales, allant de 6 à 13 syllabes en passant par 8, 9, 10, 11. Et on s'étonne que le deuxième εἴτε du v. 20 doive faire assonance avec εἰρηνοποιήσας, et non avec le premier εἴτε du même verset, qui est son parallèle naturel mais qui se trouve ici enfoui au milieu d'un stique. On comprend qu'une structure aussi arbitraire n'ait pas, elle non plus, enlevé les suffrages du monde exégétique.

L'insuccès de tels essais devrait dissuader de vouloir plier notre hymne à une forme rigoureuse. Mais il reste une issue à cette impasse: celle de transpositions qui procurent un ordre jugé plus satisfaisant. Nous en avons un exemple dans la reconstruction de J. M. Robinson.

Pour celui-ci il suffit de reporter 18a (sans τῆς ἐκκλησίας) + 18c à la fin de l'hymne, après le v. 20, pour obtenir une suite meilleure des idées et des parallélismes, à condition aussi de supprimer, outre τῆς ἐκκλησίας de 18a, les mots τὰ ὁρατὰ ... εἴτε ἐξουσίαι de 16c et les mots εἰρηνοποιήσας ... τὰ ἐν τοῖς οὐρανοῖς de 20b-c, à condition encore d'ajouter καί devant τὰ πάντα en 16f, de substituer, au v. 19, κατοικεῖ à εὐδόκησεν et τῆς θεότητος (σωματικῶς) à κατοικῆσαι, et de corriger en 20a ἀποκαταλλάξαι en ἀποκατήλλαξε. On obtient ainsi deux strophes comportant chacune six stiques se faisant parallèle d'une strophe à l'autre:

---

[13] Je reconnais moi-même une "charnière": 17-18a, mais elle est différente car les deux membres associés ne sont qu'une conclusion *récapitulative* (17) de la première strophe ὅς ἐστιν ... (15-16) et l'*amorce* (18a) de la deuxième strophe ὅς ἐστιν ... (18b-20), disposition qui respecte l'intégrité des deux strophes ὅς ἐστιν κτλ. En supprimant 18a et incorporant 18bc à sa strophe charnière, Masson n'obtient pas le même équilibre.

I. 15a/15b/16a-b/16f/17a/17b
II. 18b¹/18b²/19/20a/18a/18c

Mais à quel prix! L'arrangement ainsi obtenu est ingénieux et l'argumentation qui le justifie ne manque pas de pénétration. Nous retrouverons plus loin certains des arguments d'ordre doctrinal. Sur le plan formel de la structure littéraire, les transpositions proposées sont entièrement arbitraires. Devant l'hymne ainsi mis en forme, le problème n'est plus de savoir s'il est de l'auteur de Col., ou de Paul lui-même, ou d'une source paulinienne ou pré-chrétienne; il est l'oeuvre du Prof. J. M. Robinson.

En fait, la plupart des chercheurs respectent davantage la forme traditionnelle du texte et s'efforcent d'en dégager la structure sans violence. Depuis Schleiermacher et Norden, le parallélisme si manifeste des deux ὅς ἐστιν . . . ὅτι ἐν αὐτῷ s'est imposé à l'attention, faisant conclure à deux strophes qui commencent en 15a et 18b. Ainsi pensent, par exemple, Käsemann, Schille, Jervell, Hegermann, Eckart, Bammel, Conzelmann, Feuillet, Gabathuler, Deichgräber, Lohse, J. T. Sanders.

Il reste cependant un élément perturbateur qui gêne dans la délimitation exacte de la première strophe: c'est le troisième parallélisme que nous avons relevé plus haut des deux stiques commençant par καὶ αὐτός ἐστιν (17 et 18a). Les auteurs que je viens de nommer les incorporent tout simplement à la première strophe; mais, outre qu'ils rendent celle-ci trop longue par rapport à la deuxième, ils oblitèrent un parallélisme antithétique qui devrait être exprimé d'une certaine manière: le v. 17 se rattache bien à ce qui précède, concluant tout ce qui vient d'être dit de la primauté cosmique du Christ, mais 18a amorce ce qui suit en donnant un premier énoncé de sa primauté sotériologique. Beaucoup d'exégètes évitent cette difficulté en supprimant τῆς ἐκκλησίας,[14] ce qui permet, pensent-ils, d'entendre 18a en un sens cosmique qui le rattache à la première strophe. Mais pour ceux qui maintiennent ces mots et qui veulent rendre compte de l'antithèse susdite, la seule solution est de faire commencer la deuxième strophe avec 18a. Ainsi Dibelius-Greeven. Toutefois, cette division n'est qu'à

---

[14] Solutions plus radicales encore: suppression de l'un des deux καὶ αὐτός ἐστιν par omission de 17a (Hegermann), voire des deux par omission de 17ab et 18a (Harder, Bornkamm).

moitié heureuse si elle met dans l'ombre le parallélisme principal des deux ὅς ἐστιν [15]: ce sont bien là les vrais commencements des deux strophes.

Si bien qu'en définitive la meilleure solution est celle qui détache légèrement 17-18a du contexte pour en faire une sorte de petite strophe intermédiaire faisant charnière entre les deux strophes principales. Je l'ai déjà suggéré plus haut et je suis heureux d'apprendre par Gabathuler 71-75 que O. Piper et Ch. Maurer, dans des articles qui ne sont pas à ma disposition, ont soutenu une manière de voir analogue.[16] Il est remarquable que E. Schweizer TLZ 243, tout en supprimant τῆς ἐκκλησίας, adopte, lui aussi, cette strophe intermédiaire 17-18a.[17]

Au regard de ce résultat, la structure proposée par Gabathuler 129 [18] et reprise par D. von Allmen 39 paraît moins heureuse. Elle inclut 16f dans la strophe intermédiaire, qui comporte ainsi quatre stiques:

16f τὰ πάντα δι᾽ αὐτοῦ καὶ εἰς αὐτὸν ...
17a καὶ αὐτός ἐστιν ...
17b καὶ τὰ πάντα ἐν αὐτῷ ...
18a καὶ αὐτός ἐστιν ...

Le double parallélisme ainsi obtenu séduit au premier abord. Il a cependant le double inconvénient d'oblitérer quelque peu la situation contrastée des deux καὶ αὐτός, et de distendre l'étroite relation de 16f avec 16a par-dessus 16b-e.[19]

Cette critique vaut encore davantage pour la dernière structure proposée, celle de Pöhlmann 56. Il répartit le texte de l'hymne en quatre strophes:

---

[15] Voir la critique de Robinson 275: "His (Dibelius) second strophe displays the awkward procedure of beginning to give the correspondences to the first strophe in reverse order, and then immediately shifting to the parallel order."

[16] On peut d'ailleurs leur ajouter: J. Dupont, *Gnosis. La connaissance religieuse dans les épîtres de saint Paul* (Louvain: Nauwelaerts; Paris: Gabalda, 1949) 422; L. Cerfaux, *Le Christ dans la théologie de saint Paul* (Paris: Cerf, 1961) 299; Kehl 43.

[17] Il est suivi par Schnackenburg 35s, Lähnemann 38.

[18] Voir déjà Lamarche, *Christ Vivant* 64.

[19] Les mêmes critiques sont faites par Kehl 44, approuvé par Schnackenburg 35.

I. 15a/15b/16a
 II. 16b/16c/16d/16e
III. 16f/17a/17b/18a (om. τῆς ἐκκλησίας)
 IV. 18b¹/18b²/19/20a (om. 18c et 20b-c)

Outre que la troisième strophe de cette distribution reprend le groupement de quatre stiques que nous venons de critiquer, on remarquera que la première strophe n'a que trois stiques au lieu de quatre comme les trois autres, et aussi que la deuxième strophe a un contenu doctrinal qui ne fait pas le poids dans l'équilibre général de l'hymne.

Pour ma part, je persiste à voir dans une strophe intermédiaire de trois stiques 17a 17b 18a [20] — avec ou sans τῆς ἐκκλησίας, nous allons y revenir, — le moyen le plus heureux de respecter les divers parallélismes du texte, les deux ὅς ἐστιν ... ὅτι ἐν αὐτῷ qui charpentent les deux strophes principales 15-16//18b-20, et les deux καὶ αὐτός qui insèrent entre elles une petite strophe charnière.

III. — J'ai déjà fait plusieurs fois allusion aux suppressions pratiquées dans l'hymne par beaucoup d'exégètes. Les premiers chercheurs gardaient le texte tel qu'il est, et l'attribuaient à l'auteur de Col., qui pour eux était Paul. Ainsi J. B. Lightfoot, Abbott, Norden, Lohmeyer, Dibelius, et encore à des époques récentes Maurer, Moule, Larsson.

D'après Gabathuler 41, Harder est le premier qui a vu en Col. 1,15-20 la citation d'un hymne antérieur à l'épître et en a éliminé plusieurs expressions à titre de gloses. Beaucoup de critiques l'ont suivi dans cette voie, et il est peu de passages qui n'aient pas été suspectés par l'un ou par l'autre. Un échantillonnage des principales options peut être commodément présenté sur un tableau où chaque croix indique quel critique omet quel élément de l'hymne.

---

[20] On pourrait parler de deux stiques 17ab et 18a comme font Dupont et Cerfaux cités plus haut. Je préfère distinguer trois stiques pour mieux marquer que 17a et 17b reprennent ou complètent respectivement 15b et 16a. Schnackenburg 35 trouve harmonieux ce groupement de trois stiques commençant chacun par καί. Kehl 39 refuse le distique comme un "unausgewogener Zweizeiler", mais on s'étonne qu'à la page 42 c'est le tristique qui devient pour lui "eine ganz unausgewogene Anordnung", tandis que le distique retrouve sa faveur parce que répondant mieux au calcul de syllabes dont il est friand.

	H. von Soden	Harder	Käsemann	Masson	Robinson	Bornkamm	Jervell	Eckart	Schweizer	Hegermann	Bammel	Conzelmann	Schenke	Gabathuler	Schattenmann	Deichgräber	Lohse	Vawter	Lähnemann	Pöhlmann
15 a																				
b																				
16 a																				
b								×		×										
c					×			×	×	×			×	×		×				
d	×				×			×	×	×			×	×		×				
e	×				×			×	×	×			×	×		×				
f	×								×							×				
17 a	×	×				×			×											
b	×	×				×														
18 a		×	(×)	×	(×)	×	(×)	(×)	(×)	(×)	(×)	(×)	(×)	(×)	(×)	(×)	(×)	(×)	(×)	(×)
b																				
c		×						×		×			×						×	×
19																				
20 a																				
b		×	(×)		×	(×)		(×)	×	(×)		×	(×)	×		(×)	(×)	(×)		×
c		×			×				×	×			×	×						×

La croix × indique que le stique correspondant est omis. Mise entre parenthèses (×), elle signifie que l'omission porte seulement sur τῆς ἐκκλησίας en 18a et sur διὰ τοῦ αἵματος τοῦ σταυροῦ αὐτοῦ en 20b.

Comme on le voit sur le tableau ci-joint, les seuls éléments qui ont échappé à la suspicion sont 15-16a et 19-20a. Ils constituent en effet le noyau indispensable, le squelette sans lequel l'hymne cesserait d'exister. Mais le reste, la chair qui revêt ce squelette en est détachée par lambeaux au gré des conjectures critiques. Les raisons apportées pour retirer tel ou tel élément à l'hymne "primitif" sont de deux sortes: littéraires et doctrinales. Littéraires, selon que cet élément paraît échapper à la structure d'ensemble telle qu'on croit la percevoir ou la restituer; doctrinales, selon que cet élément semble introduire une théologie différente de celle qu'on attribue à l'hymne primitif. Pour examiner et apprécier ces éliminations de "gloses", je les répartirai en cinq groupes: 1. 16f-17; 2. 16b-c et 20c; 3. 19c; 4. 18a en entier ou seulement les mots τῆς ἐκκλησίας; 5. 20b en entier ou seulement les mots διὰ τοῦ αἵματος τοῦ σταυροῦ αὐτοῦ.

1. *16f-17ab*. Ces trois stiques sont rarement suspectés, et ils ne devraient pas l'être. Littérairement, ils ne gênent pas, ils sont plutôt nécessaires. Nous avons vu plus haut qu'ils reprennent et complètent 16a: parallélisme des τὰ πάντα, progression des trois formes verbales ἐκτίσθη, ἔκτισται, συνέστηκεν, jeu des trois prépositions ἐν αὐτῷ, δι' αὐτοῦ, εἰς αὐτόν, jeu qui reparaîtra en parallèle dans les vv. 19-20a non suspectés. Doctrinalement, ces trois stiques développent heureusement la pensée de 15-16a, à savoir la priorité cosmique du Christ (ἐστιν πρὸ πάντων reprenant πρωτότοκος πάσης κτίσεως) et sa causalité non seulement formelle (ἐν αὐτῷ ἐκτίσθη τὰ πάντα), mais aussi efficiente (δι' αὐτοῦ) et finale (εἰς αὐτόν), qui aboutit à une subsistance en lui de toute la création (τὰ πάντα ἐν αὐτῷ συνέστηκεν).

Aussi bien, les raisons avancées par Hermann von Soden pour éliminer 16f-17 sont-elles peu convaincantes. Il a raison de souligner le parallélisme des deux ὅς ἐστιν ... ὅτι ἐν αὐτῷ, mais il a tort de penser que les stiques 16f-17 portent préjudice à ce parallélisme. De fait, en omettant 17a il en supprime un autre, celui des deux καὶ αὐτός; et celui qu'il propose entre 14 et 18a ne saurait le remplacer, car il n'y a entre ces deux stiques aucun parallélisme littéraire. Quoi qu'il en dise (p. 28), les stiques 16f-17, en reprenant 15-16a, apportent quelque chose de nouveau.

Puisque Harder n'apporte aucune justification à sa suppression du v. 17 — je le sais seulement par Gabathuler 40 —, il est inutile de chercher à le réfuter.[21]

Quant à Hegermann 92, il reconnaît que 16f prépare 20a et que 17a reprend 15b, mais il voit là des additions de l'auteur de Col. — qui pour lui est Paul —, rendues nécessaires, comme une sorte de retour au texte, par l'addition de 16b-e à l'hymne "primitif". Cette explication, qui reconnaît le caractère paulinien de ces textes, n'est valable — et encore! — que si le caractère adventice de 16b-e est prouvé. Or ceci est aussi en question.[22]

---

[21] Je ne sais non plus que dire à Bornkamm 197 note 20 dont je comprends mal les raisons. Il supprime 17 et 18a sous prétexte que ces stiques se détachent syntaxiquement (?) et qu'ils rétrécissent l'horizon cosmique des deux strophes parallèles 15-16 et 18b-20 (?).

[22] La même mise en garde vaut pour Deichgräber 147, qui supprime 16f (en même temps que 16c-e) parce que cette récapitulation de ce qui précède (*Zusammenfassung*) est typiquement paulinienne (cf. 1 Cor 3, 22; 9, 22; 12, 11; Phil 4, 12.13) et doit donc être ajoutée à l'hymne antérieur reçu par Paul (auteur de Col). Cet argument tombe si l'hymne et en particulier 16c-e sont de la main de Paul.

2. *16b-e et 20c.* Hegermann 91-92 condamne 16b-e à titre d'ornements contournés (*schnörkelhafter Putz*) qui font surcharge. A la suite de Norden, à qui il emprunte cette expression, il reconnaît le caractère paulinien de leur style: πάντα (-ντες) ... εἴτε ... εἴτε ... πάντα (-ντες), cf. 1 Cor. 3,21-23; 12,13; Gal. 3,26-28.[23] Mais précisément il les déclare ajoutés parce qu'il postule l'existence d'un hymne prépaulinien. L'argument ne vaut que ce que vaut cette hypothèse, à prouver par ailleurs.

Eckart (d'après Gabathuler 109) supprime, lui aussi, 16b-e, pour la raison littéraire que ces stiques interrompent le climax qui monte de 16a à 16f-17 (stiques qu'Eckart conserve), et pour la raison doctrinale qu'ils affaiblissent la portée de τὰ πάντα "le Tout, le Cosmos", en le réduisant à n'être plus que "toutes choses". La deuxième de ces raisons ne convainc pas. A supposer — l'hypothèse reste au moins légitime! — que Paul ait composé cet hymne pour affirmer la suprématie du Christ sur les Puissances célestes qu'on vénérait trop à Colosses, il était naturel qu'il explicitât les êtres spécialement visés par lui dans l'évocation de "toute créature". Au fait, les catégories énumérées en 16b, ciel-terre, et en 16c, visibles-invisibles, restent coextensives à la totalité créée énoncée en 16a; c'est seulement 16d-e qui introduit une restriction, mais elle paraît légitime à titre d'application. L'autre raison invoquée par Eckart, d'ordre littéraire, est plus pertinente; elle ne vaut cependant que si l'on exige de l'hymne un rigoureux équilibre de structure, exigence qui nous a paru excessive. Il faut remarquer aussi que la suppression de 16b-e, en juxtaposant 16a et 16f, provoque un heurt de deux τὰ πάντα qu'il est littérairement difficile d'admettre.

Cette dernière difficulté est évitée par Robinson 276.282s, Schweizer TLZ 243, et Gabathuler 130 qui conservent 16b et ne suppriment que 16c-e.[24] J'applaudis au maintien de 16b, tout en doutant de la raison invoquée par Gabathuler 94 à la suite de Robinson 283: un parallélisme qu'il croit trouver entre 16b et 19, mais qui ne s'impose guère à mon avis. Mais l'omission de 16c-e a la même faiblesse que nous avons déjà rencontrée à propos de Hegermann: ces stiques, nous dit-on, sont un développement de τὰ πάντα (*loosely appended appositions*, Robinson 276), par adaptation à l'hérésie colossienne: ils sont donc ajoutés à l'hymne primitif.

---

[23] Cf. Percy 65.
[24] De même Schenke 401.

Oui, si l'existence de cet hymne est prouvée par ailleurs; non, si l'on accepte d'envisager que l'hymne ait été composé précisément comme une réponse à l'église de Colosses.

Plus sérieux est le grief proposé entre autres par Deichgräber 146: une rupture stylistique entre 16b et 16c-e: aux catégories bibliques ciel/terre sont apposées les catégories hellénistiques de choses visibles/invisibles (déjà Norden 254.261). Si l'on ajoute à cela que 16c-e allongent considérablement le v. 16 et éloignent trop 16f de 16a, on avouera que l'hypothèse d'une addition mérite de rester envisagée.[25]

Les deux stiques de 20c sont en parallélisme manifeste avec 16b (οὐρανοί/γῆ) et 16d (εἴτε/εἴτε). On pourrait donc s'attendre qu'ils subissent le même sort de la part des critiques. De fait, cela ne se vérifie que dans le cas de Hegermann. Eckart, qui supprime 16b, maintient 20c, j'ignore pourquoi. Robinson, Schweizer, Schenke, Gabathuler, qui maintiennent 16b, suppriment 20c; Robinson, suivi par Gabathuler, pour le même motif que ci-dessus: ces "loosely appended appositions" adaptent l'hymne à la situation de Col.; Schweizer, parce qu'il englobe 20c dans la même condamnation que 20b, sans autre justification. Pöhlmann 56 condamne de la même manière 20c en même temps que 20b, bien qu'il maintienne tout 16b-e: 20c en serait une reprise due à l'auteur de Col. qui aurait retouché l'hymne en l'adoptant. Cette reprise est certaine, mais elle peut aussi bien être le fait de l'auteur de l'hymne, et celui-ci pourrait bien être Paul lui-même, car rien ne permet de lui refuser la formulation de 20c: voir ses fréquents εἴτε ... εἴτε et en particulier I Cor 8,5 εἴτε ἐν οὐρανῷ εἴτε ἐπὶ γῆς.

3. *18c:* ἵνα γένηται ἐν πᾶσιν αὐτὸς πρωτεύων.

Du point de vue littéraire, cette proposition est assurément suspecte. Elle vient s'insérer entre la proposition relative ὅς ἐστιν κτλ. et la proposition causale ὅτι ἐν αὐτῷ κτλ. d'une façon qui interrompt la marche de la pensée et qui n'a aucun correspondant dans la première strophe. Cette observation amène plusieurs critiques à y voir une addition qu'a faite l'auteur de Col lorsqu'il

---

[25] Cependant Lähnemann 37s maintient l'appartenance de 16b-e à l'hymne original. Il invoque précisément, à la suite de Wengst, sa "charakterische plerophorische Redeweise", et aussi le fait que les Puissances sont présentées ici d'une manière plus positive que dans le reste de Col (par ex. en 2, 15), argument qui vaut pour lui parce qu'il suppose l'hymne composé par un autre auteur que celui de Col.

a inséré l'hymne dans son épître. Ainsi Harder, Schweizer TLZ 243. 245 et EKK 20, Bammel 89, Gabathuler 94.128; Lähnemann 36; Pöhlmann 55; Schnackenburg 36s hésite.

Bammel 94 ajoute que cette expression d'une finalité détonne dans un hymne qui constate, acclame, mais ne cherche pas à prouver. C'est pour la même raison que Lähnemann 36 récuse le précédent du ἵνα en Phil 2,10, invoqué par Deichgräber 148 pour légitimer son usage en Col 1,18c. Lähnemann estime, en effet, que l'hymne de Phil énumérant des *faits* est une cas différent de l'hymne de Col qui décrit l'*être* du Christ. De son côté, Schweizer EKK 20.27 s'étonne de cette primauté du Christ qui d'après 18c serait encore à conquérir, alors que selon 15 elle lui est acquise depuis la création.

Ces considérations, qui du style s'élèvent à la marche de la pensée, sont intéressantes; je doute qu'elles soient décisives. Elles négligent une différence pourtant bien nette entre les deux strophes de l'hymne. La première assurément décrit et acclame une situation acquise du Christ premier dans l'ordre créé. Mais la seconde concerne une nouvelle étape dans le déroulement du plan divin. Une péripétie non exprimée mais manifestement sous-entendue entre les deux strophes a introduit dans le monde un désordre, auquel on sent que les Puissances célestes ont pris part. Dieu veut que ce désordre soit réparé et que le Christ retrouve la primauté *en tout*: ces derniers mots sont essentiels, parce qu'ils englobent le domaine où cette primauté a été mise en échec. Après la phase statique de la première strophe, il y a là, n'en déplaise à Lähnemann, un mouvement, ou, n'en déplaise à Schweizer, une reconquête qui légitime pleinement le ἵνα de 18c. Cette proposition finale exprime l'intention de Dieu qui a présidé à la suprême étape de son plan de salut: le Christ assumant en lui tout l'univers (πλήρωμα) par son incarnation (ἐν αὐτῷ εὐδόκησεν (s.e. ὁ θεὸς) πᾶν τὸ πλήρωμα κατοικῆσαι) et y rétablissant la paix par sa mort et sa résurrection (18b et 20). Comme le dit très justement Vawter 76 note 30, le ὅς ἐστιν ἀρχή de 18b a introduit une dimension nouvelle, tout autre que celle des vv. 15-17, dimension qui exige les explications de ἵνα κτλ. (18c) et ὅτι κτλ. (19-20).

Lähnemann écrit encore que le πρωτεύων de 18c ne fait que reprendre les πρωτότοκος de 15 et 18b. Il n'en est rien. πρωτεύω dit davantage, ou autre chose, que πρῶτος: non seulement la priorité temporelle ou locale, mais la primauté de rang, de dignité. Ici πρωτότοκος désigne la priorité temporelle du Christ, non seulement au v. 18b mais déjà au v. 15b.[26] γένηται πρωτεύων de 18c exprime l'accès à une primauté nouvelle, en tous les ordres, non seulement dans l'ordre de la création (15-17) mais encore dans celui du salut.

Sous un vêtement rythmé et peut-être liturgique, cet hymne recèle une argumentation serrée, dont je vais me risquer à schématiser les articulations maîtresses. Il met en oeuvre les notions de principe, de priorité et de causalité, pour aboutir à celle de primauté. Discutant le sens du mot πρωτότοκος, les exégètes se sont souvent partagés entre le sens de priorité temporelle et celui de primauté d'excellence. En fait, ces deux qualités sont connexes et s'entraînent l'une l'autre, — du moins dans le cas du Christ, — et si l'on insiste sur l'une on n'entend pas par là nier l'autre. Mais précisément c'est seulement dans le cas du Christ que la priorité entraîne une primauté, car de soi toute priorité ne s'accompagne pas de primauté, ni réciproquement. S'il en est ainsi dans le cas du Christ, c'est parce qu'il est Principe, dans l'ordre de la première comme de la deuxième création, car dans les deux ordres il a valeur de cause pour ce qui vient après lui. Telles sont donc les étapes de cette quasi-démonstration:

Dans les deux ordres le Christ est 1) *Principe*: image (εἰκών), modèle, prototype, de tout l'ordre créé; commencement (ἀρχή), prémices, prototype dans l'ordre de la nouvelle création. — 2) *Premier* temporellement; le premier-né de toute créature (πρωτότοκος πάσης κτίσεως), le premier-né d'entre les morts (πρωτότοκος ἐκ τῶν νεκρῶν). — 3) *Cause* de toute la création (ὅτι ἐν αὐτῷ ἐκτίσθη τὰ πάντα κτλ.), et cause de la réconciliation universelle au sein de la Plénitude (c'est-à-dire Dieu et l'Univers) que Dieu a fait habiter en lui (ὅτι ἐν αὐτῷ εὐδόκησεν πᾶν τὸ πλήρωμα κατοικῆσαι) — 4) De tout cela résulte sa *Primauté* d'excellence: ἐν πᾶσιν πρωτεύων.

Cette marche de la pensée, si on l'admet, légitime et exige même la proposition ἵνα κτλ. Ce qui ne veut pas dire que cette proposition gênante du point de vue du rythme n'est pas le fruit d'une mise au point rédactionnelle.

4. *18a*: καὶ αὐτός ἐστιν ἡ κεφαλὴ τοῦ σώματος τῆς ἐκκλησίας.

Peu de critiques éliminent tout ce stique. Masson Comm. 105 le fait, sous prétexte que ces mots "compromettent irrémédiablement

---

[26] Cf. P. Benoit, "Préexistence et Incarnation", *RB* 77 (1970) 5-29 aux pp. 14s.

l'équilibre" de l'hymne, tel qu'il croit pouvoir le structurer, et aussi parce qu'ils marquent "un resserrement subit de la pensée qui au v. 18b s'élargit de nouveau aux dimensions de l'univers." Ces mêmes raisons avaient déjà amené Bornkamm 197 note 20 à supprimer 18a en même temps que 17 à titre d'"Interpretamente".[27]

Mais la plupart des critiques, et cette fois le grand nombre, se contentent, à la suite de Käsemann 36s, de retirer de l'hymne primitif les mots τῆς ἐκκλησίας.[28] Selon eux, le texte original de l'hymne parlait du corps du cosmos, selon le thème hellénistique, connu depuis Platon et diffusé notamment par le stoïcisme, qui conçoit le monde comme un être intelligent, un organisme vivant, un corps ayant pour tête un principe divin plus ou moins assimilé par le syncrétisme avec le Logos, la Sagesse, l'Image, l'Homme Primordial. C'est ce Principe, créateur et organisateur du monde selon les vv. 15-17, que le v. 18a dans sa teneur primitive désignait comme la Tête du Corps cosmique. Selon Käsemann, suivi entre autres par Wilckens et Barrett, l'hymne primitif était gnostique, pré-chrétien, et ne faisait aucune référence au thème paulinien du "Corps du Christ". Selon d'autres, comme Schweizer TWNT 1072s,[29] l'hymne était déjà chrétien, et même post-paulinien. Le milieu judéo-chrétien de culture hellénistique auquel on l'attribue, avait cru pouvoir élargir le thème paulinien du Corps du Christ aux dimensions universelles du corps cosmique, dont le Christ Tête devenait ainsi supérieur aux Puissances célestes. Dans l'une comme dans l'autre hypothèse, l'auteur de Col (qui n'est Paul, ni pour Käsemann, ni pour Schweizer) aura cru nécessaire de ramener l'hymne qu'il empruntait aux catégories de la théologie paulinienne en ajoutant à τοῦ σώματος l'apposition τῆς ἐκκλησίας: pour lui, le véritable Corps dont le Christ est la Tête, ce n'est pas le cosmos, c'est l'Eglise (cf. 1,24; Eph 1,22; 5,23.29).

Ces hypothèses ont leur intérêt mais sont à discuter. L'usage cosmique du mot "corps" dans la philosophie du syncrétisme gréco-romain est certain.[30] L'usage du mot Tête pour dégager le

---

[27] D'après Gabathuler 40, Harder supprime aussi 17-18a.
[28] Ainsi Schille 61; Schweizer Erniedrigung 103, TLZ 245, EKK 8; Robinson 281; Jervell 199 note 101; Eckart 106; Hegermann 89; Bammel 94s (avec réserve); Conzelmann 137; Schenke 401; Gabathuler 74.127; Schattenmann 17; Deichgräber 148; Lohse Comm. 95s; Schnackenburg 36; Lähnemann 37; Vawter 75; Pöhlmann 55.
[29] Voir le résumé de la pensée de Schweizer par D. von Allmen 41ss.
[30] Schweizer, TWNT VII 1029, 9ss.

principe divin qui anime et unit souverainement ce corps est déjà moins bien attesté avant le Nouveau Testament, mais il est possible.[31] If faut encore concéder que la relation grammaticale de τῆς ἐκκλησίας avec τοῦ σώματος n'est pas claire et qu'on a l'impression d'une addition. Ceci dit, il faudra voir si une autre explication de cette expression difficile ne peut être envisagée, et même trouvée plus satisfaisante. Avant d'y venir, il nous faut encore examiner les dernières suppressions proposées, dans le v. 20b.

5. *20b* : εἰρηνοποιήσας διὰ τοῦ αἵματος τοῦ σταυροῦ αὐτοῦ δι' αὐτοῦ.

Ici encore il faut distinguer entre les critiques qui suppriment tout le stique: Harder 48, Robinson 284, Schweizer TLZ 243 et EKK 8, Conzelmann 136, Gabathuler 131, Pöhlmann 56,[32] et ceux qui se contentent de supprimer les mots διὰ τοῦ αἵματος τοῦ σταυροῦ αὐτοῦ : Käsemann 37, Bornkamm 197 note 20, Eckart 106, Hegermann 89, Schenke 401, Deichgräber 149, Lohse 102, Schnackenburg 33, Vawter 75.

Ne connaissant Harder que par Gabathuler, je perçois mal ses raisons. Celles de Robinson sont d'ordre stylistique: 20b n'a pas de correspondant dans la première strophe de l'hymne (tel qu'il le restitue) et sa forme participiale ne se rencontre pas ailleurs dans l'hymne, mais bien dans le reste de Col (2,13-15). Il semble que pour Schweizer, Conzelmann et Gabathuler εἰρηνοποιήσας ait un sort lié à celui des mots διὰ τοῦ αἵματος τοῦ σταυροῦ αὐτοῦ et doive disparaître avec eux.

Au fait, c'est essentiellement la mention du "sang de la croix" qui est ici en question. Si bien des critiques omettent ces mots, à la suite de Käsemann, c'est qu'ils voient là encore un retour à la théologie paulinienne, imposé par l'auteur de Col à un hymne qui l'ignorait ou s'en était écarté. Pour Käsemann 42s l'hymne gnostique primitif ne songeait qu'à une réconciliation du cosmos par la résurrection et l'intronisation du Rédempteur qui, après être allé chercher les hommes dans la captivité de la mort, les en délivre en les attirant après lui dans son triomphe. En ce "Sauveur sauvé", Chef ayant regagné son rang de Cosmokrator, les hommes, les Puissances, bref tout l'univers est "réconcilié", "pacifié", subjugué. Point question d'une mort sanglante sur la croix. C'est là une conception paulinienne de la rédemption que l'auteur de Col a

---

[31] Schweizer, TWNT VII 1036, 11ss; cf. Schlier, TWNT III 675ss.
[32] Voir aussi Wagenführer d'après Deichgräber 149 note 5.

introduit dans l'hymne en insérant διὰ τοῦ αἵματος τοῦ σταυροῦ αὐτοῦ.

La plupart des critiques ont refusé de reconnaître ici un hymne primitif "gnostique". Non seulement des expressions chrétiennes telles que πρωτότοκος ἐκ τῶν νεκρῶν [33] et ἀποκαταλλάξαι semblent s'opposer à une telle origine, mais encore le monisme de la première strophe et l'idée d'une réconciliation des mondes terrestre et céleste paraissent inconciliables avec la perspective foncière de la gnose.[34] Enfin plusieurs observent que, si le thème de l'Homme Primordial peut être considéré comme pré-chrétien, la fusion de ce thème avec celui de la rédemption, c'est-à-dire en somme le thème du "Sauveur sauvé", n'apparaît que dans une gnose plus tardive et pourrait bien avoir sa source dans la sotériologie chrétienne plutôt qu'en être la source.[35]

Les critiques qui maintiennent ainsi le caractère chrétien et non gnostique de l'hymne primitif postulé n'en admettent pas moins qu'il concevait la réconciliation d'une autre manière que Paul: non par le sang de la croix, mais par le triomphe de la résurrection et de l'exaltation céleste du Christ. C'est en remontant de la terre au ciel que le Christ a réuni, pacifié, ramené sous sa primauté toutes les catégories de l'univers, y compris les Puissances célestes. Conception naturelle, nous assure-t-on, pour des judéo-chrétiens d'origine hellénistique qui, de par leur milieu, étaient spécialement anxieux d'échapper à la tyrannie des Puissances mauvaises régissant le cosmos. Tout en profitant de cet hymne qui l'aidait à remettre sous la domination du Christ les Puissances cosmiques auxquelles les hérétiques de Colosses accordaient trop d'intérêt, — sans doute pour les neutraliser par de bons offices, — l'auteur de Col aura tout de même voulu réintroduire par une glose le point de vue plus anthropologique de la sotériologie paulinienne: la vraie réconciliation concerne avant tout les hommes et c'est "par le sang de la croix" du Christ qu'elle s'est opérée.

---

[33] Cependant Käsemann 39.42 prétend que ce titre peut fort bien être dit du Sauveur gnostique qui "als Wegbereiter und Führer der Seinen die Bresche in die Todessphäre schlägt".

[34] Schweizer, TLZ 244 note 11, EKK 9; Gabathuler 57; Deichgräber 153s. Pöhlmann 54 estime même qu'on ne songe plus aujourd'hui à un hymne primitif pré-chrétien, "weder ein gnostischer Anthroposhymnus noch ein jüdischer Sophiahymnus".

[35] Cf. Jervell 136 note 63, 145 note 91; 210.211; Gabathuler 56s; J. T. Sanders 86. Voir en outre H.-M. Schenke, *Der Gott "Mensch" in der Gnosis* (Göttingen: Vandenhoeck & Ruprecht, 1962) passim.

On le voit, même fortement retouchée, la théorie de Käsemann a été largement acceptée, et elle continue à dominer la recherche. Il faut reconnaître que les anomalies littéraires donnent de la vraisemblance aux gloses qu'elle postule. Nous l'avons déjà concédé à propos de τῆς ἐκκλησίας. Cela se vérifie encore plus au sujet des mots διὰ τοῦ αἵματος τοῦ σταυροῦ αὐτοῦ. Ils ne peuvent se juxtaposer à l'expression δι' αὐτοῦ qui les suit sans produire une redondance intolérable.[36] L'omission de δι' αὐτοῦ par des témoins respectables de la tradition textuelle (B DG L vss. latines, sahidique, arménienne, Origène, Ambrosiaster etc.) pourrait résoudre cette difficulté, mais elle est suspecte d'être la correction intentionnelle de copistes qui auront senti cette redondance.

Ici et en d'autres endroits de l'hymne nous nous sentons donc en présence de remaniements rédactionnels, dus en général à des éléments qui semblent être des surcharges. Nous avons relevé en particulier: 16c-d τὰ ὁρατὰ ... εἴτε ἐξουσίαι, 18a τῆς ἐκκλησίας, 18c ἵνα γένηται ἐν πᾶσιν αὐτὸς πρωτεύων, et 20b διὰ τοῦ αἵματος τοῦ σταυροῦ αὐτοῦ. Tout en maintenant la convenance de ces éléments dans la marche de la pensée, nous avons reconnu que leur présence gênait l'équilibre du style. Mais il n'est pas sûr que la meilleure solution soit de supprimer les expressions susdites pour retrouver un hymne primitif qui présenterait une parfaite harmonie.

Käsemann 40 n'exagère-t-il pas quand il admire "die hymnische Durchformung des völlig abgerundeten und in seinen Zeilen wie Strophen ausgewogenen Stückes"?[37] Tous les exégètes relèvent, et j'ai relevé moi-même, la manifeste correspondance des instruments grammaticaux ὅς ἐστιν ... ὅτι ἐν αὐτῷ ... καὶ αὐτός ἐστιν qui se répondent d'un bout à l'autre de l'hymne et lui construisent un cadre stylistiquement ferme. Mais ce cadre si bien tracé ne donne-t-il pas le change sur les pensées qu'il renferme? Y a-t-il entre ces pensées, de la première à la deuxième strophe, le parfait parallélisme que ce cadre permet d'attendre et que cherchent à

---

[36] J. B. Lightfoot, *Comm. ad loc.* voit ici une reprise du δι' αὐτοῦ qui commence 20a et il invoque des cas analogues: 2, 13 ὑμᾶς; Rom 8, 23 καὶ αὐτός; Gal 2, 15.16 ἡμεῖς; Eph 1, 13 ἐν ᾧ καί; 3, 1.14 τούτου χάριν. Mais dans tous ces cas la reprise d'une expression déjà un peu éloignée était exigée par son rôle dans une nouvelle proposition, tandis qu'ici δι' αὐτοῦ est presque synonyme des mots qui précèdent immédiatement et n'est nullement exigé par ceux qui suivent.

[37] Voir la réaction de Gabathuler 52.

retrouver les divers essais de restitution d'une forme primitive ? Ce parallélisme des pensées se constate bien en 15ab//18b et d'une certaine manière en 16a//19 ; mais 18a introduit une pensée nouvelle et non exploitée pour elle-même dans la suite de l'hymne ; 20a et b parlent de réconciliation et de pacification, alors que la première strophe n'avait laissé soupçonner aucun désordre ; quant à 18c, c'est une affirmation qui vaut pour les deux strophes. Le traitement drastique que Robinson inflige à l'hymne pour retrouver une forme primitive bien balancée, prouve assez que la chose n'est pas facile, et je doute de sa réussite, car je ne vois pas de vrai parallélisme de pensée entre 16f et 20a, entre 17a et 18a, entre 17b et 18c. La répétition de δι' αὐτοῦ et εἰς αὐτόν en 16f et 20a, de καὶ αὐτός ἐστιν en 17a et 18a, de (πᾶς) et (αὐτός) en 17b et 18c crée des parallèles formels qui ne suffisent pas à établir de réels parallèles de pensée entre création et réconciliation (16f et 20a), entre "être avant toutes choses" et "être la tête du corps" (17a et 18a), entre la subsistance de tout en Lui et la primauté en tout (17b et 18c).[38]

Plus je considère cet hymne, plus je suis frappé par la différence entre ses deux parties. Autant la première (15-17)[39] est bien centrée sur une seule idée : celle de la création et de la subsistance de toutes choses en, par, pour, celui qui est l'Image de Dieu et le premier-né de toute créature, autant la deuxième (18-20) met en oeuvre des idées diverses et comme disparates : Christ Tête du Corps, de l'Eglise ; résurrection (premier-né d'entre les morts) ; primauté universelle ; habitation du Plérôme ; réconciliation et pacification universelle ; sacrifice de la croix. Dans la première partie on entend résonner un thème connu par les spéculations judéo-hellénistiques sur la Sagesse [40] ; dans la deuxième on assiste à un jaillissement de thèmes pauliniens, non préparés et mal joints entre eux. Le péché, des hommes et des anges, cause nécessaire du désordre à réparer dans le monde, n'est même pas mentionné ! La résurrection n'est évoquée que par des expressions dérivées, peut-être traditionnel-

---

[38] Je ne trouve pas plus de vraisemblance aux correspondances par "chiasmes" que Bammel 89 croit découvrir entre 15a et 16f, 15b et 16a, 18b¹ et 20a, 18b² et 19.

[39] Parlant à présent de la pensée par delà la forme littéraire, je rattache le début (17ab) et la fin (18a) de la strophe intermédiaire respectivement à la première (15-16) et à la deuxième (18b-20) strophe principale, conformément à ce que j'ai dit plus haut (pp. 228 et 236) du rôle charnière de cette strophe intermédiaire.

[40] Voir, après bien d'autres, les excellents développements de Feuillet 172ss.

les [41] mais plutôt de caractère paulinien (cf. 1 Cor, 15,20-23; Rom 8,29). La réconciliation est exprimée par le mot très rare ἀποκαταλλάσσειν — qui apparaît pour la première fois chez Paul (Col Eph) et pourrait bien être sa création —, sans qu'on voie clairement ce qu'il s'agit de réconcilier et pourquoi. Après la "pacification" qui pose le même problème, vient la mention du "sang de la croix" qui évoque évidemment le sacrifice du Christ (cf. Rom 3,25; 5,9), sans que soit expliqué comment ce sacrifice pacifie. Le tout est situé dans le cadre cosmique de la terre et des cieux, description bien connue mais également paulinienne (cf. 1 Cor 8,5).

On observera en outre que, parmi ces thèmes ou ces expressions, il en est qui n'apparaissent que dans Col ou Eph: le Christ Tête du Corps (Eph 1,22; 5,23), l'Eglise Corps du Christ (Col 1,24; Eph 1,22s; 5,23.29s), l'habitation en lui du Plérôme (Col 2,9), la forme composée ἀποκαταλλάσσειν (Col 1,22; Eph 2,16), le rare εἰρηνοποιεῖν qui a son meilleur parallèle en Eph 2,15 ποιῶν εἰρήνην, de même l'association verbale de αἷμα et σταυρός (Eph 2,13 et 16), le couple ἐπὶ τῆς γῆς/ἐν τοῖς οὐρανοῖς (Eph 1,19 et 3,15, plus proches que 1 Cor 8,5 par le pluriel οὐρανοί).

Or précisément ces affinités particulières de la deuxième partie de l'hymne pourraient nous mettre sur la voie d'une solution. Elles n'ont certes pas échappé à bien des critiques, mais ils ont conclu à des gloses pauliniennes introduites par l'auteur de Col, ou bien à des commentaires par lesquels l'auteur de Col utilisait dans son épître les données de l'hymne. Cela, parce qu'ils considéraient comme évidente l'antériorité de l'hymne par rapport à l'épître.

Quelques-uns, à vrai dire, particulièrement sensibles à cette différence entre les deux strophes, pour le fond comme pour la forme, ont entrevu que l'hymne pourrait bien être le résultat d'une évolution en deux étapes. Lähnemann [41] envisage que la deuxième strophe représente l'élément premier (*Urbestand*) à partir duquel l'hymne se sera construit en remontant (*nach vorn*). Jervell 210s, dans des pages qui sont parmi les plus pénétrantes que j'aie lues sur la question, suggère au contraire que la deuxième partie de l'hymne n'était pas à l'origine attachée à la première, mais lui a

---

[41] Cf. Apoc 1, 5 où πρωτότοκος τῶν νεκρῶν figure dans la titulature quasi-liturgique du Christ, juste après ὁ μάρτυς ὁ πιστός, qui se retrouve en 3, 14 associé à ἡ ἀρχὴ τῆς κτίσεως, autre titre qui évoque à son tour Col 1, 15b et 18b. Mais il se pourrait que Apoc s'inspire de Col, notamment en 3, 14 dans la lettre adressée à l'église de Laodicée. Allo, *Comm.* 53s voit là un "emprunt intentionnel à Paul".

été attachée après coup, pour en recevoir comme introduction le thème, de soi non paulinien, du Christ Premier Homme. Ces deux opinions paraissent se contredire. En fait, elles se complètent si l'on distingue l'ordre de l'invention et celui de l'exécution. On dirait alors, en s'inspirant de Lähnemann, que la pensée de l'auteur de l'hymne est partie des thèmes de la deuxième strophe et a voulu les compléter, ou mieux les préparer, en écrivant la première; et, en s'inspirant de Jervell, que dans l'exécution rédactionnelle il est parti de la première partie, morceau reçu d'ailleurs, et lui a ajouté la seconde, conforme aux idées pauliniennes. Il y a là une intuition que j'estime très importante et que je reprendrai tout à l'heure. Mais, autant que je puis voir, les deux auteurs mentionnés ne sont pas allés jusqu'aux dernières conséquences de cette intuition, parce qu'ils sont restés prisonniers de la thèse classique selon laquelle l'hymne 1,15-20 est une pièce antérieure au reste de l'épître.[42]

Et si l'on renonçait à cette manière de voir? Si l'on acceptait d'envisager que l'hymne soit contemporain de l'épître, ou mieux légèrement postérieur à sa rédaction primitive? *Ayant mûri sa pensée et rédigé sa lettre en réponse à la crise colossienne, l'auteur de Col aura jugé bon de ramasser et de compléter cette pensée dans un hymne de caractère poétique, qu'il insérerait vers le début de son texte, le construisant à l'aide d'un texte reçu (première strophe) et d'un condensé de ses propres idées (deuxième strophe).* Telle est l'hypothèse que je voudrais expliciter quelque peu.

IV. — Mais auparavant je crois nécessaire de rappeler d'un mot ma position concernant l'authenticité et la genèse littéraire de Col et Eph, telle que je l'ai exposée dans des travaux antérieurs.[43]

---

[42] Lähnemann 38: "Es lässt sich nun der Hymnus darstellen, wie er wahrscheinlich dem Briefschreiber vorgelegen hat." — Jervell 209s: "So ist auch Kol 1, 15-20 als ein Stück der Theologie der hellenistischen Gemeinde anzusehen. Dass der Verfasser hier zitiert, geht schon aus dem auffallenden Stilunterschied zwischen V.12-14 und 15-20 hervor. Das ist wieder deutlich durch den Neuansatz in 1, 21: καὶ ὑμᾶς ποτε ... Was er schon in einer festen Form vor sich hatte, überführt er nun auf die Gemeinde."

[43] "L'horizon paulinien de l'épître aux Ephésiens", *RB* 46 (1937) 342-361; 506-525 = *Exégèse et Théologie* (Paris: Cerf, 1961) II 53-96. — *Les épîtres de saint Paul aux Philippiens, à Philémon, aux Colossiens, aux Ephésiens* (Bible de Jérusalem; Paris: Cerf, 1949, 3ᵉ éd. 1959); *Bible de Jérusalem* en un volume (Paris 1955, 2ᵉ éd. 1973). — "Corps, Tête et Plérôme dans les épîtres de la captivité", *RB* 63 (1956) 5-44 = *Exég. et Théol.* II (1961) 107-153. — "Epître aux Colossiens", *Supplément au Dictionnaire de la Bible* (Paris: Letouzey) VII, fasc. 36 (1961) col. 157-170. — "Epître aux Ephésiens", *ibid.* col. 195-

Je ne vois aucune raison de refuser à Paul la paternité de Col. Sans doute trouve-t-on dans cette épître des conceptions et des expressions qui ne se rencontrent pas dans les épîtres antérieures, mais Paul n'est pas monolithique, et il a bien pu évoluer. Il l'a déjà fait dans ses premières épîtres, où on le voit passer d'une attente de la Parousie prochaine (1.2 Thess) à une perspective plus prudente de sa mort et de son union au Christ avant la Parousie (Phil 1,21ss; 2 Cor 5,1ss), ou encore passer des problèmes de l'eschatologie (1.2 Thess) et de la pastorale communautaire (1.2 Cor) à celui de la justification par la Loi ou par la foi (Gal Rom). Paul n'élabore pas une théologie à priori; il adapte et approfondit son message au gré des circonstances concrètes de son apostolat. La crise de Galatie l'avait obligé à réfléchir sur la situation de la Loi juive dans le salut chrétien. Celle de Colosses l'amène à réagir sur un nouveau terrain.

On s'intéresse trop à Colosses aux Puissances cosmiques et aux observances qui les honorent ou les apaisent. Cela met en danger la suprématie du Christ. Paul revendique donc celle-ci avec énergie. Il affirme que par sa mort sur la croix le Christ a dépouillé les Puissances célestes (Col 2,14-15) du gouvernement qu'elles exerçaient par le moyen des lois religieuses anciennes, y compris la Loi mosaïque. Ressuscité et monté aux cieux, il est devenu le Chef, la Tête de ces Puissances (Col 2,10).

Mais Paul avait par ailleurs élaboré en 1 Cor 6,12-20; 10,17; 12,12-27; Rom 12,4-5 le thème du "corps du Christ", non certes à partir du "corps cosmique" du syncrétisme hellénistique, ni même à partir de l'apologue classique sur l'Etat corps social, mais à partir de l'idée proprement chrétienne de l'union des chrétiens jusque dans leurs corps au corps crucifié et ressuscité du Christ, dont ils deviennent les "membres" par la foi et les sacrements, baptême et eucharistie; il était dès lors spontané de joindre ce thème à celui du Christ "Tête des Puissances" et de parler du Christ "Tête du Corps". Peut-être cette jonction était-elle déjà dans l'esprit de Paul tandis qu'il écrivait ou faisait écrire Col. Cependant, — si nous exceptons pour le moment 1,18a qui est notre problème,

---

211. — "Rapports littéraires entre les épîtres aux Colossiens et aux Ephésiens". (Festschrift Josef Schmid; Regensburg: Pustet, 1963) 11-22 = *Exég. et Théol.* III (1968) 318-334. — "L'Eglise corps du Christ", dans *Populus Dei. Studi in onore del Card. Alfredo Ottaviani.* Vol. II *Ecclesia* (Roma, 1969) 971-1028.

et 2,18-19 où je dénoncerai tout à l'heure une influence d'Eph, — elle n'y figure pas encore. Elle apparaît pour nous en Eph 1,22; 5,23, dans l'épître soeur que je crois presque contemporaine de Col encore que légèrement postérieure. De même, en effet, que Paul a écrit Rom peu après Gal, comme une synthèse bien ordonnée des idées nouvelles qu'avait fait jaillir en lui la crise de Galatie, de même il aura éprouvé le besoin de fixer en Eph, avec une sérénité dégagée de la polémique, le nouvel horizon du salut que lui avait fait contempler la crise de Colosses. La fusion des thèmes de "Corps du Christ" et du Christ "Tête des Puissances" pourrait être un des fruits de cette maturation qui s'opère en son esprit entre Col et Eph.

Mais le principal progrès que marque alors sa pensée est un retour à l'ecclésiologie. Paul ne s'intéresse que peu au cosmos et aux Puissances qui le régissent. Son regard n'a embrassé cet horizon nouveau que pour répondre au danger des spéculations colossiennes. L'alerte passée, et la réponse donnée en Col par l'affirmation de la souveraineté du Christ sur les Puissances, Paul ramène dans Eph sa pensée au seul sujet qui l'intéresse vraiment: le salut des hommes. Mais il le fait avec un regard élargi. Au lieu de revenir au problème du salut individuel par le foi et la grâce, déjà traité en Gal et Rom, il va insister sur l'aspect collectif du salut et parler plus qu'auparavant de "l'Eglise" au singulier. Il l'identifiera explicitement à ce Corps dont le Christ est la Tête (Eph 1,22s), chef et principe nourricier (Eph 4,15s). Bien plus, il la considérera dans l'horizon cosmique où s'est élevée sa pensée en Col, et il en viendra à l'identifier au Plérôme de l'univers (Eph 1,22s).

Ce Plérôme, qui est également une notion nouvelle et propre à Col Eph, n'est pas selon moi la plénitude de la vie divine ou de la grâce, ainsi qu'on l'entend d'ordinaire. Soit qu'il vienne de l'hérésie colossienne, comme quelques-uns le veulent, soit plutôt que Paul l'emprunte au langage du stoïcisme déjà adopté dans les milieux bibliques sapientiaux, ce terme sert à Paul pour désigner la totalité de l'Etre, Dieu et la création. Le "corps" du Christ ne pouvait concerner que la race humaine. Pour englober tout l'univers qui est le cadre de l'humanité et marquer que le Christ l'assume tout entier par son incarnation et sa résurrection rédemptrice, en même temps qu'il contient par nature le monde divin, il fallait un terme plus vaste que $\sigma\tilde{\omega}\mu\alpha$. Paul adopte alors $\pi\lambda\acute{\eta}\rho\omega\mu\alpha$. Ce mot apparaît en Col 2,9 (ici encore je réserve 1,19 qui fait problème) avec toute son ampleur divine (τῆς θεότητος) et cosmique (σωματικῶς). Il reparaît en Eph 1,23 au service de cette ecclésiologie cosmique dilatée que nous avons dite: l'Eglise n'est plus seulement le Corps du Christ, elle est son Plérôme; par elle le Christ remplit l'univers et est rempli par lui.

Avant de poursuivre et d'appliquer ces considérations à la genèse de notre hymne, je dois encore m'expliquer sur l'aspect littéraire et rédactionnel de cette évolution doctrinale. En parlant de "Paul", je ne prétends pas que l'apôtre travaille seul. Comme dans ses épîtres antérieures, il se fait aider par des disciples, et sans doute davantage maintenant qu'il est âgé et prisonnier. Ce recours à des "secrétaires" est souvent traité de "deus ex machina", d'expédient trop facile pour expliquer des différences de vocabulaire, de style, voire de pensée, tout en maintenant l'identité du principal auteur. Pourtant cette intervention de mains différentes est vraisemblable, voire certaine. On peut certes s'interroger sur la part de Tertius dans la rédaction de l'épître aux Romains (Rom 16,22), sans doute celle d'un simple scribe écrivant sous la dictée. Peut-être encore les frères que Paul s'associe dans les adresses de plusieurs de ses lettres, Silvain (1.2 Thess), Timothée (1.2 Thess, Phil, 2 Cor, Col), Sosthène (1 Cor), ne sont-ils mentionnés que pour l'honneur, sans être vraiment responsables du contenu de ces lettres. Le cas d'Eph est assez différent, du fait qu'une main étrangère se laisse nettement percevoir dans son style, sans que ce changement compromette le fond. La pensée reste trop géniale, trop homogène dans ses développements mêmes à la pensée de Paul, pour qu'on renonce facilement à reconnaître l'inspiration de l'Apôtre. Mais d'autre part, la façon laborieuse, et parfois maladroite, dont sont reprises, accouplées, dissociées, des formulations des épîtres antérieures, notamment de Col, oblige à supposer l'activité littéraire d'un disciple qui travaille sous la direction du maître, recevant ses pensées maîtresses et les mettant en forme de son mieux.

Il faut aller plus loin. Je pense que ce disciple, ou un autre, toujours peut-être avec le consentement de Paul, a repris certains passages de Col pour faire profiter cette épître des enrichissements acquis dans la composition d'Eph. Les deux épîtres, je l'ai dit, sont à mes yeux pratiquement contemporaines. L'épître dite "aux Ephésiens" est cette lettre que Tychique et Onésime auront apportée à l'église de Laodicée (Col 4,16) en même temps qu'ils apportaient Col à celle de Colosses. Mises ensemble sur le chantier, ces deux épîtres ont exercé l'une sur l'autre des influences qui se reflètent dans leurs relations littéraires. La dépendance est surtout du côté d'Eph, qui reprend et prolonge dans un sens plus ecclésiologique les vues cosmiques de Col. Mais sur plusieurs points le disciple rédacteur d'Eph — ou un autre disciple du groupe paulinien — aura jugé bon de retoucher Col pour la faire bénéficier de ces prolongements.[44] C'est ainsi que s'expliquent, par exemple, le corps "qui est l'Eglise" de Col 1,24, et le Christ "Tête du Corps" en Col 2,19.[45]

Cet excursus sur les relations doctrinales et littéraires de Col et Eph était nécessaire pour expliquer la genèse littéraire de l'hymne Col 1,15-20, telle que je veux maintenant la proposer.

V. — Ayant achevé une première rédaction de son épître, l'auteur de Col — Paul ou le disciple qui l'assiste — aura donc voulu ramasser et compléter sa pensée dans un hymne poétique. La ramasser en exprimant d'une manière vigoureuse l'affirmation majeure qu'il oppose à l'hérésie colossienne, à savoir la suprématie universelle que le Christ a reconquise en triomphant des Puissances cosmiques par sa résurrection; la compléter en montrant que cette suprématie eschatologique ne fait que reprendre une suprématie protologique qui remonte à la création. Ce dernier thème n'est pas absolument

---

[44] Cette hypothèse d'une première rédaction de Col complétée par l'auteur d'Eph a été avancée jadis par H. J. Holtzmann, *Kritik der Epheser- und Kolosserbriefe auf Grund einer Analyse ihres Verwandtschaftsverhältnisses*, Leipzig 1872. Reprise de diverses façons par quelques auteurs, entre autres C. R. Bowen et C. Masson (voir la Bibliographie), cette hypothèse n'a pas retenu l'attention qu'elle mérite. Je ne me rallie pas moi-même aux conclusions précises de ces auteurs, mais j'estime que l'hypothèse repose sur la juste perception d'une situation littéraire complexe qu'il faut expliquer.

[45] En ce dernier cas le contexte de Col suppose l'idée première du Christ Tête des Puissances (2, 10), que les hérétiques de Colosses manquent de saisir quand ils se soucient trop d'observances qui rendent un culte aux anges (2, 16-18). En ajoutant le v.19, le nouveau rédacteur s'est inspiré d'Eph 4, 16 pour adopter une idée qui était bien mieux en place dans le contexte d'Eph, celle du Christ Tête non plus comme chef (des Puissances) mais comme principe nourricier (du Corps Eglise). Il ne l'a d'ailleurs pas fait sans maladresse, gardant matériellement le ἐξ' οὗ (Χριστός) d'Eph, alors que l'antécédent en Col était féminin (κεφαλή). J'admets par ailleurs que la formulation d'Eph 4, 16 est plus chargée que celle de Col 2, 19; peut-être le transfert d'Eph à Col s'est-il fait à partir d'un état plus ancien et plus simple de la rédaction d'Eph. Cf. mon art. du *Suppl. Dict. Bible*, VII, col. 208.

nouveau chez Paul. Il l'avait déjà énoncé en passant, 1 Cor 8,6: "un seul Seigneur Jésus Christ par qui tout existe et par qui nous sommes" [46] mais il n'avait pas eu l'occasion de le développer. L'occasion lui est ici offerte par l'horizon cosmique auquel la crise de Colosses a élevé sa pensée. Il va mettre en valeur l'arrière-fond cosmologique de sa sotériologie.

Dans les expressions du Christ "Image", "Premier-né de toute créature", en qui, par qui, pour qui tout a été créé, la plupart des exégètes reconnaissent, avec diverses nuances, l'écho de spéculations sur le Logos et la Sagesse, élaborées dans le judaïsme hellénistique. Les textes bibliques exploités sont notamment Gen 1,26s et Prov 8,22. Cette thématique n'était pas, elle non plus, tout à fait nouvelle pour Paul, qui avait déjà plusieurs fois pensé le Christ et sa préexistence à l'aide de la Sagesse.[47] Cependant le style bien frappé des vv. 15-17 fait penser qu'il emprunte ici un texte déjà fait. Bien qu'il ne lui soit pas étranger (cf. 1 Cor 8,6; Rom 11,36), le jeu des particules ἐν, διά, εἰς rappelle bien des formules stoïciennes.[48] La répétition de τὰ πάντα sous diverses formes trouve aussi de nombreux parallèles dans les hymnes contemporains, grecs et juifs.[49] Tout cela peut donc relever d'un morceau déjà rédigé que reçoit et cite l'auteur de Col. Il aura seulement jugé bon d'en préciser l'application au problème majeur de son épître, en ajoutant 16c-e τὰ ὁρατά ... εἴτε ἐξουσίαι, appositions dont, après bien d'autres, j'ai reconnu qu'elles allongent et surchargent.[50]

Ceci fait, l'auteur va *composer de lui-même* une deuxième partie en parallèle avec la première. Pour cela, il copie soigneusement le cadre du texte emprunté, en reprenant ses formules d'articulation: ὅς ἐστιν, ὅτι ἐν αὐτῷ, καὶ αὐτός ἐστιν. Selon moi, la répétition de ces formules qui structurent l'hymne en deux strophes parallèles est

---

[46] Ou: "par qui nous (allons vers le Père)". Cf. F. M. M. Sagnard, "A propos de I Cor., viii, 6", *Eph. Theol. Lov.* 26 (1950) 54-58.

[47] Cf. A. Feuillet, *Le Christ Sagesse de Dieu d'après les épîtres pauliniennes* (Paris: Gabalda, 1966).

[48] Cf. J. Dupont, *Gnosis* 335-345. — C. F. Burney, "Christ as the ARXH of Creation (Prov. viii 22, Col. i 15-18, Rev. iii 14)", *JTS* 27 (1926) 160-177 aux pages 173-177, envisage que ces trois particules grecques soient trois façons de traduire le *be* de *berēshît*, terme de Gen 1, 1 évoqué dans l'esprit de Paul par *rēshît* de Prov 8, 22. Cette exégèse, d'inspiration rabbinisante, est plus ingénieuse que convaincante.

[49] Voir l'art. de Pöhlmann (Bibliographie).

[50] Je n'incorpore pas 16b dans cette addition, parce que je juge impossible que le morceau primitif ait écrit côte à côte le τὰ πάντα qui termine 16a et celui qui commence 16f.

le fait de l'auteur de Col, qui imite volontairement le texte qu'il complète. Puis, dans ce cadre ainsi harmonieusement dessiné, il insère, voire accumule, ses propres pensées, avec une richesse de thèmes qui ne permet guère d'obtenir un véritable parallélisme avec le contenu simple et un peu monolithique de la première strophe. Les seuls parallèles frappants sont les deux titres de 18b: ἀρχή καὶ πρωτότοκος ἐκ τῶν νεκρῶν, qui offrent le double avantage de reprendre une pensée paulinienne (1 Cor 15,20 νυνὶ δὲ Χριστὸς ἐγήγερται ἐκ νεκρῶν, ἀπαρχὴ τῶν κεκοιμημένων, tout en faisant un excellent pendant à 15ab εἰκών ... πρωτότοκος πάσης κτίσεως. Principe et Premier dans l'ordre de la création, le Christ l'est aussi dans l'ordre de la nouvelle création.

Ainsi s'avère qu'il possède la Primauté en tout, c'est-à-dire dans les deux ordres, de la création et du salut. Tel est le but du plan divin, ainsi que l'énonce l'incise 18c: ἵνα γένηται ἐν πᾶσιν αὐτὸς πρωτεύων. J'ai montré plus haut (p. 243) la nécessité de cette proposition, tout en reconnaissant qu'elle sort du parallélisme des deux strophes. Si l'on admet que ce parallélisme est l'oeuvre de l'auteur de Col, qui construit une deuxième strophe d'après la première, il n'est pas surprenant qu'il ait pris quelque liberté là où il le jugeait opportun.

Ayant ainsi mis au compte de l'intention divine cette Primauté universelle du Christ qui lui tient essentiellement à coeur, il en vient à expliquer comment Dieu a rétabli cette primauté apparemment compromise (par un désordre qui n'est pas exprimé, mais manifestement supposé): en faisant habiter dans le Christ toute la Plénitude de l'Etre, le monde divin et le monde créé, et en opérant en sa personne la réconciliation de tout ce qui était divisé. Je tiens Dieu pour sujet de εὐδόκησεν plutôt que πλήρωμα.[51] L'auteur redit dans l'hymne avec une concision presque sibylline ce qu'il avait dit plus clairement dans sa rédaction en prose (2,9). Quant au mot ἀποκαταλλάξαι, je pense de même qu'il trouve au v. 22 sa source plutôt que son commentaire. On s'est souvent et longuement interrogé sur ce que peut bien signifier cette réconciliation cosmique.[52] Ni le syncrétisme hellénistique, ni encore

---

[51] *RB* 63 (1956) 34 note 1 = *Exég. et Théol.* II 141 note 1.
[52] Cf. J. Michl, "Die 'Versöhnung' (Kol 1, 20)", *Theol. Quartalschrift* 120 (1948) 442-462; Vögtle 213-232.

moins la gnose, ni la liturgie juive [53] n'en offrent une explication suffisante. Selon moi, elle n'est qu'un élargissement, assez accommodatice d'ailleurs, de la vraie réconciliation à laquelle Paul s'intéresse avant tout, celle qui ramène les hommes à Dieu. Après avoir développé ce thème en 2 Cor 5,18-21 et l'avoir repris en Rom 5,10-11, il vient de l'utiliser une troisième fois en Col 1,21-22, et selon le même sens précis: la réconciliation avec Dieu des hommes devenus ses ennemis par le péché. Dans l'hymne qui veut replacer cette sotériologie dans un cadre cosmique, il ne craint pas de reprendre le même terme en le dilatant pour l'appliquer implicitement à d'autres êtres qui ont dérangé l'ordre divin, évidemment les Puissances célestes mentionnées clairement au v. 16 et plus discrètement en 20c.

On voit mal, à vrai dire, quel a été le tort de ces Puissances et en quoi doit consister leur réconciliation. Il est douteux que Paul et ses collaborateurs en Col et Eph soient tout à fait au clair sur ce point.[54] Il paraît du moins certain qu'elles sont en quelque manière associées au péché de l'homme, ce qui autorise à présenter leur retour à l'ordre comme une "réconciliation". Cette transposition approximative du terme reste quelque peu maladroite et ne devrait pas être prise en rigueur.[55] De fait Eph 1,10 trouvera un terme plus heureux et plus exact, ἀνακεφαλαιώσασθαι: le Christ

---

[53] Reprenant et prolongeant une thèse de Lohmeyer, le P. St. Lyonnet (Bibliographie) recourt à la liturgie juive du Nouvel An et du Yôm Kippour qui associait le pardon des péchés au pouvoir créateur et pacificateur de Dieu. Cette association des aspects cosmologique et sotériologique aurait inspiré Paul dans l'hymne Col 1, 15-20. Pour intéressante que soit cette explication, je ne pense pas qu'elle soit ici la meilleure.

[54] En Col les Puissances ne figurent pas sous un jour mauvais, mais neutre, voire bon. Assimilées aux Anges de la tradition biblique, elle apparaissent chargées d'administrer la Loi mosaïque et les autres lois religieuses du monde ancien, avec ces observances qui concernent les "éléments du monde", dont les Puissances elles-mêmes font indirectement partie (Gal 4, 3.9s; Col 2, 8.16-23). En s'acquittant de cette fonction de pédagogues et d'économes (Gal 3, 24s; 4, 2), elles n'ont fait que jouer leur rôle. Ce sont les hommes qui ont commis la faute d'exagérer leur autorité et de leur vouer une obéissance qui revient à un culte (2, 18). Peut-être les Puissances ont-elles eu, aux yeux de Paul, le tort de favoriser, voire d'exiger cette soumission des hommes et de la maintenir même après la venue du Christ? Toujours est-il qu'en Eph 6, 12 (cf. 2, 2) elles revêtent une figure franchement mauvaise. Cf. *RB* 63 (1956) 30s = *Exég. et Théol.* II 137. Voir encore B. N. Wambacq, " 'Per eum reconciliare ... quae in coelis sunt' (Col. i, 20)", *RB* 55 (1948) 35-42.

[55] Ainsi que l'a fait W. Michaelis, *Versöhnung des Alls* (Gümligen/Bern: Verlag Siloah, 1950). Voir ma recension *RB* 59 (1952) 100-103 = *Exég. et Théol.* II 172-177.

est la Tête de toutes choses, y compris des Puissances célestes, ce qui peut s'entendre de la soumission par force comme du ralliement dans l'amour.

C'est par la mort du Christ que s'est opérée la réconciliation des pécheurs; voir 2 Cor 5,19.21 préparés par les vv. 14-15; Rom 5,10. L'auteur de Col, qui vient de le redire en 1,22, le reprend dans l'hymne à propos de la réconciliation universelle, mais cette fois avec des expressions qui rappellent curieusement Eph 2,13-17.[56] En ce passage qui traite de la réconciliation des juifs et des païens, entre eux et avec Dieu, on trouve, en effet, la réconciliation (v. 16, même mot très rare ἀποκαταλλάξῃ), le sang du Christ (v. 13; cf. déjà 1,7), sa croix (v. 16) et une quadruple mention de la paix (vv. 14.15.17 bis), notamment l'expression ποιῶν εἰρήνην (v. 15) qui explique (et prépare?) le rare εἰρηνοποιήσας de Col 1,20. On pourrait certes penser qu'ici comme ailleurs l'auteur d'Eph reprend un bref passage de Col en le développant. Mais on peut aussi songer à une réaction en sens contraire, de l'auteur de Col retouchant son texte, ici son hymne, à l'aide des acquisitions d'Eph. Il faut reconnaître, en effet, que le thème de réconciliation par le sang et par la croix du Christ, celui surtout de la paix, appelé par la double référence à Is 57,19 (vv. 13 et 17), trouvent un meilleur contexte dans le passage d'Eph que dans Col 1,20, où ces termes non préparés, non expliqués, donnent l'impression d'un résumé trop concis. Nous avons remarqué, après bien d'autres, que la redondance avec δι' αὐτοῦ donne l'impression d'une surcharge. Il se pourrait donc bien que nous ayons ici une addition, non de l'auteur de Col à un hymne antérieur comme on l'imagine d'ordinaire, mais de cet auteur ou de l'auteur d'Eph remaniant et complétant son hymne.

J'attribuerais volontiers au même remaniement dépendant d'Eph le stique 18a καὶ αὐτός ἐστιν ἡ κεφαλὴ τοῦ σώματος τῆς ἐκκλησίας. Ces combinaisons littéraires de "Tête du Corps" et de "Corps Eglise" nous ont paru plus haut s'être fixées avec l'épître aux Ephésiens. Ici leur apparition ni préparée, ni attendue, ni même nécessaire, a de quoi surprendre. Nous avons vu bien des critiques s'en débarrasser, en tout ou en partie. Je propose de voir là une retouche relevant du dernier remaniement rédactionnel de l'hymne.

---

[56] Cette affinité littéraire a amené E. Testa (voir Bibliographie) à reconstituer un hymne judéo-chrétien qui comportait trois strophes: Col 1, 15-17; 18-20; Eph 2, 14-16.

Pour ne pas rattacher immédiatement son deuxième ὅς ἐστιν κτλ. au v. 17 et marquer plus clairement par un καί que l'on passe d'une étape à une autre du plan divin, l'auteur aura trouvé habile de reprendre καὶ αὐτός ἐστιν du texte cité, comme il avait repris ὅς ἐστιν et ὅτι ἐν αὐτῷ, et de le faire suivre d'un titre du Christ qui lui semblait introduire assez bien, d'un seul coup, dans l'horizon de la deuxième partie, sotériologique et ecclésiologique.

La conclusion de l'hymne, 20c εἴτε τὰ ἐπὶ τῆς γῆς εἴτε τὰ ἐν τοῖς οὐρανοῖς pourrait encore trahir une influence d'Eph 1,10 ; 3,15 ; mais elle peut aussi bien appartenir à la première rédaction de l'hymne par "inclusion" imitative et chiastique de 16b. Ceci est même plus vraisemblable, car il convenait d'évoquer une nouvelle fois en terminant, le panorama cosmique dans lequel se situe la primauté universelle reconquise par le Christ.

Nous voyons donc, selon l'hypothèse que je viens de proposer, l'hymne de Col 1,15-20 se construire sous nos yeux à partir d'une première strophe reçue d'ailleurs, que l'auteur de Col adapte et complète par une deuxième strophe. Cette élaboration progressive a entraîné des surcharges ou des maladresses perceptibles ; mais, au lieu de les attribuer à des auteurs bien différents par leur époque et par leur milieu, j'y vois le travail, homogène et relativement harmonieux dans sa croissance, qui s'est fait dans l'entourage de Paul prisonnier durant la période relativement courte où les épîtres aux Colossiens et aux Ephésiens ont été conçues et rédigées.

J'ai essayé de percevoir la marche de cette croissance littéraire, mais il est évidemment impossible de déterminer ses étapes dans leur ultime précision, de même qu'il est difficile de retrouver exactement l'état du contexte préalablement rédigé où l'auteur de Col a inséré son hymne. Il se peut bien qu'il ait aménagé des sutures afin de rendre cette insertion possible et agréable. Les vv. 13-14, voire 12-14, auraient été écrits pour servir d'introduction à l'hymne, ainsi que l'ont pensé plusieurs critiques. On peut aussi envisager, avec Bowen 203, un texte primitif qui passait tout simplement du v. 14 au v. 21 : ainsi raccourci, le texte se lit assez aisément.[57]

La façon de concevoir la genèse de Col 1,15-20 me dispense évidemment d'y voir un hymne déjà en usage dans la communauté

---

[57] En revanche, la restitution de H. J. Holtzmann, rapportée par Bowen 178, paraît heurtée et tout à fait arbitraire.

de Colosses,[58] voire dans toutes les communautés d'Asie mineure,[59] dont l'auteur de Col se serait servi pour rendre sa réfutation plus topique. Mais quand il l'a composé comme un bouquet recueillant les pensées maîtresses de son épître, cet auteur n'a-t-il pu du moins le destiner aussi à un usage liturgique précis, baptismal par exemple? J'en doute, car les allusions possibles au baptême que Käsemann a relevées en 12-14 et les allusions certaines que Jervell 201ss souligne en 2,9-15; 3,9-10 ne trouvent dans l'hymne qu'un écho très lointain. Il se peut bien que la forme rythmée donnée à cet hymne l'ait destiné à être prononcé dans l'assemblée liturgique. Mais il suffit que, complétant et couronnant l'enseignement de l'épître, il y ait servi à proclamer, avec une solennité et une densité magnifiques, la Primauté universelle et définitive de Celui qui, par son rôle créateur comme par son sacrifice rédempteur et son triomphe sur les Puissances du cosmos, est vraiment le Premier en tout.

BIBLIOGRAPHIE

F. Schleiermacher, "Über Koloss. 1, 15-20", *ThStKr* 5 (1832) 497-537.
Hermann von Soden, *Hand-Commentar z. N.T.* III/1 (Freiburg-Leipzig: Mohr, 1893) 27-34.
E. Norden, "Liturgisches im paulinischen Schrifttum. A. Eine liturgische Stelle im Kolosserbreife", in *Agnostos Theos* (Berlin-Leipzig: Teubner, 1913) 250-254.
C. R. Bowen, "The Original Form of Paul's Letter to the Colossians", *JBL* 43 (1924) 177-206.
E. Lohmeyer, *Der Brief an die Kolosser. Der Brief an Philemon* (Meyers Kommentar 9/2; Göttingen: Vandenhoeck & Ruprecht, 1930) 40-68.
I. M. Bissen, "De primatu Christi absoluto apud Coloss. 1, 13-20", *Antonianum* (1936) 3-36.
G. Harder, *Paulus und das Gebet* (Gütersloh: Mohn, 1936) 46-51.
M. A. Wagenführer, *Die Bedeutung Christi für Welt und Kirche. Studien zum Kolosser- und Epheserbrief* (Leipzig: Wigand, 1941) 68-78.
G. Bornkamm, "Das Bekenntnis im Hebräerbrief", *Theol. Bl.* 21 (1942) 56s = *Studien zu Antike und Urchristentum. Gesammelte Aufsätze* (München: Kaiser, 1959) II 188-203, aux pp. 196-197 (cité d'après cette réédition).
E. Percy, *Die Probleme der Kolosser- und Epheserbriefe* (Lund: Gleerup, 1946) 68-78.
C. Masson, "L'hymne christologique de l'épître aux Colossiens", *Rev. Théol. Phil.* 36 (1948) 138-142 (cité: Masson RThPh).
N. A. Dahl, "Anamnesis. Mémoire et commémoration dans le christianisme primitif", *StTh* 1 (1948) 69-95, aux pp. 86-87.
E. Käsemann, "Eine urchristliche Taufliturgie" (*Festschrift Rudolf Bultmann*; Stuttgart: Kohlhammer, 1949) 133-148 = *Exegetische Versuche*

---

[58] Ainsi, par exemple, Stanley 202, Vawter 78, 80.
[59] Ainsi Lohse 84.

und Besinnungen (Göttingen: Vandenhoeck & Ruprecht, 1960) I 34-51 (cité d'après cette réédition).

O. Piper, "The Saviour's Eternal Work. An exegesis of Col. 1:9-29", *Interpretation* 3 (1949) 286-298.

C. Masson, *L'épître de saint Paul aux Colossiens* (Commentaire du N.T. 10; Neuchâtel: Delachaux et Niestlé, 1950) 83-159, aux pp. 97-106 (cité: Masson Comm.).

L. Cerfaux, *Le Christ dans la théologie de saint Paul* (Paris: Cerf, 1951) 298-301.

G. Schille, *Liturgisches Gut im Epheserbrief* (Diss. Göttingen, 1952) 61.

M. Dibelius, *An die Kolosser Epheser An Philemon*, Dritte, von H. Greeven neubearbeitete Auflage (Hdb z. N.T., 12; Tübingen: Mohr, 1953) 10-21.

E. Unger, *Christus und der Kosmos. Exegetisch-religionsgeschichtliche Studie zu Kol. 1, 15ff* (Diss. Wien, 1953).

C. Maurer, "Die Begründung der Herrschaft Christi über die Mächte nach Kolosser 1, 15-20", *Wort und Dienst* (Jahrb. d. Theol. Schule Bethel) n.f. 4 (1955) 79-93.

E. Schweizer, *Erniedrigung und Erhöhung bei Jesus und seinen Nachfolgern* (Zürich: Zwingli Verlag, 1955) 102-103, 110-111, 129-130 (cité: Schweizer Erniedrigung).

A. Feuillet, "L'Eglise plérôme du Christ d'après Ephés., 1, 23", *NRTh* 78 (1956) 449-472, 593-610, aux pp. 463-470.

Serafin de Ausejo, "Es un himno a Cristo el prologo de San Juan?", *Est. Bibl.* 15 (1956) 223-277, 381-427, aux pp. 244-255.

J. M. Robinson, "A Formal Analysis of Colossians 1, 15-20", *JBL* 76 (1957) 270-287.

E. Lohse, "Imago Dei bei Paulus", *Libertas Christiana* (Festschrift F. Delekat; München: Kaiser, 1957) 122-135, aux pp. 126-130.

C. F. D. Moule, *The Epistles of Paul the Apostle to the Colossians and to Philemon* (The Cambridge Greek Testament Commentary; Cambridge: University Press, 1957) 58-71.

U. Wilckens, *Weisheit und Torheit* (Tübingen: Mohr, 1959) 200-202.

J. Jervell, *Imago Dei. Gen 1, 26f. im Spätjudentum, in der Gnosis und in den paulinischen Briefen* (FRLANT 76; Göttingen: Vandenhoeck & Ruprecht, 1960) 197-203, 209-211, 218-226.

S. Lyonnet, "L'hymne christologique de l'épître aux Colossiens et la fête juive du Nouvel An (S. Paul, Col., 1, 20 et Philon, De spec. leg., 192)", *Rech. Sc. Rel.* 48 (1960) 93-100.

K. G. Eckart, "Exegetische Beobachtungen zu Kol. 1, 9-20", *Theol. Viatorum* (Berlin-Stuttgart) 7 (1960) 87-106.

K. G. Eckart, "Urchristliche Tauf- und Ordinationsliturgie (Col 1, 9-20; Act 26, 18)", *Ibid.* 8 (1961/2) 23-37.

E. Bammel, "Versuch zu Col 1, 15-20", *ZNW* 52 (1961) 88-95.

H. Hegermann, *Die Vorstellung vom Schöpfungsmittler im hellenistischen Judentum und Urchristentum* (Berlin: Akademie Verlag, 1961) 88-157.

E. Schweizer, "Die Kirche als Leib Christi in den paulinischen Antilegomena", *TLZ* 86 (1961) 241-256, aux pp. 241-246 (cité: Schweizer TLZ).

E. Schweizer, "The Church as the Missionary Body of Christ", *NTS* 8 (1961/2) 1-11, aux pp. 6-9.

D. M. Stanley, *Christ's Resurrection in Pauline Soteriology* (Analecta Biblica, 13; Rome: Pont. Inst. Bibl., 1961) 202-208.

P. Ellingworth, "Colossians i.15-20 and its Context", *ExpTimes* 73 (1961/2) 252-253.

E. Larsson, *Christus als Vorbild. Eine Untersuchung zu den paulinischen Tauf- und Eikontexten* (Acta Semin. NT. Upsal., 23; Uppsala: Almqvist & Wiksells, 1962) 188-196.

C. K. Barrett, *From First Adam to Last* (London: Black, 1962) 83-88.

H. Conzelmann, *Der Brief an die Kolosser* (NTD 8; Göttingen: Vandenhoeck & Ruprecht, 8ᵉ éd. 1962, 12ᵉ éd. 1970) 131-156, aux pp. 136-140.

J. M. Robinson, "Heilsgeschichte und Lichtungsgeschichte", *EvgTh* 22 (1962) 113-141 aux pp. 129-130.

G. Schille, *Frühchristliche Hymnen* (Berlin: Ev. Verlagsanstalt, 1962, 2ᵉ éd. 1965) 81ss.

B. Rigaux, *Saint Paul et ses lettres* (Studia Neotestamentica, Subsidia 2; Paris-Bruges: Desclée De Brouwer, 1962) 189-193.

F. Durrwell, "Le Christ, premier et dernier (Colossiens 1, 13-20)", *Bible et Vie chrétienne* (Paris) n⁰ 54 (déc. 1963) 16-28.

E. Lohse, "Christologie und Ethik im Kolosserbrief", *Apophoreta* (Festschrift E. Haenchen, Beih. ZNW 30; Berlin: Töpelmann 1964) 156-168, aux pp. 160-164.

H.-M. Schenke, "Der Widerstreit gnostischer und kirchlicher Christologie im Spiegel des Kolosserbriefes", *ZfThK* 61 (1964) 391-403, aux pp. 400-403.

R. P. Martin, "An Early Christian Hymn (Col. 1, 15-20)", *Evangelical Quarterly* (London) 36 (1964) 195-205.

E. Schweizer, art. σῶμα, *Theol. Wört. z. N.T.*, VII (1964) 1072-1075 (cité: Schweizer TWNT).

W. Schmauch, *Beiheft zu E. Lohmeyer, Die Briefe an die Philipper, Kolosser und an Philemon* (Meyers Kommentar 9; Göttingen: Vandenhoeck & Ruprecht, 1964) 47-59.

H. J. Gabathuler, *Jesus Christus Haupt der Kirche — Haupt der Welt. Der Christushymnus Colosser 1, 15-20 in der theologischen Forschung der letzten 130 Jahre* (ATANT 45; Zürich: Zwingli Verlag, 1965).

J. Schattenmann, *Studien zum neutestamentlichen Prosahymnus* (München: Beck, 1965) 16-18.

F. B. Craddock, " 'All Things in Him': a Critical Note on Col. i.15-20", *NTS* 12 (1965/6) 78-80.

M. H. Scharlemann, "The Scope of the Redemptive Task (Colossians 1:15-20)", *Concordia Theol. Monthly* 36 (1965) 291-300.

P. Lamarche, *Christ Vivant. Essai sur la christologie du Nouveau Testament* (Lectio Divina, 43; Paris: Cerf, 1966) 55-72.

P. Lamarche, "La primauté du Christ (Col 1, 12-20)", *Assemblées du Seigneur* (Bruges) n⁰ 88 (1966) 18-32.

A. Feuillet, *Le Christ Sagesse d'après les épîtres pauliniennes* (Etudes Bibliques; Paris: Gabalda, 1966) 163-273.

M. E. McIver, "The Cosmic Dimensions of Salvation in the Thought of Saint Paul", *Worship* (Collegeville, Minn.) 40 (1966) 156-164.

R. Deichgräber, *Gotteshymnus und Christushymnus in der frühen Christenheit. Untersuchungen zu Form, Sprache und Stil der frühchristlichen Hymnen* (Stud. z. Umwelt d. N.T. 5; Göttingen, Vandenhoeck & Ruprecht, 1967) 78-82, 143-155.

N. Kehl, *Der Christushymnus im Kolosserbrief. Eine motivgeschichtliche Untersuchung zu Kol 1, 12-20* (Stuttgarter Biblische Monographien 1; Stuttgart: Katholisches Bibelwerk, 1967).

G. Giavini, "La struttura letteraria dell'inno cristologico di Col. 1", *Riv. Bibl.* 15 (1967) 317-320.

K. Wengst, *Christologische Formeln und Lieder des Urchristentums* (Diss. Bonn, 1967) 163-174.

E. Lohse, *Die Briefe an die Kolosser und an Philemon* (Meyers Kommentar 9/2; Göttingen: Vandenhoeck & Ruprecht, 1968) 77-103.

D. von Allmen, "Réconciliation du monde et christologie cosmique, de II Cor. 5:14-21 à Col. 1:15-23", *RHPR* 48 (1968) 32-45, aux pp. 38-43.

E. Schweizer, "Kolosser i 15-20", *Evangelisch-Katholischer Kommentar zum N.T.* Vorarbeiten Heft 1 (Zürich: Benziger & Neukirchen: Neukirchener Verlag, 1969) 5-31 (cité: Schweizer EKK).

R. Schnackenburg, "Die Aufnahme des Christushymnus durch den Verfasser des Kolosserbriefes", *Ibid.* 33-50.

E. Testa, "Gesù Pacificatore universale. Inno liturgico della chiesa madre (Col. 1, 15-20 + Eph. 2, 14-16", *Studii Bibl. Franciscani Liber Annuus* (Jérusalem) 19 (1969) 5-64.

A. Vögtle, *Das Neue Testament und die Zukunft des Kosmos* (Düsseldorf: Patmos Verlag, 1970) 208-232.

H. Langkammer, "Col 1, 15-20. L'œuvre de deux auteurs différents" (en polonais), *Roczniki Teologiczno-Kanoniczne* (Lublin) 17 (1970) 61-101.

A. Urban, "Kosmische Cosmologie", *Erbe und Auftrag* (Beuron) 47 (1971) 472-486.

J. Lähnemann, *Der Kolosserbrief. Komposition, Situation und Argumentation* (Gütersloh: Mohn, 1971) 34-42.

J. T. Sanders, *The New Testament Christological Hymns. Their Historical Religious Background* (SNTS Monogr. Ser. 15; Cambridge: University Press, 1971) 12-14, 75-87.

B. Vawter, "The Colossians Hymn and the Principle of Redaction", *CBQ* 33 (1971) 62-81.

W. Pöhlmann, "Die hymnische All-Prädikationen in Kol 1, 15-20", *ZNW* 64 (1973) 53-74.

N.B. Je regrette de n'avoir pas eu accès direct aux travaux de Bissen, Harder, Wagenführer, Piper, Maurer, Eckart, Schille (Frühchr. Hymnen), Martin, Scharlemann, McIver, Wengst, Langkammer, Urban.

PAUL AND HIS OPPONENTS
Trends in the Research

E. EARLE ELLIS

Among the Protestant reformers John Calvin distinguished between the 'different gospel' of Paul's adversaries in 2 Cor. 11:4 and the 'different gospel' mentioned in Gal. 1:6-8. In the Pastorals also he discerned two groups of heretics: there were Jewish legalists (Tit. 1:14) and—in the prophecy at 1 Tim. 4:3— Encratites and Montanists who, though not imposing a law on Christians, attached 'overmuch importance on superstitious observances like avoiding marriage and not eating flesh.' However, most early Protestant expositors seem to have been content to identify the false teachers in the Pauline letters rather generally with representatives of Jewish (Christian) legalism.[1]

Henry Hammond of Oxford apparently marks the first thoroughgoing break with this tradition. In his essay, *de Antichristo*, published in 1651, he discerned behind Paul's reference to the 'mystery of lawlessness' (ἀνομία; II Thess. 2:7) an allusion to Gnosticism.[2] In that [3] and a subsequent work,[4] he went on to identify as Gnostics certain other false teachers and/or libertines referred or alluded to in Romans, Corinthians, Galatians, Ephesians, Philippians, Thessalonians and the Pastoral letters. For example, when in I Cor. 8:1f. the *gift of knowledge* results in puffing men up, Paul uses γνῶσις with reference to those who call themselves γνωστικοί. Earlier, in I Cor. 6 the Apostle speaks against *dissension* in the congregation 'in opposition to the compliances and apostasies of the Gnostics'[5] and in I Cor. 16:22 makes them the object of his

---

[1] J. Calvin, *II Corinthians, Timothy, Titus, Philemon*, Edinburgh 1964 (1550), pp. 42, 238f., 365; cf. M. Luther, *Galatians*, London 1953 (1535), p. 70.

[2] Henrico Hammond, 'de Antichristo,' *Dissertationes Quatuor*, London 1651, pp. 1-51, referring to such texts as Rom. 12:9; II Cor. 11:13; Eph. 3:19; Phil. 3:2; II Thess. 2:10; I Tim. 3:6; II Tim. 3:3f.; 4:3; cf. Rom. 13:11. The false teachers in the Johannine epistles, II Peter, Jude and Revelation also are identified as Gnostics (p. 5).

[3] *Ibid.*, pp. 11-28.

[4] H. Hammond, *A Paraphrase and annotations upon ... the New Testament*, 4 vols., Oxford 1845 (1653, ²1659), IV, 89, 200, 517f.

[5] *Ibid.*, p. 164.

anathema. In condemning *libertines* in Rom. 16:18; Gal. 5:15, 20f.; Eph. 5:3-6; Phil. 3:18f. he has the Gnostics in view. Hammond refers to most of the texts that are adduced by subsequent works and also foreshadows some later scholarship in ascribing to the Gnostics virtually all of the false teaching alluded to in Paul's letters. Indeed, he was apparently so obsessed with the subject that (Archbishop) James Ussher and other colleagues were apprehensive of meeting him 'lest they should again be troubled with this eternal mention of the Gnostics.'[6] However, Hammond treated the texts rather briefly and did not develop a comprehensive thesis.[7]

In the following century J. L. von Mosheim of Göttingen joined a more cautious expression of Hammond's thesis to the Reformation tradition about the opponents of Paul.[8] He saw two heretical tendencies in first century Christianity, one that molded Christian doctrines into conformity with philosophical γνῶσις and another that combined Christianity with Jewish opinions. The former appeared in Col. 2:8; I Tim. 1:3f.; 6:20; II Tim. 2:16. The Judaizers were less significant and, as a schismatic movement, a second century manifestation (the Ebionites). The Gnostics, however, 'went out from us' (I Jn. 2:19), that is, formed separate societies already in the apostolic period. According to the Fathers these heretics were a novelty, arising only in the time of Hadrian (Hegesippus, in Eusebius, *HE* 3, 32, 7f.; Clem. Al., *Strom.* 7, 17; Tert. *de Praes.* 29f.). But in fact—writes Mosheim—though small in number until the second century, they were infecting the Church already in the time of Paul. They drew their tenets from a pre-Christian 'Oriental philosophy,' not from Platonism as the Fathers, knowing only Greek philosophies, mistakenly thought (e.g. Tert., *de Praes.* 7).

---

[6] E. Burton, *An Enquiry into the Heresies of the Apostolic Age*, Oxford 1829, p. xxvi.

[7] Hammond's views were soon discussed in Germany as is evident in the thoroughly documented survey of early (mainly second century) heresies by Thomas Ittigius, *De heresiarchis aevi Apostolici & Apostolico proximi*, Lipsiae 1690, p. 166. The increasing interest in this aspect of early Christianity is also reflected in M. de Beausobre, *Histoire critique de Manichée et du Manichéisme*, 2 vols., Amsterdam 1734, 1739.

[8] J. L. von Mosheim, *Institutes of Ecclesiastical History*, 4 vols., London 1845 (1755), I, 115-129; *Historical Commentaries*, 2 vols., New York 1852 (1753), I, 214-221, 228-235: Hammond applies 'several passages in the New Testament to the Gnostics, on no other ground, as it should seem, than that of a very slight accordance in terms. There are, however, many observations of his from which it would be inconsistent with candour to withhold our assent' (p. 229).

In 1773 C. C. Tittmann responded that 'no traces of the Gnostics are to be found in the New Testament' [9] and offered an alternative thesis. Gnosticism originated in second century Egypt, the background of most of the heresiarchs mentioned in the ancient Christian writings. It drew its doctrines from three sources, Greek philosophy, Jewish cabalistic theology, and certain re-interpreted Christian doctrines (393-399). If in the first century Philo agreed with the Gnostics in certain views (301f.) and if some Christians, influenced by Jewish allegorical interpretations of Scripture, denied the resurrection (395f.; I Cor. 15:12; II Tim. 2:17f.) and even if Simon Magus had gnostic elements in his teachings (Epiph. *Panarion.* 21; 27), they are not thereby made Gnostics. The heresy of Gnosticism emerged from obscurity in the early second century. Had it existed from the beginning of the Church, it could not have been successfully opposed as a novelty. And the term Gnostic could not have continued to be used by Clement of Alexandria for any learned Christian teacher.

Of those who saw Gnosticism in the New Testament, and some even in the Old Testament, Tittmann had further criticisms. Hammond, he concluded, was simply 'blinded by attachment to [his] own preconceived opinion' (318). Against Mosheim he offers not only the testimony of the Fathers but also of Josephus who, when treating the Jewish sects, never mentions any Oriental or Gnostic philosophy—nor does Philo. How can Mosheim identify this philosophy with the Essenes [10] when they, unlike the Gnostics, are faithful adherents of the law (395f.)?

Tittmann contended that New Testament texts that are alleged to reflect Gnosticism (e.g. Col. 2:8; I Tim. 6:20) are better explained as judaizing tendencies (317-393). In Colossians Paul is concerned to show 'the excellence of Gospel doctrine above the Jewish law' (324) which, having been deformed, can be termed a 'philosophy' or 'elements of the world' or (with regard to its regulations of abstinence) a 'worship of angels' (Col. 2:18; cf. Gal. 3:19; Lk. 20:36). Indeed, everything in Colossians 'is to be understood as relating to the ceremonial law and its zealous supporters' (344). One must not jump to the conclusion that terms later used by the Gnostics (e.g. πλήρωμα, γνῶσις) had, therefore, a Gnostic connotation in the New Testament. The 'falsely-named

---

[9] C. C. Tittmann, *Essays and Dissertations*, New York 1829 (Leipzig 1773), I, 275-399.

γνῶσις' in I Tim. 6:20 is associated with 'teachers of the law' (I Tim. 1:7) and 'Jewish myths' (Tit. 1:14) and must refer, therefore, to 'contentions of the Jews respecting the ceremonial law and religious subjects in general' (351).[11]

Mosheim and Tittmann are representative of viewpoints that in a number of ways set the course of subsequent studies of Paul's opponents. (1) They identified two mutually exclusive heretical tendencies in early Christianity, judaizing and gnosticizing, and chose between them for the most likely explanation of the false teachings attacked in the Pauline letters, viz. Colossians and the Pastorals. (2) They raised the question of the relationship of the Essenes to Gnosticism. (3) Tittmann, particularly, posed the problem of the definition and the chronological context of the terms and concepts used. Both writers also revealed weaknesses in their reconstructions, Mosheim in not being able to establish the existence of a pre-Christian Oriental Gnostic philosophy and Tittmann in making—rather too easily—a sharp distinction between (first century) gnostic teachings and the (second century) Gnostic heresy.

The British scholar, Nathaniel Lardner, provides a contrast to Mosheim and Tittmann. Writing about the same time, he ascribed to the apostolic period the 'seedling' teachings of both gnosticizing (cf. I Cor. 15:12; Gal. 4:9; Col. 2:18; I Tim. 1:4; II Tim. 2:3) and judaizing (Gal. 5:2; I Tim. 4:3) heresies.[12] However, Lardner concerned himself almost altogether with the second century situation.

II

In the Bampton Lectures for 1829 Edward Burton, the Regius Professor of Divinity at Oxford, offered a masterly and comprehensive analysis of 'the heresies of the apostolic age.'[13] He viewed these heresies essentially as varieties of Gnosticism. Admittedly, he rejected (174f.) the statement of Epiphanius (*Panarion*

---

[10] Cf. also J. D. Michaelis, *Introduction to the New Testament*, London 1802, IV, 82.

[11] Following Tertullian, *de Praes.* 33f.

[12] N. Lardner, *Historie of the Heretics*, ed. J. Hogg, London 1788 (c. 1765), pp. 17-19. His work apparently was influenced in considerable measure by M. de Beausobre (above, n. 7).

[13] Burton, *op. cit.* To the eight lectures (pp. 1-253) were appended 103 special notes (pp. 255-594) elucidating particular points. The introduction includes a valuable survey of previous studies.

28, 2, 3f.) that it was the Gnostic Cerinthus who 'seduced the Galatians to Judaism,' and formed the opposition to Peter and Paul in Acts 11:2; 15:1; 21:27f. On the other hand he apparently regarded judaizing in the heretical sense to be of little significance in the first century (165). Like Mosheim, he located this movement in the second century among the Nazarenes 'whose faith had gradually become corrupted' (518) and the Ebionites, who themselves were Gnostics with origins perhaps among the Essenes (501-519).

Although the name was applied only later, Gnosticism originated in the Platonic school of Alexandria in pre-Christian times (contra Tittmann). It was not a distinct Oriental philosophy, as Mosheim thought, but rather a combination of Platonic ideas, Jewish mysticism (Cabala) and the Iranian 'two principles' of good and evil (68-78, 111, 263). Probably this mixture was first joined with Christian ideas and terminology by Simon Magus, a student in Alexandria (*Clem. Homil.* 2,22), who in this sense is to be regarded as the father of all Gnostic heresies (88ff.).[14] In Ephesus and Corinth Gnostic doctrines may have been preached by Simon, together with the name of Christ, before Paul's arrival there.[15] According to Acts 19:19 Ephesus, at any rate, 'seems to have been particularly infected with Gnostic doctrines' (103). Only if Simon's apostasy were widespread (94) would Luke tell of its origin (Acts 8) and later writers of its presence in Rome in the reign of Claudius (Justin, *I Apol* 26).

Paul's letters, then, might be expected to reflect the battle with Gnosticism (80-85, 113ff.). The γνῶσις of I Cor. 8:1; I Tim. 6:20 and the genealogies and contentions about the Law in I Tim. 1:4-7; Tit. 3:9f. are so applied by the Fathers, and certain other references to γνῶσις (II Cor. 10:5; 11:6) and to false teachers motivated by greed may have Gnostics in view (Acts 20:29; Rom. 16:18; II Cor. 2:17; I Thess. 2:5; Tit. 1:11; Jude 16). The denial of the resurrection in II Tim. 2:14-18 is to be similarly interpreted. But in I Cor. 15 it is the product of philosophical speculation though, as Paul knew, once denied, the resurrection might in the

---

[14] Cf. Irenaeus, *adv. Haer.*, 1, 23, 2; cf. Epiphanius, *Panarion*, 21, 7, 2; 27, 2, 1. In another work, *Ecclesiastical History of the First Century*, Oxford 1831, pp. 75-82, 206, 310, Burton discusses the important adversary role in earliest Christianity that he gives to Simon Magus.

[15] *Ibid.*, pp. 176f.

future be explained away 'by the allegorical subtleties of the Gnostics' (133).[16] II Thess. 2 and I Tim. 4:1 likewise have in view the future dangers of Gnosticism to the congregation. In Col. 1:16 (*Christus creator*), Col. 2:3, 18 (φησαυροί, ἄγγελοι) and Eph. 3:18f.; 4:13 (πλήρωμα) Paul had in mind 'notions of the Gnostics' which he re-applied 'to a higher and holier sense' (83f.). By this re-application 'the system of the Gnostics was totally subverted' (113, cf. 416ff.). I Cor. 1-2, however, probably is alluding to 'ordinary disputes of Grecian philosophers' (416) and can be traced to the Gnostics only at the risk 'of indulging our fancy' (85). Likewise, the Galatians, who evidently had 'a fondness for Judaism' seem to have suffered 'merely from Jewish teachers' (120f.; Gal. 4:9). However, Gal. 5:13, 19f. may refer to the Gnostic danger (102, 143n.), and it is possible that the ecclectic Gnostics 'made a boast of observing [Mosaic] ordinances' in order to win the Jews (120).

Standing in succession to Hammond and Mosheim, Burton offered the most thoroughgoing presentation of their thesis: Paul's opponents were, with insignificant exceptions, the devotees of Gnosticism. More than those before him, he sought an historical explanation for Christian Gnosticism by underscoring the role of Alexandrian Platonism and of Simon Magus. He apparently was the first to identify the views of the false teachers, on a large scale, by interpreting the Apostle's statements as adversary theology, i.e. the employment and re-application of his opponents' terms and concepts. On the negative side, Burton also falls under Tittmann's criticism of Hammond and Mosheim. At times he too easily accepted the later Gnostic understanding of a term or concept as a key to its (adversary) use in the Pauline letter, and he too easily transferred the Fathers' anti-Gnostic application of a Pauline passage to the intention of Paul himself. One must add, however, that in such instances Burton usually expressed himself with cautious and qualified judgements.

In the early nineteenth century two continental writers [17]

---

[16] In his *History* (p. 214) Burton changes his mind and inclines to attribute the error in I Cor. 15 as well as the Corinthians' sexual attitudes in I Cor. 6-7 to Gnostic influences.

[17] Cf. also M. J. Matter, *Histoire critique du Gnosticisme*, 3 vols., Paris 1843 (1828), I, 187-216, who gives brief attention to the Pauline texts and concludes that Paul's adversaries in Corinth, Ephesus and elsewhere generally manifest 'the germs of Gnosticism' and may be regarded as 'the precursors of the Gnostics' (200); M. Schneckenburger, *Ueber das alter judischen Prose-*

signaled important developments in the research, Augustus Neander of Berlin and F. C. Baur of Tübingen. Through J. B. Lightfoot, Neander influenced later British and American scholarship; Baur was a dominant factor in German studies for the rest of the century. Accepting an earlier interpretation that the dissensions of I Cor. 1:12 reflected general sectarian divisions within the Church—parties 'of Paul,' 'of Apollos,' 'of Cephas,' 'of Christ,' Baur made this passage, in the words of Professor Käsemann,[18] the Archimedean point from which the history of early Christianity was to be pried open. 'Die Christuspartei' (1831)[19] was not, however, neutral nonsectarian Christians (Eichhorn) nor wisdom-seeking Gentiles who, rejecting Paul's authority, appealed solely to Jesus' teachings (Neander). Nor was it Sadducean Christians (Grotius), for the opponents in I Cor. 15 who denied the resurrection were Gentiles, influenced by materialistic Greek philosophies (19). Following J. E. C. Schmidt, Baur recognized in I Cor. 1:12 only two opposing parties, the Pauline-Apollonine and the Petrine-Christine. The opponents of Paul were the latter group (24), Judaizers who adhered to Peter as the first of the original apostles and claimed, thereby, to have a more direct relation to Christ: οἱ τοῦ Χριστοῦ of I Cor. 1:12 are those professing Χριστοῦ εἶναι in II Cor. 10:7.

From this adversary dialectic Baur developed a critique, along the lines of Hegelian philosophy, of the whole course of Paul's ministry and writings.[20] In his work on *Paul* (1845)[21] he sets this forth in clearest fashion. 'Judaizing opponents' of Paul, Jews or Jewish Christians who in Galatians sought to impose circumcision on the Gentile Christians, later appear in Corinthians. Since 'the conflict has entered on another stage' (I, 253, 256), they no longer raise the issue of circumcision but rather attack Paul's apostolic authority. These ψευδαπόστολοι (II Cor. 11:13), who

---

lyten-Taufe und ... die Irrlehrer zu Colossä, Berlin 1828, pp. 189-234; C. E. Scharling, *De Paulo Apostolo ejusque Adversariis*, Havniae 1836. Schneckenburger, elaborating Mosheim's view, showed the affinity of the Colossian false teachers with the Essenes, e.g. their astrological interest and attitude to angels.

[18] In F. C. Baur, *Ausgewählte Werke*, 4 vols., Stuttgart 1963-1970, I, ix.

[19] *Ibid.*, I, 1-76, 14-24. For a summary of the German discussion of the 'parties' cf. H. A. W. Meyer, *Epistles to the Corinthians*, New York 1884, pp. 19-24 (on I Cor. 1:12).

[20] And of early Christian history as a whole. Cf. W. G. Kümmel, *The New Testament: ... Investigation of its Problems*, Nashville 1972, pp. 127-143.

[21] F. C. Baur, *Paul*, 2 vols., London ²1876 (1845).

now appeal to the authority of Peter, thus reveal their relation to the Jerusalem apostles and probably are their 'disciples and delegates.' The ὑπερλίαν ἀπόστολοι (II Cor. 11:5) are either the opponents or (like the στῦλοι in Gal. 2:9) James, Peter and John as they are regarded by their party (I, 277). But did Baur have adequate reasons to tie 'the Christ party' (I Cor. 1:12) to Peter or to the opponents in II Cor. 10-13? And did the professed pedigree of the opponents—apostles of Christ, Hebraioi, Israelites, seed of Abraham, ministers of Christ (II Cor. 11:13, 22f.)—point to the Jerusalem apostles or at most to the Palestinian church?

In the more systematic and conciliating presentation of Paul's teachings in Romans the opponents are only alluded to; the Judaizing false teachers in Rom. 16:17-20 are a non-Pauline addition (I, 365). The kind of opposition that appears in Colossians, Philippians and the Pastorals, as well as the presence of Gnostic terms and concepts, witness to the post-Pauline origin of these letters. In Colossians the adversaries are best identified with Ebionites rather than with the earlier Judaizers (II, 28); this is made clear by the polemic against the regulations of food and days, the exaltation of angels, and circumcision (Col. 2:11-21). The 'Jewish opponents' in Philippians (3:2, 18) appear to be a rather vague imitation of those in II Corinthians (II, 55). In the Pastorals the opposition is clearly second century Gnosticism since, as Hegesippus (Eusebius. *HE* 3, 32) witnesses, that heresy had hardly appeared in Paul's time (II, 21, 98-101). What then of Simon Magus? He is a fiction, a personification of heathenism read back into the apostolic period by the second century author of Acts (I, 219ff.).[22]

Baur, very much like Burton, understood Gnosticism as a pre-Christian complex of Hellenistic (and Oriental) speculation.[23] However, in restricting the influence of Gnosticism on Christianity to the second century and in identifying Paul's opponents virtually exclusively as Judaizers, he stands in succession to Tittmann. Baur was the first to make Paul's opponents a decisive

---

[22] Cf. F. C. Baur, *The Church History of the First Three Centuries*, 2 vols., London 1878 (1853), I, 93; *Die christliche Gnosis*, Tübingen 1835, p. 310n., which was published the same year as his essay on the Pastoral epistles. In it Baur pointed to the Gnostic opponents as an objection to the origin of the Pastorals in the Pauline period.

[23] Baur, *Gnosis*, p. 52.

key to the whole of the Apostle's writings.[24] In this lay both the strength and the weakness of his presentation. With his key Baur brought the whole of Paul's ministry into a unified historical presentation of unusual power and appeal. But outside Germany he gave most scholars the impression that, in substantial measure at least, his exegesis had become too much the servant of his theory.

Within German-speaking scholarship a further question was raised: did Baur's identification of Paul's opponents provide the right key? Supported by his teacher, W. M. L. de Wette of Basel,[25] Daniel Schenkel[26] argued that Paul's Corinthian opponents, the Christ party, were Jewish Christian libertines who rejected all apostolic authority and claimed a special wisdom and γνῶσις based on visions and revelations (II Cor. 12:11). These pneumatics or Gnostics, whose gnosis probably was of a Jewish-Alexandrian sort, were similar to the false teachers at Colossae and probably came with letters of recommendation from a congregation in Asia Minor. The party 'of Cephas' was Jewish-Christian 'weaker brothers' (I Cor. 8-10) and allies of Paul who, in their opposition to the Christ party, appealed to Peter to decide the question.

A. Neander[27] also discerned in Corinthians, in addition to the Judaizers, 'the germ of that Gnosis which sprung up in the soil of Alexandria' (230). It appeared among the followers of Apollos, 'wisdom seeking Greeks' (232, 241) who, appealing to their γνῶσις and ἐξουσία, disregarded the weaker brothers, abused their Christian

---

[24] His views are elaborated, with minor modifications, by O. Pfleiderer, *Paulinism*, 2 vols., London 1877, II, 3f., 95-99, 194f. Cf. also A. Stap, 'L'apôtre Paul et les Judéo-Chrétiens,' *Origines du Christianisme*, Paris 1864, pp. 39-115. On the heavy impact of Baur's views in the German discussion cf. C. Machalet, 'Paulus und seine Gegner. Eine Untersuchung zu den Korintherbriefen,' *Theokratia* 2 (1970-1972), 184f. Unavailable to me were H. Lisco, *Paulus Antipaulinus*, Berlin 1894 (on I Cor. 1-4) and *Judaismus Triumphatus*, Berlin 1896 (on II Cor. 10-13); F. Mejan, *L'Apôtre Paul et les Judéo-Chrétiens . . . aux Galates*, 1892.

[25] W. M. L. de Wette, *Briefe an die Corinther*, Leipzig 1855 (1840), 256 (on II Cor. 10:7): 'probably the leaders of the Christ party boasted that they stood in a mysterious, immediate relationship with Christ through visions.'

[26] D. Schenkel, *de ecclesia Corinthia*, Basel 1838, as discussed in de Wette (*Corinther*, pp. 3-6), Baur (*Paul*, I, 286-290) and A. Neander (*Planting and Training of the Christian Church*, 2 vols., London ³1880 (1832), I, 237-240). Schenkel's work was unavailable to me.

[27] Neander, *Planting*, I, 220-253, 319-328.

freedom, engaged in immoral excess, and (together with the Christ party) perhaps believed only in a spiritual resurrection (238, 253). This group contained the seed of 'a later pseudo-Pauline Gnostic tendency' (244), even as the similar Colossian false teachers were the forerunners of a judaizing Gnosticism (319-328). In the face of Baur's continuing influence these views did not receive immediate success in German scholarship. But in the next century Schenkel's opinions were revived by Wilhelm Lütgert, and Neander exercised a considerable influence on the British scholar and bishop, Joseph Barbour Lightfoot.

In the English-speaking world of the later nineteenth century the most influential Pauline commentator was J. B. Lightfoot of Cambridge and Durham. Like F. C. Baur, Lightfoot placed the controversies of Paul within the context of the whole of early Christian history. In a brilliant monograph on 'St. Paul and the Three,' appended to his commentary on Galatians (1865), he set forth his reconstruction and provided, in the process, a devastating critique of the views of Baur.[28] From his first battle at Antioch, Lightfoot writes, 'St. Paul's career was one life-long conflict with judaizing antagonists,' Pharisaic Judaizers and Gnostic Judaizers (311). Although among the Galatians (5:13), 'as in the Corinthian Church, a party opposed to the Judaizers had [perhaps] shown a tendency to Antinomian excess' (208), the significant error in Galatia was Pharisaic judaizing. In Corinthians also the Pharisaic party is present, although 'party' may be 'too strong to describe what was rather a sentiment than an organization.'[29] It is the

---

[28] J. B. Lightfoot, *Epistle to the Galatians*, London 1892 (1865), pp. 292-374. This monograph (and his other work) largely accounts for the failure of Baur's Tübingen School ever to gain a sizable following among English speaking scholars, as E. Haenchen (*Acts*, Philadelphia 1971, p. 22) has rightly noted. It remains instructive today, especially for a generation that 'knew not Joseph' and is attracted to the views of a more recent Bauer on *Orthodoxy and Heresy in earliest Christianity* (Philadelphia 1971).

[29] Influenced perhaps by H. Alford, *The Greek Testament*, 4 vols., London 1849-1861, II (⁴1861), 476: the designations in I Cor. 1:12 'are not used as pointing to actual parties formed and subsisting among them but representing the spirit with which they contended with one another, being the sayings of individuals and not of parties' (ἕκαστος). This is confirmed by I Cor. 4:6 where two leaders can be samples to show a proper attitude toward *any* leaders. Against this is only 'the determination of the Germans' to regard their 'parties' as historical facts (499). Alford viewed the opponents to have evolved from one group, Judaizers in the earlier letters who in Colossians (2:16) add various Essene-like superstitions, in Philippians (3:13) reflect doubts about the resurrection and in the Pastorals reflect a heresy intermediate between the Judaizers and the later Gnostics (III, 75-77).

Christ party (I Cor. 1:12), extreme Judaizers whom Paul opposes in II Cor. 10-11. The party of Cephas, on the other hand, is simply Jewish Christians of rather strict ritual observance, predecessors of the later (orthodox) Nazarenes (372f., cf. 317-321).[30]

In his work on Philippians (1868)[31] Lightfoot identified Paul's opponents in Phil. 1:15-17; 3:2 also as Pharisaic Judaizers not, to be sure, within the Philippian church but within Paul's own situation at Rome (88ff., 144). However, in Phil. 3:12-19 'the persons denounced are not the judaizing teachers, but the Antinomian reactionists' (155). They appear 'to belong to the same party' to which Rom. 6:1-23; 14:1-15:6 is chiefly addressed and who in I Corinthians (1:17; 4:18f.; 8:1f.; 10:15) make a claim to 'wisdom'. Some of them are condemned in Rom. 16:17-19 in language similar to that used in Phil. 3:17-20 (155). They 'professed the Apostle's doctrine but did not follow his example [and] availed themselves of his opposition to Judaism to justify the licentiousness of Heathenism' (70). Such licentious speculators are at first Epicurean in their denial of a resurrection (I Cor. 15:12), but afterward they spiritualize it by applying it to the present new birth of believers (II Tim. 2:18). Their immoral practices are reflected in the Pastorals (II Tim. 3:2-7), in Rev. 2:6, 14f., 20, 24 and, later, in the antinomian Gnosticism condemned in the Epistle of Polycarp 7.[32]

Following Neander,[33] Lightfoot views 'the Colossian heresy' (1875)[34] as the product of a pre-Christian Oriental theosophy that had found expression in Judaism among 'the Essenes'[35] and

---

[30] Lightfoot appears to be influenced here by W. J. Conybeare and J. S. Howson, *The Life and Epistles of St. Paul*, 2 vols., London 1852, I, 476-492, a remarkable work that went through countless printings and continues to be published today. It views the Paul party as tending toward licentiousness and as paving the way for the Gnostic heresy, an exegesis to be elaborated in the next century by W. Lütgert.

[31] J. B. Lightfoot, *Epistle to the Philippians*, London 1888 (1868).

[32] J. B. Lightfoot, *The Apostolic Fathers*, 3 vols., London 1889, II, i, pp. 586f.

[33] Cf. also F. Godet of Neuchatel, disciple of Neander: the same ascetic Judeo-Christianity that appears in Rom. 14 ('the weak') and achieves developed form in Colossae arrives at a 'deeper degree of decadence' in the Pastorals (*Introduction to the New Testament: the Epistles of Paul*, Edinburgh 1894, pp. 565f.; cf. 301, 432.

[34] J. B. Lightfoot, *Epistles to the Colossians and to Philemon*, London 1886 (1875), pp. 71-111.

[35] *Ibid.*, pp. 347-417.

Essene types and, through them, among some Jewish Christians (91ff.). In *The Jewish War* Josephus, who was for a time a member of a group of Essenes (*Vita* 2), describes the sect as strict legalists, exceeding even the Pharisees in regard for the sabbath, reverence for Moses, observance of kosher food requirements (2, 143f.) (According to Hippolytus the same is true of their zeal for circumcision).[36] In addition they were ascetics, some renouncing marriage (2, 120) and some (the closely allied Therapeutae) refraining from wine and meat, and fasting in the pursuit of wisdom (σοφία).[37] They were also speculators, reverencing the names of angels and some rejecting a belief in resurrection for philosophical notions of immortality (2, 128-158; cf. Eusebius, *HE* 2, 23).

Lightfoot concludes (85) that 'in the asceticism of the Essene we seem to see the germ of ... Gnostic dualism,' a germ that found its christianized form in the false teachers at Colossae. Like the Essenes, these Gnostic Judaizers manifested an ascetic, speculative, exclusivist tendency and, as Christians, added two new elements to their speculations, the idea of redemption and the person of Christ (78). Although the heresy in Colossae is vague and undeveloped (111) and may have received its name only later (79), it is the forerunner of the full-blown second century (Jewish) Christian Gnosticism (103).[38]

'The heresy combated in the Pastoral epistles' (1865) is one and the same as that in Colossae, although in a 'more advanced and definite' form.[39] Promulgated chiefly by converts from Judaism and rooted in a claim to a superior γνῶσις,[40] it engaged in speculative

---

[36] Hippolytus, *Ref.* 9, 21: some Essenes threatened to slay Gentiles who engaged in a discussion of the law but refused circumcision. Cf. Josephus, *Ant.* 20, 2, 4, where one Jewish missionary to Adiabene counsels a convert not to be circumcised (for safety's sake) but another insists on it: to read Torah and not be circumcised is impiety.

[37] Philo, *vita cont.* 34-39, 69-74; cf. Hegesippus in Eusebius, *HE* 2, 23: abstinence from wine and meat also characterized James of Jerusalem. Cf. Lk. 1:15.

[38] Cf. Lightfoot, *Fathers*, II, i, pp. 373-388: the false teaching attacked by Ignatius appears to be 'a closely allied form of Gnostic Judaism' opposed in the Pastoral epistles (375). Cf. B. Jowett, *The Epistles of St. Paul to the Thessalonians, Galatians, Romans*, 2 vols., London 1855, p. 83: the second century heresies 'would be more correctly regarded not as offshoots of Christianity but as the soil in which it arose.' Lightfoot devoted one of his earliest articles (1856) to an analysis of this book.

[39] J. B. Lightfoot, *Biblical Essays*, London 1893, pp. 411-418, 413.

[40] I Tim. 1:4ff.; 4:7; 6:4, 20f.; II Tim. 2:14ff., 23; 4:4; Tit. 3:9.

disputations, including a denial of the resurrection (II Tim. 2:18) and perhaps a regard for mediating beings (I Tim. 1:4; cf. 1:17). For the most part its adherents were ascetics (I Tim. 4:3; Tit. 1:15), included sorcerers (II Tim. 3:13, γόητες) and promoted magical rites (I Tim. 4:1) as well as an observance of the law.[41] But unlike the false teachers in Colossae, they included persons who, from the same dualistic principle that matter is evil, followed the opposite extreme of licentious antinomianism (Tit. 1:16; II Tim. 3:6). Only in the second century Gnostic systems do the 'ascetic' and 'libertine' forms become clearly distinct and separate, when the libertine Gnosticism broke with Jewish practice completely and became anti-Judaic.

In his later writings Lightfoot recognized the 'germs' of this libertinism 'in the incipient Gnosticism which S. Paul rebukes at Corinth.'[42] Thus, (1) from the dualism that was fundamental to all Gnostic thinking and (2) from the undeniable unity of a heretical group in the Pastorals (and in Ignatius) that incorporated both ascetic-legalistic and libertine manifestations, Lightfoot was able to find a rationale by which both of these dispositions in certain other Pauline communities could be traced to the one heretical tendency of judaizing Gnosticism.[43] The question about the Essenes raised a century earlier by Tittmann now was answered.

It would be incorrect to say that Lightfoot's views dominated the later nineteenth century[44] since Anglo-American scholarship has been traditionally a rather independent enterprise, less attracted to 'schools' than its German counterpart. For example, F. J. A. Hort of Cambridge,[45] Lightfoot's friend and sometime colleague, is of a completely different mind. Skeptical of 'parties'

---

[41] I Tim. 1:7f.; Tit. 1:10, 14; 3:9.

[42] Lightfoot, *Fathers*, II, i, pp. 378, 586f. Cf. I Cor. 7:12-18; 8:1f.; 15:12.

[43] *Ibid.*, II, ii, p. 124 on Ignatius, *Mag.* 8:1; cf. 10:3 (p. 134) where this 'Judaism crossed with Gnosticism' that Paul opposed in Colossae is described as ἰουδαΐζειν, even as is the pharisaic judaizing in Galatians (2:14).

[44] H. L. Mansel of Oxford, *The Gnostic Heresies of the First and Second Centuries*, London 1875, pp. 48-63, for which Lightfoot wrote a preface, generally followed the views of E. Burton. The Corinthian epistles contain the 'germs' of the later Gnostic teaching (48), and I Cor. 13:8, 10; II Cor. 11:6 are best understood 'if we recognize in the Corinthian opponents ... the precursors of the Ebionite Gnostics' ... (50). In Colossae 'Gnostic speculations were accompanied by a spurious asceticism based on the Jewish law' ... (57). The work of J. J. Skeet (1866) on the third chapter of Philippians was unavailable to me.

[45] F. J. A. Hort, *Judaistic Christianity*, Cambridge 1894, pp. 116-146.

in I Cor. 1:12, he ventures only that the passage indicates a certain partisanship. Judaizing traducers do appear in Corinthians (95-99), as they do in Colossians and in the Pastorals (181f.). Nowhere, however, is there 'clear evidence of speculative or Gnosticizing tendencies' (146) although it is 'probable enough that a misunderstanding of the language of [Ephesians] contributed to the Pseudo-Gnostical terminology' of the early second century.[46] American writers of the period, although not uninfluenced by Lightfoot's views, likewise take an independent line.[47]

Nevertheless, Lightfoot is the most significant and representative figure of the later nineteenth century. (1) In understanding the Pauline controversies within a broad historical context, he marked a clear advance beyond F. C. Baur. 'By a more thorough exegesis and by a more faithful adherence to the actual sources, Lightfoot constructed a picture of the development of the early Church which was plainly more reliable than anything the Tübingen school had been able to produce.'[48] (2) Building upon earlier insights, he showed that the dichotomy between 'judaizing' and 'gnosticizing' (Hilgenfeld) had been wrongly drawn, and he distinguished in the Pauline texts two kinds of judaizing, pharisaic (Galatians, II Corinthians, Phil. 3:1f.) and Essene-Gnostic (Colossians, Romans, Phil. 3:12-19, I Corinthians, the Pastorals), the latter expressed both in an ascetic-legalistic and in a licentious-libertine form as the individual or circle might be moved.

---

[46] F. J. A. Hort, *The Romans and the Ephesians*, London 1895, p. 120.

[47] A. C. McGiffert of Union, *A History of . . . the Apostolic Age*, New York 1897: the 'rival factions' in I Cor. 1:12 are due to the converts of Apollos; the Christ party is nonsectarian, the Cephas party Jewish-Christian but not judaizing; in Philippians there are only unbelieving Jews (3:2) and antinomians (3:18) (389-393); the Colossian false teachers, like those in I Tim. 4:3, are not Essene but Alexandrian, 'the first appearance of that syncretism of Oriental theosophy and Christian faith' that characterized a later Gnosticism (369, 502). G. T. Purves of Princeton, *Christianity in the Apostolic Age*, New York 1900: with the coming of 'Judaistic emissaries' in II Corinthians (3:1; 10-13) there appears 'a distinct anti-Pauline party' (222); the heresy at Colossae is 'not the old Judaistic error' but, like the Essenes, 'combines Jewish rites with a mystic theosophy' and is 'the crude beginnings of what afterward became Gnosticism' (243f.). B. W. Bacon of Yale, *The Story of Paul*, Boston 1904: Gnosticism, as it was later called, was essentially Alexandrian in type and Hellenistic in derivation; it was present already in Paul's day in Ephesus and in the Corinthian church among the converts of Apollos who exaggerated their enlightenment (γνῶσις) (176ff., 299f., 315f.).

[48] J. W. Hunkin in *Beginnings of Christianity*, 5 vols., ed. F. J. Foakes Jackson and K. Lake, London 1920-1932, II, 420.

Lightfoot's reconstruction of a judaizing Gnosis is strengthened by the fact that he was not seeking to reduce the errors in the Pauline communities to one heresy across the board. At the same time he thereby left other questions unresolved. In addressing the error in Galatians, Paul appears to reckon both with visions of angels (1:4), ascetic ritualism and subjection to the στοιχεῖα (4:9f.) and with libertinism (5:13ff.). The former traits appear in Colossians (2:8, 16ff.) and both kinds appear in the Pastorals. Is the error in Galatians, even with the added element of circumcision, so different then from that in Colossians and in the Pastorals? Even if Galatians shows a relationship with the (pharisaic) Palestinian 'circumcision party,'[49] is the attitude of the Galatian opponents identical with it? As Lightfoot himself had shown, judaizing could not be defined solely in terms of pharisaic Christians. And, apparently, the line of distinction between the attitudes of the Essenes and of the Pharisees was not always entirely clear in first century Judaism.[50]

III

In German studies of the early twentieth century there was an increasing shift away from F. C. Baur's estimate of Paul's opponents. Wilhelm Lütgert of Halle, in a series of clearly written and closely argued essays, poses the sharpest alternative. Although he apparently was unacquainted with the work of Lightfoot, he reaches conclusions that in a number of respects are remarkably similar to those of the English scholar. He is not concerned to identify a heretical system of thought but to demonstrate the presence of a religious 'type' that appears in a variety of forms in the various Pauline churches.[51] Thus, when he identifies the opponents as 'Gnostics' he defines them as pneumatics who view Christianity as a higher knowledge that emancipates one from moral and churchly authorities—whether of Scripture, Jesus or apostles.[52] Such persons have their background in liberal, probably Alexandrian Judaism and teach a Jewish Gnosis in the form of haggadic exposition and expansion of Scripture.[53]

---

[49] Gal. 2:12; cf. Acts 11:2; 15:5.
[50] Cf. K. Kohler in *The Jewish Encyclopedia*, 12 vols., ed. I. Singer, New York c. 1966 (1901), V, 225.
[51] W. Lütgert, *Die Vollkommenen im Philipperbrief und die Enthusiasten in Thessalonisch*, Gütersloh 1909, p. vii.
[52] W. Lütgert, *Die Irrlehrer der Pastoralbriefe*, Gütersloh 1909, pp. 91ff.
[53] *Ibid.*, pp. 21f., 65, 92f.

As did Baur, Lutgert began with a study of the Corinthian letters.[54] Against Baur's thesis he objects (51-62) that the verbal parallels, 'another gospel' (II Cor. 11:4; Gal. 1:6) and 'belonging to Christ' (II Cor. 10:7; I Cor. 1:12), are not sufficient to identify the opponents in II Corinthians with a judaizing Christ party or with the Galatian Judaizers. Indeed, the preaching of 'another spirit' precludes Judaizers since the preaching of the law and the reception of the Spirit are mutually exclusive (Gal. 3:2). In II Cor. 5:12-16 the opponents are not Judaizers who deny Paul's personal acquaintance with Jesus but pneumatics who deny his spiritual knowledge of Jesus. The opponents are not accused of judaizing tendencies and, on the assumption that they are Judaizers, never reveal any clear image in the text. The self-conception of the opponents also is not established by Schenkel although he had a better insight into the Corinthian situation.

What, then, is the opponents' view of themselves as it appears in II Cor. 10-12 (62-101)? By claiming to give 'the spirit' (11:4), by disparaging Paul's gnosis (11:6) and by attacking him as 'weak' (10:10) and as lacking the miraculous and visionary 'signs of an apostle' (12:11f.), the opponents present themselves as pneumatics who offer a higher gnosis. But the gnosis of these persons, Paul counters, is separated from obedience to God. Like that which Satan offered to Eve (11:3), it manifests an arrogant presumption that raises itself against the true knowledge of God (10:4ff.). The opponents, then, are not Judaizers but Gnostics who in claiming to be 'of Christ' (10:7) suppose that they are exempt from obedience to authority. The fact that Paul, too, claims to be 'of Christ' and in his preaching of freedom (Freiheitspredigt) has encouraged believers not to be slaves to men (e.g. I Cor. 7:23) suggests that the opponents represent an excessive, libertine extention of Paul's own viewpoint. This is confirmed by II Cor. 6:14-7:1, which is original to the letter and directed against a sexually immoral libertinism that despises the fear of God (7:1; cf. 5:11).

From this foundation Lütgert proceeds to I Corinthians. He assumes the identity of those who claim to be 'of Christ' with the Christ party of I Cor. 1:12 and concludes that in I Corinthians it is they who scorn the weakness of the cross (1:18), pursue a false, hellenistic, philosophical wisdom (1:17; 3:18), by dissension

---

[54] W. Lütgert, *Freiheitspredigt und Schwarmgeister in Korinth*, Gütersloh 1908.

destroy God's temple (3:16f.), ignore the authority of Scripture (4:6ff.), engage in immoral practice (6:9, 20) and deny the resurrection (15:12). With its dualism of spirit and nature this libertinism can also incorporate an asceticism that is inwardly bound together with it (102-135).

This indeed occurs among 'the false teachers of the Pastoral epistles' (1909),[55] who represent the same Gnostic libertinism 'veiled' by a cloak of asceticism (36ff., 92). Their 'other teaching' (I Tim. 1:3, ἑτεροδιδασκαλεῖν), reminiscent of the term 'another gospel' in Gal. 1:6; II Cor. 11:4, is not a denial of Paul's gospel but a going beyond it. To pharisaic Judaizers Paul teaches, as he does in Galatians, freedom from the law; to antinomians Paul stresses that the law still has significance for the Christian community when sin is found in it (I Tim. 1:8-11). So is it in the Pastorals (11f.). Like the opponents in Corinthians, these false teachers question Paul's apostleship (I Tim. 2:7), appeal to a false gnosis (I Tim. 6:20), deny the resurrection (II Tim. 2:18), misuse the Scripture (Tit. 1:14) and accent an emancipation from authority characterized by immoral sexual practices (II Tim. 3:6f.). Like I John (2:18; 4:3), Paul warns that the false teaching prophesied [? in earlier oracles] for the 'last days' (I Tim. 4:1-3; II Tim. 3:1, 5) is already active in the present (I Tim. 1:6; Tit. 1:15f.; cf. II Tim. 4:10).

Here, as elsewhere, Lütgert may weaken his case at times by excessively reading an adversary theology out of Paul's statements. If Paul must remind them to be obedient (I Tim. 2:1f.; Tit. 3:1), that means they were not. If he teaches that God is invisible except in Christ (I Tim. 3:16; 6:15f.), the opponents must have been stressing visions of God. If he underscores Christ's death (II Tim. 2:8) or salvation for all (I Tim. 2:4), perhaps they—like the later Gnostics—have a docetic Christology and restrict salvation to one class of mankind (54f., 60f.).

'The perfect ones in Philippians and the enthusiasts in Thessalonians' (1909)[56] reflect some of the same characteristics. In Phil.

---

[55] Lütgert, *Pastoralbriefe*. Although he regards the Pastorals as Pauline, Lütgert seeks to identify the false teachers from the text without prejudging the question, what kind of false teachers could have existed at the time of the letters.

[56] Lütgert, *Vollkommenen*, pp. 1-54. Does Paul, however, give up his 'Jewishness' or only his 'confidence' in the law as a way to 'righteousness' (Phil. 3:4ff.)?

3 two groups of opponents are addressed. The first (3:2ff.) are probably Jews (not judaizing Christians) who persecute the community in Philippi, since Paul proceeds to show 'not why he is not a Judaizer but why he is not a Jew' (7). In brief, Paul exchanged Judaism for a gnosis, a gnosis of Jesus Christ (3:10). Lest this be equated with the views of the libertines or enthusiasts, he proceeds (3:12-21) to distinguish his teaching from theirs. Paul taught that by faith the believers already were resurrected with Christ (cf. Gal. 2:20; Rom. 6:11, 13; Col. 2:12f.; 3:1, 9f.). Some misunderstood this to preclude a future resurrection (as some today misunderstand the Gospel of John, e.g. 5:25) and to convey a present perfection in which all is permitted (12-14, 31f.). In consequence they have become 'enemies' of the gospel of the cross and have given way to licentiousness (3:19). In response to such views Paul stresses the future resurrection hope (3:10, 21) and denies that he has been 'perfected' (3:12, τετελείωμαι). For Paul, to be 'perfect' (3:15, τέλειος) is not to have reached the goal but to share Christ's sufferings and to strive toward a future goal.

Only in his analysis of 'law and spirit' (1919) in Galatians does Lütgert see evidence of (Christian) pharisaic Judaizers.[57] Following de Wette,[58] he regards Paul to be fighting against two 'fronts,' libertines who have perverted Paul's gospel of freedom and a pharisaic legalism that—as in Rom. 2 and Mt. 5-7—does not really (6:13) take the law seriously (103). The libertine tendency is clearly present, and not just a hypothetical possibility, in 5:15, 21 where dissension and immorality are connected with an emphasis on freedom and the Spirit (cf. I Cor. 3:3; 6:12-20). From the latter emphasis one may infer that the 'pneumatics' (6:1)[59] form a part of the group of 'free spirits' (14-22) who have, like the similar group in Corinth, made accusations against the Apostle: he still preaches circumcision (cf. 5:11), re-establishes the law (cf. 2:18), has his gospel from men (cf. 1:11f.), yields Christian freedom in the face of pressures from Jerusalem (cf. 2:5). They are those

---

[57] W. Lütgert, *Gesetz und Geist. Eine Untersuchung zur Vorgeschichte des Galaterbriefes*, Gütersloh 1919.

[58] *Ibid.*, p. 14ff. Cf. W. M. L. de Wette, *An die Galater*..., Leipzig 1864 (1841), p. 110, on Gal. 5:13: apparently the freer Pauline Christians and those tending toward Judaism lay in conflict and the Pauline group acted with arrogance.

[59] Lütgert does not explain how, then, Paul could call upon the pneumatics to restore those who have fallen into such sins.

who preach 'another gospel' (1:6) and, in turn, are warned (4:8-20) by Paul that their 'backsliding into paganism' (67-89) places them no less than the Judaizers under the curse of the law. For the 'seasons' and the 'weak and beggarly elements' in Gal. 4:9, like the similar passage in Colossians (2:16, 20f.), probably refer to ascetic practices and pagan astrological interests of the free spirits who 'regarded [Christian] participation in pagan cults to be allowed' (80).

Because of such libertine conduct the Galatians, or the Jewish Christians among them, have come under Jewish persecution (4:29; cf. 5:11; 6:12). To avoid it and to come under the state's protection of the Jewish *religio licita*, the judaizing false teachers urge circumcision on the Galatians (96-106). Paul responds that, if they accede to this, they would reject the cross (5:11; 6:12), fall away from grace (5:4), deny the gospel and be obligated to keep the whole law (5:2f.). Paul, then, stands between the two fronts: he fights for freedom but against licentiousness, for obedience but against legalism (106).

Against the traditional 'Judaizer' interpretation of the Galatian opponents Lütgert scores some impressive points, but he also raises some questions. (1) In inferring an adversary's viewpoint from certain of Paul's statements, he is not always convincing. (2) Although he recognizes the pneumatic (6:1) as a specially gifted Christian, he appears to confuse and thus to connect the term with ζῆν πνεύματι (5:25), a characteristic of all Christians. That is, he apparently fails to distinguish εἶναι πνευματικός (I Cor. 14:37) from ἔχειν πνεῦμα (Rom. 8:9). This error will re-appear in the studies of subsequent scholars (e.g. Schmithals). (3) The supposition of 'two fronts' of opponents contains an inherent improbability and requires a frequent shift of reference that is not always clear from the text. (4) The question raised above about Lightfoot's view of the Galatian situation applies also to Lütgert: has he defined 'Judaizer' too narrowly? It is quite conceivable that one group might have been both ritually strict (regarding circumcision) and at the same time theologically syncretistic and morally lax.

Lütgert's view of Paul's opponents was shared by K. Lake [60]

---

[69] K. Lake, *The earlier Epistles of St. Paul*, London 1914 (1911), pp. 219-232, 227f. M. Rauer, *Die 'Schwachen' in Korinth und Rom*, 1923, was unavailable to me.

with respect to II Corinthians and by J. H. Ropes [61] with respect to Galatians. With modifications it was followed also by A. Schlatter [62] and F. Büchsel.[63] But in the subsequent research it was overshadowed by the views of the *religionsgeschichliche Schule*.

C. Machalet [64] has rightly remarked that twentieth century studies on Paul's opponents sound like a replay of the same musical scale, reminiscent of the world of Ecclesiastes. His observation may be illustrated by the use of such terms as Gnostic and Gnosticism. For a century scholars—from Neander to Lütgert—who called Paul's opponents Gnostics qualified their usage to distinguish the term from the later, developed second century Gnostic systems. At about the time that Lütgert was writing, however, scholars of the 'history of religions' school began to minimize or discount this distinction. They defined such Pauline concepts as 'pneumatic' and 'gnosis' in terms of a Gnosticism that was found only in post-Christian and/or Christian-influenced sources but that was, nevertheless, asserted to be 'a pre-Christian movement which had its roots in itself.' [65] From this perspective these scholars offered a reconstruction of early Christianity equally as far-reaching as that of F. C. Baur and one that had considerable significance

---

[61] J. H. Ropes, *The Singular Problem of the Epistle to the Galatians*, Cambridge (Mass.) 1929.

[62] A. Schlatter (*Die korinthische Theologie*, Gütersloh 1914, pp. 94-100, 117-125) argued that the opponents were not, however, an extreme extention of Paul's viewpoint but had their origin in anti-pharisaic elements in the Palestinian church. This view was developed further by E. Käsemann, 'Die Legitimät des Apostels,' *Paulusbild*, ed. K. H. Rengstorf, Darmstadt 1969, pp. 475-521 (= *ZNTW* 41, 1942, 33-71): the opponents are pneumatics but not Gnostics since they do not appear to represent a specific mythological and speculative doctrine of salvation (pp. 36, 40).

[63] F. Büchsel, *Der Geist Gottes im Neuen Testament*, Gütersloh 1926, pp. 394f., who supposes that the Judaism of the opponents had gone 'beyond that which is written' (I Cor. 4:6) into a syncretistic form through the influence of the ἄνθρωποι θεῖοι of the hellenistic world, a view to be espoused a generation later, e.g., by D. Georgi (*Die Gegner des Paulus im 2. Korintherbrief*, Neukirchen 1964, pp. 220-234); cf. J. F. Collange (*Énigmes de la deuxième épître de Paul aux Corinthiens*, Cambridge 1972, pp. 69-72, 320-324). But was there such a fixed concept of the 'divine man' in the first century hellenistic world? Cf. H. C. Kee in *JBL* 92 (1973), pp. 421f.; D. L. Tiede, 'The Charismatic Figure as Miracle Worker,' *SBL Dissertation Series* 1, Missoula (Mont.), 1972.

[64] C. Machalet, 'Paulus und seine Gegner ... [in] den Korintherbriefen,' *Theokratia* II (1970-72), 185.

[65] W. Bousset, *Kurios Christos*, Nashville 1970 (1913), p. 245; cf. R. Reitzenstein, *Die hellenistische Mysterienreligionen*, Stuttgart 1966 (1910), pp. 299f., 379.

for the present theme. For, when writers who shared these assumptions, such as Professor Bultmann of Marburg,[66] spoke of Paul's opponents as pneumatics and Gnostics, they reflected a viewpoint quite different from that of Lightfoot or of Lütgert and more reminiscent of Mosheim's 'Oriental philosophy.' But, also like Mosheim, they were unable to find first century evidence for this (later) Gnosticism and reconstructed their picture of Paul's opponents largely from the concepts and motifs of second and third century sources. Such a method warranted the criticism of A. D. Nock[67] that 'it is an unsound proceeding to take Manichean and other texts, full of echoes of the New Testament, and reconstruct from them something supposedly lying back of the New Testament.' However, in spite of this weakness the approach of the 'history of religions' school became a prominent, if not a dominant factor in the German discussion of Paul's opponents during the third quarter of the twentieth century.

IV

Since mid-century the interest in Paul's opponents has continued to evoke extensive discussion and to manifest a wide diversity of opinion.[68] While one may call attention to some of the

---

[66] R. Bultmann, *Theology of the New Testament*, London 1952, I, 168-172; 'γνῶσις,' *TDNT* I, 708-711; *Exegetische Probleme des Zweiten Korintherbriefes*, Uppsala 1947, pp. 23-30 (= *Exegetica*, Tübingen 1967, pp. 315-321). Cf. G. Bornkamm, 'Die Häresie des Kolosserbriefes,' *Das Ende des Gesetzes*, München 1961 (1948), pp. 139-156; H. Köster, 'Häretiker...', *RGG* 3 (1959), 17-21.

[67] A. D. Nock, 'Gnosticism,' *Essays on Religion and the Ancient World*, 2 vols., Oxford 1972, II, 958 (= *HTR* 57, 1964, 278). Similarly, against Reitzenstein, J. G. Machen, *The Origin of Paul's Religion*, Grand Rapids 1947 (1925), pp. 247-250: ... 'it is very precarious to use the [post-Christian] Gnostic systems in reconstructing pre-Christian paganism in detail—especially where the Gnostic systems differ from admittedly pagan sources and agree with Paul. In reconstructing the origin of Paulinism it is precarious to employ the testimony of those who lived after Paul and actually quoted Paul' (p. 250).

[68] J. J. Gunther (*St. Paul's Opponents and their Background*, Leiden 1973, pp. 1-5) lists from eight (Galatians) to forty-four (Colossians) different opinions on the identity of the false teachers in the Pauline letters. The lists are inflated, however, since a number of his categories represent a distinction without a difference. For the German discussion cf. Machalet, *op. cit.* W. Schmithals, *Gnosticism in Corinth*, Nashville 1971 (1956, ²1965), and *Paul and the Gnostics*, Nashville 1972, contain extensive bibliographies with useful, if partisan discussion. Cf. also D. Guthrie, *New Testament Introduction: the Pauline Epistles*, London 1961, pp. 162-166 (on Colossians); W. G. Kümmel, *Introduction to the New Testament*, Nashville 1966, *passim*; R. M. Wilson, *Gnosis and the New Testament*, Philadelphia 1968, pp. 1-59.

more frequent contributors to the topic such as Professor Barrett of Durham [69] and Professor Schmithals of Berlin,[70] it is difficult, standing in the midst of the developments, to delineate any clear trends in the research. The concluding segment of the essay will, then, seek to present the state of the question as the writer sees it, incorporating and interacting with the various contributions as they bear upon the several matters considered.

Of the various Pauline letters in which opponents or false teachers appear, II Cor. 10-13 presents perhaps the most detailed picture. The section gives both Paul's accusations against the opponents and, in one or two instances, their own perception of their status and mission. It provides, then, the best starting point from which similar persons and groups in other Pauline letters may be compared.

The false teachers are generally recognized to be outsiders (11:4) of Jewish Christian background (11:22) who represent themselves as 'apostles of Christ' and 'ministers (διάκονοι) of Christ' (11:13, 23). On the basis of their pedigree and visionary experiences they apparently boast of a privileged authority that the Corinthians accept and Paul rejects, scornfully labeling them 'super apostles'

---

[69] C. K. Barrett, 'Paul and the Pillar Apostles,' *Studia Paulina*, ed. J. N. Sevenster, Haarlem 1953, pp. 1-19; 'Cephas and Corinth,' *Abraham unser Vater*, ed. O. Betz, Leiden 1963, pp. 1-12; 'Christianity at Corinth,' *BJRL* 46 (1963-64), 269-297; 'Things Sacrificed to Idols,' *NTS* 11 (1965), 138-153; 'Ψευδαπόστολοι (II Cor. 11:13)', *Mélanges Bibliques B. Rigaux*, ed. A. Descamps, Gembloux 1970, pp. 377-396; 'Paul's Opponents in II Corinthians,' *NTS* 17 (1970-71), 233-254; *Signs of an Apostle*, London 1970, pp. 36-40: 'Such envoys [of the Jerusalem apostles like those in Gal. 2:12; Acts 15:22f.], possibly out of hand and acting *ultra vires*, are probably to be seen in those who were unsettling the Galatian churches (Gal. 1:7) and in the false apostles whom Paul condemns in II Cor. 10-13' (p. 40). They are Judaizers even though in Corinth they do not, for their own reasons, emphasize circumcision ('Opponents,' pp. 252ff.). In I Corinthians Paul stands between a Jewish Christian legalism (Peter group) and a Gentile, gnostic rationalism (Christ group) within the Corinthian congregation ('Idols,' p. 152). In important respects Barrett is reminiscent of Baur.

[70] W. Schmithals, *Gnosticism*; *Gnostics*; *Paul and James*, London 1965. Schmithals, elaborating the view of his teacher R. Bultmann, seeks to establish the thesis that Paul's opponents throughout seven letters—Romans, Corinthians, Galatians, Philippians, Thessalonians—were Jewish (Christian) Gnostics (cf. *Gnostics*, pp. 244f.). His many acute insights on individual points often depend, however, on the validity of the method of the 'history of religions' school. Like it, he appears to define 'Gnostic' in terms of the mythological gnosis found in second and third century systems and to assume, thereupon, that this is the concept and context of the usage in the Pauline letters. See above, note 67.

(ὑπερλίαν ἀποστόλων).⁷¹ Probably they disparage Paul's apostolic credentials and conduct (10:2, 10-12) and, in any case, their behavior has encouraged some of the Corinthians to do so (11:5; 12:11f., 16).

The principal questions about the opponents appear to be these. What is their precise teaching? Do they come from the Jerusalem church (Schlatter, Käsemann, Dupont) or from the diaspora Christian mission (Bultmann, Georgi)? Are they pharisaic Judaizers (Barrett), pneumatics (Käsemann) or second-century-type Gnostics (Bultmann, Schmithals)? What is their relationship to the intruders in II Cor. 1-9, to the dissidents in I Corinthians and to the opponents and false teachers in other Pauline letters?

The intruders in II Cor. 1-9 who 'huckster the word of God' (2:17; cf. 11:7), present 'letters of recommendation' (3:1; cf. 10:12, 18) and 'boast in appearance' (5:12; cf. 11:18) are not to be distinguished from the opponents in II Cor. 10-13, even if the latter section was originally a separate letter. In I Corinthians, on the other hand, there are individual dissensions (1:12, ἕκαστος) and erring children but no opponents nor, in the strict sense, false teachers.⁷² For, (1) in contrast to II Cor. 10-13 Paul speaks as a father (4:15), differs by concession and qualification (7:1f.) and engages in no invective. The desire to 'examine' (4:3; 9:3, ἀνακρίνειν) Paul is not an exception but apparently represents only the Corinthians' attempt, that Paul will not allow, to 'test' Paul's apostolic message as they would that of any other pneumatic (cf. 14:29, 37).⁷³ Also, (2) the so-called 'Christ party' (1:12) can hardly be

---

⁷¹ II Cor. 11:4f., 20; 12:11. Following Baur and Käsemann, Barrett ('Christianity,' pp. 294f.) translates ὑπερλίαν ἀπόστολοι ironically as 'greatest apostles' and identifies them with the pillar apostles (cf. Gal. 2:2, 9) of Jerusalem. But this is precluded by the fact that the 'super apostles' were those relating their visions to the Corinthians and, thereby, forcing Paul to relate his (II Cor. 12:11). The 'super apostles' are identical with the false teachers. So, Bultmann, *Probleme*, pp. 27ff., and the commentaries of Windisch, Plummer, and Lietzmann-Kümmel.

⁷² The ἄλλοι (I Cor. 9:2) are possibly an exception since they may be the same opponents that (later) appear in II Corinthians. But there is apparently no indication that they are already present in Corinth. Probably Paul is alluding to his experience elsewhere.

⁷³ See note 8 in my essay, 'Wisdom and Knowledge in I Corinthians,' *Paulus und Jesus, Festschrift für W. G. Kümmel*, ed. E. Grässer, Göttingen, forthcoming 1975. Cf. J. C. Hurd, *The Origin of I Corinthians*, London 1965, pp. 108-113; J. Munck, *Paul and the Salvation of Mankind*, Richmond 1959, pp. 166f.

identified with the opponents in II Corinthians (10:7) on the uncertain basis of the idiom, 'to be Christ's,' especially since Paul applies the idiom to himself in the same text. But (3) there is some probability that the self-professed 'wise' (4:10, φρόνιμοι) Corinthians who 'boast' of their spiritual status (4:7; cf. 14:36) are the same 'wise' (φρόνιμοι) in II Corinthians who are receptive and favorable to the opponents, who also boast in their spiritual status.[74] On the basis of this vaunted status, probably connected with their pneumatic charism of γνῶσις (8:1, φυσιοῦν), these Corinthians have displayed (cf. 4:6, 18f. with 5:2, φυσιοῦν) and may continue to display contentious and licentious practices (II Cor. 12:20f.; cf. 7:1).

The opponents, who find supporters among such Corinthians, probably share their libertine sentiments. (1) 'The secret things of shame,' that Paul has renounced, appear to refer to such practices of the opponents.[75] (2) By the description, disguised as 'servants of righteousness' (δικαιοσύνη, II Cor. 11:15), Paul implies that they are actually ἄδικοι (cf. I Cor. 6:9) or ἄνομοι (cf. II Cor. 6:14), terms that he associates with immoral and idolatrous practices. (3) The references to the Church as Christ's 'chaste virgin' being corrupted (φθείρειν) from its purity (ἁγνότητος) may have similar connotations.[76] (4) Lütgert may be right in connecting the opponents with the admonition given at II Cor. 6:14-7:1 (cf. 7:1 with 5:11f., 'fear of the Lord;' 'boast in outward appearance'). At least Paul suspects that the influence of the false teachers will tend in this direction (II Cor. 12:21).

A number of characteristics mentioned in II Corinthians identify the opponents' spiritual status (like that of their Corinthian promoters) as pneumatics, i.e. persons with charisms of inspired speech and discernment.[77] This is implicit in their claim to visions and revelations (12:1, 11) and to be 'apostles' (a charism that includes such manifestations) and 'ministers' (διάκονοι, a term used of pneumatics).[78] It is probably to be inferred from Paul's

[74] II Cor. 11:18f.; cf. 5:12. Cf. Kümmel, *Introduction*, p. 209.
[75] II Cor. 4:2. See below, note 92.
[76] At least an idolatrous disloyalty is to be inferred. Cf. II Cor. 11:4; Jas. 3:15-17; E. E. Ellis, *Paul's Use of the Old Testament*, Edinburgh 1957, p. 63.
[77] Cf. E. E. Ellis, ' "Spiritual" Gifts in the Pauline Community,' *NTS* 20 (1973-74), 128-144.
[78] II Cor. 11:13, 23; cf. E. E. Ellis, 'Paul and his Co-Workers,' *NTS* 17 (1970-71), 441-444.

comparison of the opponents' teaching with Satan's temptation of Eve (11:3), i.e. to get 'knowledge' (cf. Gen. 2:9, γνωστόν/דעת) apart from obedience to God, and from Paul's comment about 'every proud obstacle against the knowledge (γνῶσις) of God' (10:5).[79]

One can, then, speak of the opponents not only as pneumatics but also as gnostics in the sense of offering a gnosis of God based upon the prophet's discernment of Yahweh's purpose, e.g. by inspired exposition of Scripture,[80] by oracles and inspired teaching, and by visions and revelations. (In this sense, of course, Paul also is a gnostic, 11:6). But as Käsemann has observed,[81] in II Corinthians there is nothing of the mythological speculations of the second century Gnostic systems.[82]

The claim to be 'apostles of Christ' fixes the origin of the opponents in Palestine. In Paul's usage the term ἀπόστολοι may be used of persons commissioned and sent out by churches (e.g. II Cor. 8:23). But where it is qualified as 'apostle of Jesus Christ,' it

---

[79] That is, if Paul, as one suspects, is implying that the opponents' false gnosis is the obstacle to the true gnosis of God. Cf. II Cor. 2:14, 17 where Paul contrasts his preaching of God's gnosis with the many who huckster the Word of God. It is significant that, with the exception of the qualified usage in I Tim. 6:20, Paul does not concede the term γνῶσις to the false teachers but always uses it in a good sense (also in I Cor. 8:1; cf. II Cor. 12:7).

[80] Thus, in the exposition of Exod. 34 in II Cor. 3 Paul reads Scripture without a 'veil' (3:15f.) in the light that the gnosis of God produces (4:6, Plummer) or in the enlightenment that gives the gnosis of God (cf. Windisch). Such exposition is a manifestation of Paul's gnosis. Whether it is adversary theology, i.e. a reworking of what Paul regards as a perverse exposition by the opponents, as Schultz thinks, is less clear to me. Cf. S. Schultz, 'Die Decke des Moses,' *ZNTW* 49 (1958), 1-30; G. Friedrich, 'Die Gegner des Paulus im 2. Korintherbrief,' *Abraham unser Vater*, ed. O. Betz, Leiden 1963, pp. 181-215, 184.

[81] Käsemann, 'Legitimität,' pp. 36, 40f.: that the opponents were pneumatics in the sense of the hellenistic Gnosis, as Reitzenstein asserted, is anything but certain (p. 40).

[82] For the thesis that the conceptual background of wisdom and gnosis in Corinthians lies in the prophetic and apocalyptic traditions of Judaism, with special affinities with the Qumran literature see my essay cited above, note 73. To be avoided in any case is the error of an earlier generation that sharply contrasted 'Palestinian' and 'Hellenistic' as though Palestine and the diaspora were culturally or theologically isolated from one another. Cf. I. H. Marshall, 'Palestinian and Hellenistic Christianity,' *NTS* 19 (1972-73), 271-287; Ellis, 'Circumcision' (note 86), p. 392n.; H. J. Schoeps, *Paul*, London 1959, p. 35; W. D. Davies, *Paul and Rabbinic Judaism*, London ²1955, pp. 1-16; J. N. Sevenster, *Do You Know Greek*, Leiden 1968.

means a direct commission from (the risen) Jesus.[83] In all likelihood the term is so applied to the opponents and thereby presupposes their personal acquaintance with Jesus.[84]

The opponents apparently make no demands about circumcision and the law of Moses. Whether an underlying Judaizing attitude is implied in their superior airs and their boast of being *Hebraioi* (11:22) depends on the significance of that for their background. When used to distinguish certain Jews from other Jews, *Hebraios* in pre-Christian usage appears to denote a dignity or status associated with traditional Jewish values and customs, perhaps including priestly or religious class, Palestinian background and/or the Hebrew language.[85] The term occurs in three New Testament passages, among which Acts 6:1 appears to be an important key to its usage in early Christianity.[86] Several lines of evidence suggest that the dispute in Acts between the *Hebraioi* and the Hellenists reflects primarily a difference not in language or geographical origin but in attitudes toward the Jewish cultus and customs. (1) The term, Hellenist, rarely found in the literature of the period, probably is connected to the meaning of the verb form, 'to live according to the Greek manner' (Cullmann); the term *Hebraios* would, then, have a connotation correspondent to it. (2) The dispute is over foods and probably is not an isolated

---

[83] I Cor. 9:1; 15:8f. It is conceivable that the opponents claim apostleship on the basis of a vision of Christ and that Paul, standing on the same ground, does not contest it. But Paul speaks of Christ's appearance to him as 'last of all' and as 'an abortion,' i.e. without a prior period of apprenticeship under Jesus. He evidently regards this as unique and knows no other 'apostles of Christ' of this sort. Furthermore, the opponents boast in a way that implies an apostolic relationship to Christ (II Cor. 11:13, 23) superior to that of Paul. This probably included not only a claim to superior apostolic signs, which Paul can and does contest, but also a personal acquaintance with and commission from Jesus, which Paul could not and does not contest. Had the opponents claimed only a sometime vision of Christ, would Paul have let that pass and would the Corinthian pneumatics have been so impressed?

[84] So, Kümmel, *Introduction*, p. 209.

[85] Cf. K. G. Kuhn and W. Gutbrot in *TDNT* 3 (1966/1938), 367ff., 372-375. Cf. Josephus, *bell.* 1, 3: 'I Josephus, son of Matthias, by race a Hebraios, a priest from Jerusalem' . . .; Philo, *vit. Mos.* II, 31ff., 36f.: The high priest sent to Alexandria *Hebraioi*, educated in their ancestral lore and in Greek, to translate the Hebrew Scriptures. Tested in wisdom (σοφία), they accomplished their task under inspiration.

[86] Cf. E. E. Ellis, ' "Those of the Circumcision" and the Early Christian Mission,' *TU* 102 (1968), 390-399; O. Cullmann, '. . . Beginnings of Christianity,' *The Scrolls and the New Testament*, ed. K. Stendahl, New York 1957, pp. 18-32, 26.

event but in Luke's mind is a part of the continuing tension in the Jerusalem church over this issue and the related problem of the temple.[87] (3) The episode is connected to the Hellenist Stephen's polemic 'against the holy place and the [ritual] law' (6:13) and 'the customs Moses delivered' (6:13f.), a polemic that evoked a persecution primarily against Hellenist Christians (8:1; 11:19f.) led by Paul the *Hebraios* (Phil. 3:5). (4) Since strict and lax attitudes toward the cultus and the ritual laws existed in Palestinian as well as in diaspora Jewry, such differences probably were present in the Church from the beginning.[88]

When coupled to their claim to be apostles of Christ, the opponents' title *Hebraioi* very likely refers to their association with the ritually strict segment of the primitive Church. Likewise, their pneumatic powers have their (professed) background in the pentecostal manifestations of the Jerusalem church (Schlatter, Dupont), manifestations that included the same pneumatic powers.[89] Like Paul (Gal. 1:18; 2:2), the opponents have some connection and stand in continuity with the Palestinian church even if they, also like Paul, pursue their mission in the church of the diaspora.[90]

Paul does not deny the background of the *Hebraioi* opponents in Corinth or their pneumatic powers. He does not make an issue of their 'theology.' But in their arrogance, their huckstering of the word of God (2:17; 4:2), their opposition to his apostleship, their libertine practices or sympathies he discerns a demonic perversion of what may once have been valid gifts of the Spirit. In a word he views them as false prophets and his own role also as a prophet whose struggle, in the words of Ephesians (6:12), 'is not against flesh and blood, but against the principalities,

---

[87] Later in Acts Peter is commanded by God to eat unclean food (10:14), is criticized by the circumcision party because he ate with Gentiles (11:2f.; cf. Gal. 2:12) and recalls the event at the Jerusalem council, a meeting that compromises a problem over circumcision and food laws (15:1, 15-29). Later, James reminds Paul of this agreement in asking him to demonstrate that he is not, as alleged, alienating diaspora Jews from 'Moses,' 'circumcision,' and the 'customs,' doubtless including the food laws (21:20-26). That is, he implies, we made concessions for you, now you do this for us. The attitude toward the temple, circumcision and the food laws is all part of one divisive and continuing problem within the Jewish Christian church.

[88] Cf. Ellis, 'Circumcision,' pp. 392n., 394f.

[89] Cf. Acts 2:4, 17; 6:3f., 8, 10, 15; 8:13-19; 10:10f., 44ff. The author of Acts was acquainted with the Palestinian church (21:17, 'we') and gives important, if partial and episodic disclosures of its piety and practice. Cf. J. Dupont, *Gnosis*, Paris 1949, pp. 261ff.   [90] See above, note 82.

against the powers, against the world rulers of this present darkness, against the spiritual manifestations (πνευματικά) of wickedness in the heavenly warfare.'

The opponents in II Corinthians are not isolated teachers but, as their letters of recommendation (3:1) and their self-designation as 'apostles,' 'ministers,' and 'workers' show, they are part of a larger group of missioners.[91] Their antagonism to Paul and his rather strong opinions about them imply that they are workers in a rival mission that Paul has encountered elsewhere. There is, then, a certain presumption that they are associated or identical with false teachers mentioned in other Pauline letters.[92]

The opponents in Phil. 3, who probably are one group throughout the chapter,[93] are described in terminology strikingly similar to that used of the adversaries at Corinth:

	II Corinthians		Philippians
4:2	'hidden things of shame'.[94]	3:19	'whose glory is in their shame'.
10:7, 18	'being confident in himself,' 'boast according to the flesh.'	3:3	(unlike them) 'we boast in Christ Jesus and put no confidence in the flesh.'
11:13	'deceitful workers'.	3:2	'evil workers'.
11:22	'Are they *Hebraioi*? So am I.'	3:5	(like them, I am) 'a *Hebraios* born of *Hebraioi*.'

With Lütgert one may draw other, less certain inferences from Paul's teachings in Phil. 3, especially if one assumes that the

---

[91] Georgi, *Gegner*, pp. 31-38, 49ff.; Ellis, 'Co-Workers,' pp. 440ff. (on the mission praxis).

[92] Like Burton, Baur and Lütgert, Professor Schmithals (*Gnostics*, pp. 242-245) seeks a comprehensive understanding of the opponents as they appear in the various Pauline letters (during the Aegean mission) and assumes one type of opponent unless the sources require a multiplicity. In this he is methodologically quite justified, however one may judge the success of his efforts.

[93] There is no hint in the chapter of a shift to a different type of false teacher. So, Schmithals (*Gnostics*, pp. 85f.), H. Köster (*NTS* 8, 1962, 318), and J. Gnilka (*BZ* 9, 1965, 276). Most scholars infer two groups of opponents, Judaizers (3:2f.) and libertines (3:18f.), because they suppose that one group could not incorporate both tendencies. A few obtain one group by eliminating one tendency or the other.

[94] 'Αισχύνη appears in Paul only here and in the Philippian parallel and apparently refers to some kind of ethical corruption, whether greed (cf. 2:17) or deception (11:2f.) or immorality. A contrast to the practices of the opponents is implied. So, A. Plummer, *Second Corinthians*, Edinburgh 1951 (1915), p. 111; H. Windisch, *Zweite Korintherbrief*, Göttingen 1970 (1924), p. 132.

intruders in II Corinthians share (or come to share) some of the ideas of their Corinthian supporters. But the above parallels are sufficient to show that in both letters Paul refers to 'workers' who combine libertine attitudes and a boasting in their Jewish pedigree, with its attendant ritual strictness and (in Philippians) judaizing tendencies. It is highly probable that the same type of false teacher, if not precisely the same persons, are in view in both letters.[95]

Romans (16:17-19) warns against persons that also are described in terms similar to those used in II Corinthians and Philippians and Titus. These persons make dissensions against (Paul's) teaching and deceive by fair and flattering words (cf. Tit. 1:9f.; II Cor. 11:3). They do not serve Christ but their own belly (cf. Phil. 3:19), a term that appears to refer to some ethical corruption or a perverse kind of asceticism.[96] They may promote a wrong kind of 'wisdom,' and the defeat of their teaching or the power behind it is a defeat of Satan (cf. II Cor. 11:15). Since the letter was written from Corinth within a few years of II Corinthians, at most, the similar descriptions strongly suggest that the same type of opponent is in view.[97]

Galatians and Colossians are more problematic. Both letters have a provenance and destination outside of the Aegean basin, and both may stand chronologically at a somewhat greater distance from Paul's Aegean mission.[98] But the importance of these differences can be overdrawn. The total work of Paul, i.e. during the

---

[95] This is true whether Philippians is given a dateline of Rome in the early sixties or of Ephesus (or Caesarea) in the later fifties. In either case the false teachers would be workers in the Aegean area well within one decade, whose apostasy and present activities were known to Paul.

[96] Cf. Col. 2:21. It cannot refer merely to the observance of Jewish food laws which for Jewish Christians Paul never opposes, or to an ascetic lifestyle as such, which Paul allows (Rom. 14). Nor do the words 'their own' appear to be appropriate for describing a judaizing attitude.

[97] So E. Käsemann, *An die Römer*, Tübingen 1973, p. 398: the conclusion suggests itself that there occurs here an early battle with heretics which, as in Cor. 10-13 and Phil. 3, is directed against (libertine) gnosticizing Jewish Christians. His conclusion is strengthened if Rom. 16 is destined for Ephesus, as seems likely, but if the destination is Rome (so K. P. Donfried, 'A Short Note on Romans 16,' *JBL* 89, 1970, 441-449), it is not rendered improbable.

[98] I take Galatians to have been written before the Jerusalem meeting of Acts 15 (so, F. F. Bruce, 'Galatian Problems. 4. The Date of the Epistle,' *BJRL* 54, 1971-72, 250-267, 266f.) and, with less certainty, accept the traditional Roman provenance of Colossians.

period covered by his letters, occupies less than two decades. If his opponents represent a mission (or a perversion of a mission) rooted in an important Hebraist segment of the primitive Jerusalem church, as II Corinthians indicates, they would not have begun their work in the mid-fifties and would hardly have limited their activities to the Aegean area. Admittedly, in the varied atmosphere of the diaspora they may have altered their emphases or character in this or that time or place. But they could be expected to have remained reasonably true to type.

In Galatians the false teachers also are outsiders.[99] They bring 'another gospel' (1:6), perhaps based on or supported by angelic visions (1:8), and persuade some Galatian Christians to serve the στοιχεῖα by calendrical observances (4:10), to be circumcised (5:2, 12; 6:12f.) and, thus, to be justified (5:4). To this end they zealously court (ζηλοῦν) the Galatians, not for their good but to elicit their allegience to themselves (4:17) so that the false teachers may 'boast (καυχᾶσθαι) in your flesh' (6:13).

Several of these features resemble the *Hebraioi* opponents described in II Corinthians: the 'other gospel,' boasting 'according to the flesh' (II Cor. 11:4, 18), appeal to (angelic) visions,[100] and disparagement of Paul's apostleship.[101] The Galatian Judaizers probably are a part of or related to the group opposing Paul in Gal. 2, who originate in the Jerusalem church.[102] If so, further parallels with II Corinthians (11:20,22) appear in the phrase, 'bring us into bondage' (2:4), and in the reference to 'the circumcision party' (2:12, οἱ ἐκ περιτομῆς).

---

[99] Note the third person; the second person is used when referring to the Galatians. E.g. 1:7; 5:10, 12; 6:12. Cf. F. F. Bruce, 'Galatian Problems. 3. The "Other" Gospel,' *BJRL* 53 (1970-71), 259f.; otherwise, J. B. Tyson, 'Paul's Opponents in Galatia,' *NoT* 10 (1968), 254.

[100] In 'Spiritual Gifts' (see above, note 77) I have sought to show that Paul identifies the power at work in the pneumatics with angelic spirits (I Cor. 14:12, 32), and that in Corinth (and clearly in Colossians) he detects among the pneumatics a tendency to wrongly exalt or misuse these spirits and a failure to distinguish good from evil spirits (I Cor. 12:3). The intruders in Corinth, who impart a 'different spirit,' probably belong to the same context of pneumatic experience.

[101] II Cor. 10:10: 'weak'; cf. Gal. 1:10ff., 18ff.: 'from men.'

[102] Bruce ('Other Gospel,' pp. 270f.) supposes that Judaizers who visited Antioch (Gal. 2:12; Acts 15:1) extended their mission on to Antioch's daughter churches in Galatia. This is likely although 'those from James' (Gal. 2:12) probably are not active Judaizers but only ritually strict Jewish Christians who do not wish to offend the Judaizing or segregationist faction in their party (Acts 11:2). See below, note 105.

The στοιχεῖα (4:3, 9) have been identified with the 'elementary teaching' of legal observances (Lightfoot); with 'the law and the flesh' understood as cosmic forces that, prior to Christ, held Jew and Gentile alike under their sway (Bandstra); and with angelic powers standing behind the cosmic elements and/or planetary bodies that regulated the religious life of both Jew and pagan (Schlier, Bruce).[103] Favoring the interpretation, 'angelic powers,' are (1) the earlier connection of angels with the giving of the law (3:19) and with the 'other gospel' (1:8) and (2) the use of στοιχεῖα in Col. 2:8, 20 in close association with the invocation of angels and with the angelic 'principalities and powers.' As Schlier (p. 136n.) rightly observed, the role of the angelic στοιχεῖα distinguishes the opponents from the rabbinic (pharisaic) Judaism and associates them more with the practices of apocalyptic Judaism and, indeed, with the Qumran Essenes where strict calendrical observances and a studied emphasis upon the role of the angels go hand in hand.[104]

The relation of the Galatian opponents to the Essenes is further strengthened if 'the circumcision party' (Gal. 2:12) is an equivalent designation for *Hebraioi*, the ritually strict segment of the primitive Jerusalem church.[105] For there is some evidence that the term

---

[103] Cf. G. Delling, *TDNT* 7 (1971), 670-687; Lightfoot, *Galatians, in loc.*; A. J. Bandstra, *The Law and the Elements of the World*, Kampen 1964, pp. 57-68; Bruce, 'Other Gospel,' pp. 266-270; H. Schlier, *An die Galater*, Göttingen 1951, pp. 133-137; E. Lohse, *Colossians and Philemon*, Philadelphia 1971, pp. 96-99. On the angelic regulation of seasons and years in apocalyptic Judaism cf. I Enoch 43; 60:11-22; 75:3; II Enoch 19:4; (III Baruch 9:1-4). On verbal similarities with the role of angels at Qumran cf. Y. Yadin, *The Scroll of the War*, Oxford 1962, p. 241. Cf. W. M. Brownlee, *NTS* 3 (1956-57), 207. The explicit identification of στοιχεῖα with angelic powers apparently does not occur, however, before the second century. Cf. C. F. D. Moule, *To the Colossians and to Philemon*, Cambridge 1958, pp. 90ff.

[104] The role of the angels in regulating the stars does not appear to be clearly attested in the Qumran literature, but 'the concrete contacts in theology, terminology, calendrical peculiarities, and priestly interests [with] Enoch, Jubilees and the Testaments ... are so systematic and detailed that we must place the composition of these works within a single line of tradition' (F. M. Cross, *The Ancient Library of Qumran*, Garden City 1961, p. 199).

[105] Cf. Ellis, 'Circumcision,' pp. 190ff. The phrase οἱ ἐκ περιτομῆς appears in the New Testament at Acts 10:45; 11:2, 18 (ritually strict Jewish Christians, some with Judaizing and/or segregationist tendencies); Rom. 4:12 (Jews and Jewish Christians); Gal. 2:12 (ritually strict Jewish Christians with segregationist or judaizing tendencies); Col. 4:11 (ritually strict but not judaizing Jewish Christians); Tit. 1:10 (gnosticizing Judaizers with ascetic and probably immoral practices). Cf. Justin, *Dial.* 1:3; Trypho is an Ἑβραῖος ἐκ περιτομῆς. The 'Gospel of the *Hebraioi*,' which appears in the first half of the second century, reflects a Jewish Gnosticism with an emphasis

Hebraios is associated in early Christianity not only with ritual strictness but also with those interested in exalting angelic powers.[106]

While the Galatian opponents apparently do not reveal any libertine tendencies,[107] they are sufficiently similar to the adversaries in Paul's (later) Corinthian correspondence to warrant the conclusion that they are of the same type. They are not pharisaic Judaizers (Acts 15:5) but Judaizers that combine circumcision and ritual strictness with an unhealthy attention and subservience to angelic powers. Such teaching points more to an Essene and/or Qumran background. In this context it implies an interest in divine γνῶσις even if the term is not used and the interest is less explicit than in Corinthians and Colossians.

'As J. B. Lightfoot suspected, and recent discoveries have confirmed, the error combated by the epistle to the Colossians appears to be tainted with Essenism. A return to the Mosaic Law by circumcision, rigid observance concerning diet and the calendar, speculations about angelic powers; all this is part and parcel of the doctrines of Qumran.'[108] To these words of Père Benoit, one may add the theme of knowledge and wisdom in God's mysteries.[109] Whether the errors in Colossae are the work of (outside) false teachers, as in II Corinthians, or—less likely—the result of tendencies within the church, as in I Corinthians,[110] the situation has

---

on angelic powers (cf. P. Vielhauer, *New Testament Apocrypha*, ed. W. Schneemelcher, Philadelphia 1963, I, 158-165). The canonical letter 'to the *Hebraioi*' addresses a ritually strict, Jewish Christian group that may tend to exalt angelic powers (Heb. 1:4; 13f.; 2:5).

[106] See above, note 105. Cf. M. Black, *The Scrolls and Christian Origins*, London 1961, p. 79; J. H. Moulton and J. Milligan, *Vocabulary of the New Testament*, Grand Rapids 1950, p. 178.

[107] The warnings in Gal. 5:13-21 seem to have no reference to the Judaizers except in so far as any departure from the Spirit and faith results in a state in which the 'works of the flesh' become manifest.

[108] P. Benoit, 'Qumran and the New Testament,' *Paul and Qumran*, ed. J. Murphy-O'Connor, London 1968, pp. 16f.

[109] E.g. I QH 2:13-15; 11:9f., 13; 12:11ff.; I QS 4:20, 22. Cf. Col. 2:2ff.; W. D. Davies in *The Scrolls and the New Testament*, ed. Stendahl, New York 1957, pp. 166-169. *Conflict at Colossae*, ed. F. O. Francis, Missoula (Mont.) 1973.

[110] So, Morna Hooker ('Were there False Teachers in Colossae?' *Christ and Spirit in the New Testament, in honour of C. F. D. Moule*, ed. B. Lindars and S. S. Smalley, Cambridge 1973, pp. 315-331) who thinks that the Colossians are only 'under pressure to conform to the beliefs and practices of their pagan and Jewish neighbours' (p. 329). It seems, however, that the τις (2:8, 16; cf. 2:4, 18) alludes to false teachers who already are present or

features similar to the problem in Corinth. Like some Corinthians, some Colossians are seeking 'wisdom and knowledge' (2:2ff., 23) apart from the centrality of Christ. They are pursuing desirable manifestations of pneumatic gifts (1:9) both by 'philosophical' wisdom (2:8; cf. I Cor. 3:20) and by experiences of vision and/or ecstacy. In both Corinth and Colossae the latter course has resulted in an improper attention being given to the angelic powers, e.g. that mediate the gifts.[111] The Colossians, like the Galatians, take a judaizing (2:16) road of asceticism and apparent humility. But for Paul that attitude, no less than the boastful assurance of the Corinthians, is caused by or results in a person 'vainly puffed up by the mind of his flesh' and primed for a libertine 'indulgence (πλησμονή) of the flesh' (2:18, 23; cf. I Cor. 4:8, 10, 18f.; 8:1, φυσιοῦν). Just that type of false teacher surfaces in the Pastoral letters.

The Colossian situation is much less extreme. Since the whole pneumatic context of the Pauline mission had affinities with and— via a Christian 'pentecost'—a part of its background in Essene prophetism,[112] it was not always easy for Paul to distinguish a deficient teaching in need of helpful correction from what to him was a perverse heresy demanding excision. The Colossian pneumatics have apparently picked up some unhealthy tendencies but are regarded by Paul as genuine and teachable and without the ethical aberrations present in Corinth. This may account for the relative mild admonitions in the face of potentially dangerous errors. In several respects these errors reflect the type of false teaching found in the earlier Pauline letters: the (Essene) judaizing character, the displacement of Christ from his proper central role, the tendency to misuse and thus to pervert the Christian pneumatic (prophetic) experiences.

The Pastoral letters probably reflect the state of the Pauline mission in the Aegean basin in the mid-sixties of the first century.[113]

---

who may soon appear to exploit a weakness in the church. For a more probable case against opponents in Thessalonica cf. E. Best, *Thessalonians*, New York 1972, pp. 16-22.

[111] Col. 2:18; cf. I Cor. 14:12 (πνεύματα). Cf. E. E. Ellis, 'Christ and Spirit in I Corinthians,' *Christ and Spirit in the New Testament*, ed. B. Lindars, Cambridge 1973, pp. 275ff.

[112] Cf. Ellis, 'Spiritual Gifts,' pp. 134-137.

[113] The non-Pauline literary expression and theological emphases look more like an amanuensis incorporating traditions of Paul's circle under the

Throughout the letters the false teachers represent one general type of opposition.[114] Some are from 'the circumcision party' (Tit. 1:10; cf. Col. 4:11), and others represent a defection from a Pauline viewpoint. Cf. I Tim. 1:3; II Tim. 1:15f.; 2:17; cf. 4:10. Unlike the earlier letters, the opponents appear to include a considerable number of former co-workers whose apostasy creates an especially bitter situation.

They are 'teachers of the law' who engage in disputes about it and, in haggadic fashion, expound Jewish 'fables (μῦθοι) and genealogies.' Cf. I Tim. 1:4, 7; 6:4; II Tim. 2:14, 23; Tit. 1:14; 3:9. That they are pneumatics is confirmed in the claim to give γνῶσις and in Paul's application to them of an earlier oracle, i.e. that their teaching is the product of 'erring spirits and teachings of demons' that brings one into the 'snare of the devil.' Cf. I Tim. 4:1-3, 7 (II Cor. 11:4, 18); II Tim. 2:26; cf. 3:8, 13, γόητες; Gal. 3:1, βασκαίνειν. They are 'puffed up' (τυφοῦσθαι), motivated by greed, and promote a perverse asceticism that issues, perhaps, in a subtle licentiousness. Cf. I Tim. 4:3; 6:4f.; II Tim. 3:4ff.; Tit. 1:11 (Phil. 3:19).

The description of the false teaching differs considerably from earlier Pauline letters. There are few verbal parallels and no references to (angelic) visions or ecstatic phenomena. The haggadic exposition of Scripture and the opposition of Paul's own converts and co-workers also is hardly found elsewhere, although intimations of the latter appear in Corinthians and Philippians (3:18). Nevertheless, the description does conform in some measure to the type of error encountered in the other letters. The opponents are pneumatics. Like Colossians, there is an (even more rigid) asceticism reminiscent of some Essenes and, like Corinthians, there is a claim to give γνῶσις whose source Paul believes to be 'another spirit,' an 'erring' demonic spirit.

V

The Pauline mission was an enterprise of pneumatics, persons who claimed special understanding of the Scripture and who

---

Apostle's eye in the sixties than like a later 'disciple' exercising his second century imagination about Paul's work in the sixties or about Paul's attitude toward issues in the pseudepigrapher's own time. Cf. J. N. D. Kelly, *The Pastoral Epistles*, London 1963, pp. 6-10, 30-34.

[114] So, Kelly, *Pastoral*, pp. 10f.; M. Dibelius-H. Conzelmann, *The Pastoral Epistles*, Philadelphia 1972, pp. 65ff. Otherwise: W. Lock, *The Pastoral Epistles*, Edinburgh 1952 (1924), p. xvii.

experienced manifestations of inspired, ecstatic speech and of visions and revelations. The primary opposition to that mission arose from within a segment of the ritually strict *Hebraioi* in the Jerusalem church and with variations in nuance continued to post, sometimes as a counter mission and sometimes as an infiltrating influence, a settled and persistent 'other' gospel. It also laid claim to pneumatic powers and experiences. Each group claimed to be the true voice of Jesus, each claimed to give the true γνῶσις of God and, on occasion, each made its higher appeal to apostolic status. It was, in a word, a battle of prophets, and the congregations were called upon to choose—Paul or his opposition. The dust of their warfare has settled and history has recorded the choice of the churches, at least of the continuing churches. If scholars are still drawn to the ancient debate and to the issues it raised, they are influenced in no small part, one suspects, by the attraction of the one unsilenced voice in the conflict, Paul the Jew of Tarsus, who in his letters continues the battle for his messiah.

THE PRESENT STATE OF SCHOLARSHIP ON HEBREWS

GEORGE WESLEY BUCHANAN
Wesley Theological Seminary

Introduction

Since scholars have had access to the Dead Sea Scrolls, there has been an upsurge of interest in Hebrews.[1] The Scrolls have provided a new perspective from which to examine the nature, meaning, and authorship of the document entitled "To the Hebrews." The general revival of interest in Hebrews has also motivated other research which has not been directly influenced by the Scrolls. During the first half of the twentieth century scholars did not flood the market with research on Hebrews, but that does not mean that their successors could examine Hebrews *de novo*. So many excellent researchers had previously devoted years of their lives to this study that as early as 1856 Delitzsch was able to list ten pages of bibliography of works that had been written since the Reformation which he had selected and used.[2] Since Delitzsch's time still more insights have been published, many of which are illuminating. Some of these earlier major works will be surveyed to provide a background against which recent scholarship began. Material published prior to 1955 will be examined book by book in chronological order. From 1955 on, important works will be evaluated as they are related to major categories of interest in Hebrews.

Scholarship before the Scrolls

Earlier Scholars

Wetstein.—As early as 1752, Wetstein published his *Novum*

---

[1] Research for this survey was first done in preparation of the Anchor Bible Commentary *To the Hebrews* (Garden City, 1972), hereafter referred to as ABC. Discussions summarized here are treated more fully in the commentary. I am grateful to my former professor, Morton Smith, who first introduced me to the variegated background of pre-Christian Judaism necessary for understanding such NT documents as Hebrews. Dr. Smith was my professor when the Dead Sea Scrolls were first being made available for general scholarly examination. This is the point in time which I have arbitrarily chosen as the division between earlier and more recent scholarship.

[2] F. Delitzsch, *Commentary on the Epistle to the Hebrews*, tr. T. L. Kingsbury (Edinburgh, 1878), I, 25-35.

Testamentum Graecum which contains an analysis of Hebrews.[3] This invaluable resource surveys the views of church fathers on the subject, analyzes OT passages quoted, compares Hebrews with the works of Paul, and lists parallel passages from rabbinic and classical literature. Most significant commentators who wrote after 1752 have been dependent upon Wetstein. One such scholar was Friedrich Bleek.[4]

Bleek.—At the time Bleek wrote, the authorship of Hebrews was evidently a live issue, because the major thrust of his study was intended to show that Paul could not have written this document. He traced the arguments pro and contra from the second century until his own day. He also examined proposals made to defend others, such as Clement, Luke, or Barnabas, as authors. He finally rejected them all except Apollos who, he believed, wrote the document from Egypt.

Stuart.—One of Bleek's contemporaries in America was Stuart, whose commentary provides an excellent analysis of the text of Hebrews in comparison with the Hebrew and Greek OT texts used.[5] His familiarity with classical Greek also cast new light on the text.

Turner.—Turner's small volume is important for its etymology of words used in Hebrews.[6] He studied carefully each important word to learn the fullest possible force the word might bear, and, in its context, the most likely meaning intended.

Delitzsch.—Delitzsch's years of OT scholarship were aptly applied to Hebrews. Delitzsch not only examined each text to determine its authenticity and the OT quotations to learn their meaning for the author, but he also interpreted the text in the light of OT sacrificial customs and Rabbinic interpretations. Delitzsch was convinced that the document was written early, so he was therefore predisposed to believe that Paul wrote it. This was confirmed by the Pauline ending, although Delitzsch admitted that the main document had many non-Pauline features and had not always

---

[3] J. J. Wetstein, *Novum Testamentum Graecum* (Amsterdam, 1752), II, 383-446.

[4] F. Bleek, *Der Brief an die Hebräer* (Berlin, 1828) three volumes. Vol. I is devoted to introduction and II and III, to the commentary.

[5] M. Stuart, *Commentary on the Epistle to the Hebrews* (Andover, 1828), two volumes.

[6] S. H. Turner, *The Epistle to the Hebrews in Greek and English* (New York, 1852).

been accepted as Pauline by the early church. He thought the recipients lived somewhere in Palestine.

Vaughan.—With a preface of only nineteen pages, Vaughan made no attempt to identify the author or original readers of Hebrews, although he believed the latter lived in Jerusalem.[7] He considered the document a homily rather than a letter and probably non-Pauline. He offered no suggestion for its date and purpose of composition. Vaughan was admittedly dependent upon Delitzsch. The importance of his work is his careful commentary on each word, not etymologically but against its context and the background of other usages of the same term in the OT and other ancient literature.

Westcott.—In many ways the most important commentary composed in the nineteenth century was that of Westcott.[8] Westcott's introduction deals thoroughly with texts used, the use of the title in the earliest sources, its position in the canon, its organization, original language, and peculiarities. Westcott thought that recipients were members of a small group in Palestine, at or near Jerusalem, before the fall of that city. The document was not written by Paul, in Westcott's judgment. He astutely observed, "The place of writing must be left in complete uncertainty. Plausible conjectures unsupported by evidence cannot remove our ignorance even if they satisfy our curiosity." [9] His survey of documents, authorship, and history is excellent. Westcott's commentary is distinguished by two points: 1) Westcott's comparison of terms with similar usages in OT, Josephus, Philo, and the apocrypha, and 2) his judicious selection of quotations from later church documents which interpreted Hebrews. This commentary will not cease to be useful for later scholarship.

Riggenbach.—The earliest major work on Hebrews in the twentieth century was Riggenbach's commentary.[10] This is a thorough and careful commentary, well-documented with footnotes, and a fair presentation of different opposing arguments when the meaning of the text is uncertain. Riggenbach has presented the history of the document and its textual support. He noted that this is

---

[7] C. J. Vaughan, *The Epistle to the Hebrews* (London, 1890).
[8] B. F. Westcott, *The Epistle to the Hebrews* (London, 1892).
[9] Westcott, *op. cit.*, xliv.
[10] E. Riggenbach, *Der Brief an die Hebräer* (Leipzig, 1913,1917,1922). The 1922 edition was used here.

one of the earliest NT documents discussed by church fathers.[11] Although he noticed the break between chapters 12 and 13,[12] he insisted that Hebrews is a unified letter and not a homily.[13] He assumed that the original title to the document was lost in antiquity,[14] and he thought the name "To the Hebrews" was no clue to the location of the recipients, since Hebrews might have lived anywhere.[15] Like most scholars, Riggenbach recognized the close parallel between the "rest" mentioned in the OT and that offered by the author of Hebrews, but he also decided arbitrarily that the author could not have meant Canaan when he promised "rest," but he invisaged something spiritual, a goal in heaven.[16] The author was a born Jew who wrote and thought in Greek.[17] He was probably Barnabas who wrote from Rome to Jewish Christians in Cyprus, perhaps between A.D. 66-70.[18] There are similarities between Philo and Hebrews, but also differences. Hebrews belongs to the sphere of Heilsgeschichte, whereas Philo was a Platonic allegorist.[19] The author's purpose was to prevent the readers from reverting to Judaism.[20] Riggenbach compensated with thoroughness for his deficiency in originality, having produced a commentary that has been useful for many scholars.

Moffatt.—Moffatt's useful commentary includes a careful listing and examination of the texts used, a new English translation, and a good commentary on the Greek text.[21] Moffatt reached two important conclusions as a result of his study: 1) "The identity of the author and of his readers must be left in the mist where they already lay at the beginning of the second century," [22] suggesting further that hypotheses attributing authorship to one of the early NT leaders were made "in the main due to an irrepressible desire to construct NT romances." [23] 2) The writer "knew no Hebrew, and his

---

[11] Riggenbach, *op. cit.*, v.
[12] Riggenbach, *op. cit.*, 428.
[13] Riggenbach, *op. cit.*, xv.
[14] Riggenbach, *op. cit.*, xvii.
[15] Riggenbach, *op. cit.*, vi
[16] Riggenbach, *op. cit.*, 84-85, 97-98, 415.
[17] Riggenbach, *op. cit.*, xviii, xxiv.
[18] Riggenbach, *op. cit.*, xl-xlviii.
[19] Riggenbach, *op. cit.*, xxxvi.
[20] Riggenbach, *op. cit.*, xxiii.
[21] J. Moffatt, *A Critical and Exegetical Commentary on the Epistle to the Hebrews* (Edinburgh, 1924).
[22] Moffatt, *op. cit.*, lx.
[23] Moffatt, *op. cit.*, xx.

readers were in no sense 'Εβραῖοι." [24] Although he admitted that chapters 1-12 could be classed as a homily,[25] and he said of 12:28, "With this impressive sentence Πρὸς 'Εβραίους really closes,"[26] he strangely denied that 1-12 was a pure treatise [27] and insisted that the whole document was a unit composed by one author.[28] He believed the author's world view was fundamentally Platonic, and the author was strongly influenced by Philo. The document has nothing to do with the Jewish temple or the Palestinian Christians. Moffatt denied that the author believed in a severe, angry God that had to be appeased.[29] The document was post-Pauline, but surely written before A.D. 85.[30] The original readers were members of a small group of non-Jewish Christians.[31] Moffatt provided few new insights, but his commentary is a compilation of materials useful for research in Hebrews and will continue to be valuable.

Windisch.—Windisch prepared a brief, but good, analysis of Hebrews, with a brief introduction, followed by a commentary, and finally conclusions.[32] He thought the title may have been added by a later editor and may say nothing about the original recipients.[33] In Windisch's judgment, the document itself was a sermon or tractate to which an epistolary conclusion had been added. The sermon had been written down because the author was absent from the community, though it was directed to a special community.[34] The author was not Paul. The most likely candidate for authorship was Barnabas.[35] The document was probably written during the rule of Domitian (A.D. 81-96).[36] The similarity between Hebrews and the works of Philo means that the author was not simply a Palestinian, but also a Hellenist.[37] Windisch did not have the benefit of the Dead Sea Scrolls to help him decide the source of Hebrews' dualism.

---

[24] Moffatt, *op. cit.*, ix.
[25] Moffatt, *op. cit.*, xxxviii.
[26] Moffatt, *op. cit.*, 224.
[27] Moffatt, *op. cit.*, xxix.
[28] Moffatt, *op. cit.*, xxix.
[29] Moffatt, *op. cit.*, xxxv.
[30] Moffatt, *op. cit.*, xxii.
[31] Moffatt, *op. cit.*, xvi.
[32] H. Windisch, *Der Hebräerbrief* (Tübingen, 1931).
[33] Windisch, *op. cit.*, 6-7.
[34] Windisch, *op. cit.*, 122-123.
[35] Windisch, *op. cit.*, 124-125.
[36] Windisch, *op. cit.*, 126-127.
[37] Windisch, *op. cit.*, 132-133.

Michel.—Michel prepared an excellent verse-by-verse commentary that made good use of Rabbinic and OT sources for interpretation of the text.[38] He also recognized poetic passages in Hebrews that had been sources for the author. Michel believed chapters 1-12 comprised a homily that had been written by someone who was unable to deliver the message personally, so he sent it with an accompanying note (now chapter 13).[39] He held that the author lived near Rome about the time of Clement of Rome, at the end of the first century.[40] He was a Jewish Christian leader, trained in Alexandrian thought, although he held apocalyptic views; and he was familiar with Pauline theology, although he was also an independent thinker.[41] He wrote to a specific Italian community.[42] The central theme is eschatological in nature and also Christocentric, the Son and the high priest being very closely related.[43] Jesus was the Son; he would *become* the high priest.[44] Michel's conclusions were not as important as his commentary.

Käsemann.—The title of Käsemann's book, *Das wanderende Gottesvolk*, seems like a pregnant title by which to relate the pilgrimages of the sons of Abraham to Zion as a background for the homily, "To the Hebrews."[45] Käsemann recognized the type/antitype relationship between the exodus generation and the people to whom Hebrews was addressed in that both were seeking the promised rest, but he believed the nature of the rest involved was quite different. The document includes a discussion with Judaism that is more or less historically oriented, to be sure, but this was only necessary to prevent the readers from being attracted to Judaism and leaving the true faith.[46] Käsemann admitted that there was no external criterion for distinguishing between already realized and still unfulfilled promises in Hebrews, but he insisted that it was necessary to make such a distinction.[47] The earthly

---

[38] O. Michel, *Der Brief an die Hebräer* (Göttingen, 1957), the edition used here. The first edition was 1936.
[39] Michel, *op. cit.*, 2-3, 8-9.
[40] Michel, *op. cit.*, 15-16.
[41] Michel, *op. cit.*, 16.
[42] Michel, *op. cit.*, 16.
[43] Michel, *op. cit.*, 17-18, 20-21.
[44] Michel, op. cit., 21.
[45] E. Käsemann, *Das wanderende Gottesvolk* (Göttingen, 1939)
[46] Käsemann, *op. cit.*, 10, 110-111.
[47] Käsemann, *op. cit.*, 17.

elements of the promise to Abraham had been fulfilled.[48] The better promises, belonging to the new covenant, were eschatological. These promises involve a heavenly rest, an inheritance, a heavenly fatherland, a heavenly Jerusalem, a world to come, and an entrance to the way of the saints.[49] The blood of Jesus offered in Jerusalem established and guaranteed the new covenant, but the goal of the Christian pilgrimage is never earthly, but only heavenly, Jerusalem.[50] In disagreement with Michel, Käsemann held that both the form and content of Hebrews is Hellenistic.[51] The rest and inheritance promised is never Canaan but always the heavenly world.[52] The true background for Hebrews is in gnostic thought and the wandering of the Christian is a gnostic ascension of the soul from the dark material world of demons to the heavenly city of light.[53] The Son in Hebrews is the gnostic *Anthropos*, the little Jehovah, Savior, Leader, *Sophia*, *Logos*, and *Urmensch* as in Philip. 2.[54] Concepts like "enlightened," "psychic," and "perfect" are gnostic terms referring to those who are advanced in the gnostic myth.[55] Jesus is the *telos* of the Hellenistic myth in Hebrews, just as he is the *telos* of the Jewish law in other documents.[56] Käsemann was convinced that there was a tradition of Melchizedek as the incarnation of the *Urmensch*.[57] The curtain mentioned in Hebrews was not part of the earthly temple, according to Käsemann, but the division that separated earth from heaven.[58]

Käsemann described with great confidence a gnostic pilgrimage in terms of Hebrews, even though he admitted that there was no external evidence for such spiritualization. Since he wrote this book more insights have been gained into the nature and variations of gnosticism, as well as the meaning of its terms, than was known in 1939. The Dead Sea Scrolls have also directed scholars to a more historical, geographical, temporal understanding of NT literature than was customarily understood when Käsemann wrote. Conse-

[48] Käsemann, *op. cit.*, 17.
[49] Käsemann, *op. cit.*, 18-19, 23, 30.
[50] Käsemann, *op. cit.*, 30-31, 87.
[51] Käsemann, *op. cit.*, 40.
[52] Käsemann, *op. cit.*, 41.
[53] Käsemann, *op. cit.*, 54, 58, 145.
[54] Käsemann, *op. cit.*, 61, 71-72, 114, 147.
[55] Käsemann, *op. cit.*, 84-87.
[56] Käsemann, *op. cit.*, 114.
[57] Käsemann, *op. cit.*, 130.
[58] Käsemann, *op. cit.*, 135, 145.

quently the elaborate interpretation of the pilgrimage in Hebrews as a gnostic ascension of the soul has not been followed by many recent scholars.

Spicq.—By far the most extensive and scholarly commentary of the twentieth century was composed by Spicq.[59] Vol. I deals with the introductory deductions, and vol. II is the verse by verse commentary. Spicq believed the letter was not a unit. It was written by a scholarly Bible teacher.[60] It began abruptly without the usual salutation. The true end of the epistle is chapter 12, and chapter 13 is an appendix,[61] added as an epilogue by some other author. Spicq thought Hebrews was dependent upon the gospels, especially John.[62] He also believed the author used I Peter and Paul, but he did not copy from them.[63] For authorship, Spicq carefully examined the usual possibilities—Barnabas, Peter, Luke, etc., but opted for Apollos who wrote it from Alexandria.[64] The readers were first of all members of a group of priests [65] who had been converted to Christianity [66] by Stephen and were originally from Jerusalem [67] but moved to Caesarea [68] or Antioch,[69] probably about A.D. 66-67.[70] Spicq further dealt with the theology of the epistle, its use of the OT, and its style and language. He concluded with an excellent bibliography. Spicq has demanded the attention of most later scholars dealing with Hebrews.

Manson.—Manson's little book was first delivered as a series of lectures and shows a popular style and organization. Like other scholars, Manson abandoned the Pauline authorship.[71] He also denied the claim that the Hebrews were Palestinians.[72] More than likely, he held, the recipients were members of a strong Jewish

---

[59] C. Spicq, *L'Épître aux Hébreux* (Paris, 1952, 1953). References are to vol. I.
[60] Spicq, *op. cit.*, 22-24, 125.
[61] Spicq, *op. cit.*, 37.
[62] Spicq, *op. cit.*, 94, 109-110, 123-124, 132.
[63] Spicq, *op. cit.*, 143.
[64] Spicq, *op. cit.*, 199-219.
[65] Spicq, *op. cit.*, 226.
[66] Spicq, *op. cit.*, 228.
[67] Spicq, *op. cit.*, 231.
[68] Spicq, *op. cit.*, 248.
[69] Spicq, *op. cit.*, 252.
[70] Spicq, *op. cit.*, 260.
[71] W. Manson, *The Epistle to the Hebrews* (London, c1953), 11.
[72] Manson, *op. cit.*, 18.

community in Rome.[73] Manson related Hebrews to Stephen, who *"grasped and asserted the more-than-Jewish-Messianic sense in which the office and significance of Jesus in religious history were to be understood"* [italics his].[74] This transcends the nationalistic, local view of Palestine and the temple, but the mobile tent of the wilderness is reinterpreted.[75] The author "will have been a fervent upholder of the world-mission gospel, who writes to warn this disaffected group" of Jewish Christians who held to traditional Jewish views.[76] The new exodus of which the author speaks is "not to an earthly place of rest ... but to a heavenly rest." [77] The readers were probably Jewish converts.[78] The author understood the Son of Man to have experienced death on behalf of universal man.[79] Manson noted that Ps 110 had its root in the time when David took over the religious and political rights of Jerusalem, but he further said that the author of Hebrews had an apocalyptic view of a heavenly world.[80] Christ's ministry is a transcendent and heavenly one.[81] The author contrasted Jewish holy sanctions with spiritual Christian worship.[82] The readers were Jewish Christians.[83] The author was an ardent "adherent to the principles of Stephen and the world-mission."[84] The letter was probably written about A.D. 49 when Claudius made the edict evicting Jews from Rome.[85] Manson thought the most likely author was Barnabas,[86] who was "essentially an eschatologist" whereas "St. Paul at the centre of his being is a mystic." [87]

Manson's views have the merit of recognizing the importance of eschatology in the document, but his understanding of that eschatology was soon to be rendered obsolete by an examination of the Dead Sea Scrolls and their implications for Hebrews.

---

[73] Manson, *op. cit.*, 24.
[74] Manson, *op. cit.*, 31.
[75] Manson, *op. cit.*, 35.
[76] Manson, *op. cit.*, 44.
[77] Manson, *op. cit.*, 55.
[78] Manson, *op. cit.*, 62-63.
[79] Manson, *op. cit.*, 99.
[80] Manson, *op. cit.*, 118-119.
[81] Manson, *op. cit.*, 126.
[82] Manson, *op. cit.*, 140.
[83] Manson, *op. cit.*, 157.
[84] Manson, *op. cit.*, 160.
[85] Manson, *op. cit.*, 163.
[86] Manson, *op. cit.*, 170.
[87] Manson, *op. cit.*, 195.

Scholarship since the Scrolls

Insights from the Scrolls

Early reactions.—At the time the scrolls were discovered, two of the best informed living scholars of Hebrews were Michel and Spicq. Both had completed their commentaries before the Scrolls had been made available to most scholars. In his large two-volume work, Spicq had suggested Palestine as the background for the recipients of the document. With the discovery of the Scrolls, he needed only to make his conclusions more precise to hold that the same Apollos he had earlier concluded to have been the author of Hebrews addressed it to some Essene Christians, among whom were Jewish priests from Qumran.[88] Shortly after the publication of the major Scrolls, Michel revised his commentary and published a new edition, but made few changes as a result of the Scrolls either in his commentary or conclusions.

The relationship between the literature found near the Dead Sea and Hebrews is so obvious that many scholars noticed it almost simultaneously. Like Spicq, Daniélou also thought the recipients of Hebrews were Essene priests.[89] In Israel, Flusser quickly recognized important relationships between some materials among the scrolls and NT documents. Among the correspondences, Flusser related the doctrines of the new covenant, baptism, and the Holy Spirit directly to Hebrews.[90] At the same time in Jerusalem, Kosmala was composing a book relating the insights from the scrolls to the origins of Christianity.[91] His beginning chapter dealt with the relationship between the Essenes and the recipients of Hebrews. The recipients of this document, he held, if not Jews who had formerly been Essenes, were at least Jews of Essene-like beliefs who were at the time of writing being trained in Christianity. They were not yet Christians, and were tempted to revert to Judaism.[92] Another of Flusser's close friends was Yadin, who noted numerous parallels between various scrolls and Hebrews.[93] He concluded

---

[88] C. Spicq, "L'Épître aux Hébreux, Apollos, Jean-Baptiste, les Hellénistes et Qumran," *RQ* 1 (1958-1959), 365-390.

[89] J. Daniélou, *Les Manuscrits de la Mer Morte et les Origines du Christianisme* (Paris, c1957), 106-109.

[90] D. Flusser, "The Dead Sea Sect and Pre-Pauline Christianity," *Scripta Hierosolymitana* IV (1958), 215-266, esp. 237-242, 245, 246-248.

[91] H. Kosmala, *Hebräer-Essener-Christen* (Leiden, 1959).

[92] Kosmala, *op. cit.*, 1-43, 77, 80.

[93] Y. Yadin, "The Dead Sea Scrolls and the Epistle to the Hebrews," *Scripta Hierosolymitana* IV (1958), 36-55.

that Hebrews was directed to a group of Jews who had originally belonged to the Dead Sea Scroll sect, which he, like Kosmala, identified with the Essenes. He differed from Kosmala in that he thought the recipients were already converts to Christianity at the time Hebrews was written.[94]

Although the insights observed in the late fifties were thought-provoking and important, still more important was the publication of a scroll on Melchizedek found in cave 11, which identified Melchizedek with the Messiah.[95] This document disclosed the expectation of a jubilee at the end of days for the "captives," who were the sons of light and belonged to the lot of the heritage of Melchizedek. Melchizedek was expected to come and proclaim release to those captives and atonement for their sins. This would take place in the year of the last jubilee, which was the appointed time of favor for Melchizedek. The herald of good news was not only the figure, Melchizedek, but the herald was also the one who had been anointed by the spirit. This was the fulfillment of II Isaiah, who anticipated the restoration of the land to the chosen people.

Yadin had believed that the recipients of Hebrews were former members of the Qumran sect, which he believed to be composed of Essenes. Kosmala was more conservative in suggesting that they were of "Essene-like" origin. Since Essenes were principally characterized by their strict observance of the Pentateuchal rules, any Jew who did the same would have been "Essene-like". There were probably several different groups of such Jews, both in Palestine and in the Diaspora. The recipients of Hebrews had many similarities to such groups as the Essenes and those ruled by the Rule of the Community. They seemed to have belonged to a very strict, communistic, monastic sect. They were called such names as "brothers" and "beloved," terms not limited to brotherhoods, but regularly used by them (6:10, 19). This does not mean they had been Essenes.

Christian Zionism.—The recipients were reminded that they had come to Zion (προσεληλύθατε Ζιών), the city of the living God, heavenly Jerusalem (12:22). Literally understood, this would mean that the readers were still in Jerusalem when they received

---

[94] Yadin, *op. cit.*, 38.
[95] A.S. van der Woude and M. de Jonge, "11Q Melchizedek and the New Testament," *NTS* 12(1965-66), 301-303 and J. A. Fitzmyer, "Further Light on Melchizedek from Qumran Cave 11," *JBL* 86 (1967), 25-41.

this document. They had come too late to have heard Jesus, personally, but in Jerusalem they and the author could receive the message of salvation second-hand from those who heard it from Jesus himself (2:3). These faithful saints, like Abraham and Moses, had left their homeland to come to the promised land. They had expected the promise made to Abraham to be fulfilled in their day.[96] These Zionists were impatient that the kingdom had not come. The stern exhortations of the author were intended to reduce their impatience and prevent their reverting to Judaistic festivals or returning to their former homelands.

Insights from Philo

Philo and Hebrews.—As early as Wetstein scholars have noticed many similarities in thought-form and terminology between Hebrews and the works of Philo. Scholars have assessed these data variously, but none had previously examined the question so thoroughly as Spicq. As a result of his massive collection of parallels, Spicq concluded that the author of Hebrews had been a Philonic student before he became a Christian. In his analysis of Spicq's work, Schröger acknowledged that there were many close similarities between Hebrews and Philo's works.[97] He listed these, but he also listed the differences between the two and concluded that the two developed through different branches of Judaism, Philo through an allegoric direction and Hebrews through a *heilsgeschichtliche* direction that was associated with an apocalyptic branch, which, in turn, was related to the people of Qumran. Sowers, observing that there were readings attested only in Philo and Hebrews, concluded that "this plus the fact that Heb. follows Codex Alexandrinus seems to indicate a geographical proximity of both writers."[98] This would be valid if the term "geographical proximity" were considered inclusive enough to allow for the distances that written materials might have been transported in NT times, i.e. anywhere in the Roman Empire. Barrett contrasted the ethical-allegorical interpretation of Philo to the eschatological outlook of Hebrews.[99]

---

[96] ABC, 256.

[97] F. Schröger, *Der Verfasser des Hebräerbriefes als Schriftausleger* (Regensburg, 1968), 301-307.

[98] S. G. Sowers, *The Hermeneutics of Philo and Hebrews* (Zürich, c1965), 66.

[99] C. K. Barrett, "The Eschatology of the Epistle to the Hebrews," *The Background of the New Testament and its Eschatology*, ed. W. D. Davies and D. Daube (Cambridge, 1956), 363-393.

In order to refute Spicq it would have been necessary to study Philo, Hebrews, and Spicq's logic as carefully as Spicq has done. Williamson did precisely that.[100] With well-reasoned judgments, Williamson challenged, and convincingly refuted, Spicq's view that the author of Hebrews was a Philonian before he became a Christian and was influenced by Philo's views. Williamson analyzed words, phrases, themes, and ideas used, and he examined the use made of scripture both by Philo and by the author of Hebrews. In each case Williamson dealt with Spicq's claims and evidence directly. He showed discrepancies in Spicq's logic all along the line. Williamson said that the author of Hebrews was a competent, original scholar, non-Philonic, and heavily dependent on the OT, but with a different view of time and history and a different method of exegesis from that of Philo.

Like the Dead Sea Scrolls, Rabbinic Literature, and the works of Josephus, the works of Philo will continue to be useful in general for studying Hebrews, because they represent a part of the Jewish thought of the period, but no one will be able to make a sound case for direct dependence upon Philo by the author of Hebrews without fully taking Williamson's arguments into account.

Geographical Backgrounds

Scholars continue to conjecture such non-Palestinian Backgrounds for Hebrews as Alexandria,[101] Ephesus,[102] and Rome,[103] but the internal evidence, increased contemporary literature made available, and recent scholarly logic make these conjectures increasingly less probable.

Style and Literary Structure

Hebrews was recognized at a very early dates as a document composed by a good literary artist, although scholars differed in their reconstruction of its outline. Indeed Moffatt held that it was impossible to find a definite plan for the document.[104] Michel, however, in the first edition of his commentary, had a different

---

[100] R. Williamson, *Philo and the Epistle to the Hebrews* (Leiden, 1970); also "Platonism and Hebrews," *SJT* 16 (1963), 418-419.

[101] For a list see Spicq, *op. cit.*, I, 237, fn. 2.

[102] H. Montefiore, *A Commentary on the Epistle to the Hebrews* (New York and Evanston, c1964), 28.

[103] F. F. Bruce, *The Epistle to the Hebrews* (Grand Rapids, c1964), xxxiv.

[104] Moffatt, *op. cit.*, xii-xiv.

opinion. He observed the good style of Hebrews although he did not show the author's artistry in detail.[105] Vaganay studied the document more thoroughly and discovered its inclusions and catch-words used to relate one unit to the next.[106] On this basis, he concluded that the work was composed according to the following outline:[107]

Introduction (1:1-4).
    I. Jesus, superior to angels (1:5-2:18).
    II. Jesus, compassionate and faithful high priest (3:1-5:10).
        1. Jesus, faithful high priest (3:1-4:16).
        2. Jesus, compassionate high priest (5:1-10).
    III. Jesus, author of eternal salvation, perfect high priest great priest according to the order of Melchizedek (5:11-10:39).
        [Hortatory admonitions just before the main subject 5:11-6:20].
        1. Jesus, great priest according to the order of Melchizedek (7:1-28).
        2. Jesus, perfect high priest (8:1-9:28).
        3. Jesus, author of eternal salvation (10:1-39).
    IV. Perseverance in the faith (11:1-12:13).
        1. Faith (11:1-12:2).
        2. Perseverance (12:3-13).
    V. The great task of holiness and peace (12:14-13:21).
Concluding counsel (13:22-25).

Motivated by Vaganay, Vanhoye made a much more extensive study of the structure than Vaganay had done,[108] having first surveyed previous attempts to explain the outline and structure of Hebrews.[109] Vanhoye basically accepted Vaganay's method and outline, but he dealt with both areas much more precisely. Furthermore, he appreciated the artistry of the author of Hebrews more than Vaganay did. Vaganay believed this style to have been influenced by Semitic form and to be somewhat artificial.[110] Vanhoye, however, considered the work to be both "solid and harmonious, whose unity is not simple, whose complexity is not confusing, but who has been able to express, with an admirable fulness,

---

[105] O. Michel, *op. cit.*, 1936 ed., 5-8.
[106] L. Vaganay, "Le Plan de L'Épître aux Hébreux," *Mémorial Lagrange*, ed. L.-H. Vincent (Paris, 1940), 269-277.
[107] *Ibid.*, 270-271.
[108] A. Vanhoye, *La Structure Littéraire de L'Épître aux Hébreux* (Paris, c1963).
[109] Vanhoye, *op. cit.*, 11-32.
[110] Vaganay, *op. cit.*, 269-270, 277.

the living richness of the mystery of Christ." [111] A recognition of this style, in Vanhoye's opinion, enables the reader to "grasp the movement of the whole and to discern the relative importance of the various developments." [112] In dealing with concentric structure, Vanhoye set out to show that Hebrews was "not just one case, among others, in the utilization of concentric structure, but truly the chief work of the genre." [113]

To discern the proper divisions in Hebrews, Vanhoye looked for the following indications: 1) An announcement of the subject that was to follow immediately, 2) the use of catch-words to relate the end of one unit to the beginning subject in the next, 3) characteristic terms which the author used to confer upon a unit its distinct appearance, and 4) the inclusions, which reproduced at the end of a unit a term or terms used also at the beginning.[114] These were not always exact. Sometimes the author used at the end a slightly different part of the same quotation from the OT from the one he used at the beginning, but the reader was expected to recognize their origin and see the connection. At other times he used at the end a different form of the same Greek root from the one used at the beginning, but the intended relationship is clear. For example, one unit begins with the following: "Wherefore, holy brothers, sharers of the heavenly (ἐπουρανίου) calling, consider Christ Jesus (Ἰησοῦν), the apostle and high priest (ἀρχιερέα) of our confession (ὁμολογίας)," and concludes as follows: "Having, then, a great high priest (ἀρχιερέα), who has gone through the heavens (τοὺς οὐρανούς), Jesus (Ἰησοῦν), the Son of God, let us hold fast the confession (τῆς ὁμολογίας)" (Heb 4:14). As part of the same summary that included the key words of an inclusion, the author regularly used also important terms intended to prepare the reader for the subject in the following unit. These were the terms Vaganay called "catch-words."

Although the author of Hebrews sometimes used simple and euphonic chiasms (4:16), Vanhoye found in Hebrews a much more involved concentric symmetry than that, and he demonstrated it at great length. For example:

" 'You are my Son; today I have begotten you;' (and again) 'I

---

[111] Vanhoye, *op. cit.*, 258.
[112] Vanhoye, *op. cit.*, 259.
[113] Vanhoye, *op. cit.*, 63.
[114] Vanhoye, *op. cit.*, 37.

will be his Father; and he will be my Son' " (1:5). This passage has two obvious parallels:

$$-\dot{\varepsilon}\gamma\omega \ldots \qquad\qquad -\dot{\varepsilon}\gamma\omega \ldots$$
$$\gamma\varepsilon\gamma\dot{\varepsilon}\nu\nu\eta\kappa\alpha \qquad\qquad \varepsilon\dot{\iota}\varsigma\ \pi\alpha\tau\dot{\varepsilon}\rho\alpha$$

but its external phrases also form a concentric series:

$$-\upsilon\dot{\iota}\dot{o}\varsigma \qquad\qquad\qquad\qquad\qquad\qquad \varepsilon\dot{\iota}\varsigma\ \upsilon\dot{\iota}\dot{o}\nu.^{115}$$
$$\mu o\upsilon \qquad\qquad\qquad\qquad\qquad\qquad\qquad \mu o\iota$$
$$\varepsilon\tilde{\iota} \qquad\qquad\qquad\qquad\qquad\qquad\qquad\quad \dot{\varepsilon}\sigma\tau\alpha\iota$$
$$\sigma\dot{\upsilon} \qquad\qquad\qquad\qquad\qquad\qquad\qquad -\alpha\dot{\upsilon}\tau\dot{o}\varsigma$$

An *a fortiori* exhortation (2:1-4) is even more detailed in its symmetry:

$$\ldots\ldots\ldots\ldots\ldots\ldots\ldots\ldots\ldots\ldots\ldots\ldots\dot{\varepsilon}\beta\varepsilon\beta\alpha\iota\dot{\omega}\theta\eta$$
$$.\dot{\eta}\mu\tilde{\alpha}\varsigma\ldots\ldots\ldots\ldots\ldots\ldots\ldots\ldots\ldots\ldots\varepsilon\dot{\iota}\varsigma\ \dot{\eta}\mu\tilde{\alpha}\varsigma$$
$$^{1}.\tau o\tilde{\iota}\varsigma\ \dot{\alpha}\kappa o\upsilon\sigma\theta\varepsilon\tilde{\iota}\sigma\iota\nu \ldots\ldots\ldots\ldots\ldots\tau\tilde{\omega}\nu\ \dot{\alpha}\kappa o\upsilon\sigma\dot{\alpha}\nu\tau\omega\nu$$
$$^{2}.\delta\iota'\ \dot{\alpha}\gamma\gamma\dot{\varepsilon}\lambda\omega\nu \ldots\ldots\ldots\ldots\ldots\ldots\delta\iota\dot{\alpha}\ \tau o\tilde{\upsilon}\ K\upsilon\rho\dot{\iota}o\upsilon$$
$$^{3}.\lambda\alpha\lambda\eta\theta\varepsilon\dot{\iota}\varsigma\ldots\ldots\ldots\ldots\ldots\ldots\ldots\lambda\alpha\lambda\varepsilon\tilde{\iota}\sigma\theta\alpha\iota$$
$$^{4}.\lambda\dot{o}\gamma o\varsigma \ldots\ldots\ldots\ldots\ldots\ldots\ldots\ldots\sigma\omega\tau\eta\rho\dot{\iota}\alpha\varsigma$$
$$^{5}.\beta\dot{\varepsilon}\beta\alpha\iota o\varsigma\ldots\ldots\ldots\ldots\ldots\ldots\ldots$$
$$^{6}.\pi\alpha\rho\dot{\alpha}\beta\alpha\sigma\iota\varsigma \ldots\ldots\ldots\ldots\ldots\ldots\dot{\alpha}\mu\varepsilon\lambda\dot{\eta}\sigma\alpha\nu\tau\varepsilon\varsigma$$
$$^{7}.\mu\iota\sigma\theta\alpha\pi o\delta o\sigma\dot{\iota}\alpha\nu \ldots\ldots\ldots\ldots\ldots\dot{\varepsilon}\kappa\varphi\varepsilon\upsilon\xi\dot{o}\mu\varepsilon\theta\alpha$$
$$^{8}\ldots\ldots\ldots\ldots\pi\tilde{\omega}\varsigma\ \dot{\eta}\mu\varepsilon\tilde{\iota}\varsigma \ldots\ldots\ldots\ldots\ ^{116}$$

The first two paragraphs of Hebrews follow this scheme:

a) Christ   (1:5)   a) Christ   (1:13)
b) Angels   (1:6)   b) Angels   (1:14)
b) Angels   (1:7)   b) Angels   (2:2)
a) Christ   (1:8)   a) Christ   (2:3-4).[117]

The author's effective skill in repetition is apparent in the following passage:

7:11:   "according to the order of
                                      Melchizedek;
7:15:   according to the likeness of
                                      Melchizedek;
7:17: You are a priest for the age according to the order of
                                      Melchizedek;

---

[115] Vanhoye, *op. cit.*, 70, see also 152 and Heb 9:18-22.
[116] Vanhoye, *op. cit.*, 76.
[117] Vanhoye, *op. cit.*, 85.

7:21: You are a priest for the age
7:24: for the age
7:28: for the age." [118]

Michel, who had earlier expressed approval of the style and form of Hebrews, later appreciated the excellent scholarship of Vaganay and Vanhoye.[119] Vaganay's original outline and approach was worked out with careful precision by Vanhoye. Two improvements might still have been made in understanding the method of the author. The first would have been to recognize that the original document comprised only twelve chapters. The attempt to include chapter thirteen in the structure was strained. The second would have been to see this careful artistry as a part of a homiletical midrash, based on Ps 110. Vanhoye noticed that the author repeated important themes, such as the exhortation in 3:13 and 4:1. He might also have noticed important summaries that not only formed inclusions with immediate units, but also echoed earlier themes or prepared the reader for later ones. For example, the word *Christ* at the beginning and ending of 9:24-28 frames this unit with an inclusion, but this passage also summarizes 9:10-23 and echoes such terms as "once" (6:4; 9:7, 26, 28; 10:2; 12:26, 27), which was used both before and after this unit. The expression, "At the end of the ages" (ἐπὶ συντελείᾳ τῶν αἰώνων) (9:26) refers to the same period as the expression, "At the last of these days" (ἐπ' ἐσχάτων τῶν ἡμερῶν τούτων) (1:2). The heirs of the promise (6:12, 17) are the same as those who receive the promise of the inheritance of the age (9:15).

A short passage in chapter ten echoes chapters four and six, as the following comparisons indicate:

1. Since then, we have a great high priest	1. Therefore ... since we have ... a great priest (10:19, 21)
2. [who] has gone through the heavens (4:14)	2. ... for entering the holy [precincts] ... which way he inaugurated for us [that is] new and living, through the veil (10:19, 20)
3. ... Jesus the Son of God (4:14),	3. ... by means of the blood of Jesus (10:19),
4. Let us hold fast the confession (4:14)	4. Let us hold fast unmoved the confession of hope (10:23)

---

[118] Vanhoye, *op. cit.*, 129.
[119] O. Michel, "Zur Auslegung des Hebräerbriefs," *NovTest.* 6 (1963), 189-191.

5. Then let us approach the throne of grace with boldness (4:16).	5. Let us approach [the altar] with a true heart in fullness of faith (10:22); therefore, brothers, since we have [the] boldness [necessary] for entering the holy [precincts] ... (10:19).
Which we have as a secure and steadfast anchor of the soul, and entering into that which is within the curtain, where Jesus [as] the forerunner has entered in our bahalf, being a priest for the age according to the order of Melchizedek (6:19-20).	By means of the blood of Jesus, which way he inaugurated for us [that is] new and living, through the veil, that is, his flesh (10:19-20).

The following themes are repeated in effective places in the document: 1) The origin of the ages (1:2; 11:3); exaltation (1:3; 4:14; 7:26; 8:1); high priest (2:17; 3:1-2; 4:14-15; 6:20; 7:26; 8:1; 9:11); holding fast (3:6; 3:14; 10:23); and the promises (4:1; 6:11-12; 6:15, 17; 8:6; 9:15; 10: 36; 11:9, 13, 17, 39). In this way the author of Hebrews has composed his document as intricately and as carefully as a musical composer might, with many themes woven throughout. As one melody fades into the background, another theme is raised to prominence so as to blend, vary, and move dramatically from one score to another. This is typical of midrashic style. These literary artists seldom said all that they had to say on a subject at one time and place, even though their units were well structured. This is true both of running commentaries, such as Sifra, Sifré, Mekilta, and some of the writings of Philo, and of homiletical midrashim, such as Pesikta de Rav Kahana and Prov 2-7.[120] Vanhoye is probably right in claiming that the author of Hebrews was the chief of the literary artists in his use of concentric symmetry, but the genre to which this type of symmetry belongs is, in this case, also midrash.

Since the task of the literary artist was not only to provide concentric symmetry and a well-ordered argument but also to interpret the OT midrashically, NT scholars have also given attention to the author's use of the OT.

Midrash

The Scrolls and the OT text.—For years scholars have realized that the OT texts used by the author of Hebrews followed the LXX

---

[120] See "Midrashim Pré-Tannaïtes," *RB* 72(1965), 227-239.

more closely than the Massoretic text, but they also knew that in some places it agreed with neither. Among the Dead Sea Scrolls were OT Hebrew texts that agreed more closely with the LXX than with the MT. This led Howard to reexamine every use of the OT in Hebrews to learn the facts involved.[121] According to his study,

> "A. There are 35 different quotes in Hebrews.
>   11 (possibly 14) quotes from the law
>   6 (possibly 8) quotes from the Prophets out of 10 possible sources
>   14 (possibly 17) quotes from the Writings
> B. There are 41 possible sources for the 35 quotes.
>   Out of the 41 possible sources:
>   24 are unlike either Hebrew or LXX
>   8 are identical to both Hebrew and LXX
>   6 are identical to Hebrew against LXX
>   2 are identical to LXX against Hebrew
>   18 possible LXX influences
>   10 possible Hebrew influences."[122]

Analyzed according to divisions, the references to the Pentateuch are the most frequent and the least accurate according to the standard of the MT and the LXX; the references to the Writings are second in frequency and most accurate by the same standard; and the Prophetic books stand in between.[123] After examining individual passages, Howard concluded that it is not correct to say that the quotations in Hebrews are always Septuagintal. Many do not correspond to any extant LXX text, and some agree with a known Hebrew text against the LXX.[124]

Howard was not the only or first to formulate a list of OT references in Hebrews.[125] Scholars do not agree completely in their deductions, because it is sometimes difficult to distinguish a quotation from an allusion. The author frequently changed tenses and varied

---

[121] G. Howard, "Hebrews and the Old Testament Quotations," *NovTest*. 10 (1968), 208-216.

[122] Howard, *op. cit.*, 211.

[123] Howard, *op. cit.*, 212.

[124] Howard, *op. cit.*, 215. Hebrews is exhibit A for illustrating the *pesher* method of exegesis, employing a Christological use of the OT, since the first twelve chapters constitute a homily based on Ps 110, supported by Ps 2 and others. Nevertheless, M. Black, "The Christological Use of the Old Testament in the New Testament," *NTS* 18 (1971), 1-14, never mentioned Hebrews even though he discussed Ps 110, Ps 2, and the Son of Man in relationship to *pesher* exegesis in the NT. What a strange omission!

[125] Spicq, *L'Épître aux Hébreux*, I, 331, Schröger, *op. cit.*, 251-252, *et al.*

quotations in other ways to suit his message.[126] He also sometimes paraphrased a LXX quotation, as is evident from the following two examples of a quotation from the same OT passage:

ὅτι αὕτη ἡ διαθήκη ἥν διαθήσομαι τῷ οἴκῳ Ἰσραήλ
 μετὰ τὰς ἡμέρας ἐκείνας, λέγει κύριος,
διδοὺς νόμους μου εἰς τὴν διάνοιαν αὐτῶν,
 καὶ ἐπὶ καρδίας αὐτῶν ἐπιγράψω αὐτούς (Jer. 31:33; Heb 8:10).
αὕτη ἡ διαθήκη ἥν διαθήσομαι πρὸς αὐτούς
 μετὰ τὰς ἡμέρας ἐκείνας, λέγει κύριος
διδοὺς νόμους μου ἐπὶ καρδίας αὐτῶν,
 καὶ ἐπὶ τὴν διάνοιαν αὐτῶν ἐπιγράψω αὐτούς (Jer 31:33; Heb 10:16).

Instead of "with the house of Israel," 10:16 has "with reference to them," and it has "hearts" and "minds" in reverse positions. This does not change the meaning of the passage, but it is not very likely that the author of Hebrews used one text for 8:10 and a different one for 10:16. Since this variant is quite likely to have been made by the author of Hebrews himself, the question of variant texts becomes more obscure. When did he actually use a variant LXX text that is no longer extant, and when did he vary the text by arbitrarily paraphrasing it? No one knows; the possibilities are just more numerous than scholars knew before the discovery of the Scrolls.

Williamson examined the author's use of the OT in comparison with the exegetical methods of Philo and found great differences: Philo seldom used the Psalms, Prophets, or Writings, whereas Hebrews used Psalms and Prophets extensively; Philo frequently wrote running commentaries, whereas Hebrews is a homily; Philo often identified his source by mentioning the book, personage, or division in which the passage was contained, whereas Hebrews always quoted anonymously, with one exception. He referred to a passage "in David" (4:7), meaning "in the Psalms." Hebrews never followed Philo's pattern of saying, "The scripture says" or "As it is written." Philo's method of exegesis is allegorical, whereas Hebrews regularly avoided allegory and interpreted typologically.[127] These differences further question the dependence of Hebrews on

---

[126] Schröger, *op. cit.*, 201-206.
[127] Williamson, *op. cit.*, 498-538.

Philo, but they also clarify the method of exegesis employed by the author. It was midrashic artistry at its best.

Schröger examined extensively the use of scripture by the author of Hebrews, studying each quotation and allusion in different LXX texts as well as the MT to learn which texts the author used and the way he used them. Schröger prepared very helpful charts to show the results of his study. He found that the author used his texts in various ways: sometimes he followed the literal sense; sometimes he used it directly or indirectly to apply to the Messiah; sometimes he related the text to the event in a promise-fulfillment relationship; and at still other times, he employed the text typologically.[128] In Hebrews Schröger found elements of rabbinic exegesis, elements of apocalyptic-pesher exegesis, and elements of Hellenistic-late Jewish-synagogue exegesis.[129]

Hebrews is not a document that was hastily or simply composed. The author was a literary artist who used his OT passages as skillfully as he employed inclusions and *a fortiori* arguments. He employed the literary genius of both Greeks and Jews, but his goal was clear and steadfast: he wanted to bring about the fulfillment of God's promise to Abraham. This was possible because of Christ's sacrificial death. Michel was correct in saying that Hebrews was Christocentric, and Black was negligent in over looking the author's Christological use of the OT.[130] The Christ who was central to the author's theology was Jesus, whom the author understood to be both Son and high priest. These two roles will be examined to learn the author's Christology.

Son of Man

Commentators generally have paid little attention to the term, Son of man, in Heb 2:6. Several have ignored it. Others have insisted that it has no messianic significance. It is an accidental term that happened to be in Ps 8 which the author of Hebrews quoted. It has no further significance to Hebrews than it did to the Psalmist.[131] Some admitted that it was a messianic title and

---

[128] Schröger, *op. cit.*, 259-262.
[129] Schröger, *op. cit.*, 269.
[130] Michel, *Der Brief an die Hebräer, passim*; "Zur Auslegung des Hebräerbriefs," 189-191; Black, *op. cit.*
[131] See Moffatt, *op. cit.*, 23; Stuart, *op. cit.*, 69; Westcott, *op. cit.*, 42-43; Windisch, *op. cit.*, 20. This entire discussion is dealt with much more fully in ABC, 38-51.

identified with Jesus, but they did not say how.[132] Michel erroneously noted that Ps 8 was not used by the rabbis to refer to the Messiah.[133] Laubach said Ps 8 was used in Hebrews to call attention to Jesus as "the man," the second from Adam, but he noticed also a resemblance between the subjection element in Ps 8 and that of Ps 110. He did not follow through, however, to show what that meant.[134]

Major studies on the Son of man, such as those of Jeremias,[135] Higgens,[136] Bultmann,[137] Cullmann,[138] and Tödt,[139] have used Heb 2:6 for their analyses no more than commentators have. Vielhauer separated the concept of "Son of man" so far from that of messiahship that he said the heavenly Son of Man was not at all related to the concept of the Kingdom of God.[140] It was only in reaction to Vielhauer's extreme position that scholars like Marshall[141] and Walker[142] took steps to restore the close relationship between messiahship and Son of Man theology that is evident in Hebrews and the gospels. The identification of the title, Son of man, with the title, king, is supported by the use of these terms in Daniel and Enoch as well.[143]

The superior attributes of the Son in Hebrews are those normally given to a mighty king. Enthronement Psalms, like Ps 2, which identified the son as a king on Mt. Zion who would break the enemy nations to pieces and rule them with power, and Ps 110, which

---

[132] C. Kuss, *Der Brief an die Hebräer* (Regensburg, 1966), 40-41; Spicq, *L'Épître aux Hébreux*, II, 31.

[133] O. Michel, *Der Brief an die Hebräer*, 70-71. See San. 98a.

[134] F. Laubach, *Der Brief an die Hebräer* (Wuppertal, 1966), *loc. cit.*

[135] J. Jeremias, *New Testament Theology*, tr. J. Bowden (London, c1971), I, 265.

[136] A. J. B. Higgins, *Jesus and the Son of Man* (Philadelphia, c1964), 146.

[137] R. Bultmann, *Theology of the New Testament*, tr. K. Grobel (New York, c1951), I, 5, 7, 9, 26-37, 40, 42-44, 47 49, 51-53, 79-80, 124, 172.

[138] O. Cullmann, *The Christology of the New Testament*, tr. S. C. Guthrie and C. A. M. Hall (Philadelphia, c1957), 188.

[139] H. E. Tödt, *The Son of Man in the Synoptic Tradition* (Philadelphia, c1964).

[140] P. Vielhauer, "Gottesreich und Menschensohn in der Verkündigung Jesu," *Aufsätze zum Neuen Testament, Theologische Bücherei* 31 (München, 1965), 55-140.

[141] I. H. Marshall, "The Synoptic Son of Man Sayings in Recent Discussion," *NTS* 12 (1965-66), 347.

[142] W. O. Walker, Jr., "The Kingdom of the Son of Man and the Kingdom of the Father in Matthew," *CBQ* 30 (1968), 577. See also E. Bammel, "Erwägungen zur Eschatologie Jesu," *Studia Evangelica* III (1964), 3-32.

[143] The defense of these claims is not directly related to the topic discussed here but can be found in ABC, 38-51.

described the son as a king who sat at God's right hand while God made his enemies his footstool, were supportive proof texts. The author also used texts from II Samuel and Ps 45. II Sam 7:14 originally was applied to Solomon as God's son when he ruled from Jerusalem. Ps 45 was addressed to an anointed king (Ps 45:8), who was encouraged to gird on his sword in glory and ride forth victoriously (Ps 45:4-5). He was assured that his enemies would fall before his sharp arrows (Ps 45:6). From his divine throne he was destined to rule justly (Ps. 45:8). The son of God was to be a king like Solomon for whom God would make his enemies a footstool (Ps 110:1). In the same context, the author of Hebrews identified the son of God with the son of man for whom God would put all things under his feet.[144] Since the author also identified Jesus with the king mentioned in these expressions, it seems likely that he understood the expressions, Son of God and Son of man, to have the same meaning and to describe a messiah or king. This is consistent with the usage of the term in Daniel, Enoch, and the gospels.

Many scholars have avoided the political associations of the Son of man designations by claiming him to be a corporate personality or a heavenly figure, but the Son of man in Hebrews was a king who ruled over a nation and had such power that other kings would be subject to him.[145] Like the gospel writers, the author of Hebrews identified the Son of God with the Son of man and Jesus, accepting the political nature of that figure described in Daniel, Enoch, and the gospels.[146] This is consistent with the eschatology of Hebrews and the concept of Jesus as the high priest. The earliest reference to a son of man on record probably refers to Judah the Maccabee, who was also a Levite and whose brothers became high priests. In Hebrews Jesus was also both Son and high priest.

---

[144] In a larger context of conditions under which the Messiah, the son of David, or redemption would come Dan 7:13 was quoted by the Rabbis, identifying the son of man with the Messiah (San. 98a).

[145] So C. K. Barrett, *The Gospel According to St. John* (London, 1967), 60; R. Bultmann, *Theology of the New Testament*, I, 49; Sjöberg, *Der Menschensohn im Äthiopischen Henochbuch* (Lund, 1946), 50, 58-59; 141-143; 193-194; H. Teeple, "The Origin of the Son of Man," *JBL* 84 (1965), 219, 243; E. Schweizer, "The Son of Man," *JBL* 79 (1960), 122; T. W. Manson, *The Teaching of Jesus* (Cambridge, 1951), 311-336, and *BJRL* 32 (1949-50), 171-193; *et al.*

[146] S. Mowinckel, *The Psalms in Israel's Worship*, tr. D. R. Ap-Thomas (New York, c1962), I, 48-49, 54, 60, 62-63, 125, related the king to the son of God in the OT and related theology of kingship in the ancient Near East, generally.

Great High Priest

Hebrews, Paul, and the Gospels.—Although other tradition classifies Jesus as a son of David who had been teamed with John the Baptist, a son of Aaron, in accordance with the two-messiah expectation (Lk 1:5-13, 26-33), the author of Hebrews made no mention of Jesus as a son of David. In the letters of Paul, the crucifixion and resurrection of Jesus was very important, but the author of Hebrews mentioned the cross only once (12:2), and there only as an example similar to that of Moses who was reported to have accepted disgrace instead of the position of wealth available to him (11:24-25). It was only when Jesus' death was reinterpreted in terms of an atonement offering that it captured the author of Hebrews' attention. It was important that Jesus be understood as a high priest so that his sacrifice could be understood as an atonement offering. This meant his death was related to the Day of Atonement rather than the Passover Feast, as the gospels record. Since Jesus was not from the priestly line of Aaron, the author attributed the office of high priest to him on the basis of Ps 110 (5:10). As a priest of the confession (3:1), he became forerunner and pioneer (2:10; 6:10-20), having gone through the veil as the high priest did when he entered the holy of holies. As a priest he offered blood, but not that of bulls and goats. He offered his own blood in the greater and more perfect tent (9:11-12). Like other offerings that went up to God in the heavens, Jesus, the perfect sacrifice, also went through the heavens to God (4:14). This ascension displaced the resurrection of the gospels and placed Jesus at the right hand of God (1:3, 13; 4:14; 5:8; 8:1; 10:12; 12:2). His self-offering not only opened the heavens to Jesus, but it also provided a cleansing for his sins so that he could be sinless (1:3; 4:15), holy, undefiled, and separated from sin (7:26-27).

The Dead Sea Scrolls.—The priestly role of Jesus in Hebrews has puzzled scholars who have tried to make sense out of this document in a way that is consistent with the gospels and the letters of Paul. With the discovery of the Dead Sea Scrolls Yadin and Kosmala offered explanations for this phenomenon. Yadin held that since the Essenes considered the priestly messiah to have a higher status than the administrative messiah, the author of Hebrews interpreted Jesus' function as a high priest as a direct challenge to the two-messiah doctrine of the Dead Sea sect. That sect considered both messiahs to be inferior to the archangel Michael. The author of Hebrews countered this doctrine with such a superior picture of Jesus as the high priest that the author's statement of 9:25-26 "requires no further comment." [147] Yadin might have implied, but he did not say, that the author of Hebrews' claim that Jesus was superior to the angels would also have included superiority over Michael.

Kosmala related the claim that Jesus was "the apostle and high priest" to the book of Malachi which discussed the Lord's messenger and the Day of the Lord (Mal 3:1, 23). Malachi said the priests should keep knowledge and that the Torah should be received from the priest who was the messenger of the Lord of Armies (Mal 2:7). Kosmala noted that the author of Hebrews also considered Jesus to be both an apostle or messenger as well as a priest (Heb 3:1). Like Hebrews, literature from the Dead Sea Scrolls indicates that the community also anticipated the creation of a new community in which the law of Moses was to be kept uprightly. Malachi was central to the theology both of Hebrews and of the Dead Sea sect.[148] Malachi expected no royal messiah, but only Elijah. The book of Malachi was basically oriented toward the priesthood.[149] Since Elijah was considered the high priest of the end time, sometimes identified with Phineas (Sifra §131), the author of Hebrews had this concept as background for his theology.[150] T. Levi also gave the priestly leader superiority over the royal messiah, although the Testaments of the Twelve Patriarchs accepted the two messiah doctrine. Like the Dead Sea documents, the Testaments gave top position to the priestly messiah. This means that the author of Hebrews' conception of Jesus as the high priest was not such a uniquely oriented doctrine as scholars have previously thought,[151] but there is one distinctive factor: in Hebrews there is "only *one* leader of their salvation" (Heb 2:10), rather than two, "The Messiah of the Epistle to the Hebrews had no political-national assignment to fulfill further, and the high priestly atonement had already been completed through him." [152] Since Jesus had come from Judah, thus fulfilling the royal requirement, and was a

---

[147] Yadin, *op. cit.*, 48-53, quotation from 53.
[148] Kosmala, *op. cit.*, 76-79.
[149] Kosmala, *op. cit.*, 80.
[150] Kosmala, *op. cit.*, 81.
[151] Kosmala, *op. cit.*, 88.
[152] Kosmala, *op. cit.*, 89.

priest from the order of Melchizedek, Jesus therefore satisfied all the requirements that were common to Jewish circles of that time.[153]

The Hasmoneans.—The ideas of Yadin and Kosmala are thought-provoking, but both scholars overlooked an important Jewish expectation related to the Hasmoneans, who were the most recent leaders to capture and rule the promised land. These leaders gradually conquered and liberated the entire Davidic kingdom from the Syrians, and some of them accepted the roles of kings and high priests. To be sure, these leaders were political-national leaders, but Kosmala, in claiming that the function of Jesus was not at all political, overlooked the role of Jesus as Son in Hebrews. As Son he received all the attributes of an ideal king of Israel. He was to rule over all his enemies, who would become as a footstool for his feet (1:13; 2:7-9). His willingness to give up his life for his religion made him a martyr, like one of the faithful who resisted the Greeks in the Maccabean Revolt. Like the Hasmoneans, he filled the role both of high priest and royal leader for his people. The author of Hebrews, like the supporters of the Hasmoneans, justified on the basis of scripture a position for Jesus that he could not have merited on the basis of family lineage. Both used Ps 110 to support their views.

According to Gen 14:18, Melchizedek was called "priest of the Most High God"; according to Ps 110, the enthroned person who would sit at the Lord's right hand was a "priest for the age according to the order of Melchizedek." There is quite a firm tradition that the Hasmoneans were to be identified with both of these passages. Rabbis called John Hyrcanus "John, high priest of the Most High God" (RH 18b). Josephus also referred to John Hyrcanus as "high priest of the Most High God" (*Ant.* XVI [163]). According to Jubilees 32:1, Levi, from whom the Hasmoneans descended, dreamed that he had been ordained (*ordinatus*) priest of the Most High God, he and his sons, continually for the age (*usque in saecula*). Simon was called "the great high priest" (I Mac. 13:43) and a "priest for the age" (I Mac. 14:41) with the apparent intention of identifying him with the hero in that enthronement Psalm (Ps 110). This would be especially applicable, since the one described in that Psalm may not have been called "king," but his activity was described as that of a king, and, like Simon, he was called "a priest for the age." Because the Hasmoneans did

---

[153] Kosmala, *op. cit.*, 90.

not fit the traditional expectation, they had to defend their position continually. This was accomplished partly through the subtlety of the author of Maccabees. He did not call Simon a king, but he quoted from an enthronement Psalm intended for a king and which described the activity of a king.

The anti-Hasmoneans, however, did not feel the same way about the Hasmoneans. They called their leadership "iniquity in the holy of holies" (Assump Mos. 6:1; see also *Ant.* XIII [372-376]). They objected that these Hasmoneans, who were only Levites, had assumed the position reserved for the sons of Zadok (Gen. R. 97; 99:2). These purists were more sensitive about their priestly lineage than about their royal lineage. Some were willing for John Hyrcanus to be king even though he had no basis for tracing his ancestry to David's line at all, but they objected to his being high priest (*Ant.* XIII[288-297]). This resistance caused the Hasmonean supporters to be defensive about their claims and to use scripture for justification.

The author of Hebrews followed the same practice as the Hasmonean defenders. Jesus apparently had a legitimate claim to royal lineage from the family of David, but he had no priestly ancestry. The author of Hebrews wanted to claim for him the same type of heroism claimed for the Hasmoneans, which included both sonship and priesthood. Imitating the methods of the Hasmoneans, his exegesis of the same Ps 110 gave scriptural authority to his belief. This would not follow the practice of the sect governed by the Rule of the Community who insisted on having a priest from the line of Aaron and Zadok (1QS 1:18-21; 2:2, 5, 11, 20-21). The point at which Hebrews and the Dead Sea Scrolls are in agreement was not mentioned by Yadin or Kosmala. Their eschatology was similar. Both expected the promise made to Abraham to be fulfilled and the land restored to the children of Abraham.

Eschatology

The promise.—In Num 14:23, 29-30, the Lord swore that those who had rebelled against him would not enter into the land, which meant the inheritance, the promised land. The Lord took an oath the Israelites would not enter into his "rest" (Ps 95:11). The Israelites were reminded that they had not yet come to the "rest and inheritance" which the Lord would give them, but after they crossed the Jordan and entered the land, and after the Lord had given them rest from their enemies, then they should offer sacrifices to the Lord (Dt 3:20; 12:10-11; 25:19; 29:9; Josh 1:15; 22:4). Later the Lord "gave to Israel all the land which he swore to give to their fathers" (Josh 21:43), "and the Lord gave them rest on every side . . . not one of all their enemies had withstood them" (Josh 21:44). This meant that "not one of all the good promises which the Lord made to the house of Israel had failed" (Josh 21:45). It was possible to live on the land without rest from the enemies, but it was not possible to have rest without the acquisition of the Land of Canaan. The rabbis understood that this was the case. "R. Judah says, 'If Israel had been virtuous, in three days they would have entered the land, as it is said, "and the ark of the covenant of the Lord goes before them, a journey of three days, to spy out for them a rest" (Num 10:33)—and there is no rest but the Land of Israel, as it is said, "For you have not entered into rest until now, into the inheritance which the Lord your God gives you" (Dt 12:9)' " (Sifré Dt 1:2, 65b §2).

The promised "rest."—The word "rest" belonged to the terminology associated with sabbath rest. Just as there was one day of rest in every seven, so there was also one year of rest in every seven. Israelites who had allowed themselves to be enslaved by their Israelite brothers to pay back the money they had borrowed were released to "return home" every seventh year, and in Jubilee years, those who had sold their property because of indebtedness had their property returned to them or to their posterity. In this same thought-form, the Lord announced that the Hebrews could return to Palestine. Their period of "servitude" was over; they were allowed to return "home"; and their land was to be restored. The good news was that their jubilee had arrived (Heb 4:2; Isa 61:1-6), but when they tested the Lord in the wilderness, he withheld the fulfillment of his promise. He swore that he would not let them enter the land while that generation was alive.

The expected fulfillment.—The author of Hebrews assured his readers that the promise was still left unfulfilled and available for their generation. There is no indication from the context to suggest that the author expected a different rest from the one denied to the first Exodus generation (4:1-9). Since, however, the author referred to Palestine and Jerusalem as "heavenly," even scholars who have acknowledged the close relationship between the "rest" of the Israelites and the "rest" promised the readers have almost consistently insisted that the author of Hebrews anticipated a rest in heaven rather than any nationalistic-political entity.[154] This prompts an examination of the passages dealing with heavenly promises.

The heavenly land.—When Abraham and his family left Haran, they were reaching out for a "better" [fatherland], that is a heavenly [one]" (11:16). Just as the author of Hebrews was the only author in the Bible who called the Land of Canaan "the land of the promise" (11:19), so he was the only one to call it a "heavenly" land (11:16), but it is clear in both instances that Palestine was the land intended. The covenant made with Abraham promised his seed the Davidic kingdom (Gen 15:18), which was the same land Abraham's group reached out for when it left Haran. Just because it was called "heavenly" does not mean it was not on earth, any more than the sharers of the heavenly calling (3:1) who had tasted the heavenly gift (6:4) were not those who lived on earth. Indeed, it was the very land on which the patriarchs dwelled as strangers and wanderers (11:13), but it means that it was a divine land which God himself had promised. Delitzsch said, "It must be confessed that we nowhere read of the patriarchs, that they expressed a conscious desire for a home in heaven. The nearest approach to anything of the kind is in Jacob's vision of the angel-ladder, and his wondering exclamation (Gen 28:17) *zeh šaʿar haššamāyim* [This is the gate of heaven]; but even there no desire is expressed for an entrance into the heavenly land, but the promise renewed of future possession of earthly Canaan: 'The land whereon thou sleepest will I give to thee.' "[155] Although this seems obvious, Delitzsch, as well as scholars generally, both before and after him, have interpreted this passage spiritually.

The heavenly city.—In contrasting Mt. Sinai with Jerusalem, the author of Hebrews called Jerusalem "[the] city of [the] living God" (12:22). As in Gal 4:24-26, Mt. Zion was contrasted with Mt. Sinai

---

[154] For spiritualizing views of recent eschatologists, see Bruce, *op. cit.*, 297-299, 305-307, 373-376; Barrett, "The Eschatology of the Epistle to the Hebrews," 378-393; J. Gnilka, "Die Erwartung des messianischen Hohenpriester in dem Schriften von Qumran und im Neuen Testament," *RQ* 2 (1959-60), 395-426; E. Grässer, *Der Glaube im Hebräerbrief* (Marburg, 1965), 106-107, 174; Montefiore, *op. cit.*, 193-197, 230; Vanhoye, *L'Epître aux Hébreux*, I, 187; Williamson, *Philo and the Epistle to the Hebrews*, 192-193, 491. See S. Nomoto, "Herkunft und Struktur der Hohenpriestvorstellung im Hebräerbrief," *NovTest.* 10 (1968), 10-25, for a different emphasis.

[155] Delitzsch, *op. cit.*, II, 246.

(Horeb), and by implication, the old covenant with the new. Although only a few words of 12:18-21 are actually identical to the ones describing the theophany in Ex 19-20 and Dt 4-5, the description was accurately paraphrased, with an additional notation from Dt 9:19. Christians were assured that it was not Mt. Sinai or Mt. Horeb, but Mt. Zion which they had approached. Philo called Jerusalem "The City of God" (*De Som.* II [250]), That was the city of David which the author of Hebrews called "[the] city of [the] living God." This was none other than the capital city of the promised land, "heavenly Jerusalem" (12:22), where the Lord had chosen to dwell. Zechariah promised that when the Lord became king, Jerusalem would remain aloft upon its site as a city without a curse (Zech 14:9-11). In Ezekiel's vision of the restored temple (40-48), he saw the glory of the Lord entering the temple (43:4), and Ezekiel was told that the temple would be the place of the Lord's throne where he would dwell with his people forever (43:6-7, 9). "Heavenly Jerusalem" was not used to mislead the reader into thinking that Mt. Zion was in heaven—although Jews and Christians believed there was also a Jerusalem in heaven—but to affirm its divine origin, just as the heavenly gift (6:5) was something believers on earth had tasted, meaning it was a teaching considered divine or heavenly. The Jerusalem which the author of Hebrews had in mind was the city which had the foundations (11:10) which God had prepared for the children of Abraham (11:16). Whenever the Israelites succeeded in capturing and ruling the land of the promise and entered into their "rest," they would be dwelling securely in the heavenly land whose capital city was heavenly Jerusalem (11:16; 12:22).

Christians at the end time.—For hundreds of years Jerusalem has been a place where pilgrims and migrants have gathered, particularly at times when they expected the Messiah to appear and restore the kingdom to Israel (Ps 122:1-7; 68:35; 42:4; 84:1-7). Whenever Jews believed the signs of the times were exactly right for God to gather the Jews from the Diaspora and return them to Palestine, some of the most pious and sincere were willing to give up their positions, sell their land, and move to Jerusalem. In order to stimulate these movements, rabbis said those who died outside of Palestine would not live again (Ket. 111a-b) or would experience a twofold death (Gen. R. 96:5), whereas the dead of the land of Israel would be the first to rise in the days of the

Messiah (Gen. R. 96:5; Ex. R. 32:2). The concern which the author of Hebrews had shown for the promised land and the heavenly city would have been attractive to such Jewish idealists as these. The merit which the author ascribed to Abraham's willingness to leave his homeland in search of a city that had the foundations would have been shared by migrant Israelites who had done the same. If they had been attracted by the Christian message to believe that Jesus provided the merits needed for salvation and moved to Jerusalem to be there when the promise was received, they might afterwards have become discouraged by the delay and have begun to wonder if their hopes had been in vain.

"But you have come to Zion," the author said to these migrants, "to [the] city of [the] living God, heavenly Jerusalem... to a festal gathering and a church of firstborn [people]" (12:22-23) Since Israel was called the first born, and since Paul observed that the gospel came to the Jew first and then to the Greek (Rom 1:16), the "church of firstborn [people]" was probably the name applied to the Christian church at Jerusalem. Zion was the capital city of the heavenly fatherland which was the goal of Abraham's migration. In the author's judgment, it was the ultimate goal of all sons of Abraham..

Conclusions

Recent scholars have had at their disposal both the insights published by earlier laborers in the same vineyard and the insights provided by the Dead Sea Scrolls. The Scrolls have helped to clarify the background against which to examine the history and thought-forms that were customary in NT times. They have not been a direct resource for identifying the author or readers. With these and other resources, modern scholars, like Vanhoye, have examined the literary style more carefully than it has ever been studied before and have thereby demonstrated a literary unit that was more artistically composed than anyone realized before. Williamson has probably made a definitive case for showing that the author of Hebrews was not a student of Philo and was not a Platonist. The author and recipients seem more closely related to monastic Zionists than has been previously thought, and there is more reason than before for locating both in Palestine before A.D. 70. Yadin has probably jumped too quickly to the conclusion that the recipients were formerly Essenes, without considering the wide possibility for orthodox practices in Judaism and Christianity. The royal priesthood of Jesus in Hebrews seems to have been more closely patterned after a Hasmonean ideal than has been recognized by earlier scholars, and the Son of Man figure now seems more closely related to an earthly king than a heavenly being. The eschatology of the document, which many have considered very important, now seems more closely related to the promised land than to heaven, even though heavenly terms are used.

The Dead Sea Scrolls have been the stimulus that has prompted scholars to reexamine the history, theology, and political views prevalent in NT times. One of the fringe benefits of this study has been a reappraisal of Hebrews. Although many new insights have been gained in the last twenty years, the vein has not been exhausted. Future scholars will reappraise, clarify, and correct these views and add still further insights to these conclusions.